The Future of Public Housing

Jie Chen • Mark Stephens • Yanyun Man
Editors

The Future of Public Housing

Ongoing Trends in the East and the West

Springer

Editors
Jie Chen
School of Public Economics
and Administration
Shanghai University of Finance
and Economics
Shanghai, People's Republic of China

Mark Stephens
School of the Built Environment
Heriot-Watt University
Edinburgh, Scotland, UK

Yanyun Man
College of Urban and Environmental
Sciences
Peking University
Beijing, People's Republic of China
Lincoln Institute of Land Policy,
Cambridge, MA, USA

ISBN 978-3-642-41621-7 ISBN 978-3-642-41622-4 (eBook)
DOI 10.1007/978-3-642-41622-4
Springer Heidelberg New York Dordrecht London

Library of Congress Control Number: 2013956596

Printed on acid-free paper

Springer is part of Springer Science+Business Media (www.springer.com)

Preface

Introduction

This book aims to examine the recent remarkable revival in public housing in the Asian and other emerging urban economies, set against the continued stagnation and decline of the sector in the western countries.

In the twentieth century, public housing was a common response to urbanization and the urban housing problem in western capitalist, European and Asian socialist and developing countries. Yet by the Millennium it was widely perceived as a failure – criticized when it excluded the poorest and most vulnerable, yet condemned when it created concentrations of poverty. With the intellectual dominance of the 'Washington consensus', privatization became the order of the day (World Bank 1993). Mass privatization was adopted throughout almost all of the European formerly socialist states after 1990, creating a number of 'super homeownership' societies with homeownership rates exceeding the levels found anywhere in the capitalist west (Lowe 2003; Stephens 2005). Urban China followed, producing similarly spectacular changes in tenure structures, although within a very different economic and demographic context (Stephens 2010).

Yet the seeming convergence in world housing systems did not last. In the West and in transition Europe, the 'financialization' of housing was brought to a sudden halt, first as the US sub-prime crisis morphed into the credit crunch, and the credit crunch developed into what is perceived in North American and Europe as being a 'Global' Financial Crisis. Fiscal austerity has made a revival in public housing in the 'old' world unlikely, and it remains true that 'governments will be distancing themselves from direct housing provision' (Priemus and Dieleman 2002). Selective demolition, mixing tenure and stretching subsidies remain common themes in most western countries (Whitehead 1999).

In contrast, economic growth and urbanization in Asia have brought its own pressures on the housing system (Chen et al. 2010; Stephens 2010; Chen et al. 2011). And in Asia, governments have concluded that forms of public housing have a vital role to play in the urbanization process (Lui 2007).

More dramatically, for the last few years China's public housing program has been expanding at an astonishing speed. In the beginning of 2011, Chinese Prime Minister Wen Jiabao announced that the Chinese government is committed to building 36 million units of public housing during the '12th five-year plan period' (2011–2015) (Chen et al., 2013). In Chinese policymaker's minds, new model of public housing is introduced with main purpose to solve temporary and interim accommodation needs of migrants, new workers and house-poor households (Li, 2011). But the Chinese government also explicitly expects that the development of PRH would become a crucial policy tool to promote urbanization (Li 2011).

Clearly, the growing needs of public housing programs have been driven not only by political pressures, but also the urbanization process in these regions. However, lessons from Western Europe and America have suggested that the expansion of public housing would make a profound impact on the private housing market, general social-economic development as well as the morphology of cities.

The chapters in this book mark a systematic attempt to examine critically the role of the new public housing in the Asian and other emerging urban economies, whilst drawing on the context of the maturing public and social housing sectors in Europe and North America.

In the remainder of this introductory chapter, we provide an overview and commentary on the individual chapters within it, although conclusions are left to the final chapter by Forrest (2013).

Public Housing in Asia

The full spectrum of public housing that can be found in the Asian countries is examined by Chiu (2013). She notes how its role ranges from 'absolute dominance' in Singapore, through 'significant presence' in Hong Kong whilst it plays only a 'marginal' role in Japan, South Korea and Taiwan. The term 'public housing' is also applied in different ways. At one end of the spectrum it means direct government provision of housing for the poor; at the other it means any intervention that lowers the market price of housing to promote 'affordable' housing.

Chiu examines whether the conditions exist that would allow the extensive public housing models of Hong Kong (and to an extent Singapore) to be transferred to mainland China. She argues that the Hong Kong model is not adequate to cater for the greater complexity of socio-economic and urban contexts that prevail in mainland China, and this helps to explain the wider range of housing schemes adopted by Chinese cities. Chiu identifies a number of factors that allowed public housing to flourish in Hong Kong. Intervention began in the early stages of rapid urbanization in Hong Kong, its colonial government was willing to make land available for public housing and, as a city state, the pressure of migration from rural areas was muted. Chiu also casts some doubt on the financial foundations of the Chinese public housing model. In Hong Kong, publically provided home-ownership schemes allowed funds to be recycled into the development of future public housing. In contrast, in China the home-ownership schemes are provided by private developers. These schemes limit the government's up-front financial commitment, but also mean that the profits accrue to the developer. The participatory and consultative governance mechanisms that help to ensure the quality of public housing in Hong Kong may also be lacking in mainland.

Mainland China

Chen et al. (2013) first provide a summary of pre-reform and post-reform public housing development in mainland China and then discuss why the Chinese government has again turned to public housing as a solution after some 30 years of housing reform and privatization. The authors show that the recent push for public housing in mainland China should not be seen as a step backwards or as the restoration of the pre-reform welfare housing system. Instead, it represents the central authority's increasing recognition of the complexity of urban housing systems in a modern market economy. Interestingly, the 'productivist' housing policy hypothesis can be used to explain why the recent massive construction of public housing in China is widely regarded as an economic vehicle to counteract the shocks of the global economic downturn and as a regulatory tool to cool down the overheating residential property markets.

Meanwhile, the shift in housing policy exemplifies many of the trends in Chinese social and economic policies that have emerged since the Global Financial Crisis. Over the last few years, the Chinese government has apparently become more cautious of market failure and has increasingly regained more direct control of resource allocation in many economic and social sectors. The massive new public housing program is thus designed to help balance economic growth and provide stability in light of the increasingly short supply of low-cost housing, high levels of inflation, and a growing wealth gap. However, this chapter also shows that the Chinese public housing model is being reshaped under the overall transformation of the country's guiding ideology in recent years. According to the new ideology of 'harmonious society' proposed by the Chinese Communist Party since 2006, social policy is no longer subordinated to economic policy but an integral part of it. The provision of affordable housing thus has become a political task in China to alleviate the level of inequality and income disparity generated by market and growth-led development in the post-reform era. This chapter provides some preliminary evidence that the change of Chinese public housing policy could be seen as a strong signal of a shift of ideology from 'productivist' to 'developmental' welfare.

Yang et al. (2013) examine the recent development of post-reform public housing programs in Beijing, the capital of China. Their focus is to test whether public housing programs in Beijing are accessible and affordable for target households. Based on a study of two public housing programs in Beijing, namely Economic and Comfortable Housing and Capped Price Housing, the authors find that low- and medium-income families' incomes fall far short of the level needed to afford subsidized housing. They argue that, to achieve the policy objective of public housing, it is critical for the local government to integrate public housing allocation into a wider coordinated context of urban planning and to ensure that public housing communities are designed with good access to public services.

Chang and Chen (2013) trace recent experience of public housing development in Shanghai, the largest city in China. This chapter uses Shanghai as case study to elaborate the multiple purposes behind the public housing programmes in China. It focuses the roles of two major public housing programmes, namely Relocation Housing and the new public rental housing (PRH) programme, in Shanghai's recent socio-spatial dynamics. It is shown that it is mainly a result of deliberate urban development policy in line with other strategies such as city marketing and gentrification. The authors suggest that the Shanghai municipal government uses the new public housing regime as a way to buttress local economic competitiveness. The analysis is augmented with data from a questionnaire survey of PRH tenants in Shanghai. It shows that PRH is a very selective program with a clear target to attract and retain the 'talented class' to enhance the city's competiveness.

Hong Kong

Yip (2013) identifies the public housing programme in Hong Kong as being the first example of 'intensive state intervention' in Asia. He explores how housing became the 'most important pillar of social policy' in a system that generally exhibits very high levels of economic liberalism. The shortage of land, its ownership by the state as well as Hong Kong's high population density all played their part. However, the sustained support for public housing was underpinned by a strong 'productivist' ethos of the British colonial administration and the provision of housing as a means to limit unrest and to gain legitimacy. Under British administration public housing was used to clear areas of slum housing for economic development and new towns were created to house the workforce required for new industries. The end of colonial rule in 1997 coincided with the Asian Financial Crisis and SARS, which prompted a withdrawal of the new administration in 2002 from assisted home-ownership programs that had been established in the late 1970s. This was intended to signal that the government would protect property values (by limiting supply). The public housing programs were initially scaled up, reaching a peak of more than 100,000 new units in 2000/2001, but have since been reduced and at less than one-quarter of the peak. Yip argues that the 'deep-rooted government-developer nexus' inhibits measures to 'suppress' the housing market, and so tackle underlying affordability problems that have been exacerbated by rising prices and growing income inequality. Receipts from land sales and stamp duty appear to be at the root of this nexus. Nonetheless, public support for public housing remains strong not only among beneficiaries but among the population as a whole.

Taiwan

Chang and Yuan (2013) introduce the development of public housing policy in Taiwan. They argue that the Taiwan government has failed to take the housing problems of the socially disadvantaged individuals seriously and has not considered providing public housing for economically disadvantaged individuals as an approach to lowering their housing costs. To date, the public housing issue in Taiwan has not been significantly improved. The authors believe that the deficiency of public housing provision in Taiwan is largely due to the political system. This chapter suggests that the purposes of public housing policy should be simplified and political intervention should be minimized so as not to confuse the essence of public housing. Furthermore, new directions for public housing policy in Taiwan are proposed.

South Korea

Jang and Kim (2013) introduce some lessons from the recent experience of public housing in Seoul, the capital of South Korea. Since 1990, the Korean government has rapidly expanded public housing to approximately 5 % of households. Moreover, each of Korea's political parties is in competition to supply as many public housing units as possible. The Seoul city government's target is to supply 80,000 public housing units in 4 years (2011–2015), which will effectively increase the stock to 7 % of households. However, the Seoul city government has struggled to acquire sufficient land to build public housing. For this reason, the Seoul city government is introducing new methods to supply public housing, such as purchasing existing private houses, acquiring public housing units in redevelopment projects, and encouraging small-scale developments, among others. These experiments are beneficial to finding practical ways to increase the public housing supply in countries of high population concentration with less available land and in countries that belatedly began their public housing programs.

Japan

Hirayama (2013) examines the connection between public housing and the development of neoliberal policies in Japan. Japan's postwar housing policy has consistently favored the growth of middle-class home ownership, while the public rented housing sector has been residual, and rent subsidy systems have not existed. This deficiency has combined with neoliberal policies that have served to marginalize low-income housing even further. In Japan, not only public housing but also employee housing and some private rented housing have made up the low-rent housing sector. Among developed countries, Japan's housing safety net system has been particularly flimsy. However, along with prolonged economic stagnation, it has become progressively difficult for those on low incomes to find adequate housing in the sphere of the market. Moreover, a decline in public housing, as well as employee housing and low-rent private housing, has caused the system of providing affordable housing to low-income groups to disintegrate. With the reduced availability of public and other low-rent housing, a new housing crisis has provoked a sharp increase in the number of people who are unable to secure dwellings. The author concludes that it is likely that the Japanese government will be pressed to undertake a substantial restructuring of housing policy beyond neoliberalism and to increase investment in low-income housing.

Singapore

Deng et al. (2013) discuss how the development of public housing has enabled Singapore to transform itself from a nation of home seekers to home owners since its independence. This chapter documents key policies and strategies that have helped to shape Singapore's public housing landscape over the last 50 years. It also shows that public housing is an important channel through which transfers of wealth to middle- and lower-income Singaporean households are facilitated. The Singapore government's dual role as a housing developer and a financer in the Housing Development Board (HDB)–Central Provident Fund system has been instrumental in the creation of an efficient and effective public housing sector. The authors argue that Singapore's public housing success story is built on an efficient centralized planning system. This includes institutional structures such as a dominant ruling political party and a competent civil service, and is supplemented by strong governance and a structure that facilities fair distribution. The authors highlight two challenges facing the public housing system in Singapore. First, it is challenging to balance the pricing dynamics between a regulated primary market and a decentralized laissez-faire secondary market. Second, the HDB is under increasing pressure to find more public funding and resources to meet the rising housing aspirations of Singaporean families.

Europe and North America

Murie (2013) provides an overview – both geographical and historical – of public housing in Europe and North America, noting that strictly speaking 'public housing' is now relatively rare. Many countries never adopted state-owned housing as a model, whilst many that did have now retreated from it. In addition to the USA (where there was never a sufficient political constituency to create a large public sector), Sweden and the UK provide the clearest remaining models of rental housing owned and managed by the state. Public housing was never anything other than marginal in southern Europe, whilst the state-owned housing in central and eastern Europe has generally been privatized. There has been a trend towards the development of a wider 'social' sector, with provision by non-state not-for-profit landlords, which sometimes act to moderate rents in the open market. Murie observes that the transition from 'public' to 'social' has tended to shift the emphasis from the mode of provision to the people who are housed. Whereas public housing was seldom intended primarily for the poor, the implication is that this is what social housing is for.

Murie observes that it is difficult to predict the level of decommodification in a housing system by that implied by Esping-Andersen's welfare regimes. Some countries whose social security systems offer only low levels of decommodification possess highly decommodifying housing systems, although he suggests that the relationship might be partly causal. He posits that more complicated policy and practice – including that implemented at the local level – might help to explain why a housing system might diverge from a welfare regime. He identifies a wide range of contextual factors, including demography, economic environment and political pressures that influence outcomes and are driving transitions in the housing system.

The hoped-for self-financing model of social housing seems to be rather more elusive than some authors have hoped for (though see Boelhouwer's account of the Netherlands). Whilst maturing social rented sectors in principle offer lower rents, in practice rents have risen towards market levels. In some countries, social or public sectors have shrunk dramatically due to privatization. This has taken the form of discounted sales to tenants in Central and Eastern Europe and in the UK. Privatization has helped to generate 'residualization' in the public or social housing, a phenomenon that is apparent even in those countries that have not adopted mass privatization.

Murie emphasizes the diversity of experience, arguing that the nature of public or social housing varies both within and between countries. Given the difficulty that the market has, if left unaided, in housing large sections of the population, he considers it at least possible that political support for the remnants of public sector might regain political support and enjoy a new phase of growth in the future.

United States of America

Deng and Zhu (2013) examine the role of public housing in the USA, a country with a very different political culture compared with much of Europe. A belief in the superiority of the market, a distrust of government and an attachment to individualism combined to ensure that public housing has never been in the mainstream of housing policy. This reflects the country's generally underdeveloped welfare state which, save for the New Deal and Great Society initiatives of Presidents Roosevelt and Johnson in the 1930s and 1960s, has not flourished. The failed attempt by the Clinton administration to extend the coverage of health insurance in the 1990s and the fierce battle over President Obama's more recent and successful initiative, reflect the fierce partisanship in American politics, which when combined with the constitutional separation of powers between legislature and executive, as well as the federal structure, mitigates against a significant role for the state.

As with many other countries, a crisis prompted the state to intervene in the housing market. In the case of the USA, it was the Great Depression of the 1930s when, Deng and Zhu (2013) inform us, half of residential mortgages were technically in default and the construction industry had collapsed. But the response was not to turn to public housing. Instead, the government established the Federal Housing Administration, which introduced mortgage insurance, and, together with reforms to the banking sector, formed the basis for the expansion of home-ownership during the years of post-war prosperity.

Although legislation was passed to facilitate public housing in the 1930s, the plans to expand the sector following the landmark 1949 Housing Act were impeded by the competing expenditure burdens arising from the war in Korea. The formation of a federal agency for housing (Housing and Urban Development) in the 1960s was accompanied by a significant – though by international standards still proportionately small – public housing program. However, it was not long before the backlash set in and the program wound down. The sector still exists, but is widely perceived – not entirely fairly – as having been a failure. Deng and Zhu argue that this illustrates the impossibility of sustaining a public housing program that does not command widespread public support.

Consequently, the 'trick' of American housing policy since the 1970s has been to devise policy instruments that are capable of providing affordable rental housing to the poor, that also command public support. This requirement meant that the key shift in housing policy in the USA was slightly different from that which occurred in Europe. The key shift was not from supply to demand-side subsidies (although this was also to occur), but from subsidized provision by the state to subsidized provision by the market. Hence the project-based 'Section 8' assistance introduced in under the 1974 Housing Act and the subsequent Low Income Housing Tax Credit (LIHTCs introduced after 1986) focused on subsidized private provision for people on low and moderate incomes. Within this framework, the demand-side voucher program helps to provide more targeted assistance on the lowest income households, and indeed can serve to make housing that has been subsidized by LIHTCs accessible to people on very low incomes. However, in contrast to European housing allowance schemes, it should be noted that vouchers are not an 'entitlement' program, so many of those who are eligible do not actually receive them due to rationing.

The durability of LIHTCs as a policy instrument – they have now been in existence for a quarter of a century – and, following a blip during the financial crisis, appear to be robust are points in their favor. Supporters of the US system also point to the way in which these policy instruments can help to avoid the concentration of subsidized housing in the same neighborhoods, something that has been so damaging for public housing. Ironically, part of the success attributed to LIHTCs may arise from their lack of transparency, which suggests that in the US context, the government has learned to intervene by stealth.

United Kingdom

The United Kingdom (UK) has a history of public housing subsidized by central government, dating back to 1919. Providing an historical overview of the sector, Stephens (2013) highlights the dilemmas faced by any public housing program: between the depth of subsidy and the scale of the program; between rent levels and the quality and location of the housing; and between targeting housing on the poor and creating poverty neighborhoods.

As in other countries, the early public rental housing was not aimed at the poorest households – indeed they could not afford even the subsidized rents. The Government's aspiration after the Second World War that public rental housing should house a wide range of social classes soon gave way to a prioritization of rehousing people who would otherwise be rendered homeless by the demolition of slum housing (almost all of which was owned by private landlords). Public rental housing was made affordable to them by lowering space standards, locating housing on peripheral locations or by increasing density (high rise). In addition, the differential rent schemes operated by local authorities since the 1930s were transformed into a national housing allowance scheme in the 1970s. Today more than 60 % of social renters in the UK receive this benefit.

At its peak around 1980, around one-third of households lived in public rental housing. Since then two important shifts have occurred: first, the discounted sale of properties to tenants under the 'right to buy'; second, local authorities now account for only half the total stock of social rental housing. The second of these phenomena arose because it became common in the 1990s and 2000s for local authorities to transfer their housing to independent not-for-profit organizations called housing associations. Moreover, almost all new social rented housing built since 1988 has been developed by housing associations.

These changes reflect, in part, the maturity of the sector: asset value growth in relation to outstanding debt. This allowed the discounted sales to tenants without a balance sheet loss to the government, and also many of the stock transfers that could be made without subsidy; indeed they allowed the stock to be refinanced to pay for its modernization. Other stock of lower value required subsidy to facilitate transfer, but behind all of this lies a second motivation for transfers: debt acquired by housing associations does not appear on the government's books.

The British social rented sector is frequently characterized as being 'residualized': incomes and employment levels are much lower amongst social tenants than their counterparts in other tenures. Stephens argues that one reason for this is that the UK economy generates relatively high levels of relative poverty and an important function of the social rented sector is to provide a safety net for them. However, he notes that a new financial model for financing new 'affordable' housing is predicated on higher rents, reduced security of tenure, at the same time as housing allowances are being restricted.

France

French social rented housing embodies much of the country's distinctive political and cultural outlook. Le Corbusier's modernism is expressed in the architecture of France's social housing, and in her chapter, Lévy-Vroelant (2013) argues that '[i]n France maybe more strongly than in other countries, social housing history has paralleled the country's industrial and economic development.' Whilst by no means immune from international trends, French political discourse has probably resisted the fashion for neo-liberal economic thought more strongly than in any other western European country.

The complexities of social housing in France are highlighted by the apparently contradictory public opinions towards the sector. Some 80 % of the population regard social housing to be a necessity; simultaneously, 74 % believe it to have a bad image. As Lévy-Vroelant observes, 'social housing is good, but for the others.' And being 'good for others' provides a sufficient support base to ensure that – almost uniquely in Europe – the social rented sector is growing in size, both absolutely and relatively.

Certainly, French social rented housing belongs to the family of 'generalist' systems whereby it is not reserved only for the poor. Indeed, whilst other systems may be stratified informally (as in the Scandinavian countries), in France three distinct types of social housing have been produced since the 1960s: 'standard', 'upper-income' and, 'very social' for the poor. So the image of large peripheral estates built in the 1960s and 1970s, now housing poor and immigrant households, sits aside that of high quality city center housing with the whiff of clientelism hanging over it. The generalist model does not avoid the concentrations of poverty, and poverty neighborhoods became the focus of urban policy in the 1990s. However, the availability of social housing for a wider section of society than would be the case in the USA seems to assist the retention of broad public support for the sector.

Questions of access have featured prominently in the development of French housing policy. In the late 1970s, a center-right government did embark on the shift in housing subsidy away from the supply side and towards the demand side. Often presented as a means of saving money, it should be remembered that housing allowances can open up social housing to the poorest households who could not otherwise afford the (nonetheless subsidized) rents. The trend has been towards a much greater representation of people from the lowest quartile of the income distribution in social rented housing, whilst the distribution of those in the top half of the income distribution has been diminishing. More recently, France has joined the UK in the introduction of a legally enforceable 'right' to housing.

There have been important changes to the financing of French social rented housing. The state has been retreating and has been instead increasingly playing the role of 'facilitator' encouraging public-private partnerships. As elsewhere assets are being sweated, but the future of social rented housing as a mainstream instrument of housing policy seems to be more secure in France than in many other European countries.

The Netherlands

The Netherlands is notable for the size of its social rented sector. It still represents almost one-third of the stock, although it has diminished from a peak of 41 % in the early 1990s. As Boelouwer (2013) notes in his chapter, the sector started to grow later than in many other European countries, but grew rapidly in part reflecting very strong demographic pressures, so escaped the retrenchment seen elsewhere in the 1970s or 1980s. Boelhouwer argues that the Netherlands social rented sector is a product of the country's wider welfare system and reflects a kind of labour-led corporatism. Certainly the size of the social rented sector is such that it is part of the mainstream housing market, impacting certainly on the private rented sector, and probably home-ownership too.

The Netherlands social rented sector provides a good example of maturation – the phenomenon whereby the asset value of the sector outweighs its debts. In the 1980s, the state began to disentangle itself from the sector and in 1995 the 'grossing and balancing' exercise left housing associations in effect without debt, but also without the prospect of future subsidy. With a supporting guarantee fund, which allows the associations to borrow cheaply on the markets, and another fund to assist financially distressed associations to restructure, the new arrangements have been characterized as a kind of 'revolving fund'. Under this principle the surpluses generated by a maturing sector are recycled and subsidize future investment.

The housing associations prospered under the new system, an outcome greatly facilitated by its co-incidence with a long period of economic growth and rising property values. Inevitably, particularly as the desire of the government to cut its budget deficit in the aftermath of the economic crisis, the social rented sector has been seen as a potential source of revenue for the government. The image of the housing associations – as rich and unaccountable corporations – has not strengthened their position in this respect.

The sector is therefore at a junction. An intervention by the European Commission led to protracted negotiations under the state-aid rules, which interpreted the sector as providing unfair competition with private landlords. Consequently, an income limit has been placed on eligibility, although some 40 % of households remain eligible, and 10 % of allocations can be made outside the limit. Although the principle of universal access may have ended, in practice the impact is likely to be relatively small, and the sector will remain far less residualized than in countries such as the UK.

More controversial has been government attempts to extract surpluses from the sector. Some rent rises for the highest income groups have been introduced, but more controversially a property tax seeks to extract surpluses to pay for housing allowances. However this runs up against the status of housing associations as private bodies, and such a measure would be a form of expropriation. In the event the difficulty in forming governments removed the immediate threat to the housing associations.

Nonetheless there is a feeling that the sector cannot continue to exist without reform. Boelhouwer highlights the various options, which include splitting the functions between profit- and non-profit making activities, or even introducing private equity into the sector. However, he concludes that a continuation of the existing system with the government playing a stronger supervisory role would be most consistent with the form of modern corporatist welfare state that prevails in the country.

Sweden

Sweden has long since been held up of the exemplar of a 'unitary' housing system located within a 'social democratic' welfare regime. Certainly the model of public housing that was developed in Sweden was distinctive, and for a long time the label of 'social' was rejected as bringing with it misleading connotations of US-style segregation. In his chapter, Andersson (2013) reminds us of the way in which public housing (which takes the form of housing owned by municipal housing companies) was developed in Sweden. The so-called 'construction phase' was especially intense during the period of the 'million homes program' between 1965 and 1974. Although the quantity of housing built was remarkable in its own right, it was the manner of its governance that was distinctive. Rents in the municipal sector were set using 'utility' standards, which were based on cost recovery and physical standards with less emphasis on location. Rent rises were agreed using corporatist structures which took the form of annual negotiations between landlords and tenants. Crucially, the rent set for the municipal sector formed the basis of rents in the private sector. By 'leading' the market in this way, a 'unitary' rental sector was created, in which the impact of the municipal sector was far greater than its size.

However, the key foundations of the Swedish system have been undermined since the budget crisis of the early 1990s. Interest subsidies have been removed, and very little new building in the sector has occurred since then. A form of privatization was also introduced in the 1990s and reinforced in 2007 after a period when it had been made more restrictive. This has resulted in sales of municipal housing to tenants (in the form of co-operatives), notably in the capital, Stockholm. In other municipalities, some transfers to private landlords have occurred. The rent-leading role of the municipal housing companies was abolished in 2010, and they are now expected to run themselves according to 'business-like' principles.

There has been a gradual decline in the relative scale of public housing in Sweden. This is attributable to the lack of new build, demolitions in low-demand areas and privatization. Whilst the proportion of the housing stock, that is public rental, has declined from a quarter to perhaps one-fifth of the stock since the mid-1980s, only about 14 % of the population lived in it in 2008. The model of public housing developed in Sweden reflected the remarkable electoral dominance of the Social Democratic Party, which held office continuously for four decades from 1936 to 1976. However, the party's electoral hegemony is now ended. Moreover, Sweden's system of economic management is no longer so distinctive: it has been a member of the European Union (although outside the European single currency) since 1995.

Andersson advances the important arguments that as the central state withdraws from housing, the local state – in the form of Sweden's 300-odd municipalities – will become more important in determining the future of public housing. It is notable that there have been wide variations in changes in the proportion of the population housed in public housing. The reduction has been especially striking in Stockholm where the proportion of the population living in public housing fell from one-third to one-fifth between 1990 and 2010. In contrast, the proportion was stable in Malmö. Andersson (2013) demonstrates that the political control of municipalities helps to explain the level of municipal housing in 1990 and changes in its share by 2008. He concludes that although politics explains only part of the level and change in level of municipal housing, 'politics matters.'

Hungary

What happens when a country divests itself of almost all of its public housing? In common with other European transition countries, Hegedüs (2013) records that Hungary privatized almost all of its public housing after 1990. In 1990 around 23 % of the housing stock was publically owned, but this has been reduced to around 3 %. Hungary, like many other transition countries, has become a 'super-home ownership' state. This has had the effect of making the remaining stock of public housing very residualized – both in terms of the people living there who are generally very poor and its physical quality and location. Whilst there have been programs to improve its quality – notably to repair and improve the energy efficiency of panel housing – the sector is far from the mainstream of housing policy.

In the formative years of transition from communism, the Hungarian government acceded to the pressures from the banking and construction industries to introduce tax subsidies for mortgages and house-building. With a relatively strong economy from the latter part of the 1990s, the mortgage market began to develop, but with a distinctive characteristic: a high proportion of loans were denominated in foreign currencies. So, when, as a result of the financial crisis, house prices fell by a quarter and the Hungarian currency devalued, the impact on the mortgaged ownership sector was far-reaching.

These difficulties in the housing market coincided with Hungary's general economic malaise and the country required the support of a loan from the International Monetary Fund. With greater public borrowing being blocked off as a possibility, the populist government decided to assist people with mortgages by shifting the cost of currency devaluation from borrowers on the banking sector. This is part of an 'unorthodox' economic policy whereby public expenditure is boosted to the benefit of the better off by 'taxing' the banks and other corporations. As with other interventions of the transformation era, the 'unorthodox' housing policy appears to have benefitted the better off the most. Another measure by which delinquent loans would be nationalized in order to save the tenants from foreclosure involves housing being rented back to its former owners. As Hegedüs notes, the scheme could mark the biggest expansion of the social rented sector since 1989 – an ironic outcome of the push to develop owner-occupation. However, questions remain about its viability and sustainability, given that rents do not cover maintenance. Hegedüs reaches the pessimistic conclusion that unless new models of social housing are developed, housing will become an important source of social conflict.

Shanghai, People's Republic of China — Jie Chen
Cambridge, USA — Yanyun Man
Edinburgh, Scotland, UK — Mark Stephens

References

Andersson R (2013) Chapter 15: Understanding variation in the size of the public housing sector across Swedish municipalities: the role of politics. In: Chen J, Stephens M, Man JY (eds) The future of public housing: ongoing trends in the east and the west. Springer, Beijing

Boelhouwer P (2013) Chapter 14: Maturation of the Dutch social housing model and perspectives for the future. In: Chen J, Stephens M, Man JY (eds) The future of public housing: ongoing trends in the east and the west. Springer, Beijing

Chang Y, Chen J (2013) Chapter 4: Public housing in shanghai: a tool with multiple purposes. In: Chen J, Stephens M, Man JY (eds) The future of public housing: ongoing trends in the east and the west. Springer, Beijing

Chang C-O, Yuan S-M (2013) Chapter 6: Public housing policy in Taiwan. In: Chen J, Stephens M, Man JY (eds) The future of public housing: ongoing trends in the east and the west. Springer, Beijing

Chen J, Hao Q, Stephens M (2010) Assessing housing affordability in post-reform China: a case study of Shanghai. Hous Stud 25(6):877–901

Chen, J, Guo, F, & Zhu, A (2011) The Housing-led Growth Hypothesis Revisited: Evidence from the Chinese Provincial Panel Data. Urba Stud 48(10): 2049–2067

Chen J, Jing J, Yang Z, Man JY (2013) Chapter 2: Public housing in mainland China: history, ongoing trends, and future perspectives. In: Chen J, Stephens M, Man JY (eds) The future of public housing: ongoing trends in the east and the west. Springer, Beijing

Chiu RLH (2013) Chapter 1: The transferability of public housing policy within Asia: reflections from the Hong Kong-mainland china case study. In: Chen J, Stephens M, Man JY (eds) The future of public housing: ongoing trends in the east and the west. Springer, Beijing

Deng Y, Sing TF, Re C (2013) Chapter 7: The story of Singapore's public housing: from a nation of home-seekers to a nation of homeowners. In: Chen J, Stephens M, Man JY (eds) The future of public housing: ongoing trends in the east and the west. Springer, Beijing

Deng L, Zhu X (2013) Chapter 11: From public housing to joint ventures: lessons from the U.S. Housing policy development. In: Chen J, Stephens M, Man JY (eds) The future of public housing: ongoing trends in the east and the west. Springer, Beijing

Forrest R (2013) Chapter 17: Some reflections on public housing. In: Chen J, Stephens M, Man JY (eds) The future of public housing: ongoing trends in the east and the west. Springer, Beijing

Hegedus J (2013) Chapter 16: "Unorthodox" housing policy in Hungary: is there a Way back to public housing? In: Chen J, Stephens M, Man JY (eds) The future of public housing: ongoing trends in the east and the west. Springer, Beijing

Hirayama Y (2013) Chapter 9: Public housing and neoliberal policy in Japan. In: Chen J, Stephens M, Man JY (eds) The future of public housing: ongoing trends in the east and the west. Springer, Beijing

Jang Y-h, Kim S-H (2013) Chapter 8: New experiments in public housing supply in Seoul, south Korea: the possibilities and limits. In: Chen J, Stephens M, Man JY (eds) The future of public housing: ongoing trends in the east and the west. Springer, Beijing

Kemeny J, Lowe S (1998) Schools of comparative housing research: from convergence to divergence. Hous Stud 13(2):161–176

Lévy-Vroelant C (2013) Chapter 13: "Everyone should be housed": the French generalist model of social housing at stake. In: Chen J, Stephens M, Man JY (eds) The future of public housing: ongoing trends in the east and the west. Springer, Beijing

Lowe, S (2003) Introduction: housing in post-communist Europe: issues and agendas, in Lowe, S and Tsenkova, S (eds) Housing Change in East and Central Europe: Integration or Fragmentation?, xiii-xix, Aldershot: Ashgate

Li, K (2011) Massive-scale implementation of security housing program and step-by-step improvement of housing policy and provision system. Qiu Shi(in Chinese), 2011-04-16, Beijing

Lui H-K (2007) The redistributive effect of public housing in Hong Kong. Urban Stud 44(10):1937–1952

Murie A (2013) Chapter 10: Public housing in Europe and North America. In: Chen J, Stephens M, Man JY (eds) The future of public housing: ongoing trends in the east and the west. Springer, Beijing

Priemus H, Dieleman F (2002) Social housing policy in the European union: past, present and perspectives. Urban Stud 39(2):191–200

Stephens, M (2005). A Critical Analysis of Housing Finance Reform in a "Super" Home-ownership State: The Case of Armenia. Urban Stud, 42(10):1795–1815

Stephens M (2010) Locating Chinese urban housing policy in an international context. Urban Stud 47(14):2965–2982

Stephens M (2013) Chapter 12: Social housing in the United Kingdom. In: Chen J, Stephens M, Man JY (eds) The future of public housing: ongoing trends in the east and the west. Springer, Beijing

Stephens M, Chen J, Man JY (2013) Preface: The future of public housing: ongoing trends in the east and the west. In: Chen J, Stephens M, Man JY (eds) The future of public housing: ongoing trends in the east and the west. Springer, Beijing

Whitehead CME (1999) The provision of finance for social housing: the UK experience. Urban Stud 36(4):657–672

World Bank (1993) Housing: enabling markets to work. Washington, DC

Yang Z, Yi C, Wang W (2013) Chapter 3: Public housing programs and the challenge of household affordability in Beijing. In: Chen J, Stephens M, Man JY (eds) The future of public housing: ongoing trends in the east and the west. Springer, Beijing

Yip N-m (2013) Chapter 5: Challenges to public housing in post-colonial Hong Kong. In: Chen J, Stephens M, Man JY (eds) The future of public housing: ongoing trends in the east and the west. Springer, Beijing

Acknowledgement

The production of this book is supported by Lincoln Institute of Land Policy, National Science Foundation of China (NSF71173045), Key Social-Science Research Project of the Ministry of Education of the People's Republic of China (13JZD009), Ministry of Housing and Urban Development of the People's Republic of China (2012–21), and Fudan University 985-III Project (2012SHKXQN012).

Contents

Contributors

Roger Andersson Professor, Department of Social and Economic geography, Institute for Housing and Urban Research, Uppsala university, Uppsala, Sweden

Peter Boelhouwer Professor and Department Head, OTB Research Institute for the Built Environment, Faculty of Architecture and the Built Environment, Delft University of Technology, Delft, GA, Netherlands

Chin-Oh Chang Professor, Department of Land Economics, National Chengchi University, Taipei, Taiwan

Ying Chang Assistant Professor, Department of Urban Planning and Design, Xi'an Jiaotong-Liverpool University, Suzhou, Jiangsu, People's Republic of China

Jie Chen Professor and Deputy Director of the Institute of Real Estate Research, School of Public Economics and Administration, Shanghai University of Finance and Economics (SHUFE), Shanghai, People's Republic of China

Rebecca L.H. Chiu Professor, Department of Urban Planning and Design, The University of Hong Kong, Pokfulam, Hong Kong

Lan Deng Associate Professor, Urban and Regional Planning, University of Michigan, Ann Arbor, MI, USA

Yongheng Deng Provost's Chair Professor and Director, Institute of Real Estate Studies (IRES), School of Design; NUS Business School, National University of Singapore, Singapore, Singapore

Ray Forrest Chair Professor, Department of Public and Social Administration, City University of Hong Kong, Hong Kong, China

József Hegedüs Managing Director, Metropolitan Research Institute, Budapest, Hungary

Yosuke Hirayama Professor, Graduate School of Human Development and Environment, Kobe University, Kobe, Japan

Yeong-Hee Jang Vice President, The Seoul Institute, Seoul, South Korea

Juan Jing Research Fellow, China Programme of International Centre for Planning Research, Cardiff University (UK), Beijing, China

Soo-Hyun Kim Associate Professor, Graduate School of Urban and Real Estate Studies, Sejong University, Seoul, South Korea

Claire Lévy-Vroelant Professor, Centre de recherche sur l'habitat, UMR LAVUE, CNRS, University of Paris, Paris, France

Yanyun Man Professor, College of Urban and Environmental Sciences, Peking University, Beijing, People's Republic of China

Senior Fellow, Lincoln Institute of Land Policy, Cambridge, MA, USA

Alan Murie Emeritus Professor, Centre for Urban and Regional Studies, School of Geography, Earth and Environmental Sciences, University of Birmingham, Birmingham, UK

Chaoqun Ren Graduate Student, Institute of Real Estate Studies (IRES), Department of Real Estate, School of Design and Environment, National University of Singapore, Singapore, Singapore

Tien Foo Sing Associate Professor, Institute of Real Estate Studies (IRES), Department of Real Estate, School of Design and Environment, National University of Singapore, Singapore, Singapore

Mark Stephens Professor, School of the Built Environment, Heriot-Watt University, Edinburgh, Scotland, UK

Zhu Xiaodi Deputy Director, The DC Office, The Ameson Education and Cultural Exchange Foundation, Washington, DC, USA

Zan Yang Associate Professor, Hang Lung Center for Real Estate, Department of Construction Management, Tsinghua University, Beijing, China

Chengdong Yi Professor, Department of Urban and Real Estate Management, Central University of Finance and Economics, Beijing, People's Republic of China

Ngai Ming Yip Professor, Department of Public Policy, City University of Hong Kong, Hong Kong SAR, Hong Kong

Shu-Mei Yuan PhD Student, Department of Land Economics, National Chengchi University, Taipei, Taiwan

Wei Zhang Graduate Student, Hang Lung Center for Real Estate, Department of Construction Management, Tsinghua University, Beijing, China

Part I
Public Housing in the East

Chapter 1
The Transferability of Public Housing Policy Within Asia: Reflections from the Hong Kong-Mainland China Case Study

Rebecca L.H. Chiu

1.1 Introduction

The use of the terminology 'public housing' varies among Asian countries. Some refer to housing directly provided and funded under the aegis of the government, inclusive of rental and owner-occupier housing, e.g. in Hong Kong and Singapore. Some only refer to rental housing directly provided and produced with government subsidy and let to low income families or special population groups, e.g. in China, South Korea, Taiwan and Japan. To enable a more comprehensive discussion, this chapter adopts a wider definition of public housing as applied in Hong Kong and Singapore, that is, cheaper rental or owner-occupier housing provided by the government or developers involving public funding and public resources (e.g. land) not priced at market rates in the production process. Housing acquired with the support of consumer subsidy alone is excluded. This definition differs from the more embracing terminology of 'protective housing' (*baozhangxing zhufang*) used in China, which means guaranteed access to decent and affordable housing commensurate with the housing users' socio-economic status, including controlled private housing, e.g. private housing projects subject to price control or size control. Simply put, as translated by the State Council, it refers to 'affordable housing'.

The spectrum of public housing provision in the major Asian economies ranges from absolute dominance (Singapore), through significant presence (Hong Kong) to marginal existence (Japan, South Korea and Taiwan). Public housing provision is part and parcel of the general housing welfare policy. The intensity and extensity of housing subsidy is argued to be determined by how respective Asian government perceives the role of housing in the socio-economic and political development strategies, qualified by the financial and other housing resources available to the government, such as state-owned land. In the case where housing is entrusted with

R.L.H. Chiu (✉)
Department of Urban Planning and Design, The University of Hong Kong, Pokfulam, Hong Kong
e-mail: rlhchiu@hku.hk

J. Chen et al. (eds.), *The Future of Public Housing: Ongoing Trends in the East and the West*, DOI 10.1007/978-3-642-41622-4_1,

important political and social functions, the housing welfare policy covered a wider array of population groups, such as the case of Singapore. Where the economic function dominates, housing welfare is primarily targeted at the economically active groups, such as the public rental housing policy of Hong Kong in the 1960s and 1970s, and Japan's home ownership policy from 1950 to early 1990s (Chiu 2008; Chiu 2010).

In the past 15 years, Asian countries went through two financial crises and two subsequent economic recessions. A consequence of these economic shocks, especially the Asian financial crisis which had much stronger impacts on the Asian region than the global financial crisis, was the re-engineering of housing policies in most of the affected countries. The policy changes were necessary for rescuing the economy, ensuring social stability, and tackling the weaknesses of the incumbent housing policies unveiled by the drastic economic changes. In the main, by 2010, the impetus of home ownership had either mitigated (e.g. in China), stagnated (e.g. in Singapore) or even terminated (e.g. in Hong Kong). Another significant policy trend was the new emphasis given to rental subsidies (e.g. South Korea and Singapore) resultant from the deteriorated economic conditions triggered off by the two financial crises specifically, and increasing social polarization incurred by globalization and the pursuits for knowledge economy generally. Although China has been less affected by the economic crises, its housing reform underpinned by marketization since the 1980s had gradually been proved to be inadequate to meet all housing needs in the mid-2000s. Thus, subsidized housing provision was brought back to the agenda of the central government in 2007. Eventually, a national attempt to revise and expand the housing subsidy policy in all cities was launched by the central government in 2011. The most recent trend in Asia since 2011 has been, nonetheless, the restoration of home ownership subsidy to combat housing affordability problems engendered by extraordinary housing price hikes resultant from the movement of global funds from the West to the Asian region and strong domestic economic growths (Chiu 2013).

Inevitably, as in the past years, public housing policy in Asia will continue to evolve responding to societal changes. A common step in the policy re-engineering process was to find out how other governments tackled similar problems, and whether the successful experience of other countries could be borrowed. China's central government actually mandated in the 2011 affordable housing drive that in formulating the local affordable housing policy, governments should learn from the public housing policy of other Asian cities, especially Hong Kong and Singapore. Policy transferability study provides important reference for policy development.

Yet, policy transferability has been rarely discussed in the comparative housing literature. Apart from Chiu's (2010) and Pawson and Hulse (2011) recent work, the only brief conceptual discourse on transferability is found in Oxley (2001). It is therefore necessary to thrash out the transferability issues in the Asian context for understanding possible future changes in Asia's public housing policy. The purpose of this chapter is thus to pioneer the investigation of public housing transferability in Asia given its unique characteristics by examining the transferability of public housing policy from Hong Kong to Chinese cities as a case study. Direct public housing policy provision has been one of the most common methods of housing subsidy provision in the Asian countries. Since Hong Kong's public housing policy is generally regarded as successful, and the central government of mainland China has officially asked local governments to learn from Hong Kong, it is thus instrumental to begin the investigation of policy transferability in Asia from these two places.

The analysis in this chapter examines the possibility of transferring housing policy to Chinese cities, rather than the actual transfer process itself. The investigation will focus on issues concerning the reasons for transferring housing policy from Hong Kong, and the factors affecting the actual or potential successes and failures of the transferred policy. Issues examined include socio-economic factors notably the rapidly urbanizing contexts of Chinese cities; and policy environment factors such as essential resources required for a producer housing subsidy approach and the features of the decision making process in housing. The analysis elucidates the similarities and differences in housing policy and the policy environments, contributing to future consideration of policy transfer.

1.2 Conceptual Framework

The lack of attention to policy transferability in the housing literature is in part because of the intricacy of such analyses (Oxley 2001), and also because of the limited interest in cross-national policy transfer analyses in public policy studies until the 1990s (Dolowitz and Marsh 1996; Mossberger and Wolman 2003). Since then, globalization and the dramatic advancement in information technology have induced and enabled policy transfer, engendering the emergence of policy transfer literature in comparative public policy research. Based on the policy transfer literature, the pioneering work of Chiu (2010) examined the replicability of Hong Kong's public rental housing policy system. The paper argues that it is necessary to investigate the policy environment (land ownership and development control, funding mechanism and governance) of the originating countries/cities and to discern its roots in their national, social and historical contexts, that is, the macro and meso levels of investigations have to be combined. Chiu (2010) has demonstrated that the assessment of the policy environment enables the identification of the possibilities and constraints of policy replicability, which is important for the subsequent comparative analysis when the importing country/city is drawn into the investigation.

In the comparative inquiry examining the transferability of housing policy to the recipient countries and in explaining the performance of the transferred policy, Chiu (2010) suggests that the three level analysis found in the policy transfer literature can be adopted: macro, meso and micro. The macro analyses compare the compatibility of the social, political, economic, historical and ideological contexts of the originating and the borrowing housing systems. The meso analyses investigate policy transfers in their legal, institutional, cultural and financial frameworks, or in a nutshell, the policy environment. The policy targets, budgetary resources and the governance structure defining the power relations in decision making are some of the major issues to be investigated. At the micro level, the major concerns are the actual transfer processes, notably the actors and agents involved. For the purpose of this study, the micro level analysis is excluded as it pertains more to the transfer process rather than the possibility of policy transfer.

1.3 The Analysis

1.3.1 The Socio-economic and Political Contexts: Reasons for Transferring Housing Policy from Hong Kong

As pointed out in the policy transfer literature, policies selected for transfer are usually those that have proven to be successful, with important similarities, or have tackled similar problems (Mossberger and Wolman 2003:430). An obvious reason for choosing Hong Kong is its generally known success in developing and operating one of the largest public housing programs in Asia, comprised of both rental and owner-occupier housing, totaling 720,000 dwellings and 440,000 dwellings in 2013 respectively, accommodating 46.3 % of Hong Kong's households (Hong Kong Housing Authority 2013; Census and Statistics Department 2011). Apart from the scale, as discussed later, the ability of Hong Kong's public housing sector to be financially self-sufficient, largely self-contained in terms of meeting the residents' daily needs, able to maintain an orderly, clean, safe and a generally satisfying living environment are other major reasons.

Similar to large Chinese cities, Hong Kong is a high density city mainly comprised of high rises, though its compactness (in terms of development intensity and land use mix) is greater than many Chinese cities. While its legal, political and institutional systems are different from Chinese cities, Hong Kong's economic, social and ethnic ties and to a large extent cultural affinity as well, have made experience sharing easier. Given these similarities and dissimilarities, Hong Kong offers a window for Chinese cities to closely observe institutional alternatives for solving urban and housing problems.

Hong Kong went through rapid economic and urban development since the late 1960s. In its earlier years of economic take-off, it also used public housing as a way to tie down the transitional population from China in order to support the flourishing manufacturing industry for keeping up the economic momentum. In the 1970s, public rental housing was added a social objective: to enhance social and political stability. In the 1980s and 1990s, subsidized home ownership schemes were expanded to meet other social and economic concerns: the rising aspiration in home ownership and the aggravating affordability problems (Chiu 2003; Yeung and Wong (2003)). The large scale of the public rental housing programs were largely effective in solving the housing needs of the low income families, despite the housing price hikes in 1981–1982, 1990–1993, 1996–1997, and 2010–2013. Since the 1970s, with the exception of the unprecedentedly long spell of economic depression after the Asian financial crisis, the private housing market has thrived because of strong domestic demand and lately external demand as well. It may be argued that the government can retain its minimal interventionist policy in controlling the housing market and facilitating the real estate sector to become a major economic propeller because the lower income groups are already protected by the public housing programs.

Thus, problems tackled or solved by Hong Kong's housing policy are similar to those faced by the Chinese cities today. But there are more in the China context. First, the scale of urbanization, indirectly population growth, is of a much larger scale in Chinese cities. E.g. urban population grew by 8.8 million and 3.9 million between 1990 and 2012 in Beijing and Shanghai respectively, compared with a total population of a mere 7 million in Hong Kong today. Thus, housing needs and demands are of a much larger magnitude in Chinese cities. Second, the household registration system in Chinese cities also complicates the housing subsidy policies – more than 35 % of the permanent population in Beijing and Shanghai are non-registered population in 2010, mobile population excluded (Chiu 2012). Decisions on the eligibility criteria for housing subsidy do not only have huge implications on land and financial resources, but also on population policy (especially that concerning rural-urban migration), human resources policy (particularly in terms of attracting 'talented migrants'), for instance. Is the housing subsidy policy to resolve problems associated with these issues at the same time?

No doubt maintaining social stability is a common concern of the housing policy of both Hong Kong and other Chinese cities. But perhaps given China's rapidly polarizing socio-economic structure resultant from the unleashing of the market forces and its rapid urbanization process bringing into the cities the very poor from the rural areas, social stability and social conflict are greater and more complex issues than what the colonial government of Hong Kong faced in the late 1960s. Economically, China could also make use of the public rental policy to secure a large and stable supply of contented labour to support the manufacturing and processing industries (note that dormitory type of accommodation is less able to sustain stable and contented labour supply, as is happening in Guangdong). But a deeper issue is whether the public housing policy, which protects the lower income families from the tyranny of the housing market, is also tasked to enable a more market-driven and open private housing sector to stimulate the growth of the real estate sector.

Thus, apart from confirming the worthiness of the policy to be transferred by assessing its performance, it is also necessary to analyze and compare its urban, socio-economic and political contexts in the originating city and that of the potential recipient cities in order to identify and determine the potential functions of the transferred policy. Such decisions establish the fundamental validity for the transfer and what exactly to be transferred. Based on the above discussion, the broader objectives and implications of subsidized housing policy could be greater in Chinese cities than those in Hong Kong. Thus, the Hong Kong type of public housing policy could only fulfill some of the broader social objectives of the housing policy of Chinese cities. More diversified housing policy tools than a public housing program are needed to fulfill the many and complicated objectives of Chinese housing policy. The policy environment is yet another major aspect influencing policy transferability.

1.3.2 The Policy Environment

Following on from the macro analysis above, the focus of the meso level of analysis is the policy environment, which directly determines the capability of the importing city to replicate the policy and to achieve similar, if not better, performance as in the originating cities. This analysis will not examine the legal or regulatory tools and the general cultural factor as they are less instrumental to the producer subsidy approach adopted in Hong Kong. Instead, the attention is given to the factors which are fundamental to the performance of Hong Kong's public housing policy, namely, land, housing finance, governance and the institutional structure.

1.3.2.1 Land Factors

Land in both Hong Kong and mainland Chinese cities is state-owned. However, as pointed out in Chiu (2010), once leased, they become *de facto* private land as the leases are usually renewable in Hong Kong. Thus, Chiu (2010) argues that Hong Kong can operate a large scale public housing program because the program had started before the rapid growth of the city, enabling the government to build public housing on new land alongside with city expansion. Consequently, presently 74 % of the public housing flats are found in the main urban area (45 %) or the inner new towns (29 %). The rapid growth of major Chinese cities started in the early 1990s. To push for large scale development of public housing after almost two decades of rapid urbanization would be challenging. The problem aggravates if infrastructure development, especially public transport, is not well provided to reduce travelling time and to relieve the housing-job imbalance problems. Worse still, in a more developed city, there is always keener competition for land resources, making it difficult for the local governments to keep land for public housing use, not to speak of the need to generate public revenue and to spur economic growth by leasing land for private housing development. Thus, to spare land for public housing development requires great commitment from local governments in Chinese cities. Perhaps a solution to resolve this dilemma is by way of increasing land utility efficiency, that is, allowing greater development intensity over residential land earmarked for public housing development. However, the ill effects of high rise living needs to be compensated by more careful land use and residential planning and design to avoid compromising the quality of the living environment.

1.3.2.2 Housing Finance

Financially the public housing program of Hong Kong has been self-sufficient after an injection of an interest-bearing permanent capital of HK$16.4 billion in 1987. This is possible because of a number of factors (Chiu 2010). First, land is offered free for the construction of public rental housing, and at cost price for subsidized owner-occupier housing. Second, public rental and subsidized owner-occupier housing is provided and managed by one single organization in both the public sector (The Hong Kong Housing Authority) and the voluntary sector (The Hong Kong Housing Society). This enables the deployment of proceeds from home sale to fund the construction and the operation of rental housing which cannot be self-sufficient financially. Third, the indexing of the price of the subsidized home ownership schemes to market housing price, which co-incidentally had been on the upward trend generally, enables the Hong Kong Housing Authority to make windfall gains from these schemes. Fourth, the rental income from the retail properties in the public housing estates also constitute a major source of income for the public housing sector, though the rental income has to be shared equally with the government as a way of paying for the land cost of the retail property. All these factors are related to policy design.

However, except the land factor, the other factors of the policy environment identified above are not found in the mainland Chinese cities. To replicate the non-land factors, the capability to transform the organizational structure of public housing provision to that of Hong Kong is crucial as the other two factors (price indexing and income from retail properties) will not be effective in bringing about funding to public housing providers without centralizing the organizational structure. Currently, all subsidized home ownership schemes in Chinese cities are directly produced and provided by development companies in the private sector, while public rental housing is mostly provided by government bureaus. The advantage of this mode of provision is that there is no capital outlay from the government in operating the subsidized home sale schemes, but the disadvantage is that the profit from these housing schemes does not go to the government either.

An obstacle for the Chinese cities to adopt the Hong Kong model may be the requirement of an enormous starting fund which local governments cannot afford or are unwilling to pay for. Another risk is the possibility of making a loss, especially if the sale price is indexed with the volatile market prices. After all, there were historical contingency factors at play which enabled Hong Kong to accumulate a sizeable capital from the subsidized home ownership schemes and the retail properties (for details, please see Chiu 2010). However, there could be a deeper ideological issue in that at the wake of a housing system reform which upheld the market principle, it is politically incorrect to restore a subsidized housing system which is dominated by a government housing provider. But as long as a recyclable flow of housing fund is not established, a public housing program of the scale of Hong Kong or Singapore cannot be replicated in Chinese cities.

1.3.2.3 Governance and Institutional Factors

Chiu (2010) points out that as the economic urgency to operate a massive public housing program dissipated in the 1990s, the continued improvement of public housing standards in Hong Kong until today is attributed to the elitist but increasingly consultative mode of governance of the public housing system. The dominant public housing provider, the Hong Kong Housing Authority, is an incorporated organization, the operation of which abides by an ordinance. It is nonetheless supported by a government department, the Housing Department, as its executive arm. In the governing board, there are only 5 official members, but 26 non-official members who are leading professionals, politicians, academics and interest group representatives. While the new housing policy directives or major housing schemes are initiated by the Governor before 1997 or the Chief Executive after 1997, the detailed policy design and implementation, and the monitor of the execution are left to the governing board of the Housing Authority and its standing committees in charge of different aspects of the operation of the public housing program. The actual execution of the decisions of the governing board such as the implementation of the home sale exercises, and the operation and management of the public housing stock and its residents, are carried out by the Housing Department manned by civil servants.

Owing to the large population in the public housing sector, politicians are mindful of public housing affairs in order to gain support from their electorates (Chiu 2010). Thus, many of the new initiatives in public housing come from politicians; officials of the Housing Department usually have to balance the interests of different political camps. Political parties also monitor the work of the Housing Department through their elected members in the Legislative Council. At the housing estate level, the political parties are also heavily involved in the monitoring of the management of housing estates through their elected members in district councils. The Estate Management Advisory Committee and the Mutual Aid Committees at the estate level, which are mainly comprised of residents and are either set up or endorsed by the Housing Department, also have considerable influence in the management of estates. These consultative organizations directly affect the quality of the living environment of public housing. Thus, the mode of governance of the Housing Authority has a major impact on the quantitative and qualitative standards of public housing in Hong Kong and is instrumental in maintaining the good standards. As the governance mode is embedded in the political culture and the overall governance structure, this is perhaps the most difficult to replicate in Chinese cities, which usually have non-participatory governance systems. Although a few Chinese cities have set up housing authorities, it is generally consultative in nature, without decision making and executive power and community representation.

1.4 Conclusions

This chapter argues that given the much more complex socio-economic and urban contexts, the Hong Kong type of public housing policy can only partially fulfill the many social objectives associated with the subsidized or affordable housing policy of Chinese cities. Thus, the direct provision of public housing alone does not suffice. This explains why a wider array of affordable housing schemes covering more population types has been developed in most Chinese cities. In terms of the policy environment, this chapter suggests that greater commitment from the local governments in providing affordable housing and increasing the development intensity of residential blocks may be the ways to maximize land resources for public housing construction in Chinese cities. Land availability alone cannot enable a large scale of public housing supply, however. To develop a recyclable flow of funds to support the supply and operation of a large public rental housing program, a build-for-sale scheme of considerable scale needs to be operated simultaneously by the same housing providers which have to be either non-profit-making government agents or voluntary agents with a genuine interests to help provide affordable housing to the low income families. This possibility seems rather remote given the existing industrial structure in the affordable housing provision system in most Chinese cities. Lastly, to facilitate the timely supply of public housing to meet the needs of the lower income families and to improve and maintain the quality of public housing, a more participatory and consultative mode of governance of the housing system is required.

Conceptually, the analysis in this chapter focuses on the socio-economic and political contexts in the assessment of the transferability of policy goals and objectives. In the case of greater differences in historical, cultural, ideological and urban contexts, the scope of comparative analysis needs to be widened. Similarly, in examining the policy environment, the critical issues to be analyzed and compared would depend on the types of policy to be transferred and the effects to be achieved. For instance, to examine the transferability of a consumer approach for the provision of affordable housing, the analysis of the conditions and the structure of financial market and the capacity of the private housing market will be crucial. As well, the evaluation of the performance of a transferred policy will require a completely different layout of the analytical model as the focus will be set on the policy process, though the policy environment and policy goals are inevitable analysis components.

Within Asia, the above findings may imply that large scales of public housing development akin to that of Hong Kong and Singapore are unlikely to be replicated in future. Both Hong Kong and Singapore are well developed city states with clearly defined political borders and negligible rural population sectors. Housing problems incurred by uncontrolled rural-urban migration do not exist, rendering it more possible for the government to plan and fund public housing programs covering a significant or even a dominant portion of the population. Land was made available for public housing development in Hong Kong because of its unique political context as a colony. In the case of Singapore, it was because of the extraordinary political functions attached to housing by its first national government. Apart from weaker political incentives, the socio-economic roles of public housing in other Asian countries are also regarded as much lesser than that of Hong Kong and Singapore. While public housing may serve the purpose of attracting and stabilizing labour supply, it is overtaken by other economic considerations such as the desire of generating higher financial returns on land investment, or supporting real estate development, or shaping the image of the place by private housing development. What may proliferate, however, is the establishment of smaller housing organizations providing public rental and owner-occupier housing currently to enhance the recyclability of housing funds. To establish more participatory and consultative modes of governance in public housing to enhance quality may also emerge or be enhanced in countries with more democratic political systems.

Acknowledgement The work described in this paper was funded by a grant from the Seed Funding Program for Basic Research of the University of Hong Kong granted in 2011.

References

Census and Statistics Department (2011) 2011 Census Results [Online]. Census and Statistics Department, the Government of the Hong Kong Special Administrative Region, Hong Kong. Available from: http://www.census2011.gov.hk/en/main-table/E123.html. Accessed 5 May 2013

Chiu RLH (2003) Analysis on policy trends. In: Yeung YM, Wong KY (eds) Fifty years of public housing in Hong Kong: a golden jubilee anniversary public housing volume. Chinese University Press, Hong Kong, pp 221–242 (In Chinese), pp 235–258 (In English)

Chiu RLH (2008) Editorial introduction: urban housing policy issues in re-surging Asia. Urban Policy Res 26(3):245–247

Chiu RLH (2010) The transferability of Hong Kong's public housing policy. Int J Housing Policy 10(3):301–323

Chiu RLH (2012) The sustainability of the urban forms of China's leading cities: Beijing, Shanghai and Guangzhou. Urban Policy Res 30(4):359–384

Chiu RLH (2013) A comparison of housing welfare policies among major Asian countries in the modern era. LHI J Land Housing Urban Aff 4(1):23–32

Dolowitz DP, Marsh D (1996) Who learns what from whom: a review of the policy transfer literature. Political Stud 44(2):343–357

Hong Kong Housing Authority (2013) Hong Kong Housing Authority Home Page [Online]. Hong Kong Housing Authority, the Government of the Hong Kong Special Administrative Region, Hong Kong. Available from: http://www.housingauthority.gov.hk/en/public-housing/index.html. Accessed 5 May 2013

Mossberger K, Wolman H (2003) Policy transfer as a form of prospective policy evaluation: challenges and recommendations. Public Adm Rev 63(4):428–440

Oxley M (2001) Meaning, science, context and confusion in comparative housing research. J Housing Built Environ 16:89–106

Pawson H, Hulse K (2011) Policy transfer of choice-based lettings to Britain and Australia: how extensive? How faithful? How appropriate? Int J Housing Policy 11(2):113–132

Yeung YM, Wong KY (eds) (2003) Fifty years of public housing in Hong Kong: a golden jubilee anniversary public housing volume. Chinese University Press, Hong Kong

Chapter 2
Public Housing in Mainland China: History, Ongoing Trends, and Future Perspectives

Jie Chen, Juan Jing, Yanyun Man, and Zan Yang

Abstract China has a unique experience of public housing development. Before 1998, public ownership dominated the housing provision in urban China. Nonetheless, the employer-based welfare housing program was formally abolished in 1998, and the overwhelming majority of the public housing stock was quickly privatized. However, the Chinese government again committed to developing public housing in 2007, and a large-scale public housing construction program has been implemented since 2009. This chapter aims to first provide a summary of pre-reform and post-reform public housing development in China and then discuss why the Chinese government has again turned to public housing as a solution after about 30 years of housing reform and privatization. It shows that the recent push for public housing in China should not be seen as a step backward or as the restoration of the pre-reform welfare housing system. Instead, it represents the central authority's increasing recognition of the complexity of urban housing systems in a modern market economy.

J. Chen (✉)
Institute of Real Estate Research, School of Public Economics and Administration, Shanghai University of Finance and Economics (SHUFE), Shanghai, China
e-mail: chen.jie@mail.shufe.edu.cn

J. Jing
China Programme of International Centre for Planning Research, Cardiff University (UK), Beijing, China
e-mail: jing.juan@yaoo.c.uk

Y. Man
College of Urban and Environmental Sciences, Peking University, Beijing 100871, China

Lincoln Institute of Land Policy, Cambridge, MA 02138, USA
e-mail: yman@plc.pku.edu.cn

Z. Yang
Hang Lung Center for Real Estate, Department of Construction Management, Tsinghua University, Beijing 100084, China
e-mail: zanyang@tsinghua.edu.cn

J. Chen et al. (eds.), *The Future of Public Housing: Ongoing Trends in the East and the West*, DOI 10.1007/978-3-642-41622-4_2,

Keywords Public housing • Housing policy • Urban development • China

> The recent emphasis on public housing for the poor (in China) is a good example of how government resources can be used to address a pressing social need (World Bank 2012: 47).

2.1 Introduction

China has a unique experience of public housing development. Before 1978, the provision of housing in China rested on strong socialist ideologies: housing was not regarded as a commodity with an exchange value but instead as a basic need, as a right, to be allocated outside of the marketplace (Angel 2000). Since 1978, old-style public housing has been privatized and the socialist welfare housing system phased out. The housing conditions of urban residents have greatly improved since the market-oriented housing reform: the floor area per capita increased from 6.7 square meters in 1978 to 32.7 square meters in 2011,and the home ownership rate reached 89.3 % in 2011 (NBSC 2011). However, the supply of affordable housing has not kept pace with the full-fledged marketization. In recent years, the rapidly rising housing prices and lack of affordable housing for low- and middle-income urban households, particularly in big cities, have triggered widespread complaints from many would-be home buyers (Chen et al. 2010; Logan et al. 2010), thus also threatening the socioeconomic and political stability (Naughton 2010).

Correspondingly, over the last few years, the Chinese central government has shifted the emphasis of housing policies from commercial housing to public housing, and China's public housing program has been expanding at a dazzling speed.[1] Official data suggest that China started constructing 16.3 million units of public housing and finished 11 million units during its "11th Five-Year Plan" period (2006–2010) (MOHURD 2011). In the beginning of 2011, Chinese Prime Minister Wen Jiabao announced that the Chinese government is committed to building 36 million units of public housing during the "12th Five-Year Plan" period (2011–2015).

However, this chapter shows that the recent massive public housing program is very different from the old-style socialist welfare housing of the pre-reform period. New public housing is not developed and controlled by employers or work units but by the local government in partnership with commercial property developers. Public housing, even when constructed at a very large scale at certain times, is still seen as a supplementary housing sector to support the housing market rather than an equal partner of the market. Therefore, the recent push for public housing in China should not be seen as a step backward or as the restoration of the pre-reform

[1] Chinese authorities commonly label such housing as "(social) security housing" (*Bao Zhang Fang*) (Qi 2009).

welfare housing system. Rather, it represents the central authority's increasing recognition of the complexity of urban housing systems in a modern market economy.

This chapter also shows that the Chinese public housing model has been reshaped under the overall transformation of the development ideology from "productivist welfare" to "developmental welfare" in recent years. It has been widely observed that the Chinese government's overriding development priority given to economic growth has been partly shifted to social development in recent years. In 2006, President Hu Jintao proposed the idea of a "harmonious society." This strategy gives priority to promoting common people's welfare and social harmony ahead of pursuing pure economic growth. According to this new ideology of a "harmonious society", social policy is no longer subordinated to economic policy but is an integral part of economic policy. This chapter provides some preliminary evidence that the change in the Chinese public housing policy could be seen as a strong signal of a shift in ideology from "productivist welfare" to "developmental welfare," where the latter assumes that "social expenditures in the form of social investment do not detract from, but contribute positively to, economic development" (Midgley and Tang 2001).

2.2 Pre-reform Public Housing in China

The current public housing system in China is a direct legacy of that in the pre-reform era. On one hand, the pre-reform public housing stock still accounts for a bulk fraction of urban China's housing stock. On the other hand, the dominance of public housing in the urban housing stock is a key difference between formerly planned economies and market economies (Szelenyi 1987). Therefore, knowledge of pre-reform public housing and housing reform is necessary to understand the current Chinese public housing policy.

2.2.1 *Public Housing in the Pre-reform Era: 1949–1978*

When the Chinese Communist Party took control of power in 1949, the housing stock in urban China was predominantly owned by private persons (cf. Table 2.1). However, this situation was in conflict with the socialist ideology, where housing was not considered as a commodity but as a type of social welfare to be freely provided by the state (Wang and Murie 1999). The state provision of housing with low or almost free rent such that individuals are responsible for their own housing has long been proclaimed as an essential demonstration of the superiority of socialism over capitalism (Lim and Lee 1990). Nonetheless, due to various political and economic reasons, the dominance of private ownership in urban China's housing stock continued until the mid-1950s.

Table 2.1 Distribution of property rights to housing stock in major cities, 1955

	Publicly owned (%)	Privately owned (%)	Foreign-owned (%)
Beijing	44.35	53.85	1.8
Tianjin	43.41	53.99	2.6
Shanghai	25.8	66	7.6
Jinan	22	78	
Qingdao	57.9	37.9	4.16
Shenyang	64	36	
Harbin	55.31	40.2	4.46
Nanjing	37.75	61.3	0.95
Wuxi	19.75	80.25	
Suzhou	14	86	

Source: Report on "The Current Basic Conditions and Opinions of Socialist Transformation of Private Housing in Urban Areas" from the Office of the Second Secretary of the CCP (October 1955)

In late 1950s, the Chinese communist government carried out a massive nationalization of the ownership of land and private housing in all urban areas (Wu 1996). About one billion square meters of private housing were nationalized within a few years (Hou et al. 1999). Meanwhile, the government established public ownership over all new housing stock. By the end of the 1970s, private-sector housing had declined to about 20 % of the total urban housing stock and public housing had become the predominant form, accounting for 74.8 % (Hou et al. 1999).

Like other former socialist countries, the welfare housing system constituted an important pillar of the welfare system in socialist China (Wu 1996). Municipal housing authorities and employers (work units or *danwei*) were the two major providers of public housing. Nonetheless, different from the Soviet Union and East European socialist countries, public housing units were mainly allocated and administrated by work units rather than state agencies (Wu 1996). The dominance of work units in allocating social services is arguably related to the Chinese traditional clan culture (Zhao and Bourassa 2003). The integration of work and living has the purpose of facilitating the reproduction of labor, building workers' loyalty to the enterprise, promoting high productivity, and ensuring social stability (Wu 1996; Zhao and Bourassa 2003). In addition to ideological and cultural factors, the predominance of public housing was also related to economic reasons, for example, the low capacity of the construction sector, the urgent need to accommodate the increasing number of urban residents at low cost, the need to ensure State Owned Enterprise (SOE) workers' health and productivity, and households' low capability to consume adequate housing due to both income insufficiency and the lack of financial instruments for private consumption (Huang 2004; Zhang 2000; Rosen and Ross 2000).

The work unit-based welfare public housing program achieved some success in accommodating the fast-expanding public sector and SOE employees in urban China during the 1950s–1960s. However, the public housing system in China existed only in urban areas. After the *Hukou* system was introduced in 1958, rural populations were restricted from working and living in cities. Public housing was accessible only to registered urban residents (about 12–18 % of the national population from the 1950s to the 1970s). Even among registered urban households, however, the inequality of housing provision was apparent (Zhou and Logan 1996). For municipal housing that owned by the public housing agency, the level of funding depended in part on the bargaining ability of regional leaders with the central planning and housing ministries (Zhao and Bourassa 2003). The distribution of public funds for work-unit housing was also not egalitarian; "key" work units—for example, advanced enterprises in favored industries or high-ranked government institutes—usually received more public funds and additional resources (such as additional land use rights) (Wu 1996). As a consequence, the better houses were allocated disproportionately to the elites among party leaders, government officials, and managers of state-owned enterprises. The provision for workers or other underclass members was far behind schedule in almost all Chinese cities. Also, the quality of public housing significantly varied according to the work status of the tenants (Zhou and Logan 1996).

For municipal housing projects, the cost of housing development and maintenance came directly from state funds (Hou et al. 1999). The cost of work-unit housing development also came from public funds, but employers usually had the autonomy to decide on how to use those funds. In both systems, public funds paid for almost all the costs of the process of land acquisition, housing construction, and maintenance after completion (Wu 1996). The tenants had to pay only a nominal rent.

However, although the public housing provision in Chinese cities was on a limited scale, public finance could not support a sufficient supply to meet the housing demand. Because virtually all public housing was solely financed by the state through budgetary funding and allocated freely to end users, the funding for housing investment was consistently short of the growing need. Further, similar to other governments in the early stage of development (Wells 1985), the Chinese government viewed housing as a nonproductive social expenditure and a drag on the economy and hence strongly discouraged investments in housing (Hou et al. 1999). For these reasons, the investment on housing was constantly low in China before 1978: the ratio of housing investment in the total fixed investment was on average around 6.7 % during 1950–1978 (cf. Fig. 2.1), far smaller than the world average of 20–30 % over the same period (World Bank 1993).

As a result of long-term insufficient investment, the housing shortage in urban China became extremely acute in the 1970s (Wang and Murie 1999). In 1978, the mean living floor space per capita in urban China was 3.6 square meters (the living construction space per capita was 6.7 square meters), even smaller than that in 1950 (4.5 square meters); meanwhile, 41.5 % of urban households were living in poor housing conditions (Hou et al. 1999). Further, the welfare housing system became a vital impediment to economic growth (Wang and Murie 1999).

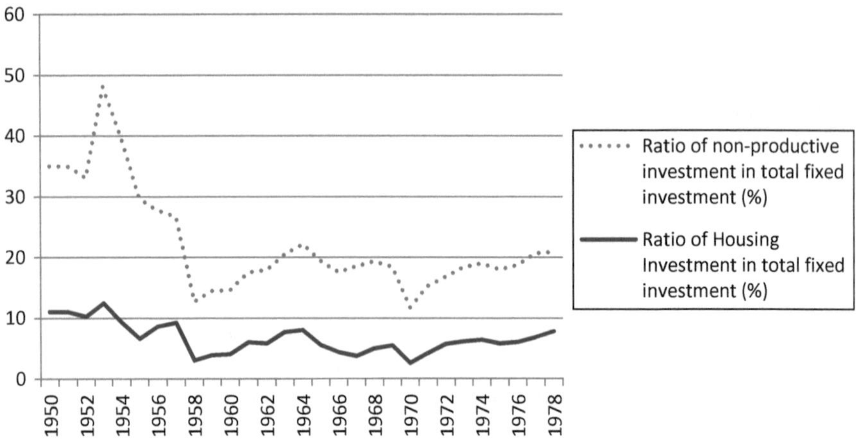

Fig. 2.1 Housing investment in urban China, 1950–1978 (Source: China Statistics Yearbook 1981)

2.2.2 Housing Reform in China: 1978–1998

At the beginning of the 1980s, the Chinese government launched market-oriented housing reform as an indispensable component of China's transition from a planned economy to a market economy. Basically, the Chinese housing reform involved six key components: the commoditization of housing goods, the monetization of housing consumption, the marketization of housing allocation, the commercialization of housing provision, the privatization of public housing stock, and the socialization of housing management (Wang and Murie 1999; Zhao and Bourassa 2003).

However, the market-oriented housing reform proceeded with strong resistance in the 1980s. Until the early 1990s, the Chinese urban housing sector was seen as the last bastion of paternalist housing (Angel 2000). According to a World Bank survey, more than 90 % of urban residents in China were living in public housing in 1990, the largest ratio in the world at that time (World Bank 1991).

In a drastic move, partly as a component of the stimulus package to counter the economic and fiscal pressures of the Asian financial crisis in 1997, the Chinese State Council issued in June 1998 the milestone policy document on housing reform (SC[1998]No.23) and formally abolished the work unit-based public housing system. Within one-and-a-half years, more than 60 % of urban public housing was sold to individuals.[2] The public housing stock privatized in 1998–1999 was estimated at 2.5 million square meter, with an implicit market value of approximately 2.5 trillion RMB, roughly equivalent to 32 % of China's 1998 GDP (Adams 2009). Given the

[2] People's Daily Online, (11 July 2000), available at: http://english.peopledaily.com.cn/english/200007/11/eng20000711_45187.html

vast literature describing the Chinese housing reform in the 1980s and 1990s, this chapter does not provide further detailed discussions on the topic.

Nevertheless, we wish to point out that the massive-scale privatization of the public housing sector turned out to be a crucial step in China's market-oriented socioeconomic reform (Gibson 2009; Adams 2009). The breaking of the link that tied workers to cheap public housing through work units is an important element of the Chinese government's drive to reform SOEs and banks (Rosen and Ross 2000). In addition, the liberalization of housing markets is also a critical step in promoting the labor mobility implied by economic reform. Particularly, it helped greatly to increase job opportunities of migrants who did not have access to work unit housing (Fleisher et al. 1997). Further, once the "unit-based society" has been dissolved under the market economy, the development of the private owner-occupied housing market becomes not only a means to boost the economy but also a central pillar in building an assets-based welfare system (Stephens 2010). Finally, the market provision of housing greatly enhances personal choice and freedom in daily life (Rosen and Ross 2000).

2.3 Post-reform Public Housing in China

After the watershed termination of welfare housing provision in 1998, the public housing sector was scaled down dramatically in urban China, and the market came to the central stage of housing provision. Although successful in expanding the urban housing stock, the predominance of the market in housing provision triggered a house price boom, making housing affordability one of most acute social issues in China and causing social instability (Chen et al. 2010). Under such social and political pressures, the Chinese government concluded in August 2007 that public housing is a necessary vehicle to meet the basic housing needs of low-income and "house-poor" urban households (SC[2007]No.24). Public housing is also considered as a key instrument in promoting urbanization, which are considered to be crucial for China's long-term development strategy (Li 2011).

2.3.1 Housing Development in Post-reform Urban China

The 1998 housing reform paved the way for the development of a market-oriented housing sector in urban China. Since then, the Chinese housing sector has experienced a building boom that has lasted until the present time. Over the period 1998–2011, 9.3 billion square meters of housing were completed in urban areas in China, roughly twice the current total housing stock in the United Kingdom or as large as that in Japan (EIU 2011). The vast increase in housing supply leads to substantial additions to the housing stock and significant improvements in housing conditions for average households in urban China. For example, the living space per

Table 2.2 Housing conditions and population in urban China (selected years)

Year	Living floor space per person (square meter)	Housing stock (million square meter)	Completion of housing (million square meter)	Urban population (million)	Urbanization (%)
1978	6.7		38.00	172.45	17.92
1982	8.2	/	138.31	214.80	21.13
1987	12.7	/	193.13	276.74	25.32
1992	14.8	/	231.40	321.75	27.46
1997	17.8	3,622	405.50	394.49	31.91
2002	22.8	8,185	597.94	502.12	39.09
2007	27.5	11,289	688.21	606.33	45.89
2011	32.7	/	1,025.13	690.79	51.27

Source: China Statistics Yearbook (various years)

Table 2.3 Official statistics on tenure distribution of housing in urban China, 2011

Tenure type	Description	Share (%)
Owner-occupied		**89.3**
Owned private housing	Self-built after 1949 or old private housing built before 1949	11.2
Owned market housing	Bought through the market and built by developers	38.0
Privatized public housing	Bought during the 1980–2000 housing reform	40.1
Rental-lease	Including both private and public rental housing	**10.7**

Note: NBSC (2011)

capita in urban China has increased by 1 square meter annually on average since 1998 (cf. Table 2.2). By the end of 2011, the average living floor space per capita in urban China had reached 32.7 square meters, more than 4 times that in 1978.

Meanwhile, largely thanks to the massive privatization of the public housing stock in the late 1990s and early 2000s (Adams 2009), China was quickly transformed from having one of the highest levels of public ownership of housing in the world to being one of the highest homeowner nations. According to a report of the National Bureau of Statistics of China (NBSC) (cf. Table 2.3), the homeownership ratio in urban China reached 89.3 % in 2011, and nearly half of owner occupied-homes had been converted from public housing (NBSC 2011).

2.3.2 *Public Housing Development Since 1998*

Since 1998, the public housing provision structure has evolved gradually along with the economic and social development (cf. Tables 2.4 and 2.7). A two-tier public housing system consisting of Cheap Rental Housing (CRH) and Economic Comfortable Housing (ECH) was introduced in 1998 (CRH and ECH are defined in the next section). ECH was even designed as the predominant form of post-reform housing

Table 2.4 Milestone documents on housing policy in post-reform China

Date	Issuing authority and policy document	Objectives and implications
July 1998	State Council: Notification on deepening the urban housing reform and accelerating housing construction (SC [1998]No. 23)	The welfare-based public housing system was to be completely abolished; ECH was designed to dominate the whole housing system
August 2003	State Council: Notification on continuing accelerating healthy and sustainable development of real estate market (SC [2003]No.18)	Market solutions dominate the housing sector; ECH and other public housing programs were downgraded to marginal sectors
August 2007	State Council: Opinions on tackling housing difficulties of low-income families in urban areas (SC[2007] No.24)	Government would again intervene in the housing sector through public housing; CRH chosen as the premier public housing scheme; ECH scheme significantly modified
December 2008	State Council General Office: Opinions on promoting steady and healthy development of real estate market (SCGO[2008]No.131)	Strive to solve the housing difficulties of 7.47 million low-income "house-poor" urban families by 2011
June 2009	MOHURD: Notification on the 2009–2011 development plan of CRH (MOHURD[2009]No.91)	Detailed annual plan to solve the housing difficulties of 7.47 million low-income "house-poor" urban families by 2011, with a target set for each province
January 2010	State Council General Office: Notification on steady and healthy development of real estate market (SCGO [2010]No.4)	Strive to meet the housing needs of 15.4 million low-to-middle income "house-poor" urban families by 2012
September 2011	State Council General Office: Guidelines on the construction and management of public housing (SCGO[2011] No.45)	Public housing planned to host 20 % of urban households by 2015; growing attention shifted to PRH
May 2012	MOHURD: Regulations on Public Rental Housing (MOHURD[2006]No.11)	Regulation details set on the construction and operation of public rental housing

Source: Author's summary based on official documents

provision (SC[1998]No.23). However, against the pressure of boosting GDP growth through a real estate boom (Rosen and Ross 2000), the actual importance of public housing rapidly waned after 1998 (cf. Table 2.4). In 2003, the State Council formally gave up the idea of establishing ECH as the main form of post-reform housing (SC [2003]No.18). Public housing has since been substantially downgraded to playing a supportive role in the whole housing system (cf. Table 2.5).

However, the successful expansion of the urban housing stock through the market has been accompanied by a rapid increase in house prices, making home purchase increasingly unaffordable for low- and middle-income households and, in particular, for migrants and young office workers (Chen et al. 2010; Yang and Shen 2008). The housing market is also polarizing property wealth between different tenures and different socioeconomic and demographic cohorts (Logan et al. 2010; Man 2011).

Table 2.5 Housing units built in urban China, 1999–2010

		Government-supported ECH built	
Year	All commodity housing units built (in thousands)	Units (in thousands)	% share in all commodity housing
1999	1,946.4	485.0	24.9
2000	2,139.7	603.6	28.2
2001	2,414.4	604.8	25.0
2002	2,629.6	538.5	20.5
2003	3,021.1	447.7	14.8
2004	4,042.2	497.5	12.3
2005	3,682.5	287.3	7.8
2006	4,005.3	338.0	8.4
2007	4,401.2	159.4	8.1
2008	4,939.2	144.6	7.2
2009	5,548.9	143.6	7.2
2010	6,019.8	163.2	6.6
2011	7,219.2	/	/

Source: China Statistics Yearbook (various years)
Notes:
1. Even after the 1998 reform, not all urban housing units in China were commodity housing. Throughout 1998–2011, around 9 billion square meter of housing (roughly 100–110 million units) were constructed in urban China, but only 59 % were commodity housing; the rest were either self-help housing or enterprise-built housing
2. Commodity housing here refers to all housing built by real estate developers. Because ECH, CPH, and RSH are built for sale and provided by developers, they are considered as commodity housing in China's official statistics. However, nationwide data on the completion of CPH and RSH were not available

There is evidence that the Chinese central government has over time reached a consensus that the imbalance between the housing sector and socioeconomic development is largely attributed to the insufficiency and inefficiency of the state provision of housing (Qi 2009; MOHURD 2011; Li 2011). In August 2007 the central government again committed to meet the basic housing needs of low-income "house-poor" urban households by developing public housing (SC[2007]No.24). This milestone document signaled the turning point of the Chinese post-reform housing history and essentially reversed the downslide trend of public housing since 1998 (cf. Table 2.5).

Over the last few years, the construction of public housing has experienced another "Great Leap Forward." Both the development target and mode have been frequently revised. For example, in December 2008 the central government pledged to provide decent housing for 7.47 million low-income 'house-poor' urban households by 2011, mainly through CRH and RSH (SCGO[2008]No.131). This plan was released as a key part of the famous 4 trillion RMB economic stimulus package to counteract the negative shocks of the 2008 global financial crisis (Qi 2009). A half year later, in July 2009, the MOHURD (Ministry of Housing and Urban-Rural Development) published a detailed provincial level annual development plan for CRH for the period 2009–2011 (MOHURD[2009]No.91), and the central

Table 2.6 The Chinese public housing scheme in the "12th Five-Year Plan" period

	Newly started (million units)	Newly started (billion square meter)	Completed (million units)	Completed (billion square meter)	Investment (billion RMB)
2011	10.43	73	4.32	30	37
2012E	7.00	49	5.00	35	25
2013E	7.00	49	4.00	28	25
2014E	6.00	42	3.00	21	21
2015E	6.00	42	3.00	21	21

Source: The 2011 data represent actual numbers, whereas the 2012E data are based on the plan announced in official documents; the rest of the data are based on the author's own estimates, assuming that the average size of a public housing unit is 70 square meter and the average cost per unit is 350,000 RMB

government doubled the housing target with the aim of meeting the housing needs of 15.4 million low-to-middle-income "house-poor" urban households by 2012 (SCGO[2010]No.4) (cf. Table 2.4). As a result, in 2010 alone, China started constructing 5.9 million units and completed 3.3 million units of public housing. Although this achievement probably set a world record in public housing construction, it was only a prelude to a much larger public housing construction program. In January 2011, Premier Wen Jiabao announced a 5-year plan to construct 36 million units of public housing from 2011 to 2015, which aims to accommodate a fifth of the Chinese urban population by 2015 (cf. Table 2.6).

However, given that as much as half of the cities' revenues come from land sales and property taxes, it is reasonable to expect local governments to resist the promotion of public housing development. There is also widespread concern that once land is allocated for public housing, property prices in their surrounding neighborhoods could take a hit. Further, considering that the local government debt in 2011 was estimated at over 14 trillion RMB, local governments openly contend that they lack the necessary funding for public housing projects.

Nonetheless, given the political importance of the public housing program, any major adjustment to the target of 36 million units over 2011–2015 can be regarded as unlikely. However, what constitutes "public housing" is still unclear.

2.3.3 Public Housing Programs in Post-reform China

Currently, housing in urban China is supplied through a diversified multilevel provision system. While CRH, ECH, and RSH have existed as public housing schemes since 1998, CPH and PRH were introduced only recently. CPH first appeared in a State Council policy document in January 2010 (SCGO[2010]No.4) and is expected to meet the homeownership needs of low-to-middle-income "house-poor" households.

PRH, which is modeled after public housing in Hong Kong, appeared in some southern cities of China around 2009 and was soon elevated to a national scheme.

Table 2.7 Types of public housing in post-reform urban China

Type	Description	
Old Public Housing	Housing built by the state between 1949 and 1998	
Privatized	Sold to sitting tenants at heavily discounted prices	
Non-privatized	Remain under the control of local housing authorities	
New Public Housing	Housing built or subsidized by the state after 1998	
	Target group	**Eligibility requirement**
For sale		
Economic Comfortable Housing (ECH)	Low-income "house-poor" urban households	residence permit (*Houkou*), income and asset threshold, living space per person threshold
Capped–Price Housing (CPH)	Low-to-middle-income and middle-income urban households	residence permit (*Houkou*), income threshold, without owned-home
Shantytown Renovation Housing (SRH)	Households relocated due to urban revitalization and major construction projects	owners of expropriated homes
For renting		
Cheap Rental Housing (CRH)	Lowest-income "house poor" urban households	residence permit (*Houkou*), income and asset threshold, living space per person threshold
Public Rental Housing (PRH)	Wide range of urban population, including new migrants	no residence permit required, loose or no income threshold

According to China's 12th Five-Year Plan (2011–2015) of public housing development (cf. Table 2.7), PRH will gradually replace ECH and become the leading form of Chinese public housing. The development of PRH is expected to benefit low- and middle-income families that are neither qualified to apply for CRH/ECH nor rich enough to buy commercial apartments.

As their names suggest, CRH and PRH are only for renting, whereas ECH, SRH, and CPH are sold at below-market prices to households eligible for each program, respectively. For example, SRH is reserved for households relocated due to urban renovation projects,[3] ECH is designed to promote homeownership among low-income households, and CPH is targeted at middle-income households (SCGO[2010]No.4). For the ECH scheme, land is freely allotted to developers, and the sale price is restricted to covering the construction cost, with a small profit (normally at 3 %).

[3] There are several debates in China on whether SRH should be regarded as "public housing" (security housing) considering that the buyers of SRH are not restricted to low-income households. Meanwhile, as relocated households are compensated by a lump-sum fund equivalent to the market value of their old housing, their affordability usually is not a problem. However, according to our definition of public housing, i.e. housing allocated by the government rather than the market, SRH qualifies as public housing in the Chinese context.

Table 2.8 Newly started public housing by type, 2009–2011 (in thousand units)

Year	Cheap rental housing	Public rental housing	Economic comfortable housing	Capped-price housing	Shantytown renovation housing	Total
2009	1,710 (51.8 %)	/	590 (17.9 %)	/	800 (24.2 %)	3,300
2010	1,800 (30.5 %)	/	1,300 (22.0 %)	/	2,800 (47.5 %)	5,900
2011	1,650 (15.8 %)	2,270 (21.8 %)	1,100 (10.6 %)	830 (8.0 %)	4,150 (40.0 %)	10,430

Data source: Chinese Statistics Yearbook (various years), MOHURD (2011), and the MOHUED website. The respective ratios of each public housing type in the total number of newly started public housing units are shown within parentheses

Note: The numbers in italics are the author's own rough estimates based on the available raw data on space measurements, assuming that the average size of an ECH unit is 85 square meter over the period 2009–2010

For the CPH scheme, land is obtained through competitive bidding, and the sale price is set at around 70–75 % of the comparable free market housing level. For both the ECH and CPH schemes, buyers are subject to certain years of resale restriction period before they can trade their housing in the market.

CRH and PRH also differ. Whereas CRH is targeted at a small number of the poorest local households at nominal rent, PRH is targeted at both low-income and middle-income households that either do not want to become homeowners or cannot afford the market price. Further, PRH is so far the only public housing program that is accessible to migrants; the rest are restricted to local permanent residents in the city (who have a local *Hukou* registration).

As shown in Table 2.8, among all newly started public housing units in 2011, SRH represents the largest segment (40 %), followed by PRH (21.8 %) and CRH (15.8 %); ECH is downgraded to the fourth position (10.6 %). This is consistent with the guidelines in the 12th Five-Year Plan, which instruct local governments to shift the priority of public housing development from ECH to PRH.

However, because the NBSC classifies built-for-sale public housing (ECH, CPH, and sometimes, SRH) as a type of commodity housing in its statistical system of housing sector, it is difficult to get an accurate estimate of the current share of public housing in the Chinese urban housing stock. However, according to a large household survey conducted by National Bureau of Statistics of China (NBSC) in 265 prefecture-level cities, on average 7.8 % urban households were accommodated by new public housing units in 2010 (cf. Table 2.9). However, the proportion of households living in new public housing varies greatly across cities. In 115 cities (43.4 % of total cities), the proportion of public housing units was lower than 5 %; only 6 cities had a proportion higher than 30 % (cf. Table 2.9). Nonetheless, a MOHURD news release published in August 2012 announced that, as of the end of 2011, about 26.5 million low-to-medium urban households had been assisted through various forms of public housing, accounting for 11 % of total urban households.[4]

[4] http://news.xinhuanet.com/2012-08/03/c_112611112.htm

Table 2.9 Proportion of public housing in 265 prefecture-level cities in 2010

Property Type	Median	Mean	Maximum	Minimum	SD
ECH	1.6 %	3.4 %	48.5 %	0 %	5.3 %
CRH	2.8 %	4.3 %	55.7 %	0 %	5.3 %
Total	5.6 %	7.8 %	58.3 %	0.2 %	7.4 %
The distribution of cities by proportion of public housing					
Below 5.0 %	5.0–9.9 %	10.0–19.9 %	20.0 – 29.9 %	Above 30 %	
115 (43.4 %)	81 (30.6 %)	57 (21.5 %)	6 (2.3 %)	6 (2.3 %)	

Source: The Large-Sample Urban Households Survey conducted by the National Bureau of Statistics of China (NBSC) in 2010, which covered all 265 prefecture-level cities

2.4 Understanding the Recent Expansion of Public Housing in China

Why does the Chinese government see public housing as a solution after almost 30 years of housing reform and privatization? What are the major driving forces behind this drastic switch? This section aims to provide some answers to these two questions.

However, it is very challenging to determine what exactly drives the dynamics of housing policy because housing policies are often championed in pursuit of nonhousing needs (Kemeny 1992). It has long been recognized that housing policy should not be limited to housing needs and that public intervention in the housing sector often occurs in response to a wide array of social and economic needs (Angel 2000: 111). Whitehead (2003) suggested that in the rationale of public economics, state intervention in housing markets has three goals: the allocation, redistribution, and stabilization of needs. This is largely because housing is typically thought of as a complex good with significant social and urban externalities (Oxley 2000; Sullivan and Gibb 2003). However, the embedding nature of housing policy makes it extremely difficult to understand what constitutes its most essential driving force.

Because China's public housing sector and housing policy are still evolving, it is premature to either assess its performance or examine its overall impacts. We can, however, highlight how new housing policies take shape in response to the economic, demographic, and societal dynamics in a fast-growing transitional economy. Particularly, in this chapter we attempt to show that there is a tendency for the Chinese public housing model to be reshaped under the overall transformation of the development ideology from "productivist welfare" to "developmental welfare" (Holliday 2000; Midgley and Tang 2001).

2.4.1 *Economic Concerns*

Based on our observations, the primary justification for public housing in China is based on economic growth needs. It has long been argued that the East Asian region as a whole is embarking on the so-called "productivist welfare capitalism," where social policy is subordinated to economic policy, there is basically no concept of "social right," and the state provision of social welfare is premised on the needs of the overriding growth objectives (Holliday 2000). As one of the most reputed examples of "productivist welfare capitalism," China has a long tradition of formulating social policies according to the needs of the overriding growth objectives. Some literature locates the Chinese housing policy within Asian models of a "developmental state" (Stephens 2010). Within this sociopolitical culture, it becomes natural that "(in China) state housing provision is seen as important economic drivers rather than socially necessary" (Wang and Murie 2011).

For example, Chinese housing policy makers expect that various forms of public housing could, by reconciling the contradiction between the profitability requirement of developers and the housing affordability of workers, promote urbanization and retain skilled or semiskilled workers in large cities (SCGO[2011]No.45). It should be noted that there is no evidence that Chinese policy makers are seeking to shrink the importance of the construction and real estate sector in the economy. On the contrary, it appears that they are interested in maintaining the economy-stimulating effects of housing investment in size through expanding the public housing sector (SCGO [2010]No.4). For example, the first wave of post-reform public housing expansion was launched as a key component of the 4 trillion RMB economic stimulus package in late 2008, explicitly aimed at reducing the negative impacts from the recent global economic slowdown (Qi 2009). This is the major reason why brick-and-mortar subsidies rather than individual-level subsidies have been favored by the central authority, as the former can be more helpful in generating GDP and jobs (Chen et al. 2011).

Further, in Chinese leaders' minds, more affordable housing in the urban area will also free up household income for consumer spending (Li 2011). Because stimulating domestic consumption is considered as the most important means to adjust the economic imbalance and promote economic transformation in the next decade, the central government has high expectations of public housing.

2.4.2 *Stabilization Concerns*

While some observers have sneered at the 36-million-unit program and belittled it as a new Great Leap Forward launched by the Chinese government, many analysts believe that the Chinese government launched its public housing program with the aim of killing two birds with one stone: to make housing affordable to those at the bottom of society and at the same time stimulate demand and cushion any slowdown after decades of breakneck growth. In many public situations, public housing is emphasized by the government authority as a means to smooth the excessive real estate cycles and stabilize the growing housing price volatility (SCGO[2008] No.131; SCGO[2010]No.4). This is obviously a lesson learned from the underlying global economic downturn triggered by the US subprime bubble burst in 2007 (Yao et al. 2010).

2.4.3 Urban Development Concerns

For local governments, the major interest in supplying public housing is driven by the urgent need to smooth relocation costs, which have soared due to the rapid increases in market housing prices. There are reasons to believe that the dominance of Shantytown Renovation Housing (SRH) in recent public housing development (cf. Table 2.8) is directly tied to the local governments' goal to promote urban renewal by providing low-cost housing to relocated residents. The local governments simply cannot afford for compensation to grow at the same rates as the soaring prices of market housing.

Subordinate to the local development strategy, urban renewal has been extensively used by municipal governments as a "growth machine" (Wu et al. 2006). During the so-called "property-led regeneration," old dilapidated houses in downtown areas are expropriated, original households are relocated to suburban areas, and residential communities in downtown areas are converted to shopping centers or other more profitable projects. By doing so, local governments obtain substantial revenues and funding sources to invest in the development of urban infrastructure and thus increase the city's competitiveness (Li 2011). Property-led regeneration reflects the emergence of the entrepreneurial and profit-seeking behavior of local governments in Chinese cities (Yang and Chang 2007). Thus, the main function of Shantytown Renovation Housing (SRH) is to rehouse expropriated urban and rural households at low costs and thus help to facilitate "growth-promoting" urban regeneration.

2.4.4 Urbanization Concerns

Official statistics suggest that China is currently experiencing the largest-scale urbanization in human history: in 2011, for the first time in Chinese history, more than half of the population—51.27 % or 690.79 million people—was living in urban areas, representing an increase of 19.36 percentage points over the 1997 figure and a net growth of 300 million urban households over this period. Further, according to the *World Urbanization Prospect 2011* by the United Nations (United Nations 2012), the urbanization ratio in China will reach 69 % in 2030, and the urban population will increase by more than 300 million over the period 2011–2030. This implies that there will be a strong and sustained momentum for the expansion of housing demand and consumption in urban China in the next few decades. However, the land available for urban residential use in China is small compared to its fast-growing urban population. Moreover, to ensure its own food security, China has a strict quota on agricultural land development. Thus there is a decreasing supply of suitable sites for residential development. The expansion of low-cost public housing programs, however, is expected to increase the supply of affordable housing to meet the accommodation needs of a growing number of new entrants who have little hope of purchasing commodity homes at market prices.

For urban residents, housing is more than just affordable shelter (Whitehead 2003); it can profoundly affect the well-being of families through its interconnections with the composition of communities and social services. Thus, its socioeconomic implications often go way beyond the housing sector. From this perspective, public housing has several positive potentials: it is considered to potentially have positive effects on childhood development (Newman and Harkness 2002; Currie and Yelowitz 2000), it could boost households' nonhousing consumption (Le Blanc and Laferrère 2001), and it may even improve health outcomes for families (Baker and Tually 2008). In addition, by reconciling the contradiction between the profitability requirement of land private ownership and the housing affordability of workers (Tutin 2008), public housing can attract and retain skilled or semiskilled workers in large cities and can thus have impacts on regional economic competitiveness (Ross 2008).

We thus argue that the current housing provision system in China is actually not very different from that in western countries if one considers the development stage the country is in. China is at a stage of rapid industrialization and urbanization. The social composition of the urban population not only includes the emerging middle class but also a re-emerging and ever-expanding working class (which differs from the socialist workers of the pre-reform period). However, whereas commercial housing targeted at the new middle class in cities flourished during the first decade of the twenty-first century, the working class housing problem was not properly addressed. The poor-quality private rental housing offered by urban villages provided a temporary solution in the past, but the alliance of local farmers, rural-to-urban migrants, and young educated professionals now represent a large proportion of the expanding urban population (PFPC 2012). It is this group of people that the new public housing is aimed at (MOHURD 2011; Li 2011). In many western countries, public housing was developed at a similar stage of rapid industrialization to accommodate industrial workers (Malpass and Murie 1999). From this perspective, one may conclude that governments across the world are taking "similar strategies" to address similar housing issues; the only difference is the timing.

2.4.5 *Redistribution Concerns*

The rapid upsurge in house prices in most major Chinese cities since 2003 has elevated the housing affordability issue to a key social concern in China (Chen et al. 2010). There is clear evidence that the Chinese housing market is increasingly polarizing property wealth between different tenures and different cohorts (Logan et al. 2010). While rising market housing prices continues to create substantial wealth for established homeowners, the residual proportion of the urban population trapped in the private rental housing and informal housing sectors due to affordability problems is expected to face declining welfare security. In 2005, home assets accounted for 71.34 % of the total family wealth of Chinese urban households (Liang et al. 2010). With the accelerated home price inflation in recent years, the wealth gap between homeowners and renters in China is expected to expand significantly. There is growing concern that the unequal housing distribution intensifies the gap in economic and social stratification, which could widen further with the rapid increase in housing prices (Man 2011).

The change in housing policy orientation should thus be understood under the overall shift in the development strategy of China. A number of researchers have pointed out that the Chinese government's overriding development priority given to economic growth has been partly shifted to social development in recent years. In 2006, President Hu Jintao proposed the idea of a "harmonious society." In 2007, during the CCP's 17th National Congress, he put forward the "scientific concept of development" as China's development strategy in the foreseeable future. This strategy prioritizes promoting common people's welfare and social harmony ahead of pursuing pure economic growth. Thus, the switch in housing policy is an integral part of the macro transition.

2.4.6 Social and Demographic Reasons

The high priority given to public housing also has to be seen in the context of societal changes and demographic transformation. During the rapid urbanization process, the "urban poor" face increasing hardships; many rural-to-urban migrants are excluded from the formal housing market and are concentrated in so-called "urban villages." The National Population and Family Planning Commission of China (PFPC) reported that in 2011, only 37 % of rural-to-urban migrants were accommodated by the private rental market; the rest lived in overcrowded dorms or shanty sheds at their workplace (PFPC 2012). Also of significance is the fact that the underdeveloped private rental market provides an ineffective solution for vulnerable households in these changing economic and social circumstances. Apart from rural migrants, many well-educated young professionals wish to join the ranks of the urban middle class, which increasingly demands a higher-quality of life. Nonetheless, most of these people could not initially afford market housing (Chen et al. 2010).

The explosion of housing demand in China in the last decade is also widely believed to be attributable to the rapid demographic transition during this period. Over the last decade, China has experienced sharp changes in demographic profiles in terms of both age structure and household size (Peng 2011). While the total dependency ratio was 48.1 % in 1997, it drastically dropped to only 34.4 % in 2011. It is reasonable to consider the fast-growing proportion of adults in the total population as another key reason for the surge in housing demand. Meanwhile, the recent downsizing of the average household size in urban China (from 3.08 in 1997 to 2.88 in 2011) may also positively contribute to the housing demand.

An increase in the public provision of urban housing may help to address the housing stress of a broader range of disadvantaged groups that acutely need public support. Such an increase can also help to influence the supply structure of housing provision by adding a large number of small-size apartments, which are currently rare in the market. "Public housing supply can alleviate the imbalance between demand and supply in the housing market and the structural problems of housing stock; thus, it is a key vehicle to promote urbanization" (Li 2011).

2.4.7 Political Reasons

Besides these economic and social justifications, the strong push for public housing also has important political implications. While housing price inflation and affordability problems appear as economic imbalances, their underlying causes are deep-rooted political problems in the society. The requirement of the working class for housing support (through public housing) has become a very important political demand that the Communist Party can no longer afford to ignore. The recent changes in the composition of the urban population, especially the large number of rural migrants and young graduates and professionals, demand significant adjustments in the ruling Party's representation and development strategies. The provision of about 20 % of public housing in urban areas could bring a large group of new residents into the system. The development of public housing could thus be one of the most important strategies to maintain social and political stability (Naughton 2010). This point is also related to the "paternalism hypothesis," which has a long tradition in China, and the wider view that housing is a merit good that more easily gets public support when state assistance is delivered in a direct form (Whitehead 2003; Hills 2007).

"Adequate housing for everyone" was for the first time set as a political promise of the Chinese government in the CCP's 17th National Congress in October 2007. It was repeatedly reiterated by Premier Wen Jiabao in his annual report to the People's Congress in 2009–2011. Of course, adequate housing for everyone does not necessarily mean private home ownership for everyone. Rather, it refers to a situation where people's basic housing demand can be adequately met, and public housing is considered as a key policy tool to achieve this target (Qi 2009). In any case, the ruling party has taken the provision of public housing as a serious political obligation. As stated by Vice Premier Li Keqiang, "the government's ability to deliver and distribute public housing fairly is an important test of its political credibility" (Li 2011).

2.4.8 Summary

To sum up, the Chinese central government appears to believe that the inadequate support for public housing at the various levels of government is a major reason for the chronic shortage in the supply of affordable housing for low- and middle-income families (Li 2011). On average, economic comfortable housing and pubic rental housing accounted for less than 7.8 % of the total housing stock in 265 cities in 2010. In more than 40 % of the prefecture-level cities, public housing represented less than 5 % of the total housing stock, indicating a severe shortage in subsidized housing for low- and middle-income families in urban China. Further, most migrant workers are excluded from any type of government-subsidized housing. In summary, public housing development in China has multiple functions. As stated by Vice Primer Li Keqiang, the top Chinese leader in charge of economic and social policy since 2007 and the person expected to take over as premier in spring 2013:

> The new public housing program is more than a major enhancement of social welfare, a vehicle to adjust income inequality and a crucial channel to improve social stability; it is also an important pillar of economic growth for the next several years as it has many economic functions such as "a tool to dampen price increases in the private housing market." …"implementing the massive public housing program is an effective approach to switch the economic growth model and improve economic structure…Public housing projects bridge economic growth and welfare, enable investment and promote consumption, and thus are decisive in expanding domestic demand. (Li 2011)

2.5 Conclusions

The recent policy attention given to the large-scale construction of public housing in China seems odd in comparison to the housing practice in most western countries, where public housing development has been kept at a minimum. Wang and Murie (2011), who examined the early stage of post-reform public housing development in China, found it difficult to locate the new phase of the Chinese housing policy ideology into any existing regimes in the typologies of comparative research on housing systems. They suggested that the Chinese approach to housing policy is distinct and hybrid. Even ECH could be seen as a residual safety net as social housing does in the liberal regime of housing system, their driving rationales are much different. While the residual status of public housing in the liberal regime is mainly underpinned by the ideology of minimizing government intervention, in China it is largely due to the needs of economic growth. Several studies attribute this difference in housing policy to the "productivist welfare" ideology prevailing in East Asia (Holliday 2000).

Interestingly, the "productivist housing policy" hypothesis can also be used to explain why the recent massive construction of public housing is widely regarded as an economic vehicle to counteract the shocks of the global economic downturn and as a regulation tool to cool down the overheating residential property markets.

Meanwhile, the shift in housing policy exemplifies many of the trends in Chinese social and economic policies that have emerged since the global financial crisis. Over the last few years, the Chinese government has apparently become more cautious of market failure and has increasingly regained more direct control of resource allocation in many economic and social sectors (Naughton 2010).

The current national prioritization of public housing in China signals a sharp change in the housing policy of previous decades so as to address negative externalities and inefficiencies in China's short-lived post-housing reform period. Although housing sector complexities can never be totally coordinated by a central authority, this massive public housing program is designed to help balance economic growth and provide stability in light of the increasingly short supply of low-cost housing, high levels of inflation, and a growing wealth gap.

Land and housing policies are among the Chinese government's most important tools for fine-tuning the economy (Chen et al. 2011). A housing policy that addresses the needs of the majority is critical for any government during in the event of an economic downturn. In the 1980s, during which China experienced massive unemployment, the country adopted a market approach to confront job creation, with debt financing as a key element to maintain employment through massive large-scale infrastructure projects. Today the government is looking at a long-term land allocation plan oriented toward economic restructuring as a tool to control economic cycles.

The current plan to rapidly increase investment and construction in public housing may result in an increased supply of affordable housing for needy families. However, we believe that the establishment of a finance system for such affordable housing is at least equally important. The Chinese government should promote the use of a variety of financing tools and instruments to attract social capital to public housing investment and lower the cost of borrowing to low- and middle-income families. A well-functioning housing finance system will contribute to the expansion of home ownership, the development of housing markets and employment, economic growth and wealth accumulation, and social and political stability.

Acknowledgment The research is supported by the funding from Peking University-Lincoln Institute Center for Urban Development and Land Policy, National Science Foundation of China (NSF71173045), Key Social-Science Research Project of the Ministry of Education of the People's Republic of China (13JZD009), MOHURD (2012–2021) and Fudan University 985-III Project (2012SHKXQN012). Biography of the corresponding author: Professor Jie Chen received his Bachelor's degree from Fudan University in 1997, Master's degree in Economics from the University of Oslo in 2001, and Ph.D degree in Economics from the University of Uppsala in 2005. His major research areas include housing and urban policy, real estate investment and finance, and housing price appraisal. His research is published in Journal of Housing Economics, Urban Studies, Housing Studies, Annals of Regional Science, and several other SSCI-listed journals. He serves an executive associate editor of the Journal of Real Estate (in Chinese), an associate editor of International Real Estate Review, and a member of the international advisory committee of International Journal of Housing Policy. He provides policy consulting services to Chinese central and local government agencies and a number of international organizations including World Bank and Asia Development Bank.

References

Adams B (2009) Macroeconomic implications of China urban housing privatization, 1998–1999. J Contemporary China 18(62):881–888
Angel S (2000) Housing policy matters: a global analysis. Oxford University Press, New York
Baker E, Tually S (2008) Women, health and housing assistance: implications in an emerging era of housing provision. Aust J Soc Issues 43(1):123–138
Chen J, Hao Q, Stephens M (2010) Assessing housing affordability in post-reform China: a case study of Shanghai. Hous Stud 25(6):877–901
Chen J, Guo F, Zhu A (2011) The housing-led growth hypothesis revisited: evidence from the Chinese Provincial Panel data. Urban Stud 48(10):2049–2067
Currie J, Yelowitz AS (2000) Are public housing projects good for kids? J Public Econ 75(1):99–124
EIU (2011) Building Rome in a day: the sustainability of China's housing boom. The Economist Intelligence Unit Limited, London
Fleisher BM, Yin Y, Hills SM (1997) The role of housing privatization and labor-market reform in China's dual economy. China Econ Rev 8(1):1–17
Gibson N (2009) The privatization of urban housing in China and its contribution to financial system development. J Contemporary China 18(58):175–184
Hills J (2007) Ends and means: the future roles of social housing in England. Centre for Analysis of Social Exclusion, London
Ho LS (1988) Towards an optimal public housing policy. Urban Stud 25(3):204–211
Holliday I (2000) Productivist welfare capitalism: social policy in East Asia. Political Stud 48(4):706–723
Hou X, Ying H, Zhang Y (1999) To meet housing needs of all people: major breakthroughs of urban housing system. Guangxi Normal University Press (In Chinese), Nanning
Huang Y (2004) The road to homeownership: a longitudinal analysis of tenure transition in urban China (1949–93). Int J Urban Reg Res 28(4):774–795
Kemeny J (1992) Housing and social theory. Routledge, London
Le Blanc D, Laferrère A (2001) The effect of public social housing on households' consumption in France. J Housing Econ 10(4):429–455
Li K (2011) Massive-scale implementation of security housing program and step-by-step improvement of housing policy and provision system. Qiu Shi (In Chinese), 2011-04-16, Beijing
Liang Y, Huo Z, Liu K (2010) An empirical study on the family wealth distribution in urban and rural China. Econ Res 10:33–47 (In Chinese)
Lim G-C, Lee M-H (1990) Political ideology and housing policy in modern China. Environ Plann C: Government Policy 8(4):477–487
Logan JR, Fang Y, Zhang Z (2010) The winners in China's urban housing reform. Housing Stud 25(1):101–117
Malpass P, Murie A (1999) Housing policy and practice, 5th edn. Palgrave Macmillan, Hampshire
Man JY (2011) China's housing reform and outcomes. In: Man JY (ed) Policy. Lincoln Institute of Land Policy, Cambridge, MA
Midgley J, Tang K-L (2001) Social policy, economic growth and developmental welfare. Int J Soc Welfare 10(2):244–252
MOHURD (2011) The minster of MOHURD's report of latest progress of public housing program on the meeting of the 11th NPC (National People's Congress) Standing Committee Held in 27 Oct 2011, Beijing. http://finance.sina.com.cn/focus/rdxwbzf/index.shtml
Naughton B (2010) The turning point in housing. China Leadersh Monitor 33(1):1–10
NBSC (2011) Series reports on China's economic and social development achievements during the 11th five-year planning period (2006–2010): No. 9. National Bureau of Statistics of China (NBSC), Beijing. http://www.stats.gov.cn/tjfx/ztfx/sywcj/t20110307_402708357.htm
Newman SJ, Harkness JM (2002) The long-term effects of public housing on self-sufficiency. J Policy Anal Manage 21(1):21–43

Oxley M (2000) The future of social housing: learning from Europe. Institute for Public Policy Research (IPPR), London

Peng X (2011) China's demographic history and future challenges. Science 333(6042):581–587

PFPC (2012) In: National Population and Family Planning Commission of P. R. China (PFPC) (ed) Report on China's migrant population development 2012. China Population Press, Beijing

Qi J (2009) Housing problems of low-income families in China. In: The 22nd Session of the Governing Council of UN-Habitat. The Governing Council of UN-Habitat, Nairobi

Rosen KT, Ross MC (2000) Increasing home ownership in urban China: notes on the problem of affordability. Housing Stud 15(1):77–88

Ross LM (2008) Quantifying the value proposition of employer-assisted housing: a case study of Aurora healthcare. Center for Housing Policy, Washington, DC

Stephens M (2010) Locating Chinese urban housing policy in an international context. Urban Stud 47(14):2965–2982

Sullivan T, Gibb K (eds) (2003) Housing economics and public policy. Blackwell Science Ltd., Oxford

Szelenyi I (1987) Housing inequalities and occupational segregation in state socialist cities. Int J Urban Reg Res 11(1):1–9

Tutin C (2008) Social housing and private markets: from public economics to local housing markets. In: Scanlon K, Whitehead CME (eds) Social housing in Europe II: a review of policies and outcomes. London School of Economics and Political Science, London, pp 47–61

United Nations (2012) World urbanization prospects: the 2011 revision. United Nations, New York

Wang YP, Murie A (1999) Commercial housing development in urban China. Urban Stud 36(9):1475–1494

Wang YP, Murie A (2011) The new affordable and social housing provision system in China: implications for comparative housing studies. Int J Housing Policy 11(3):237–254

Wells J (1985) The role of construction in economic growth and development. Habitat Int 9(1):55–70

Whitehead CME (2003) The economics of social housing. In: O'Sullivan T, Gibb K (eds) Housing economics and public policy. Blackwell Science Ltd., Oxford, pp 135–192

World Bank (1991) Housing indicator program. The World Bank, Washington, DC

World Bank (1993) Housing: enabling markets to work. The World Bank, Washington, DC

World Bank (2012) China 2030: building a modern, harmonious, and creative high-income society. The World Bank, Washington, DC

Wu F (1996) Changes in the structure of public housing provision in urban China. Urban Stud 33(9):1601–1627

Wu F, Xu J, Gar-On Yeh A (2006) Urban development in post-reform China: state, market, and space. Routledge, London

Yang Y-R, Chang C-H (2007) An urban regeneration regime in China: a case study of urban redevelopment in Shanghai's Taipingqiao Area. Urban Stud 44(9):1809–1826

Yang Z, Shen Y (2008) The affordability of owner occupied housing in Beijing. J Housing Built Environ 23(4):317–335

Yao S, Luo D, Morgan S (2010) Impact of the US credit crunch and housing market crisis on China. J Contemporary China 19(64):401–417

Zhang XQ (2000) The restructuring of the housing finance system in urban China. Cities 17(5):339–348

Zhao Y, Bourassa SC (2003) China's urban housing reform: recent achievements and new inequities. Housing Stud 18(5):721–744

Zhou M, Logan JR (1996) Market transition and the commodification of housing in urban China. Int J Urban Reg Res 20(3):400–421

Chapter 3
Public Housing Programs and the Challenge of Household Affordability in Beijing

Zan Yang, Chengdong Yi, and Wei Zhang

3.1 Introduction

As China's political, economic and cultural center, Beijing is a strong magnet for both population and industry. Due to rapid industrialization and urbanization, the city's population has reached 20.2 million at the end of 2011 (according to Statistical Bureau of Beijing), and built-up urban areas have grown to 1,425.9 km^2 in 2011 (NBSC 2012). In addition, there have been massive urban renewals, shantytown rebuilding and new town development. The increased demand for housing has resulted in higher housing prices, and corresponding higher housing prices have grown in Beijing at a rate faster than the national average. The average price for commodity housing in Beijing increased 2.6 times from 2001 to 2009, while disposable income per capita increased only 2.4 times during the same period. This has created problems of low housing affordability and poor housing consumption, especially among low- and middle-income households. Severe housing problems are increasingly threatening economic stability in Beijing (Yang and Shen 2008; Yang and Wang 2011) and also widening social stratification between different cohorts (Yang and Wang 2011; Man 2011).

Under social and political pressures, in August 2007 the Chinese government committed to meeting basic housing needs of low-income "house-poor" urban households through developing public housing (SC[2007]No.24). This document signaled the turning point of Chinese post-reform housing history and essentially reversed the downslide trend of public housing since 1998. For last few years,

Z. Yang (✉) • W. Zhang
Tsinghua-Hang Lung Center for Real Estate Studies, Department of Construction Management, Tsinghua University, 100084 Beijing, People's Republic of China
e-mail: zanyang@tsinghua.edu.cn

C. Yi
Department of Urban and Real Estate Management, Central University of Finance and Economics, Beijing 100081, People's Republic of China

J. Chen et al. (eds.), *The Future of Public Housing: Ongoing Trends in the East and the West*, DOI 10.1007/978-3-642-41622-4_3,

public housing program in China has been expanding at a dazzling speed. Official data suggests that China started constructing 16.3 million units of public housing and finished 11 million units during its "11th five-year plan" period (2006–2010) (MOHURD 2011). In 2010 alone, China started 5.9 million units and completed 3.3 million units of public housing. In the beginning of 2011, Chinese Prime Minister Wen Jiabao announced that the Chinese government is committed to building 36 million units of public housing during the "12th five-year plan period" (2011–2015). By this plan, public housing sector would accommodate roughly 20 % of Chinese urban households by 2015.

It is difficult to provide comprehensive evaluation on housing policy in China at its early stage. This paper, however, based on the unique dataset, put effort to test whether public housing programs in Beijing could to meet household affordability. In this study, a residual income approach is used to measure housing affordability of two programs: Economic and Comfortable Housing (ECH) and Capped Price Housing (CPH). In this measure, household affordability is related to a socially defined minimum market basket of goods and public housing costs. We find that in general the incomes of eligible households for public housing fall far short of the level required to access public housing. Although the price of ECH and PRH is lower than that of commercial housing, it is still too expensive for most medium – and low – income families. The development of public housing is challenged by its affordable for the eligible household.

3.2 Public Housing Programs in Beijing: Economic and Comfortable Housing (ECH) and Capped Price Housing (CPH)

As the capital of China, Beijing offers all available affordable housing programs, including Cheap Rent Housing (CRH), Economic and Comfortable Housing (ECH), Capped Price Housing (CPH) and Public Rental Housing (PRH). It indicates that the political objective of affordable housing program design is targeting low-and-medium-income households who cannot or have difficulties affording commodity housing in the private sector. At the subsidized rental level, CRH and PRH are restricted to eligible households and persons with low- and medium- income.

In Beijing, funding for affordable housing is mainly from the local government fiscal budget, 10 % of net proceedings from land granting, and loan from housing provident funds.[1] In 2011, Beijing government is given the permission to issue private debt and government bond to finance affordable housing construction.

---

[1] Public provident funds are deposits from employers and their employees' one – for – one match saving for the purpose of housing consumption. In 2011, in the 28 pilot cities, the reserves on housing provident funds is required to be invested in PRH development (MOHURD 2011).

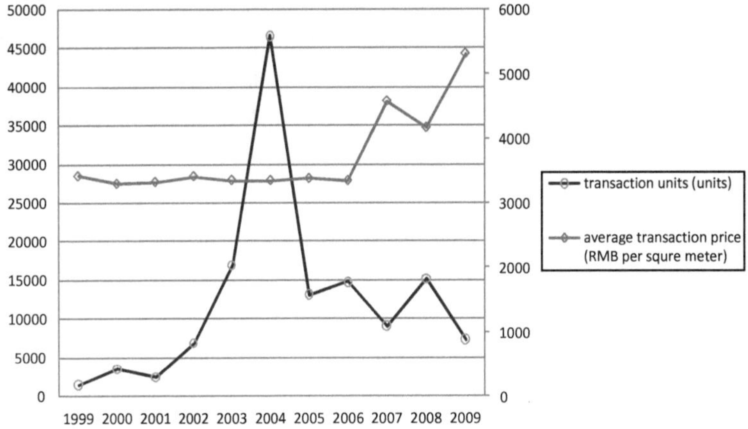

Fig. 3.1 Transaction units and average ECH transaction price in Beijing (Source: Beijing Municipal Commission of Housing and Urban – Rural Development)

3.2.1 Economic and Comfortable Housing (ECH) in Beijing

The Beijing municipal government's strategy began in 1993 with the *Kangju* (healthy living) Project and continued with the national Economic Housing Project in 1998. The objective of that project is to improve living conditions for medium- and low-income groups and encourage the establishment of an economical housing supply system (Meng and Feng 2005).

ECH is encouraged by polices that including the free transfer of land and reductions or exemptions from taxes and levies. This makes the average price of ECH units lower than that of similar quality commercial housing. The ECH price is determined by the Ministry of Housing of Urban and Rural Development (MOHURD) and the National Development and Planning Committee. The general principle of ECH price determination is to cover construction costs and limit developer profits while making the housing affordable for medium-to-low-income households. As Fig. 3.1 shows, the ECH transaction price was rather stable before 2006 and started to increase after 2007 in correspondence with the growth of commercial housing prices. We can notice that 78,121 ECH units were sold from 1999 to 2004, according for 7 % of the total commodity housing in urban China during the same period. As the ECH price is one-third that of the market price on average, this implies that 30 % of housing wealth is shifted to assisted households. However, it is clear that the importance of ECH declined rapidly after 2004, and in 2010, transacted ECH units contributed less than 3 % of total new urban commodity housing. This may due to the reselling policy. Since 2004, after owning the economic housing and land-use permits for 5 years in Beijing, homeowners have been able to list their ECH in commercial markets to local housing authorities after

Table 3.1 Eligibility conditions of applying for ECH in Beijing (2010)

Eligibility conditions		Economic and comfortable housing (ECH)
Target group		Medium-to-low-income households
Current living floor space per head		10 m^2
Annual household income (RMB)	One-person	22.7 thousand
	Two-person	36.3 thousand
	Three-person	45.3 thousand
	Four-person	52.9 thousand
	More than five-person	60.0 thousand
Total household assets (RMB)	One-person	240 thousand
	Two-person	270 thousand
	Three-person	360 thousand
	Four-person	450 thousand
	More than five-person	480 thousand

Source: Beijing Municipal Commission of Housing and Urban – Rural Development

land tax, calculated as 70 % of the difference between the original and current market prices, is duly paid [SC[2007]No.24].

Eligible candidates for ECH in Beijing require local *Hukou* registration and must meet the demarcation line standards for total income and total wealth. Their current living floor space per head must be below 10 m^2, including self-owned and rental housing. The eligible conditions are specified in Table 3.1.

3.2.2 Capped Price Housing (CPH) in Beijing

CPH was initiated in 2007 by the State Council as a new housing assistance program targeting mainly urban middle-income families. The program is also referred to as the dual-restriction commodity in which both selling price and apartment size are severely controlled. The price is set jointly by relevant local government departments, which consider the actual costs and reasonable developer profits. Generally, CPH profit is limited to 3–5 %, slightly higher than that of the comparable ECH and observably lower than the nearby ordinary commodity housing. The maximum size of a unit in CPH is limited to 90 m^2 per unit, and land for CPH is leased through tender auction at a lower price. The government's land lease tender states that finished units can only be sold to eligible homebuyers at fixed prices, and commercial developer bids are deemed unsuccessful if they do not abide by these requirements.

CPH is more flexible than ECH with regard to household income and assets. Under CPH, priority is given to households with elderly or disabled people and families whose residences were demolished by urban upgrade projects. Only local

Table 3.2 Eligibility conditions of applying for CPH in Beijing (2010)

Eligibility conditions		Capped price housing (CPH)
Target group		Medium households
Current living floor space per head		15 m^2
Annual household income (RMB)	Three-person or less	88.0 thousand
	More than three-person	116.0 thousand
Total household assets (RMB)	Three-person or less	570 thousand
	More than three-person	760 thousand

registered households are allowed to buy CPH, and they have to meet certain conditions concerning income level and housing assets. Similar to ECH, after 5 years, CPH owners can sell their housing after land tax, calculated at 35 % of the difference between the original and market prices at selling time, is duly paid. Eligible conditions for CPH in Beijing are displayed in Table 3.2.

In Beijing, CPH achieved its highest rate of development in 2009, when 64,000 units covering about 6.83 million m^2 were built. The respective supplies of CPH units were 42,000 in 2008 and 30,000 in 2007. In 2010, 30,000 CPH units were planned for construction,[2] about half that of 2009 level. This was primarily due to a shift in policy focus to public rental housing in the central government.

3.3 Previous Studies and Measures of Housing Affordability

The accurate assessment of housing affordability is important in order to formulate public policy and measure poverty. However, conceptual and empirical analysis of affordability is far from consistent in the previous studies. This is partly because of the conceptual complexity, and partly because of the weakness of the existing measuring methods.

Housing affordability is the ability of a household to pay its housing cost without compromising its standard of living (Grigsby and Rosenburg 1975). The core concept in this definition is the opportunity cost between housing and non-housing consumption. Disposable income after subtracting housing cost should not drag a household below the desirable minimum standards, defined as the "poverty standard" by Bramley (1990) and the "minimum market basket" by Grigsby and Rosenburg (1975). In other words, housing is not affordable if it cannot meet householder's requirement and utility at certain minimum level. Therefore, Bramley (1990) defines housing affordability by emphasising housing consumption that meets the "social sector norms of adequacy". This definition describes the differences in opportunity cost between

[2] Source: Beijing Municipal Commission of Housing and Urban – Rural Development.

housing and non-housing consumption and captures three critical dimensions of housing affordability: income, housing costs and non-housing expenditure.

From this point, residual income approach has been paid particular attention (e.g. Thalmann 1999; Kutty 2005; Stone 2006). It highlights the critical relationship among income, housing cost and expenditures on non-housing necessities. It is thus appealing from a political perspective because it allows us to ask the question "affordable to whom?" and to address the service standard of housing that we are applying (Stone 2006). Freeman et al. (2000) provide an international review on the study of housing affordability and discuss the residual income approach. Kutty (2005) applies this method in the American study and argues that this results in a more accurate picture of the nation's poverty. Yang and Shen (2008), Yang and Wang (2011) developed this method for a study of Beijing, and discuss its advantages in their case study of China.

Using this residual income approach in the study, firstly, we assess the minimum required expenditures for non-housing consumption of the eligible households. In this study, official poverty line of household determined by the Urban Living Standard Guarantee System (*dibao*) in Beijing is used to estimate non-housing consumption. The poverty line is used for providing social assistance to poor urban households. It is based on a "cost of basic needs" covering basic cost of cloth, food, living and compulsory education and adjusted every few years by Beijing Civil Affairs Bureau according to the changes of CPI. However, it is generally thought that the poverty line is set at an unreasonably low level and updating frequency is far behind the growing economy (Chen et al. 2010). We compare the poverty line with the average non – housing consumption for the 40 % bottom households from the Beijing Statistics Bureau and find that poverty line is much lower than the statistics level of household consumption. However, our general conclusion on household affordable for ECH and PRH is not variant much by using two different measures on non – housing consumption of household.

Secondly, average total purchase prices of ECH and PRH are used to estimate the housing costs of eligible households. Given the total cost of ECH and PRH, we can estimate the down payment and annual debt service payment respectively based on the Chinese standard repayment loan. We can thus derive a minimum required budget that is the sum of expenditures for non-housing goods and the costs of ECH and PRH after taking financing costs into account. By comparing the eligible household's actual income (obtained from the Beijing Housing Indemnity Office (BHIO) in Beijing Municipal Commission of Housing and Urban – Rural Development) with minimum required budget estimated above, we are able to measure if ECH and PRH is affordable for the eligible households.

We can also measure affordable for renting housing such as CRH or PRH, by comparing eligible household's actual income and minimum required budget including expenditures of non – housing goods and rents for LRH or PRH.

3.4 Data

The data on eligible household is obtained from Beijing Housing Indemnity Office (BHIO) in Beijing Municipal Commission of Housing and Urban-Rural Development.

More than 40,000 families were approved as eligible for ECH and 70,000 families for CPH from 2007 to the first quarter of 2010. Table 3.3 summarizes the major characteristics of the eligible households in the database for the two programs.

In the table, annual income refers to total family income including salary, subsidies, income from financial assets and unregulated income. It shows that on average the incomes and asset values of eligible households in the ECH program are lower than those in the CPH program. For example, more than half of ECH households have annual income between RMB20,000 and RMB50,000, while more than half of CPH household annual incomes are between RMB50,000 and RMB100,000. These differences reflect policy discrepancies between the ECH and CPH projects described above. With regard to family structure, child ages are similar in both groups, as shown in Figs. 3.2 and 3.3. In general, more than half of the eligible households have children old enough to attend school, and more than 80 % of families are working class.

Table 3.3 Major characteristics of eligible households for ECH and CPH in Beijing

Annual income (Thousand RMB)		Distribution (%)
ECH	0–5	7.93
	5.001–10	6.00
	10.001–20	26.58
	20.001–30	26.74
	30.001–40	23.15
	40001–50	9.00
	50.001–60	0.61
CPH	0–10	2.94
	10.001–30	13.93
	30.001–60	43.30
	60.001–70	15.21
	70.001–100	23.59
	Above 100	1.03

Family assets (Thousand RMB)	ECH	CPH
0–50	45.94	27.54
50.001–100	21.25	19.44
100.001–500	32.81	49.80
500.01–600	0.00	2.74
Above 600	0.00	0.47

Sources: Beijing Housing Indemnity Office (BHIO) work reports by the BHIO

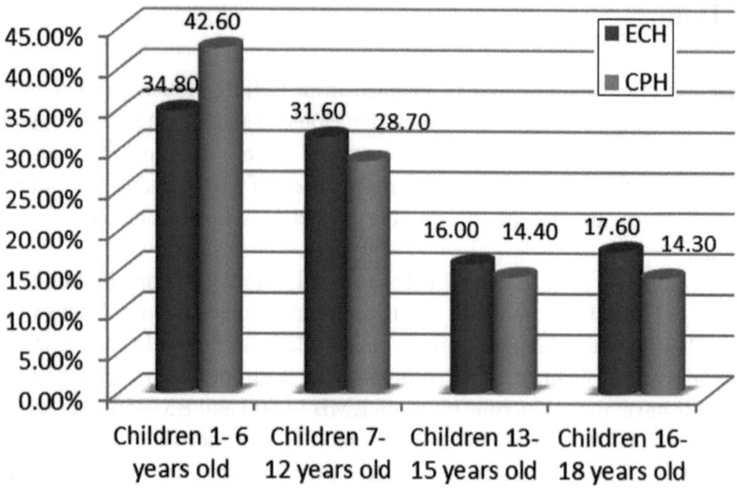

Fig. 3.2 Child age distribution in families eligible for ECH and CPH (%) (Sources: Beijing Housing Indemnity Office (BHIO) and work reports by the BHIO)

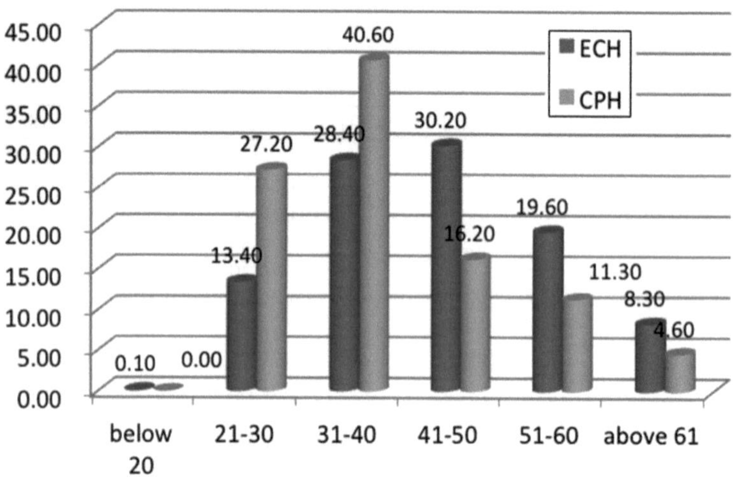

Fig. 3.3 Age distribution of households eligible for ECH and CPH (%) (Sources: Beijing Housing Indemnity Office (BHIO) and work reports by the BHIO)

3.5 Affordability of Housing Costs for Low-Income Households

In this section, we calculate the affordability of approval eligibility for ECH and CPH households from 2007 to 2009 using the residual income approach.

The average sale prices of ECH and CPH housing obtained from the BHIO are used. Average construction areas of 70 and 80 m^2 are used to calculate the total

Table 3.4 Household affordability for ECH and CPH (RMB)

	2007	2008	2009	
Year	ECH	ECH	ECH	CPH
Total price	249,603	331,731	362,529	582,465
Down payment (20 %)	49,921	66,346	72,506	116,493
Amortization (yearly)	17,454	19,156	20,731	33,309
Non-housing expenditure (yearly)	10,788	11,484	13,572	13,572
Required minimum income (yearly)	28,242	30,640	34,303	46,881

Notes:
1. Average sizes of 30 m^2 per capita (construction area) are used to calculate total ECH and CPH costs
2. Loan maturity at 30 years is assumed in the estimation. This is currently the longest term for a bank mortgage loan for affordable housing
3. The mortgage rate used in the calculation is 7.83 % at the 2007 level, 5.94 % at the 2008 level and 6.94 % at the 2009 level
4. Non-housing expenditure is calculated using the poverty line which is yearly published by Beijing Civil Affairs Bureau
5. RMB refers to Renminbi, the Chinese currency
US$1 = RMB6.154, EUR1 = RMB 8.071 up to 2013 -5 -4

costs of ECH and CPH, respectively. These are referenced by the BHIO. Given the total costs of ECH and CPH, we can estimate the down payment and annual debt service payment, respectively. A standard repayment loan, which has been the dominant credit contract for affordable house purchase in China, is one in which the down payment is less than 20 % of the total value and the loan maturity is a maximum of 30 years. Applying the annual interest rate for each year, we can estimate the annual amortization for purchasing ECH and CPH, respectively, and the annual minimum income of a family required to purchase ECH and CPH in 2007, 2008 and 2009, respectively. Because CPH began in Beijing in 2008 with very few projects, we calculate CPH affordability only for 2009. The estimated results are shown in Table 3.4. By simply measuring the gap between these minimum required budgets and the actual income of a family (shown in Table 3.3), we can obtain the affordability of ECH and CPH debt payments. Further, we can give a general overview of down payment affordability by comparing total household asset value with required ECH and CPH down payments.

If we compare the actual family income shown in Table 3.3 with the required income calculated in Table 3.4, we find that more than 67.25 % of eligible ECH households have difficulties in purchasing ECH at the price level in year 2009, indicating that the ECH supply has not successfully made home ownership affordable. The affordability of CPH is better, with nearly 61.48 % of households showing higher incomes than the minimum required income level. For most households, down payment affordability is not a severe problem given the asset value shown in Table 3.2. More than 50 % of eligible households are affordable to downs payments of ECH and CPH.

To further understand household affordability for ECH, we specify the affordability for different household sizes (shown in Table 3.5). We find that one-person

Table 3.5 Household affordability for ECH by households size (RMB)

Year	2007	2008	2009
Household size	**One-person household**		
Total price	86,070	114,390	125,010
Down payment (20 %)	17,214	22,878	25,002
Amortization (yearly)	6,018.47	6,605.62	7,148.57
Non-housing expenditure (yearly)	3,720.00	3,960.00	4,680.00
Required minimum income (yearly)	9,738.47	10,565.62	11,828.57
Household size	**Two-person household**		
Total price	172,140	228,780	250,020
Down payment (20 %)	34,428	45,756	50,004
Amortization (yearly)	12,036.93	13,211.25	14,297.14
Non-housing expenditure (yearly)	7,440.00	7,920.00	9,360.00
Required minimum income (yearly)	19,476.93	21,131.25	23,657.14
Household size	**Three-person household**		
Total price	258,210	343,170	375,030
Down payment (20 %)	51,642	68,634	75,006
Amortization (yearly)	18,055.40	19,816.87	21,445.71
Non-housing expenditure (yearly)	11,160.00	11,880.00	14,040.00
Required minimum income (yearly)	29,215.40	31,696.87	35,485.71

households have the most difficulty in housing affordability, while two-person families are relatively better. In 2009, more than 80 % of one-person households and more than 50 % of three-person households are not affordable for ECH. This level was around 40 % for the two-person households.

3.6 Concluding Remarks

China's affordable housing supply is increasingly viewed as a political issue because skyrocketing prices have raised concerns of widening inequality among households as well as unsustainable economic development. In Beijing, housing prices are challenged by rapid urbanization as well as increasing improvements to living conditions. A greater supply of affordable housing is also regarded as a measure to stabilize housing prices. About 100,000 affordable housing units were planned for construction in Beijing in 2011.

Despite the benefits it would ostensibly create, this study will show that a successful housing program is not only estimated by the number of affordable dwellings supplied, but also challenged by the extent to which the programs meet household needs concerning both affordability and accessibility. Based on the study of two affordable programs in Beijing, namely Economic and Comfortable Housing and Capped Price Housing, we find that low- and medium-income families fall far short of the level required for the subsidized housing to be affordable.

Affordable housing development in China is supported by government through preferential land supply and tax policy. The price of affordable housing is determined to ensure limited low profit for developers, nominally 3 %. It leaves little room for price decreases from the supply perspective, which suggests that demand-side subsidies, integrated with other income subsidy policies, should be complementally used in housing policy. This would provide households with more options to locate in areas that meet their affordability and accessibility demands. In addition, shared equity between low-income families and the government could be an effective policy that would decrease the financial burden of disadvantaged households and share the risk that arises from future housing values.

The responsibility of affordable housing provision in China rests almost entirely on local government. It is the role of central government to ensure that vulnerable families receive the highest quality housing and services in their time of greatest need. It is important for them to integrate affordable housing allocation into a wider coordinated context of urban planning, and to ensure that affordable housing communities are designed with good access to public services. However, this does not necessarily mean that government is the sole agent in affordable housing provision. That affordability programs in China have not successfully brought housing prices and accessibility within reach of the targeted income groups may imply that expansion of public/private partnerships could provide an effective model for the type of affordable housing that has been awarded worldwide (UNECE 2004).

References

Bramley G (1990) Access, affordability and housing need. ESRC housing studies conference, University of Surrey, September. SAUS, University of Bristol, Mimeo

Chen J, Hao Q, Stephens M (2010) Assessing housing affordability in post-reform China: a case study of Shanghai. Hous Stud 25(6):877–901

Freeman A, Kiddle C, Whitehead C (2000) Defining affordability. In: Monk S, Whitehead C (eds) Restructuring housing systems: from social to affordable housing? York Publishing Services, York, pp 42–49

Grigsby WG, Rosenburg L (1975) Urban housing policy. APS Publications, Inc./Center for Urban Policy Research Rutgers University, New York

Kutty NK (2005) A new measure of housing affordability: estimates and analytical results. Housing Policy Debate 16(1):113–142

Man J (2011) China's housing reform and outcomes. In: Man JY (ed) Policy. Lincoln Institute of Land Policy, Cambridge, MA

Meng FY, Feng CC (2005) The rudiments of affordable housing in China. J Asian Arch Building Eng 437:431–437

MOHURD (2011) Report on construction and management of urban affordable housing. http://finance.sina.com.cn/focus/rdxwbzf/index.shtml

NBSC (2012) China statistical yearbook 2000. National Bureau of Statistics of China. China Statistical Press, Beijing

State Council (2007) Several opinions on solving the housing difficulties of low-income households in urban areas. State Council of the People's Republic of China, No. 24, 2007-8-7, Beijing

Stone ME (2006) What is housing affordability? The case for the residual income approach. Housing Policy Debate 17(1):151–184

Thalmann P (1999) Identifying households which need housing assistance. Urban Stud 36(11):1933–1947

UNECE (2004) The future of social housing. United Nations Economic Commission for Europe (UNECE), Vienna

Yang Z, Shen Y (2008) The affordability of owner occupied housing in Beijing. J Housing Built Environ 23:317–335

Yang Z, Wang ST (2011) The impact of privatization of public housing on housing affordability in Beijing: an assessment using household survey data. Local Economy 26(5) 384–400

Chapter 4
Public Housing in Shanghai: A Tool with Multiple Purposes

Ying Chang and Jie Chen

Abstract Direct state provision of housing remains an important element of housing regime in many countries. This chapter traces recent experience of public housing development in Shanghai. It focuses the roles of two major public housing programmes, namely Relocation Housing and the new PRH (public rental housing) programme, in Shanghai's recent socio-spatial dynamics. It is shown that the public housing programme in Shanghai is mainly a result of deliberate urban development policy in line with other strategies such as city marketing, and gentrification. Thus we suggest that the Shanghai municipality government appropriates the new public housing regime as institutions to buttress local economic competitiveness. Our analysis is augmented with data from a questionnaire survey of PRH tenants in Shanghai. Finally, we identify challenges for the future development of public housing sector in China.

Keywords Public housing • Housing policy • Urban development • Shanghai

4.1 Introduction

It has been argued that many aspects of urban dynamics are strongly affected by local housing policy (Glaeser et al. 2006). Public housing is perhaps the most controversial housing policy as it is in direct competition with market rate housing

---

Y. Chang
Assistant Professor, Department of Urban Planning and Design, Xi'an Jiaotong-Liverpool University, 111 Renai Road, Dushu Lake Higher Education Town, Suzhou Industrial Park, Suzhou, Jiangsu 215123, People's Republic of China
e-mail: Ying.Chang@xjtlu.edu.cn

J. Chen (✉)
Professor, Deputy Director of Institute of Real Estate Research, School of Public Economics and Administration, Shanghai University of Finance and Economics, Shanghai 200433, People's Republic of China
e-mail: chen.jie@mail.shufe.edu.cn

J. Chen et al. (eds.), *The Future of Public Housing: Ongoing Trends in the East and the West*, DOI 10.1007/978-3-642-41622-4_4,

and also costly to implement and maintain (Green and Malpezzi 2003). Nonetheless, direct state provision of housing remains an important element of housing regimes in many countries. As suggested by Green and Malpezzi (2003), "political support is generally stronger for programs tied more closely to the consumption of specific goods (housing, food, and medical care) than for income support".

Being a developmental state, the Chinese state envisages economic growth as the most important means to earn the political legitimacy to govern. From 1998 to 2011, China witnessed an unprecedented construction boom with more than 9,300 million square metre (sqm) added to the residential stock, which made it possible to shelter the 280 million population that migrated from rural areas to urban areas. However, as Wu (2001) pointed out, China's post-reform housing policy has embedded two interrelated but contradictory objectives: on one hand, increase housing supply sufficiently to accommodate rapid urbanization through commoditization and marketization of housing; on the other hand, stimulate local growth through enhancing the attractions of profit-driven real estate investment (Chen et al. 2011).

In recent years, the embedded contradiction within housing policy has been aggravated to produce a number of threats to the state's political legitimacy, which include a general worsening of housing affordability, rampant property speculation as well as increased macro instability (Chen et al. 2010). To confront these threats, since 2009 the Chinese central government has been mandating all municipalities to construct large-scale public housing projects (Wang and Murie 2011). In spring 2011, the State Council promised to deliver 36 million units of public housing during the period of "the 12th Five-Year Plan [FYP]" (2011–2015). This ambitious program is expected to accommodate 20 % of Chinese urban residents by 2015.

However, it is still widely believed, in China "(the) state housing provision is seen as important economic drivers rather than socially necessary" (Wang and Murie 2011). Nonetheless, according to the new doctrine of a "harmonious society" proposed by Chinese President Hu Jingtao in 2006, social welfare policy should be more integrated with economic policy and therefore also become a new benchmark for ranking the success of Chinese local leaders. For example, a recent joint report released by the World Bank and the Development Research Center of the State Council of China [DRCSC] suggests that China's future version should be either the "active welfare society" or "developmental welfare" model (World Bank 2012, p. 298).

Like HDB housing projects in Singapore (Wang 2012), the new public housing sector in Shanghai has been designed to serve as a platform to wave together a hybrid of ideologies such as neoliberalism, interventionism, authoritarian capitalism and developmentalism. Particularly, as we show in this chapter, the new PRH (Public Rental Housing) scheme in Shanghai is a result of deliberate urban development policy aiming to contribute to city marketing as well as the making of new gated neighborhoods for the middle class. Overall, we assert that the Shanghai municipality government aligns her public housing program mainly to reinforce local economic competitiveness and provide stability.

4.2 Current Conditions and Recent Development

4.2.1 The Current Housing Conditions in Shanghai

With a total population of more than 23 million and an annual GDP of 1,920 billion RMB (ac. 297 billion US$) in 2011,[1] Shanghai is the largest as well as the most globally vibrant city in China. Like other Chinese cities, Shanghai's neoliberal transformation of housing provision since the 1980s has been primarily driven by the state-led shift from the central planning system to the socialist market system (Wang and Murie 2011). Since the late 1990s, globalization has in conjunction with market reform shifted housing demand and housing supply in Shanghai (He et al. 2010; Shen and Wu 2012; Wu 2001). Housing development since the 1990s has significantly transformed the ownership structure of Shanghai's urban housing stock. By the early 1980s, 80 % of the urban housing stock in Shanghai was owned by the state (including working units) and only 20 % belonged to private persons (Shanghai Statistics Yearbook 1983). However, in 2011, 82 % of Shanghai permanent residents owned their home (Table 4.1).

Neoliberalism stimulates investment boom in the housing sector. By the end of 2011, the total housing stock in Shanghai amounted to 550 million sqm, which is 13.4 times that in 1978 and 2.9 times of that in 1998. The living space per person in the urban area is 18.7 sqm in 2011, doubled from 1998. The quality of housing also has increased significantly. In 2011, low-standard housing (mainly shanties and old lane houses) amount to only 1.46 % of total residential stock (Table 4.2).

According to the 6th population census, Shanghai accommodated 23 million residents (8.25 million households) in 2010. Among residents, permanent

Table 4.1 Tenure distribution structure of permanent households in Shanghai (%)

Tenure type	2004	2008	2010	2011
Rental	26.6	21.6	19.9	17.19
Public rental (pre-reform public housing stock)	25.9	17.4	16.4	13.89
Private rental	0.7	4.2	3.5	3.3
Home ownership	72.9	77.6	80.1	82.09
Owned: inherited from older generation	2.2	0.7	0.7	0.89
Owned: privatized pre-reform public housing	42.9	37.8	37.4	37.9
Owned: self-purchased commodity dwellings	27.8	39.1	41.1	43.3
Other	0.5	0.8	0.9	0.69
Total	100	100	100	100

Source: Shanghai Statistics Yearbook 2005–2012

[1] By the official exchange rate Shanghai's GDP was ranked the 13th among all cities in the world in 2011. Source: http://en.wikipedia.org/wiki/List_of_cities_by_GDP

Table 4.2 The structure of residential housing stock in Shanghai (1949–2010) unit: 10,000 sqm

Year	Total	Villa	Apartment	Staff dwelling	Improved lane houses	Old lane houses	Shanties
1949	2,359	224	101		469	1,243	323
1950	2,361	224	101	1	469	1,243	323
1960	3,602	224	101	500	478	1,800	500
1970	3,871	225	101	741	492	1,853	459
1978	4,117	128	90	1,140	433	1,777	464
1990	8,901	158	118	4,884	474	3,067	123
1998	18,587	214	191	14,868	445	2,758	49
2000	20,865	250	206	17,939	428	1,896	84
2005	37,997	1,380	491	33,610	541	1,836	37
2010	52,640	2,064	492	47,951	528	1,275	29

Source: Shanghai Statistics Yearbook (1985, 2000, 2011)

households (with local registration status-*hukou*) account for 61 % and migrants (without *hukou*) account for 39 %. The overwhelming majority of the migrant population is rural – urban migrants.

The census data reveals a sharp disparity in the homeownership ratio between permanent households and migrant households: 80 % vs. 20 %. Meanwhile, among all households, 7.4 % are living in accommodations without plumbing, 15 % without toilet (7 % share toilet with others) and 27.2 % without bathroom. The demand for decent housing is still tremendous, particularly among rural – urban migrant workers.

The literature also reveals that the socialist legacy together with the force of neoliberal marketization has concentrated low income households in certain types of dilapidated urban neighborhoods (He et al. 2010; Wu and Webster 2010).

4.2.2 The Post-reform Public Housing System in Shanghai

Despite the dominating role of the market in the post-reform housing provision, the Chinese government never fully withdraws from the housing sector. In 2001, Shanghai became the first city in China to set up the Cheap Rent Housing [CRH] system. The poorest households living in overcrowded dwellings are entitled by right to receive subsidized rents or cheap accommodation from the local housing authority. However, the CRH is proposed as a residual welfare scheme with strict entry requirements. By the end of 2009, only 61,500 households were assisted by the CRH program (roughly 90 % in the form of rent allowance and only 10 % in the form of subsidized accommodation). This number accounted for only 1 % of permanent households in Shanghai.

Until 2009, municipalities in China had almost full autonomy on decisions regarding the quantity and mode of public housing provision. The incentive to provide public housing was primarily driven by internal pressures and objectives, subject to the constraints of local government's resources. However, since 2010 the central government has placed public housing provision as a priority on its social and political agenda (MOHURD 2011). The scale of public housing construction has expanded substantially: the national target has been lifted from 1 million units in 2008, to 3.3 million units in 2009, 5.9 million units in 2010 and 36 million units over the 12th FYP (2011–2015). Meanwhile, since 2010 the Ministry of Housing and Urban – rural Development has set strict guidelines as well as annual targets for public housing provision for each municipality (MOHURD 2011).

In 2008, Shanghai reintroduced the Economically Affordable Housing [EAH] programme. Similar to EAH programs in other Chinese cities (Wang and Murie 2011), Shanghai's EAH program aims to increase the homeownership ratio among "house-poor" low-middle income households. To ensure affordability, housing is built on government allocated land, exempted from various fees and taxes and the benchmark sales price is set based on construction costs. Units are also regulated at around 60–80 sqm. Occupants have restricted ownership rights over their homes and face restrictions in reselling, i.e., a 5-year resale restriction period. In Shanghai, the EAH has been sometimes called "shared-ownership" housing. This name comes from the fact the government and buyers share roughly between 50 and 70 % ownership of EAH respectively. This is a measure that helps to prevent the applicants purchasing EAH homes for investment purposes. By 2010, 10 million sqm of EAH homes had been constructed in Shanghai.

In 2010, nearly 20 years after the termination of welfare rental housing, Shanghai Municipality adopted the Public Rental Housing [PRH] Programme and branded it as one element of the 'four in one' comprehensive public housing polices. The central idea of the 'four in one' model is to provide different types of affordable housing for different groups: the Cheap Rent Housing for the poorest households; the EAH (Shared-ownership) for the low-middle income households; relocation housing for the households displaced by the government; and the PRH for those who can-not afford home ownership but are also excluded from the other three affordable housing programme. The PRH program is the only scheme open to non-*hukou* holders, however still with an eligibility condition of the possession of a long-term residence permit.

According the Shanghai Housing Development Plan for the 12th FYP (2011–2015) published on Feb.7, 2012, the supply plan for public housing in Shanghai between 2011 and 2015 is one million units in total: 400,000 units for EAH; 350,000 units for relocation housing; 75,000 units for CRH; and 200,000 units for PRH. The land supply for affordable housing, together with small-medium size commodity housing, would be about 700 to 800 hectares per year from 2011 to 2013, making up 70 % of the total land supply (Tables 4.3 and 4.4).

Table 4.3 The supply plan of the "Four-in-One" public housing in Shanghai (2011–2015)

	2011–2015 (Target of net increase)	
Types	Units (1,000)	Population coverage (%)
Cheap rental housing	75	1.5 (2.6)
Economical affordable housing	400	4.2 (7.6)
Relocation housing	350	3.5 (6.0)
Public rental	200	1.2 (1.9)
Total	1,000	11.8 (19.2)

Source: Shanghai housing development plan for the 12th Five-Year Planning Period (2011–2015)
Note: In parentheses are referring to permanent households only and out parentheses are referring to the whole resident households, including floating migrants. The population in 2015 is the author's own estimation. For Cheap rental housing and public rental housing, the figures include the additions from the purchase or conversion of existing housing stocks

Table 4.4 The planned land supply in Shanghai between 2010 and 2012 (in hectares)

Year		EAH	Relocation housing	Public rental housing	Small-medium size commodity housing	Others	Total
2010	Hectare	250	450	0	70	330	1,100
	Percent	(23 %)	(41 %)	0 %	(6 %)	(30 %)	
2011	Hectare	200	400	100	140	360	1,200
	Percent	(17 %)	(33 %)	(8 %)	(12 %)	(30 %)	
2012	Hectare	100	450	50	100	300	1,000
	Percent	(10 %)	(45 %)	(5 %)	(10 %)	(30 %)	

Source: The 12 FYP of land supply in Shanghai
Note: There is no land supply plan for the cheap rent housing and there was no land supply for PRH in 2010

4.3 Urban Redevelopment and Public Housing in Shanghai

4.3.1 Key Concepts: Entrepreneurial City, City Marketing and Gentrification

As argued by several literature, Shanghai has embraced a state-led development approach but functions as an entrepreneurial city when paving its way to reclaim it global status (Wu 2003; He and Wu 2005; Zheng 2010).

City marketing is one of the main features of an entrepreneurial city, and particularly for cities that have embraced global competition. Sager (2011) emphases the neo-liberal rationale behind it, 'city marketing, promotion and branding are means for achieving competitive advantage in order to increase inward investment and tourism' and two groups of 'placer customers', together with the visitors, are usually the targets of city marketing drives: specifically, (1) inhabitants that want an attractive place to live, work and relax, (2) companies looking for a place to locate their offices and production facilities, do business and recruit employees (Sager 2011, p. 157). Important means used in city marketing include flagship projects and mega events (e.g. a Formula One race event and the well-known World Expo 2010 were held in Shanghai). In Shanghai, the city has employed various preferential policies to create an attractive image as an ideal place for industrial development and financial investment (Marton and Wu 2006; Wu and Barnes 2008); Creative industry clusters have been tossed into a hub to host world famous cultural and artistic events (Zheng 2010). It is also suggested that Shanghai manifests a complicated relationship between gentrification, globalisation, and emerging neo-liberal urbanism, and the local state has played a leading role in the large scale gentrification in Shanghai, mainly through the strategic plan (He 2010).

4.3.2 Relocation Housing and Gentrification

Many have investigated how the Shanghai municipality, as an entrepreneurial government, uses land as an important revenue generator (Wu 2004; He and Wu 2005; Yang and Chang 2007). Meanwhile, the Shanghai municipality has a long history in using public housing to promote urban redevelopment. The following sections will elaborate on the multiple purposes which the relocation programme in Shanghai serve in the process of inner city redevelopment and gentrification.

From 1987 to 1995, Shanghai implemented a small-scale "*housing congestion alleviation*" programme for those with the problem of extreme overcrowding (MOST 1995). A total of 60,000 households were resettled under this programme (Wu 2004).[2] Since 1992, the "365 scheme" of urban regeneration was introduced with the aim of redeveloping 365 hectares of shanty housing by 2000. The successful accomplishment of this scheme was largely associated with real estate developers who sought to share the profits of land redevelopment with local governments (Wu 2004).

The redevelopment of inner city in Shanghai continued on a greater scale in the post-reform era. In 2001, the "new round redevelopment scheme" was proposed with an aim of redeveloping nearly all dilapidated neighborhoods in the central areas. However, after commodity housing prices in Shanghai began to soar from 2002, the relocation compensation costs for displaced households increased dramatically (He and Wu 2005). To reduce displacement costs and facilitate the redevelopment of inner cities, the relocation housing policy was designed in 2003.

According to the new displacement policy implemented in 2003, displaced households will receive compensation at least equal to the market value of their demolished housing and have the right to buy the relocation housing at the price usually capped at roughly 70 % of nearby comparable free-market housing. High housing prices in the center and the substantial price gap between relocation

[2] In 1987–1988, the standard to qualify for entering this programme was households with housing space less than 2 sqm per person. This standard was lifted to 2.5 sqm in 1991 and 4 sqm in 1995.

Table 4.5 Residential relocation and housing demolition in Shanghai (1995–2011)

Year	Displaced households	Demolished residential space (10,000 m^2)
1995	75,777	253.90
2000	70,606	288.35
2005	75,857	851.85
2006	81,126	848.35
2007	51,354	690.00
2008	53,583	753.71
2009	68,286	612.56
2010	39,721	389.87
2011	23,112	182.83
Total	1,159,899	7,665.2

Source: Shanghai Statistics Yearbook (2012)
Note: Data only covers nine central urban districts and Pudong new district

housing and market housing in the suburb provides large incentives for households faced with relocation to move.

In 2005, the Shanghai Municipality announced a plan to provide 10 million sqm of relocation housing and 10 million sqm of Capped Priced Commodity Housing; the so called 'two 10 million sqm' programme. However, this scheme was suspended in 2006. Nonetheless, relocation housing continued to be built on a large scale: over the 11th FYP (2006–2010), 29.6 million sqm or roughly 330,000 units of relocation housing were completed. According to the Shanghai Housing Development Plan of the 12th FYP (2011–2015), 150,000 downtown households would be displaced and 3.5 million shanty housing in the inner city would be demolished.

The following table shows that a number of 1,159,899 households were displaced from the central area between 1995 and 2011, with a constructed residential area of 76.65 million square metres being demolished. This data suggests that, roughly one in four (permanent) households in Shanghai experienced forced relocation. It can be reasonably inferred that, without large-scale population relocation and land use restructuring, the housing stock in the urban area would be much less than the current level (Table 4.5).

The 12th FYP of Shanghai points out that, relocation housing has become a central tool to promote urban redevelopment and its 400,000 unit construction target over the period of 2011–2015 is decisive for the success of urban development in the 12th FYP. Relocation housing is the one of the biggest segments of public housing supply in Shanghai and the land supply for it is prominent in the overall supply, with a total of 450 hectares, making up 45 % of the total land supply in Shanghai in 2012 (see Tables 4.3 and 4.4).

Both dilapidated neighborhoods and work compounds were the primary location of low-income households, who have been relocated to the outskirts. The original impoverished neighborhoods are replaced by high rise commodity housing that mainly accommodates the upper and upper-middle class. The blighted industry areas are also replaced by shopping centers, offices and banks.

The relocation housing programme is thus an outcome as well as a response to state-led urban development approach. There is ample evidence that the relocation-housing programme in Shanghai as a whole has contributed to alleviate the level of overcrowding of poor households in dilapidated neighborhoods (He and Wu 2005; Yang and Chang 2007; Weinstein 2009; Wang 2011). However, the price of the trade-off between good location and housing overcrowding could not be easily measured. Further, the interests of displaced poor renters are largely ignored; it must be understood that often owners of overcrowded dwellings in fact do not live there and rent out to migrant workers.

4.4 The Development of New Public Rental Housing in Shanghai

The new Public Rental Public (PRH) programme has become a national priority of housing policy in China. Since 2011, the provision of PRH has become one of the key indicators to evaluate the performance of local municipalities.

4.4.1 Features of Public Rental Housing in Shanghai

In Shanghai, the supply plan of PRH units in the 12th FYP (2011–2015) is 200,000 units, half of which is to be provided at the city level and half at the district-level. By 2012, 21 PRH companies were established in Shanghai.

These PRH companies are legal independent entities, with investments shared equally between the city and the district. The PRH company is responsible for the investment, planning, design, administration, and management of the PRH. It is financially independent, which means that for additional costs beyond the initial investment, they have to finance themselves. In this respect, the PRH Company in Shanghai resembles the municipal housing company in Sweden and social housing cooperatives in the Netherlands. However, it is still unclear who will finance the operating deficit of the PRH Company if it occurs.

According to the governmental policy statement,[3] the principles of PRH in Shanghai can be summarized as 'led by the government, supplied by multiple sectors, provided at market price, and subsidised by multiple means'. Specifically, the government is responsible for the policy making, planning, organising and coordinating different sectors in the implementation. Both public and private sectors could be the suppliers. The rental price is at market level and the gap between the market price and affordability should be met by the subsidy shared by the municipality and employers.

[3] http://www.shfg.gov.cn/fgdoc/qyfc/zfbz/201202/t20120229_540238.html

It needs to be noted that although no permanent register status (hukou) is required, the applicant has to possess a long-term residence permit and have continuously contributed to the social insurance account for at least 12 months. Since summer 2013, the application for a residence permit has changed into a points-based system, which gives higher scores for candidates who are of younger age, have higher education, higher skilled, and who work in sectors within short-listed or remote new towns. In the following sections, we borrow the term 'talented professionals' (*rencai* in Chinese) to refer to these groups who are welcomed (or selected) by the city of Shanghai. In short, the new PRH programme in Shanghai is tailored for:

1. Talented professionals who cannot afford homeownership via the market while not eligible for other affordable housing programmes, for instance, the EAH;
2. Residents who live in overcrowded housing; this implies that homeowners can also apply for PRH, as long as their construction space per person is less than 15 sqm.
3. No permanent register status (hukou) is required. However, the applicant has to possess a long-term residence permit and have continuously contributed to the social insurance account for at least 12 months.

It should be emphasized that the rental rates of PRH in Shanghai are only slightly lower than the private rental market price. We will elaborate on the implications of this point in later sections.

4.4.2 The Competition for Talented Professionals and PRH

Shanghai has been given a role by the state as the 'dragonhead' to lead the 'opening up' policy in the post-reform era, with an ambitious aim of becoming a global financial centre. A strong relation has been found between the economic globalisation and the marketization of the socialist system in China (Witt and Redding 2013). Meanwhile, it has been suggested that globalisation and competitive strategies are bound together for reshaping the landscape of Chinese cities (Xu and Yeh 2009). There is also significant literature on the diverse city marketing and place promotion methods used in Shanghai (Wu 2001; Wei et al. 2006; Yang and Chang 2007).

To meet the growing demand of an entrepreneurial city, Shanghai needs more human inputs as the engine of the city. However, if one consider only permanent residents (*hukou* holders), Shanghai has been an aging city since early 1990s. The latest Census in 2010 shows that the ratio of aged 60 and above was as high as 23 % amongst permanent residents. The natural population growth rate among permanent households was −0.6 ‰ in 2010. The impact of the aging issue is not just the reduced labor force but also pressure on the social insurance fund.

The decentralization of the fiscal regime has permitted Shanghai to embark on its entrepreneurial journey. However the lack of contributors to the social insurance fund has weakened the fiscal system. In addition, Shanghai is faced with the growing competition from neighbouring cities in the Yangtze delta for high-skilled workers.

As summarized by Sager (2011, p. 157), 'the creative class needs places for consumption, recreation, and living.... Furthermore, housing the creative class requires a shift from working class quarters to hip, varied and good quality residential areas.'

The importance of providing decent housing to talented professionals has been repeatedly highlighted in government documents and meeting minutes. The 12th FYP Development Plan of Shanghai states that, *'it is a crucial time for Shanghai to fulfill its goal of becoming 'four centres' and a global metropolitan, but we are faced with many challenges..... we need more innovative public policy for talented professionals, and improve the living and cultural environment for talented professionals.'*

The slogan above is not an initiative but a formal recognition and adoption of recent practices to link housing to employment. As early as the late 1990s, many joint ventures in Shanghai bought 'commodity' housing for their employees to attract capable staff (Wu 2001). Recently, the mass media has reported a new phase of work-unit housing (for example, the Shanghai Baoshan Iron and Steel group, Shanghai Railway Group provides dormitory for their employees by using their own land for industrial purpose).[4] On the other hand, another type of apartment, 'the apartment for talented professionals' (*rencai gongyu*) has also emerged in Shanghai in recent years. From 2001 to 2011, Zhangjiang High-Tech Industrial Park has provided apartments for talented professionals' (*rencai gongyu*) of 270,000 sq, mainly by using the industrial land.[5] In 2011, the Changning District collected 500 units of apartments for 'talented professionals' mainly by adaptive reuse of vacant office buildings, hotels, and industrial buildings. The tenants can receive a heavy rent subsidy from the government.[6]

These initiatives have helped to frame the new PRH programme. In the 12th FYP of Talents Development Plan in Shanghai, the preferential policy of PRH as a means to attract the talented professionals has been highlighted: *(We need) to improve the living environment for talented professionals. To build public rental housing, and to moderate the* ***temporary*** *poverty in housing for young talented professionals.'*

The official document of the municipal housing authority also clearly states that the main aim for PRH in Shanghai is 'to relieve the housing pressure for young employees, talented professionals and other migrant workers residing in Shanghai'.[7]

However, a rent level close to market rate has excluded those low-income households from the PRH programme. From this perspective, PRH is a very selective programme with a clear target to attract 'talented class' but gives little considerations to solving the affordability problems of those low-income migrants.

---

[4] http://www.21cbh.com/HTML/2010-1-8/161128.html

[5] http://news.hexun.com/2011-12-18/136420803.html

[6] http://sh.people.com.cn/GB/134952/211179/215602/15533216.html

[7] http://www.shfg.gov.cn/fgdoc/qyfc/zfbz/201202/t20120229_540238.html

Table 4.6 Basic information of the first two municipal PRH projects

	Shang Jingyuan Garden	Xinning Apartment
District	Yangpu	Xuhui
Investment cost (billion RMB)	14.98	22.5
Total Construction Space (m^2)	158,562	192,000
Total residential space (m^2)	151,818	172,000
Cost per sqm (RMB)	9,500	11,700
Units of apartments for rent	2,201	2,900
Units rented out by the end of 2012	1,581	843
Occupancy ratio (by 2012)	71.9 %[a]	29.1 %
Apartment size (m^2)	1-bed room: 50–68 m^2; 2-bed room: 67–72 m^2; 3-bed room: 80–82 m^2	1-bed room: 40–42 m^2; 2-bed room: 62–63 m^2; 3-bed room: 75–78 m^2
Distribution of housing size (units)	1-bed room: 100; 2-bed room: 2,001; 3-bed room: 100	Mostly are two-bed room apartments
Monthly rent per unit (RMB)	1-bed room: 1,970; 2-bed room: 2,540–2,930; 3-bed room: 2,970–3,240	1-bed room: 1,694–1,896; 2-bed room: 2,533–2,772; 3-bed room: 3,033–3,311
Monthly rent per sqm (RMB)	Ca. 40	Ca. 45
(Annualized) Rent-price ratio	1:23	1:24

Source: authors' summary based on government documents and media news reports

Note: The two PRH projects were converted from purchased completed but undistributed public housing projects; EAH in the case of Shangjing Yuan and Relocation Housing in the case Xining. The investment costs in the table refer to the purchase prices of the two PRH projects, respectively. However, the decoration costs (around 700–800 RMB per sqm), furniture and facility costs and property management costs have not been added to the two figures yet. On the other hand, the PRH tenants do not pay the property management fee separately, as it is already included in the monthly rent

[a]http://www.shgjj.com/html/zyxw/52866.html

4.4.3 PRH Projects and a Survey Report of Its Tenants

This section provides basic information on the first two municipal-level PRH projects in Shanghai (Shangjing Gardern and Xinning Apartment). The two projects provide 5,100 units of apartments in total and have been available for rental application since March 2012. Unlike most commodity housing in China which is unfurnished at the delivery stage, the PRH apartments are furnished and approved applicants can move in immediately. By the end of 2012, roughly 2,400 tenants lived in the two projects (Table 4.6).

From the table above, it can be seen that the investment cost of PRH projects in Shanghai are very high, around 10,000 RMB per sqm in both cases. Because the PRH rent has to be capped at the market level, the annualized rent-price ratio is much less than 1:20, which implies that the investment cost needs at least 20 years to be recovered from the cash flow of rent revenue.

Further, as the PRH rent rate does not have much advantage compared to that of nearby private rental housing, the two PRH projects have not received much welcome among potential users. [8]High vacancy level aggravates the financial balance of PRH owners. However, so far the municipality largely seems to treat the provision of PRH as a political task (a pilot project) and little consideration has been given to cost recovery as well as sustainability of PRH projects.

To understand who has been attracted to the new PRH project, we provide analysis of the characteristics and housing satisfactions of PRH tenants, based on a survey of the residents of the two PRH in Shanghai (sample size 333 in total, 128 from Shangjin Garden and 205 from Xinning Apartment). This survey was conducted during June-Oct of 2012 by the Center for Housing Policy Studies (CHPS) at Fudan University.

The survey shows that most PRH tenants are middle-class: 64 % of survey respondents report their personal annual disposable income as higher than 60,000 RMB, 30 % higher than 90,000 RMB and 13 % higher than 120,000 RMB (note that the mean level of annual disposable of Shanghai residents in 2011 was 36,230 RMB). Further, the PRH tenants are mostly young and middle-aged: 65 % of respondents are aged below 35 and 44 % younger than 30; only 14 % older than 50. In addition, a high education level is one of the main features of PRH tenants: 65 % of respondents have received a Bachelor degree or higher.

The recent survey also shows that, the majority of PRH feel satisfied with the overall quality of the PRH project: 59 % of respondents think PRH meet their expectations and 17 % think PRH is beyond their expectations. However, 24 % feel PRH failed to meet their expectations. The aspects of PRH that respondents are most satisfied with include security of tenure (30 %), housing quality (18 %) and community security (17 %). The aspects that tenants felt least satisfied with include rent rate (3 %), convenience for the work place (4 %) and layout and design (6 %).

Because there is very limited security of tenure in the private rental housing market in China (Man 2011), PRH has strong attractions for middle class who highly value residential stability. Further, the high ratio of housing satisfaction among PRH tenants can be also attributed to the fact that the PRH projects are "gated communities". Wu (2005) suggests that the primary reason for the new emergence of gated communities is more about the protection of life style and the self-identity of the middle class, it also occurs in the context 'wherein the local government fails to provide differentiated services to those who are better-off in the market transition'. In this respect, PRH provides an alternative to homeownership with an affordable and guaranteed leasing contract offering decent housing to the newly-emerged middle class.

However, the survey also identifies several challenging issues for the PRH programme in Shanghai. For example, about half of respondents complained that the rent is too high in their survey questionnaires. Taking the ratio of rent-to-income of 0.3 as a threshold of housing affordability, the survey shows that about 25 % of respondents could not afford the rent of PRH. In addition, PRH tenants bear other additional costs. More than half of respondents (51.52 %) reported that their commuting time from home to work increased in comparison to their previous residence; 90 % of respondents needing to spend more than half an hour to go to workplace after moving in the PRH projects (in contrast to only 57 % before moving in).

Field works also shows that the two PRH projects are located in areas with limited job opportunities and the access to the subway and other mass means of transport is not good. It is clear that besides the high rent level, the low occupancy rate of PRH projects can be also attributed to their disadvantages in terms of location. The latter however is a common problem experienced in the history of public housing development in western countries (Green and Malpezzi 2003). To save investment costs, municipalities worldwide tend to place newly-built public housing projects in areas where land is less valued. Such a strategy however makes these projects unattractive to working households.

Meanwhile, although the large-scale construction of PRH projects can be justified on cost-reduction grounds (economics of scale), we argue that it should be carefully avoided. It is difficult to attract a large pool of applicants for any one given community. Instead, we recommend scattering small-size PRH projects across mature urban areas with good transport connections. We also believe it is cost-ineffective to provide all PRH through new construction and we support purchasing or adapting old vacant properties to be used as PRH apartments. Further, a selective rent subsidy policy should be implemented by the municipality to lessen the affordability burden of PRH tenants and increase the attractions of PRH among low income households.

4.5 Conclusion

The provision of affordable housing has become a political task in China to alleviate the level of inequality and income disparity generated by market and growth-led development in the post-reform era (Chen et al. 2010). Public housing policy, as a primary urban policy, is expected to achieve the socio-economic equality by providing decent homes for all (Li 2011). This chapter uses Shanghai as case study to elaborate the multiple purposes behind the public housing programmes in China. A close examination of the two key public housing programmes, namely the relocation housing and Public Rental Housing (PRH), has proved that the recent revival of public housing in Chinese cities is mostly driven by economic growth motives.

The supply of relocation housing is coupled with the demand for land as a revenue generator; the inner city redevelopment, the economic restructuring, the mega events and flagship projects to market the city. The PRH programme is one measure of city marketing in order to attract talented professionals and involves the development of gated communities for the middle classes. Particularly, the existing PRH projects helps alleviate the pressure of homeownership for the 'young white collars' by providing a decent place to live at a price they can afford. These PRH projects resemble a temporary substitute for the homeownership of gated communities that the middle class long for. According to our survey, the PRH residents are mainly the young middle class with a high education level, a group which highly value the amenities and the privatized landscape of the gated neighborhoods with a high level of security.

However, the rents of PRH are beyond the affordability range of low-income households. With the rent level close to the market price and other conditions, PRH is a very selective programme with a clear target to attract and keep 'talented professionals' to enhance the city's competiveness. Nonetheless, more considerations of low-income households' housing difficulties should be given if the housing policy's long-term aim is to provide decent housing for all. Further, currently the cost efficiency issue seems to be given very little attention in the PRH programme. There is a serious shortage of funding sources for the construction and management of PRH projects. The designs and locations of PRH projects remain hurdles to attracting tenants.

Finally, although the PRH projects in Shanghai are still at an early stage, we believe further investigations of PRH development in Shanghai can produce many valuable policy lessons for other major cities.

Acknowledgment The research is supported by the funding from NSFC (71173045), Lincoln Institute of Land Policy, Key Social-Science Research Project of the Ministry of Education of the People's Republic of China (13JZD009), Ministry of Housing and Urban Development of the People's Republic of China (2012–21), and Fudan University 985-III Project (2012SHKXQN012).

References

Chen J, Hao Q, Stephens M (2010) Assessing housing affordability in post-reform China: a case study of Shanghai. Hous Stud 25(6):877–901

Chen J, Guo F, Zhu A (2011) The housing-led growth hypothesis revisited: evidence from the Chinese Provincial Panel data. Urban Stud 48(10):2049–2067

Glaeser EL, Gyourko J, Saks RE (2006) Urban growth and housing supply. J Econ Geogr 6(1):71–89

Green RK, Malpezzi S (2003) A primer on US housing markets and housing policy. Regulation. Madison, Wisconsin

He S (2010) New-build gentrification in Central Shanghai: demographic changes and socioeconomic implications. Popul Sp Place 16(5):345–361

He S, Wu F (2005) Property-led redevelopment in Post reform China: a case study of Xintiandi redevelopment project in Shanghai. J Urban Aff 27(1):1–23

He S, Liu Y, Wu F, Webster C (2010) Social groups and housing differentiation in China's urban villages: an institutional interpretation. Hous Stud 25(5):671–691

Li K (2011) Massive-scale implementation of security housing program and step-by-step improvement of housing policy and provision system. Qiu Shi (in Chinese), 2011-04-16, Beijing

Man JY (2011) China's housing reform and outcomes. In: Man JY (ed) Policy. Lincoln Institute of Land Policy, Cambridge, MA

Marton AM, Wu W (2006) Spaces of globalisation: Institutional reforms and spatial economic development in the Pudong new area, Shanghai. Habitat Int 30(2):213–229

MOHURD (2011) The Minster of MOHURD's report of latest progress of Public Housing Program on the meeting of the 11th NPC (National People's Congress) standing committee held in October 27, 2011. Beijing. http://finance.sina.com.cn/focus/rdxwbzf/index.shtml

MOST (1995) Housing settlement project in Shanghai. Shanghai Housing Settlement Project Office, Shanghai. http://www.unesco.org/most/asia7.htm

Sager T (2011) Neo-liberal urban planning policies: a literature survey 1990–2010. Prog Plan 76(4):147–199

Shen J, Wu F (2012) Restless urban landscapes in China: a case study of three projects in Shanghai. J Urban Aff 34(3):255–277
Wang SW-H (2011) The evolution of housing renewal in Shanghai, 1990–2010: a 'Socially Conscious' entrepreneurial city. Int J Hous Policy 11(1):51–69
Wang J (2012) The developmental state in the global hegemony of Neoliberalism: a new strategy for public housing in Singapore. Cities 29(0):369–378
Wang YP, Murie A (2011) The new affordable and social housing provision system in China: implications for comparative housing studies. Int J Hous Policy 11(3):237–254
Wei YD, Leung CK, Luo J (2006) Globalizing Shanghai: foreign investment and urban restructuring. Habitat Int 30(2):231–244
Weinstein L (2009) The changing right to the city: urban renewal and housing rights in Globalizing Shanghai and Mumbai. City Commun 8(4):407–432
Witt MA, Redding G (2013) China: authoritarian capitalism. In: Witt MA, Redding G (eds) The Oxford handbook of Asian business systems. Oxford University Press, Oxford
World Bank (2012) China 2030: building a modern, harmonious, and creative high-income society. Washington, DC
Wu F (2001) Housing provision under globalisation: a case study of Shanghai. Environ Plan A 33(10):1741–1764
Wu F (2003) The (Post-) socialist entrepreneurial city as a state project: Shanghai's reglobalisation in question. Urban Stud 40(9):1673–1698
Wu F (2004). Intraurban residential relocation in Shanghai: modes and stratification. Environ Plan A 36(1):7–25
Wu F (2005) Rediscovering the 'Gate' under market transition: from work-unit compounds to commodity housing enclaves. Hous Stud 20(2):235–254
Wu J, Barnes T (2008) Local planning and global implementation: Foreign investment and urban development of Pudong, Shanghai. Habitat Int 32(3):364–374
Wu F, Webster C (2010) Urban poverty in China. Edward Elgar Publishing, Cheltenham
Xu J, Yeh A (2009) Decoding urban land governance: state reconstruction in contemporary Chinese cities. Urban Stud 46(3):559–581
Yang Y-R, Chang C-H (2007) An urban regeneration regime in China: a case study of urban redevelopment in Shanghai's Taipingqiao area. Urban Stud 44(9):1809–1826
Zheng J (2010) The 'Entrepreneurial State' in 'Creative Industry Cluster' development in Shanghai. J Urban Aff 32(2):143–170

Chapter 5
Challenges to Public Housing in Post-colonial Hong Kong

Ngai Ming Yip

5.1 Introduction

With over seven million people crowded in a small city of 1,050 square kilometers, it would not be surprised to find housing has been an issue that most people in Hong Kong concern. In fact, the gravity of the issue is further amplified by the very uneven distribution in the spatial location of housing as well as the alarming polarization in income between the rich and the poor. Housing in Hong Kong is notoriously expensive and at the same time the big income gap between the rich and the poor is also reflected in the huge difference in the quality of housing people on different incomes enjoy. Whilst even middle class families often find housing to be unaffordable; decent housing for poorer households is definitely a big financial burden if not at all a distant dream.

Hence, it is not surprising to find Hong Kong to be the first city in Asia to have intensive state intervention in housing. Despite Hong Kong is now among the rank of economically advanced cities, its reliance on public housing in fulfilling the housing need of ordinary families has not been diminished. Not only has the sector expanded over the year, which is in sharp contrast with its neo-liberal outlook in other social policy areas, there is also an overwhelming public support for its continual growth. Recently, the eminence of public housing has risen on the policy agenda after a full decade of neglect in the 2000s when Hong Kong suffered from the longest and deepest economic recession after the Second World War. In fact, housing has returned as the top policy priority of the new Chief Executive Leung Chun Ying, in his campaign pledge.

In the last 15 years, not only has Hong Kong encountered significant changes in its political milieu in the change of sovereignty, it has also experienced several rounds of global scale economic turmoil. The Asian Financial Crisis triggered the

N.M. Yip (✉)
Professor, Department of Public Policy, City University of Hong Kong, Hong Kong SAR
e-mail: sayip@cityu.edu.hk

J. Chen et al. (eds.), *The Future of Public Housing: Ongoing Trends in the East and the West*, DOI 10.1007/978-3-642-41622-4_5,

longest economic recession after the Second World War until it touched the rock bottom in 2003 when SARS broke out. Its road to recovery was not smooth, interrupted by the global financial crisis in 2007 and 2008, but eventually being lifted by the China factor (Yip 2011). At the same time, Hong Kong has undergoing rapid social and demographic changes. The combined effect of delayed marriage, low fertility rate as well as increased divorce rate have made family size shrink by one third over the last three decades, from 3.9 in 1981 to 2.9 in 2011 (Census and Statistics 2012a) and the rising level of single person and single parent households. The population is also rapidly aging with 13 % of the population in 2011 over the age of 65 and nearly one tenth (8 %) of households consisted of only single elderly person or elderly couple.

All such changes would have repercussion in the shifting demand for housing and consequently commands a different approach and level of state intervention on housing. Yet it is not the intention of this chapter to embark on a comprehensive analysis of such impacts, which is too ambitious for a short chapter (discussion on more specific aspects of the issue can be referred to Yip (2011, 2012, 2013a, b), Forrest and Yip (2013)). This chapter would, instead, offer a short review of the changes that confronts public housing in recent years and a systematic account of the challenges to public housing development. This chapter will start with a short review of the development of public housing in Hong Kong from the early 1950s to mid 1990s then it is followed by an account of recent development from mid 1990s to the present. A discussion on the current debates will be deliberated in Sect. 5.4 and the chapter will conclude in Sect. 5.5.

5.2 A Review of the Historical Development of Public Housing

The construction of public housing started in 1954 in Hong Kong and up to 1997, the government has built nearly 880,000 rental flats (HKHA, annual report, various years). Not only does it make Hong Kong a pioneer of extensive state intervention on housing in Asia, the Hong Kong Housing Authority is still now the biggest landlord in the world. Yet, contrary to the general perception of public rental housing being housing for the poor, public housing in Hong Kong was, from the onset, not meant to be housing for the poorest. For the two parallel programmes that were initiated in 1954, none was setup that specifically catered for the poor (Yip 2003). The Resettlement Housing Scheme, which was the biggest among the two, was built to accommodate victims of slum clearance or natural disasters and no income tests were applied. The other scheme, the Low Cost Housing Scheme took in skilled blue-collar and junior white-collar workers and attached with a minimum income threshold for the applicants, apparently to guarantee that the incoming tenants were able to pay the relatively high level of rent (Yip 2003).

The existence of such a big decommodified housing sector appeared to be at odd with the laizzez faire approach to social and economic policy practiced by the colonial government in the 1960s and 1970s. Yet more critical analysis on the development of public housing demystifies the mask of public housing being provided as welfare by a benevolent state (Hopkins 1971). In fact, public housing programmes in the 1960s and 1970s were no more than the part and parcel of economic policy as well as the political manoeuvre of the colonial regime (Smart 2006). The Resettlement Programme was set up to accommodate victims of natural disaster and slum clearance, mostly on public lands which had been illegally occupied by squatters. Yet such clearance had been selective and did not connect to how poor the conditions of the slums were but rather whether the land is needed for industrial development and displaced residents were also often relocated to where new labour force was required by industries (Keung 1985; Cuthbert 1991; Drakakis-smith 1979). On the other hand, quality of the resettlement housing was only barely inhabitable (only a studio room for one family with no kitchen and residents had to share public bath rooms) in order to keep rents low. The low rent of public housing was then able to serve as social wages that indirectly reduced labour costs in helping to enhance industrial competitiveness (Castells et al. 1990) albeit this was done in an inefficient way (Wong 1991; Smart 2006).

Public housing has also been perceived as a political reaction of the colonial government in the 1950s as a gesture to counteract the increasingly political pressure both from the newly establishment Communist regime in China and its local supporters (Smart 2006). In the early 1970s onward when Hong Kong built its new towns, public housing was being mobilized as the major locomotive in accommodating a critical mass of population in the newly developed areas. This helps to support the cost of public services like public transport or retail and community services and directly boosted the value of lands for private housing developments. Again public housing was linked directly to economic development.

The 1970s was an important watershed for public housing development in Hong Kong. By early 1970s, there were already over 1.6 m people (40 % of the population) residing in public housing in which 72 % were in resettlement estates (Yip 2003). The colonial government embarked on an ambitious 10-years housing programme to build public housing for 1.8 m people. A new housing organization, the [new] Hong Kong Housing Authority (there was another organization with the same name in English existed from 1954 and the Chinese name of the new organization had changed) to amalgamate existing housing organisations both in the formulation of policy, new construction programmes as well as management of the housing estates.

The new institution also brought significant changes to the housing landscape of Hong Kong. To improve living quality, the much better facilitated low cost housing would replace resettlement blocks as the only form of public housing and old resettlement estates would be redeveloped. New towns were to be set up to accommodate the expanding population and all new towns would be public housing led. Yet perhaps an overhaul of housing policy was the introduction of the Home Ownership Scheme (HOS) in which built-for-sale flats would be sold, mainly to

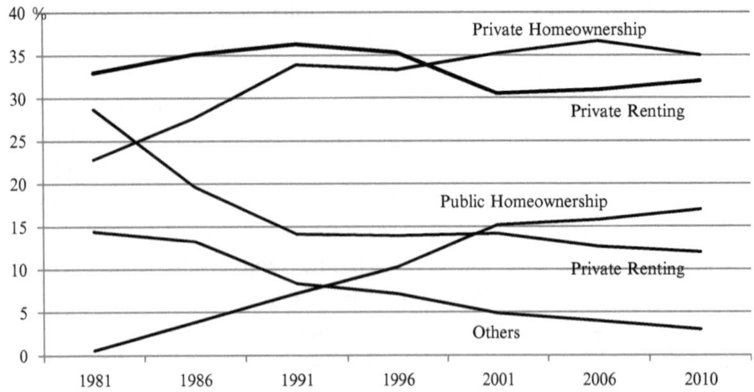

Fig. 5.1 Tenure distribution (1981–2010) (Source: Author's analysis of Censure microdata 1981–2010) (Note: Assisted Homeownership includes HOS, PSPS and TPS, Others includes temporary housing, housing provided by employers and rent free housing)

pubic tenants, but also to low middle class first time buyers roughly in the 40th to 70th household income percentiles brackets. In fact, this marked a change of course in housing policy, from rental housing towards homeownership. HOS was able to bring homeownership more affordable to middle class first time buyers as its shared equity arrangement[1] could effectively reduce the selling price and hence overcome both the wealth and income constrains in saving for the downpayment and regular repayment of the mortgage loan.

HOS was hugely successful. Not only were 200,000 flats being constructed from 1979 to 1996 and topped up the homeowner rate by another 11 %, receipts from HOS sale (both first sale and resale) was able to supply a steady stream of funds for the development of public rental housing. HOS owners were potential upgraders to the private housing, particularly for those who bought in the 1980s when house price was low. Around 20 % of HOS buyers did eventually trade up (Transport and Housing Bureau 2010). Cash subsidies to first time buyers were also introduced in the early 1990s but they are largely ineffective and the schemes were short-lived.

Yet even with state intervention in promoting and in fact, directly supplying owner occupied flats, homeownership rate of Hong Kong has been lagging behind its Asian neighbours. In 2001, only half (49 %) of all households were owner-occupier, up from 24 % in 1981 when reliable statistics on tenure was first available. In fact, in the private sector, after a sharp increase from 24 to 35 % in the 1980s, homeownership rate in the 1990s was almost stagnant in the private housing sector in the 1990s with only a 1 % increase. The overall homeownership rate of 49 % in 2001 was mainly attributed to the increase in assisted homeownership (HOS), one third of homeowners bought HOS flats (Fig. 5.1).

[1] The equity of the flat is "shared" between HKHS and the buyer. Typical share is 50–70 % for HKHA. HOS owners has to repay the share of HKHA upon resale to the open market.

The year 1997 was a watershed, not only was Hong Kong returned to China after nearly 150 years of Colonial rule, the coincidental emergence of the Asian Financial Crisis also changed the shape of the housing market, as well as housing policy. Eager to demonstrate its competence as first government under Chinese rule, the new Special Administrative Region (SAR) government has embarked on an ambitious plan with a production target of 850,000 flats in 10 years (Hong Kong Government, 1997). This was intended to demonstrate a bold and forward looking measure in offering a long term solution to the chronic problem of housing Under-supply in Hong Kong. At the same time, a target was set in boosting the rate of homeownership to 70 % and reducing waiting time of public rental housing from the then 5 years to 3 years. This homeownership target required the government to produce, in the next 10 years, a total of 500,000 rental and for-sale flats in the public sector as well as to sell off 250,000 rental flats to sitting tenants under the Tenant Purchase Scheme (TPS) with discounts as deep as 88 %.

The Asian Financial Crisis triggered a market slump and exposed the extreme vulnerability of housing assets in a volatile housing market. House price dropped by one third in 1998 alone and when SARS broke out in 2003, an average flat in Hong Kong was only worth one third of its value in 1997 (Midland Reality 2012). This created serious problem of negative equity and caught Hong Kong by surprise. Hong Kong already had an excessively prudent lending policy with standard loan to value ratios of 70 % but it seemed that it was still unable to hedge the risk of a price fall of such a high level. By 2001, negative equity affected 105,697 borrowers with total outstanding loans of US$21.2 billion (around 17 % of all mortgage debt) (HKMA 2003). Fortunately, a prudent lending policy as well as a restrained policy in foreclosure helped to cushion the impacts of the problem and mortgage repayment arrears (of more than 90 days) remained at 2.5 % in 2002 (HKMA 2003) and repossession still remained at a negligible level.

With buildings activities boosted by the strong market signals before 1997 began to turn into new supply of housing in the early 2000s, a new wave of market clash was on the making. Shrinking demand in an already over-supplied housing market further exacerbated house price fall. Property developers, with the apparent support from other stakeholders, such as the banking industry as well as homeowners in negative equity, confronted the government openly to install heavy measure in curbing housing supply in order to stabilise the market. The government bowed down and unprecedented control measures were introduced. Land sale was suspended and HOS, which was regarded by the developers as the cause of oversupply, also had to go. In fact, HOS had also suffered from shrank demand since 1997 and for the first time since its inception in the late 1970s, unsold HOS was observed. This presented a sharp contrast to the average over-subscription of 10 times from 1979 to 2000. The moratorium of HOS and TPS, and in fact the withdrawal of the government from assisted homeownership, was announced in late 2002 (HKHA 2002) as strong "political signal" on the government's will to guard the property market from further decline.

Despite the seemingly incompetent handling of the housing market, the first SAR administrative has actually brought substantial improvement in public housing. With a high production target of public rental housing, not only has the quantity of new public housing supply leapfrogged, quality of public housing has also being substantially improved with modernised design and better amenities being installed. Converting some unsold HOS flats to rental housing also significantly boosted the quality. At the same time, enhanced production has shortened the waiting time for applicants in the General Waiting List, from an average of 6.5 years in 1997, to 2.1 years in 2003 (Hong Kong Report 1997, 2003). Although there was also a high level of new applicants that joined the waiting queue in the same period- an average of nearly 35,000 households between 1999 and 2003, the high level of both rental flats and HOS flats production (allow public tenants buyers to release their rental flats), was high enough to enable the HKHA in clearing the backlog in the waiting queue (Census and Statistics Department, Annual Digest of Statistics, various years).

Hence, a highly contrasting housing scene was observed in Hong Kong. While the cost of housing has been notoriously high and housing consumption of ordinary households lag behind people in other countries with comparable level of economic development, state intervention is the highest in the developed world. Housing policy in Hong Kong does defy from what have been prompted by its liberal and non-interventionist outlook in other social and economic policies. The particular structure in land ownership has equipped the state with powerful tools in intervening in the housing market with a fairly early introduction of the public housing sector which has subsequently developed over the year to become the biggest public rental sector in the world. The year 1997 has marked, coincidentally, both a historic juncture in the political trajectories of Hong Kong when it was returned to China, and also at the same time a watershed of its housing policy when the Asian Financial Crisis forced an adjustment in its approach to state intervention in housing.

5.3 Current Development

5.3.1 Assisted Homeownership

Hong Kong recorded robust recovery after the economy hit its rock bottom in 2003 when Hong Kong suffered from SARS. A spectacular average growth of 5.6 % was achieved between 2003 and 2011. Led by the high demand on luxurious apartments, not only did general house price pick up in recent year, it also reached historical high both in nominal and real terms in 2011. The improved economic performance that reinforced consumer confidence as well as hot money from Mainland China for luxurious apartments were definitely the pushing factors, yet the major cause of such a rapid rise in house price was perhaps attributed to the much reduced supply of new housing. In fact, while the average yearly supply of new housing in the private sector from 1979 to 2007 stood at around 26,000 flat, only one third of such level was being completed in 2008 and 2009 (respectively at 8,776 and 7,157 flats)

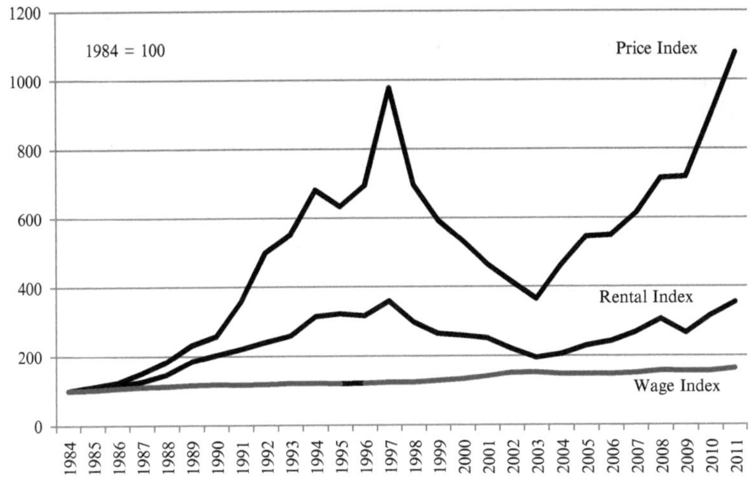

Fig. 5.2 House price, rental and wage index (1984–2011) (Source: Annual Digest of Statistics)

(Census and Statistics Department, Annual Digest of Statistics, various years). From mid 2003 to the beginning of 2013, nominal house prices have quadrupled (Centaline 2013) (Fig. 5.2).

As public frustration accumulated in late 2000s over the inability of the government in taming the soaring housing market, there was great public pressure in urging the government to take action in curbing such rapid increase. Eventually in late 2010, extra tax (Special Stamp Duties) on property transactions was introduced. Yet the relatively mild tax rate was unable to cool down the market. House price in 2012 alone has risen by one third. Despite reinforced measures being added in 2012 by increasing the tax rate (at the end of 2012, tax rate was 20 % for properties sold within 6 months between the transactions) and another tax to curb the demand from foreigner (15 % Buyers' Stamp Duties for non-resident buyers). However, despite market transaction has been curtailed a lot, there was no sign of a market U-turn at the time of writing (early 2013).

Rapid price soar and the fast lengthening of the public housing waiting queue triggered new round of public demand for the resumption of the assisted homeownership scheme HOS. Apparently, HOS has proven to be effective in helping middle to low income first time buyers to embark on the housing ladder while at the same time contributive in building up funding for public rental housing development. Yet the previous government (the Tsang Administration) was apparently very reluctant to act worrying that reverting the 2002 decision in withdrawing from the housing market too soon would be too damaging to the trustworthiness of the government when officials who made such a big decision were still in power. Instead, only a small scale scheme "My Home Purchase Plan" (modeled on the Rent to HomeBuy Scheme in the UK) of 4,000 units over 5 years to middle income households would be introduced.

Yet such a scheme was regarded to be too mild and under public pressure the Tsang Administration eventually bowed down and a new HOS was introduced in 2011. The new scheme does not follow the "shared-equity" arrangement as the "old" HOS, the discount enjoyed by buyers of the HOS buyers would be converted to an interest-bearing loan from the HKHA and be repaid at the point of reselling the property to the open market. However, since there will be no repayment before the resale, outstanding loan under the new HOS, which will accumulate over time, will be unfavourable to HOS owners who hold their flats for a long time. Though this may encourage HOS owners to sell their subsidised property sooner and accelerates the circulation of HOS, it is still unclear whether it would eventually help lower middle income first time buyers in stepping up to private homeownership. Under the new HOS, 17,000 flats will be constructed before 2017 to target households who earn less than HK$30,000 (about 1.5 times the median household income).

5.3.2 *Public Housing*

Not only was the supply of new private housing seriously affected by the economic downturn in 1997, it also created a knock on effect on the production of public sector housing. The ambitious plan in producing half a million public sector flats in the first 10 years of the new Special Administrative Region (SAR) of China has gone awry in the early 2000s. After the peak of the production in the year 2000 (a legacy of the construction work which started a few years earlier) at 46,756 flats, annual output has been dramatically reduced to 20,390 flats in 2003 when the first Chief Executive, Tung Chee Hua was forced to step down. His successor, Donald Tsang was only able to achieve a even lower target, at an average of 14,363 flats a year, which was only 60 % of what his predecessor has achieved (at 24,000 flats annually). The reduction of the production of the Homeownership Scheme (HOS) flats was even more stunning with the termination of the HOS in 2002. Whilst the first SAR government has planned a quarter of a million HOS flats in the next 10 years, only around 60,000 flats have been completed or been in the process of production when the moratorium was announced.

The abrupt cessation of HOS produced disruptive impacts on the public housing sector far more than what was reflected on the production of HOS. It actually affects both the circulation of public rental flats (as the number of rental flats vacated by public tenants who had moved to HOS has been much reduced) as well as the generation of capital from the receipt of HOS sale for public housing development. Reacting to the latter change, the HKHA has repackaged its shopping centre and car parks as REIT (Real Estate Investment Trust) to raise HK$20b (US$2.6b) to fund future public rental housing development. Together with the huge surplus it accumulated over the years (HK$22b (US$2.8b) in 2004), it should be able to cushion the unexpected turmoil in the revenue structure and bought time for the HKHA to explore new funding mode for public housing development.

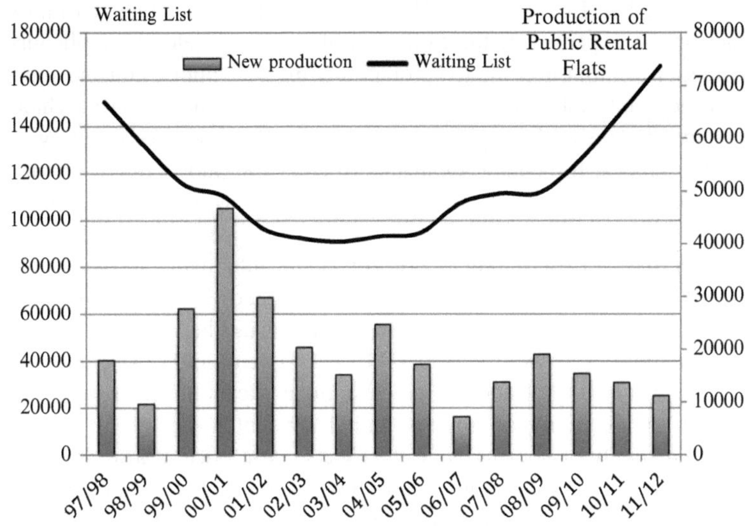

Fig. 5.3 Production of public rental flats and applicants in the general waiting list (1997–2012) (Source: Hong Kong Housing Authority Annual Reports (various years), Hong Kong Report (Various Years))

Moratorium of HOS sale dried up the recycling of public rental flats that were released from green form buyers of HOS flats (public tenants) who had to surrender their public rental flats for reallocation to applicants in the waiting list. The combined effect of the reduction of recycled and new rental flats has weakened the capacity of HKHA in clearing the waiting queue. Hence it is not surprising to find the waiting queue being lengthened substantially. Between 2003 (when HOS was terminated) and 2013, size of the public housing waiting queue has more than doubled (220 %) (Fig. 5.3). Despite such a sharp expansion in the waiting queue, HKHA was still able to maintain its pledge of 3 years waiting time, at 2.7 years in late 2012 (LCQ2 2013).

Yet the average waiting time reported in official statistics in fact does not reflect the real picture in housing need as they only include applicants in the family and single elderly waiting list. A separate waiting queue was set up for single non-elderly applicants. Whilst the former list expanded by 2.2 times between 2001 and 2012, the latter rose at a much faster rate at 4.8 times (Hong Kong Report 2001, 2003, 2012). By the fourth quarters of 2012, amongst the 199,600 applicants on the waiting list, nearly half (47 %) were single applicants under the age of 60. Single person applicants are treated very unfavourably under the "quota and point" system of allocation, set up in 2005, with the intention in restraining their accessibility to public housing. A disproportionately small quota has been allocated to this group. For instance, in respectively 2007 and 2009, only about 8 % of public housing flats assigned to applicants in the waiting list were allocated to single persons (HKHA, various years). A similar target (8 %) was kept in 2013, regardless the high proportion of this group (approaching half of the total applicants) on the general waiting list (LCQ17 2010). Hence, keeping the policy pledge of allocation is in fact on the expenses of the exclusion of single non-elderly applicants from the calculation without needing to substantially increase public housing supply.

Under the point system in the waiting queue of single non-elderly, which takes into account only age of the applicants and the time they have been waiting, there is in fact little chance for young applicants to enter the public rental sector as the factor of age has taken a much more significant weighting in the score. For instance in mid-2010, the average points of singleton applicants under 30 was only 36 whereas the corresponding score for applicants over 50 years old was 125 (LCQ17 2010). Yet a much higher score was needed to secure the allocation, an average points score of 138 was needed for applicants between the age of 31–40 whereas for those who were between 41 and 50 years old, 141 points was the threshold (LCQ17 2010). Hence, in practice, no applicant under the age of 30 was able to enter the public rental sector as an independent household.

A reduced supply of housing not only affects house price, it also drove up rents in the private rental sector. Private sector rents rose much faster than the increase in wages. Whilst average wages only moved up by 7 % between 2003 and 2011, rents in the private sector increased by 82 % during the period (Census and Statistics Department, Annual Digest of Statistics, various years). As income disparity between the rich and the poor has worsened, low-income renters were hit the most. The private rented sector has always been instrumental as a flexible tenure in adjusting to the fluctuation in the demand for housing in Hong Kong (Yip and La Grange 2006). Plywood-partitioned rooms and cage-man apartments (residents lived in triple decker bunk-beds) have widely been employed to increase the supply of housing. More recently, “sub-divided flats” of small en-suite rooms (8–12 m^2 in size) emerged to cater for the need of a new breed of tenants – salaried singles or couples able to pay higher rents for more privacy and better environment. Yet the conversion of overwhelming majority of the “subdivided” flats, most of them in tenement blocks in inner city areas and some even in industrial buildings, violate health and fire safety codes. A few fire incidents with death casualties in sub-divided flats triggered the authorities concerned to take sterner action against the illegal conversion. As most the tenants in such flats were single persons or couples, it inevitably being connected to the debate to the inadequacy of assisted homeownership flats as well as the inequitable public housing allocation policy for the young singles.

5.4 Current Debates

5.4.1 Young People

Access of young people to housing has generated concern in the developed world given the increasingly uncertain future in employment and income prospect for the young generation (Forrest and Yip 2012). Young people in Hong Kong was even hit harder as Hong Kong commands one of the most expansive housing in the world and a stringent borrowing policy which required down-payment of 30 % of the house value. Such gap has been reduced when HOS was still in place. The share-equity arranging helped to mitigate the wealth and income burden in respectively down-payment and repayment of the mortgage loans which allow many aspiring middle class young couples to step a foot onto the housing ladder.

Yet, termination of the HOS put an end to this later route. Having to pay full market price, it is nearly impossible for most young people to save enough for down-payment in home purchase with their earned income alone. Hence, assistance from their rich parents is often pivotal in realizing the home-owning dream of the young cohort. Against the context of widening disparity in income and job prospects, life chances are more important than before in homeownership attainment and the divide between people with richer and poorer parents has also intensified (Yip 2012).

Even with the reinstalling of the new HOS, not only would the small supply of HOS (even smaller for the young singles) be able to satisfy the demand of the young first time buyers, the high cost of HOS (as HOS flats would be linked to market price) would be unaffordable to most young people even after a discount. Renting thus appears to be more viable alternate for most young singles who aspire for independent living. Giving the equally high cost of private renting, it is hence not surprising to find the young singles (the post-eighties generation, a term framed by public media) has to rely on public renting as a more reliable alternative, or at least they could insure against their future housing need.

Soaring demand of young single applicants to public housing in the last few years triggered concern of the community. The initial response was largely negative as statistics on public housing application showed that nearly half (40 %) of the young single applicants under the age of 30 in 2010 had completed, or were in the process of completing, post-secondary qualifications. Hence, there is a risk of abuse of public housing from these potential middle class people. Yet subsequent public reaction portrayed a gloomier picture as such a high level of would-be middle class who came forward to request for assistance may in fact reflect the lack of confidence in solving their housing needs through their own means.

However, both the worry of abuse and pessimism on young people's housing futures may be over-stated. Given the extremely slim chance of young applicants to secure a public flat under the quota scheme, it is more likely that the act of coming forward to apply for public housing reveals other underlying need of young people. A survey conducted by the HKHA (2011) on single non-elderly applicants revealed that nearly all (90 %) applicants in 2010 who were under the age of 30 were living in their parental homes and nearly one third of them (31 %) were in fact over-qualified for public housing as they earned more than the income limit for singleton applicants (HK$9300 in 2010 which was more or less the level of the median personal income). If they did not have burning need for housing, their act of application may in fact reflect their quest for independent living. This was confirmed by the survey that most such applicants (81 %) took live independently as the main reason for their application. On the contrary, improvement of living quality and the mitigation of rent burden were the main motivations of application for applicants aged over 30 (HKHA 2011).

As the level of unmarried young people who live independently is substantially lower than their counterparts in other countries (Yip 2012), it is thus not surprising given the trend in delayed marriage, prolonged education as well as the demand for personal space and privacy, more young people in Hong Kong are aspiring for living on their own. Public housing opens up a possibility in realizing such a dream albeit it may still be remote in the near future. Even though the government seems to recognize such a need, it may not be the need of young people for independent living that draws their attention but rather the potential social and political risk created by the frustrated and discontented post-eighties generation. There is no sign of a fundamental change in policy direction concerning young people's housing. As a gestural move, the Tsang Administration initiated a pilot scheme offering youth hostels for single youths on a very small scale to be offered by NGO and this direction was reiterated in the recent Policy Address of Mr CY Leung.

5.4.2 *Residualisation of Public Housing*

Public housing as a secure safety net in solving housing problem of an average household has been recognized from the very beginning of the public housing programmes in Hong Kong (Castells et al. 1990) that people with housing need only had to wait patiently in the queue (though it may be long sometimes) and a decent, affordable and secure home would eventually be rewarded (Lee and Yip 2006). Changing rules in housing allocation may have changed the nature of public housing in Hong Kong, from a decent housing sector for the general public to a marginalized tenure. Similar to what happened in some western countries, public housing has been evolved into a residualised sector and housing sector for the poorest households. In fact, there is a risk that Hong Kong may also be heading towards such a direction.

Income profiles of public tenants have undergone an apparent downward spiral. In the early 1980s (when income breakdown by tenure was possible from Census data), public rental housing was a rather mixed tenure. In 1981, richer tenants who belonged to the top 30 % of the income spectrum took up nearly a quarter (26 %) of all tenants and there was almost the same proportion (28 %) of poorer tenants who were at the bottom 30 % (Fig. 5.4). A combination of reasons may create such a mix. The majority of public tenants at that time lived in resettlement estates which mainly accommodated households affected by slum clearance and no means test was imposed. The rest of public tenants stayed in low-cost public housing that targeted not the poorest sector but lower middle income white collar and skilled labour (Yip 2003).

Since then, profile of the public tenants began to polarize. In 2006, only one tenth of tenants belong to the richest 30 % households whereas the poorest households (who belonged to the bottom 30 %) have increased to nearly half (46 %) (Fig. 5.4). Income level between richer and poorer public tenants has also widened. Whilst income in real term for the poorest tenants (who belonged to the bottom 10 % of the income spectrum) increased by 1.8 times between 1981 and 2006, there was a 3.1 times increase among tenants at the topmost income decile group (Forrest and Yip 2013).

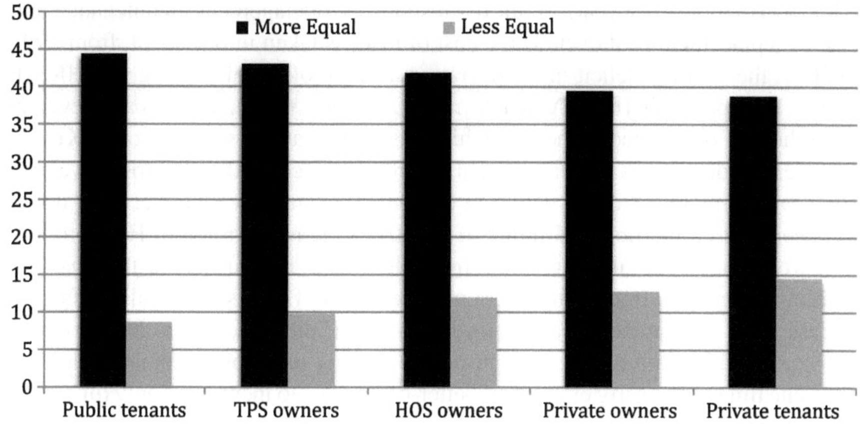

Fig. 5.4 Does public rental housing help create a more equal society? (Source: Household Survey conducted by the author) (Note: *TPS* Tenant Purchase Scheme, *HOS* Homeownership Scheme)

Such change may have reflected both the general change in income polarization of the general population (refer to Chiu and Lui 2003 for a general discussion) as well as the specific policy evolution within the public rental sector. With the graduate phrasing out of slum clearance, nearly all public tenants who entered the sector after the 1970s were subject to means tests which only allows households who earned less than the median income to enter the public sector. At the same time, HOS has acted as a pull factor in inducing better off public tenants to leave the sector whereas the "Housing Subsidies Policy" (requiring better off tenants to pay higher rents and to leave the sector if income reaches a certain threshold level) has effectively driven out better off tenants who have not been attracted by HOS. In addition, successful programme of elderly housing has also accommodated a large number of retired tenants who have no income and thus brings up the proportion of low-income tenants.

Yet it is still premature to judge whether public rental sector in Hong Kong would eventually be turning into a residualised housing sector. Though public housing is heading towards tenure for the retired working class, poor household and the disadvantaged group, there is no evidence that it would soon turn into a tenure for the long term unemployed as general unemployment rate in Hong Kong is still low and a sector of dilapidated housing as high level of reinvestment in upkeeping can still be maintained (Forrest and Yip forthcoming).

5.4.3 The Commitment to Public Housing

Public rental housing is highly subsidised. A very rough estimation shows that total economic subsidies (the difference between public and private sector rents of comparable units) of the current stock of 720,000 public rental units could cost

HK$7b (US$0.9b) per year.[2] Even if subsidies on management, maintenance and cost of replacement (but exclude the cost of land) is taken into account, from 1997 to 2011, the average deficit in the operation account of rental housing was HK$1b (US$0.13b) per year (HKHA annual report, various years). In the past, revenue from the sale of assisted homeownership flats as well as the surplus from HKHA's commercial operations and investment return of its accumulated surplus over the years were able to offset the deficit in the rental housing account. Yet great doubt has been cast on the financial future of HKHA as the moratorium of HOS production would have cut future revenue from HOS sale and turmoil in the financial market has greatly affected the return on investment of its reserve funds. In fact, to release such this financial burden in the long run, the government has seriously considered tightening up the entry to public housing to suppress demand whilst at the same time to intensify eviction of better-off tenants to increase supply (of cycled flats) in order to curtail the need to produce more public housing.[3]

With the resumption of HOS and improved investment return, there seems to be no need for the government to contemplate such a policy direction. In fact, even an attempt in raising the idea of a retreat from public housing would not be popular. Not only is public housing widely perceived as an important housing safety net in the 1970s and 1980s (Castells et al. 1990), the social function of public housing has evenly be reinforced in recent years. Public housing was regarded as having a positive contribution to a more equal society and it should also be make available to a wider spectrum of the community rather that only reserved for the poor households.

A recent survey conducted by the author indicates that roughly 40 % of respondents believed that public housing could create a more equal society whereas only around 10 % did not believe so. The support for public housing was in fact distributed quite evenly across tenure (Fig. 5.5). When asked about the target group of public rental housing, about half (53 %) of them thought public housing should be available to a wider spectrum against 42 % that public housing should only be offered to poorer households. Interestingly, there was a higher level of support for wider availability of public housing among both owners and tenants in the public sector. A clearer public support for public rental housing was reflected in the overwhelming backing of the building of more public rental housing expressed by 85 % of the respondents (Fig. 5.6).

However, despite such a high level of general support in building more public housing, locating new sites for public housing development is not straightforward. Resistance from local district councils and residents has been the major hurdle (LCQ16 2012). Development density, depriving residents of leisure facilities and

[2] Assuming public sector rents are only at one third of the market level, size of the public housing flat is 30 m^2 and the rent level of a small rental unit of 30 m^2 15 km^2 from CPD commands a monthly rent of US$40 per square meter.

[3] Information from the author's participation in a Central Policy Unit task force in 2007 on public housing policy. It is believed that the task force discussion would fit into the election pledge of Donald Tsang who was seeking for re-election of the Chief Executive.

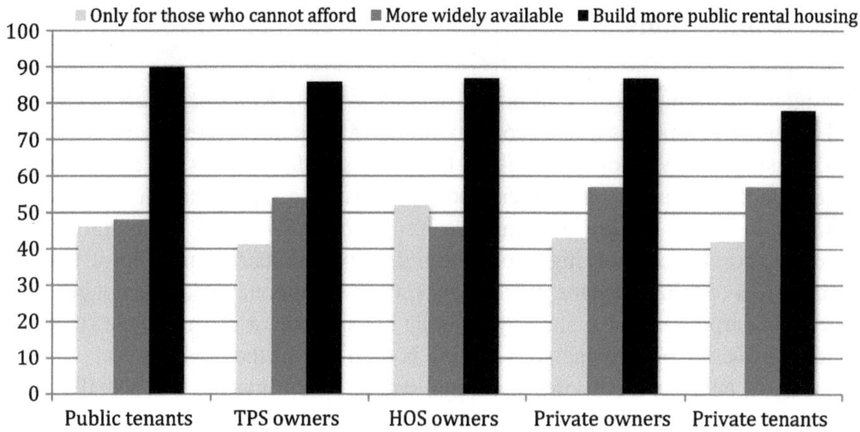

Fig. 5.5 Housing for the poor or for a wider cross section of the population? (Source: Household Survey conducted by the author) (Note: *TPS* Tenant Purchase Scheme, *HOS* Homeownership Scheme)

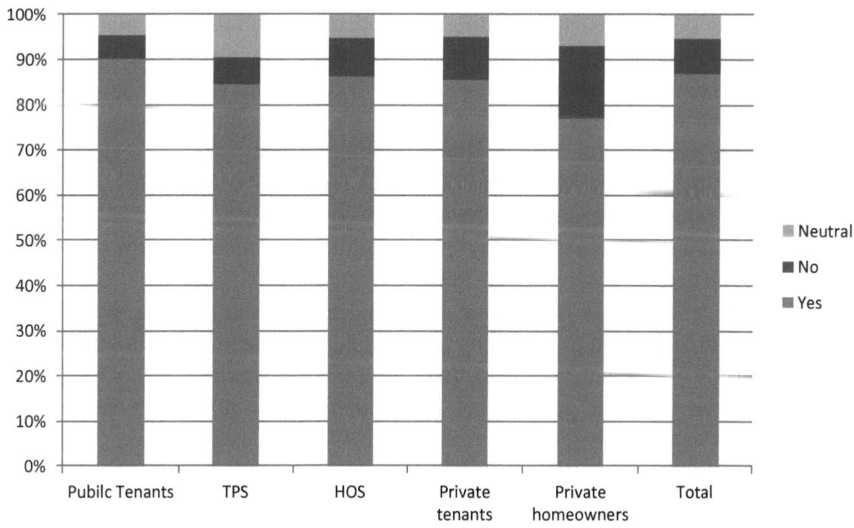

Fig. 5.6 Should the Government Build more Public Rental Housing? (Source: Household survey conducted by the author) (Note: *TPS* Tenant Purchase Scheme, *HOS* Homeownership Scheme)

open space etc was often being quoted as the rationales for the objection. Yet it is perhaps the worry of owners in the private housing estates in the neighbourhood that the presence of poor public tenants may have a negative impact on the house price, a typical NIMBY consideration (HKET 2012).

5.5 Conclusions

Despite its extreme neo-liberal policy outlook as Hong Kong has been elected for 18 consecutive years as freest economy in the world's freest (Heritage Foundation 2012), state intervention on housing has been standing out as un exceptionally intensive even among other social policy areas, like public health and income transfer in which the government also has deep involvement. Structural factors like the shortage of land, high population density and state ownership of land do explain to a certain extent the necessity of state intervention, yet it does not generate strong underpinning for sustaining a public housing sector of such scale (together with the assisted homeownership scheme housed half of the population).

Critical analysis has shown that intervention in housing did not actually stem whole-hearted as welfare effort of the benevolent state but rather driven by the productivists concern (Holliday 2000) in supporting economic development with measures in social policy. It helped to enhance the competiveness of the industry in the 1950s and 1960s, both as "social wage" (Castells et al. 1990) and to release land occupied by squatters for industrial development (Drakakis-smith 1979; Keung 1985). Likewise in the 1980s and 1990s, the development of assisted homeownership can be perceived as the same productivists approach in asset based welfare policy in supplementing the inadequate welfare provision (particularly retirement pension) with state assistance for home buying (Yip 2013b). Whilst early public housing construction was motivated by the need of the colonial government in enhancing its political legitimacy and to minimize the threat of social unrest creating by specific housing issues (Smart 2006), such motives continued to underpin the development of housing policy in the 1970s and 1980s as persistent housing shortage and periodic breakout of social unrest have sustain the instrumentality of housing policy in maintaining the political legitimacy of the colonial government (Castells et al. 1990).

The political economy of housing continued to function both on the colonial government in the period of transition and beyond to the new SAR administration. Public housing policy has been performed as a pivotal arena in the sociopolitical strategy of the Colonial government in opening up the political system in its preparation to the handover of sovereignty to China (Castells et al. 1990). Far from a coincident, the first SAR Administration also chose housing as the most important pillar of social policy. Formulated at the time when Hong Kong experienced the worst of housing affordability problem, the intention to enhance its political legitimacy is apparent for a government with a limited electoral mandate.

It is thus not surprising to find housing emerged again in the political battlefield in the recent election of the Chief Executive in 2012. As contrast to previous election, the concern has moved beyond the enhancement of the legitimacy of the government with limited suffrage (elected only by a small electoral college of 1,200 members with very limited representation). Popular support is more important than ever as universal suffrage will be introduced in the next election. Again, at a time when housing affordability is worst than ever, demonstrating a vision and the capacity in taming the housing market was being perceived to be most populist election appeal.

Yet, with the deep-rooted government-developer nexus and the reliance of public finance on property-related taxes (receipts from land sale and stamp duties from housing transaction), it is in fact political suicide for the incoming government to introduce any genuine measure to heavily suppress the housing market. However, within the context of an increasing antagonism against the hegemony of the "land-power", doing-nothing is simply not an option. The expansion of public rental housing and the installation of assisted homeownership were picked up as a convenient and effective policy instrument in pacifying public demand for intensive intervention that would produce no harm to the housing market. On the one hand, it matches with public expectation in building more public rental housing and HOS raises the hope for first time buyers who cannot afford private sector housing, on the other hand, if housing need for the most needy has already been catered, there is no need for heavy measures in curtailing house price.

It seems that public housing would continue to be at the centre of public policy of post-colonial Hong Kong albeit it is expected such demand on housing intervention would be periodic that would fluctuates with the ups and downs of the economy and housing market. Associated with the demand for increased intervention are the technical issues of locating lands for new public housing development and the redevelopment of old housing estates as well as the need for a sustainable housing finance system. The creation of new land would inevitably trigger new rounds of political debate as environmental protection as well as anti-developmentism and localism have been on a rise in the last decade, the city-wide struggle against land reclamation in protecting the harbour and marine life as well as the conversion of agricultural lands for urban development would inevitably become more intense.

References

Castells E, Lee G, Kwok YW (1990) The Shek Kip Mei syndrome. Pion, London

Census and Statistics Department (2012a) Population census 2011, domestic households by household size (table D103). www.census2011.gov.hk/en/main-table/D103.html. Accessed 23 Mar 2012

Census and Statistics Department (various years) Annual digest of statistics. Government Printers, Hong Kong

Centaline (2013) Centa-city index. http://hk.centadata.com/cci/cci_e.htm. Accessed 8 Aug 2013

Chiu SWK, Lui TL (2003) Testing the global city-social polarization thesis: Hong Kong since the 1990s. Urban Stud 41(10):1863–1888

Cuthbert AR (1991) For a few dollars more: urban planning and the legitimation process in Hong Kong. Int J Urban Reg Res 15(4):575–593

Drakakis-smith DW (1979) High society: housing provision in metropolitan Hong Kong, 1954–1979. Centre of Asian Studies, Hong Kong

Forrest R, Yip NM (forthcoming) The reluctant interventionist, Housing Studies
Heritage Foundation (2012) Hong Kong remains world leader in economic freedom, 2012 Index Shows. http://www.heritage.org/research/reports/2012/01 /hong-kong-remains-world-leader-in-economic-freedom-2012-index-shows. Accessed 20 Jan 2012
HKET (2012) Is NIMBY for public housing justified? Hong Kong Economic Times, 17 Dec 2012
HKHA (Hong Kong Housing Authority) (2011) Operation of the quota and points system for non-elderly one-person. http://www.housingauthority.gov.hk/hdw/content/document/en/aboutus/ha/paperlibrary1/shc/shc0811.pdf. Accessed 20 Dec 2011
HKMA (2003) Survey on residential mortgages in Hong Kong, 11 Nov 2003, Hong Kong Monetary Authority. http://www.info.gov.hk/hkma/eng/press/category/resident_index.htm. Accessed 16 Nov 2011
Holliday I (2000) Productivist welfare capitalism: social policy in East Asia. Political Stud 48:706–723
Hong Kong Housing Authority (various years) Hong Kong housing authority annual report. Hong Kong Housing Authority, Hong Kong
Hong Kong Housing Authority (HKHA) (2002) Memorandum for the housing authority – statement on housing policy by the secretary for housing, planning and lands on 13 November 2002, HA 59/2002. HKHA, Hong Kong
Hong Kong Government (1997) Long term housing strategy. Hong Kong Government, Hong Kong
Hong Kong Report (1997) Hong Kong report 1997. Government Printers, Hong Kong
Hong Kong Report (2001) Hong Kong report 2003. Government Printers, Hong Kong
Hong Kong Report (2003) Hong Kong report 2003. Government Printers, Hong Kong
Hong Kong Report (2012) Hong Kong report 2003, Government Printers, Hong Kong
Hopkins K (1971) Housing the poor. In: Hopkins K (ed) Hong Kong the industrial colony. Oxford University Press, Hong Kong
Keung J (1985) Government intervention ns housing policy in Hong Kong. Third World Plann Rev 7(1):23–44
LCQ2 (2013) Distribution of waiting time of Public Housing applicants. http://www.info.gov.hk/gia/general/201301/30/P201301300329.htm. Accessed 20 Mar 2013
LCQ16 (2012) Supply of public housing, Press Release LCQ16. http://www.info.gov.hk/gia/general/201211/14/P201211140251.htm. Accessed 5 Mar 2013
LCQ17 (2010) Allocation of public rental housing flats – Reply of the Government to Legislative Councilor Fred Lee Wah Ming. Press Release LCQ17, 1 Dec 2010, http://www.info.gov.hk/gia/general/201012/01/P201012010154.htm. Accessed 5 Nov 2012
Lee J, Yip NM (2006) Public housing and family life in East Asia: housing history and social change in Hong Kong 1953–1990. J Fam Hist 31(1):66–82
Midland Reality (2012) Property price chart. http://www.midland.com.hk/eng/living_in_hk/hk_property_market.shtml. Accessed 1 Feb 2012
Policy Address (1997) Policy address 1997. http://www.policyaddress.gov.hk/pa97/english/paindex.htm. Accessed 20 Dec 2011
Smart A (2006) The Shek Kip Mei myth. University of Hong Kong Press, Hong Kong
Transport and Housing Bureau (2010) Consultation on Subsidising Homeownership. http://www.thb.gov.hk/eng/policy/housing/policy/consultation/con_framework1005.pdf. Accessed 20 Dec 2011
Wong R (1991) On privatizing public housing. City University of Hong Kong Press, Hong Kong
Yip NM (2003) Managing and serving the estates. In: Yeung YM, Wong KY (eds) Fifty years of public housing in Hong Kong. Housing Authority, Hong Kong, pp 357–382
Yip NM (2011) Business nearly as usual: global financial crisis and its impacts on the households in Hong Kong. In: Forrest R, Yip NM (eds) Housing markets and the global financial crisis: the uneven impacts on households. Edward Elgar, Gloucestershire
Yip NM (2012) Homeownership, cohort trajectories and Hong Kong's post-eighties generation. In: Forrest R, Yip NM (eds) Housing and young people. Routledge, London

Yip NM (2013a) Housing policy in the Tsang administration. In: Cheng YS (ed) An evaluation of the Donald Tsang administration. City University of Hong Kong Press, Hong Kong
Yip NM (2013b) Housing in Hong Kong: intensive intervention continues. In: Ronald R, Doling J (eds) Housing in East Asia: socio-economic and demographic challenges. Palgrave, London
Yip NM, La Grange A (2006) Globalization, de-industrialization and Hong Kong's private rental sector. Habitat Int 30:996–1006

Chapter 6
Public Housing Policy in Taiwan

Chin-Oh Chang and Shu-Mei Yuan

Abstract This chapter introduces public housing policy in Taiwan after the Kuomingtang (KMT) retreated from China and took over Taiwan. The government has never put much thought into public housing policy. As a consequence, the housing rights of low- or middle-income households and minority groups were not taken seriously by the Taiwanese government. This chapter suggests that the purposes of public housing policy should be simplified and political intervention should be minimized to not confuse the essence of public housing. Furthermore, new directions for public housing policy in Taiwan are proposed.

Keywords Taiwan • Public housing • Housing policy

6.1 Introduction

There are two types of public housing concepts in Taiwan. One type refers to physical building construction by the government. The characteristics of this type of public housing are as follows: (1) very low numbers of dwelling units for disadvantaged households, (2) for sale, not for rent, and (3) loosely-defined application criteria. In Taiwan, as long as households had income lower than the median price, applicants were deemed qualified. The other type of concept refers to housing policies that spend national resources on socially or economically disadvantaged households to improve their housing well-being, such as re-settlement after natural disasters, housing for civil servants, housing for dependents of servicemen and subsidies for mortgage interest rates.

C.-O. Chang (✉)
Professor, Department of Land Economics, National Chengchi University, Taipei, Taiwan
e-mail: changchinoh@gmail.com

S.-M. Yuan
Department of Land Economics, National Chengchi University, Taipei, Taiwan
e-mail: shumeiyuan@gmail.com

J. Chen et al. (eds.), *The Future of Public Housing: Ongoing Trends in the East and the West*, DOI 10.1007/978-3-642-41622-4_6,

Taiwan's public housing policy has been neglected by the government. Compared to other countries, Taiwan's government does not put much effort into public housing. There are only approximately 6,000 dwelling units of social housing (0.08 % of Taiwan's total housing stock) provided for socially disadvantaged individuals and approximately 170,000 dwelling units of public housing (2.27 % of Taiwan's total housing stock) provided for economically disadvantaged individuals; even though the government is currently actively promoting an affordable housing policy and there will be an estimated 8,000 public housing units (0.10 % of Taiwan's total housing stock) in 2014, the total public housing stock is currently still less than 3 %. This low public housing share does not mean that the housing market in Taiwan is functioning robustly such that the government does not need to intervene. On the contrary, Taiwanese housing problems are serious. According to the "social housing demand survey" conducted by the Ministry of the Interior in 2011, the socially disadvantaged needed 330,000 dwelling units, a number that was much higher than what the government has supplied. In addition, the price/income ratio (PIR) of housing has increased to above 10 in metropolitan areas, and low- or middle-income households suffer from high financial pressure when buying houses in the market-oriented housing system.

Non-government organizations (NGOs) call for the provision of more public housing. However, the government only pursues short-term regime stability or political propaganda; it appears that the government has not taken the housing problems of the socially disadvantaged individuals seriously and has not considered providing public housing for economically disadvantaged individuals as an approach to lower their housing costs. To date, the public housing issue in Taiwan has not been significantly improved.

The rest of the chapter is organized as follows. In the following section, we introduce the housing market in Taiwan. In Sect. 6.3, we describe the historical context of the public housing policy. In Sect. 6.4, we discuss two current public housing policies. In Sect. 6.5, we explain why there are so few units of public housing in Taiwan. Finally, in Sect. 6.6, we offer some concluding remarks and propose new directions for the public housing policy for Taiwan.

6.2 Housing Market in Taiwan

Some reasons for the implementation and failure of the public housing policy relate to the development of the housing market. Taiwan's housing market has been quite volatile, with four booms over the past 40 years (Fig. 6.1). The first cycle was approximately between 1972 and 1974. The rise was commonly understood as caused by the oil embargo. The sudden increase of oil prices led directly to high inflation in most commodities. This increase also led to a sharp rise in the cost of construction and capital on the supply side and triggered the expectation of housing price increases. The second cycle was between 1978 and 1980. The factors that stimulated the increase in housing prices were similar to those that caused the first boom. Inflation caused by oil price increases again resulted in higher costs on the supply side and expectations of price increases on the demand side. The third cycle was between 1987 and 1989. The main cause of the housing price increases during this boom was the rapid expansion of the money supply. The primary reason behind

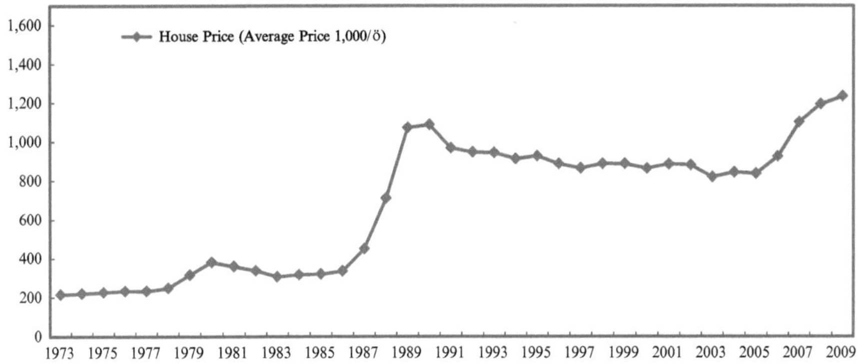

Fig. 6.1 Taipei's housing price from 1973 to 2010 (in Real Terms) (*Source*: Taiwan Real Estate Research Center, National Chengchi University)

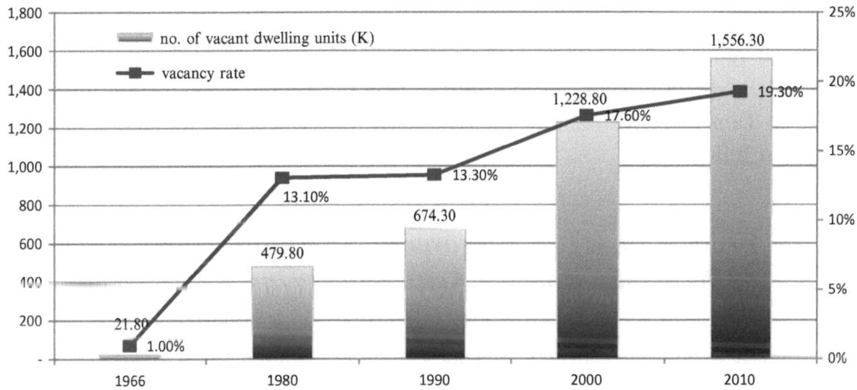

Fig. 6.2 Number of vacant dwelling units and vacancy rate in Taiwan (*Source*: Population and Housing Census 1966, 1980, 1990, 2000, 2010; Directorate General of Budget, Accounting and Statistics, Executive Yuan)

the increase of the money supply was the consistently high economic growth rate of approximately 12–13 %. The fourth cycle was between 2004 and 2010. This cycle differs from the previous cycles in that it occurred in the major metropolitan area, Taipei, but was not widespread in Taiwan. This phenomenon is fundamentally related to the unbalanced resource distribution in Taiwan's regional development because Taipei is the political and economic center and has more job opportunities than other cities. Another difference is that this cycle has lasted much longer in terms of expansion and contraction compared with the previous cycles. This cycle is basically fueled by low interest rates, which give business conglomerates and speculators leverage to play the market. Over the last 40 years, Taiwan's government passively watched the failure of the housing market. This permissive management toward the housing market contributed to rocketing housing prices, high PIR, high vacancy rates and high ownership rates (Figs. 6.2 and 6.3).

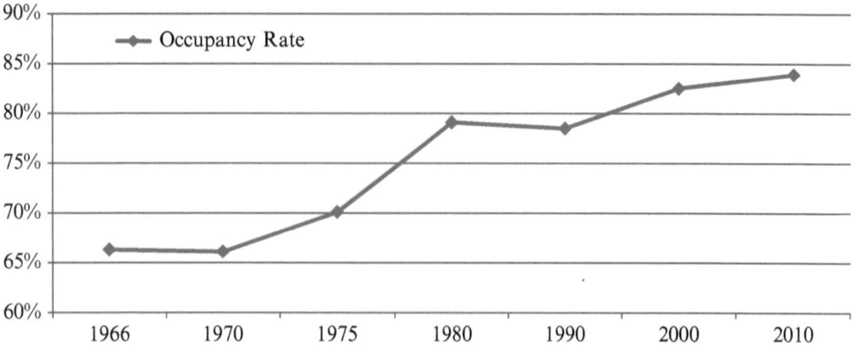

Fig. 6.3 Ownership rate in Taiwan (*Source*: Population and Housing Census 2010; Directorate General of Budget, Accounting and Statistics, Executive Yuan)

6.3 Historical Context of the Public Housing Policy

Different political systems come with different philosophies of public housing policy. The different schemes of public housing that were in place in Taiwan are listed in Table 6.1. We identify three periods in the history of the public housing policy as follows:

6.3.1 From the KMT[1]'s Takeover to the Enforcement of the Public Housing Act, 1940s–1970s

Since the KMT retreated from China and came to Taiwan in 1949, after World War II, the party limited social activities by martial law and put most of Taiwan's resources into national defense.[2] Regarding economic policy, the government focused on economic growth and tried to escape poverty. Taiwan was considered a springboard to retake mainland China and a temporary place to stay after the retreat. The public housing that the KMT actively planned and constructed only included residences and dependents' dormitories provided for officials, congress-persons and officers, and the party did not provide public housing for the general public.

[1] KMT is the abbreviation of Kuomintang via the Pinyin transcription system, and translated as the Chinese Nationalist Party. KMT was founded in 1894 and established the Republic of China in mainland China in 1911. After World War II, the Communists controlled almost all of mainland China, as by the end of 1949 the KMT retreated to Taiwan.

[2] Earlier national statistics were not public; however, according to the accessible and earliest data "Government Finance Statistics Yearbook (IMF) 1987" it was estimated that more than 40.7 % of the governmental budget was used for national defense in the beginning of the KMT's takeover.

Table 6.1 Different schemes of public housing

Scheme (Responsible authorities)	Details
Housing for Civic Servants (Human Resources Bureau)	Eligibility • Employees of the central government and public schools for at least 1 year Modes of Subsidy • Subsidized interest loans (varied with ranks) Output • Up to 2000, 88,385 loans and housing units were provided
Housing for Dependents of Servicemen (Ministry of Defense)	Eligibility • Servicemen's families who own no private properties Modes of Subsidy • Subsidies for sitting tenants in former Estates for Dependents • Mortgage interest subsidy scheme to purchase private homes Output • Up to 2000, 55,153 loans were rendered
Public Housing for Sale	Eligibility • With ownership of housing units • Holders of local resident registration for more than 6 months • Lower income household (standard set by Executive Yuan – below median household income) Modes of Subsidy • Reduced interest mortgage • Exemption on transaction tax Output • Up to 2000, 165,545, units were directly constructed by the government
Mortgage interest subsidy for home purchase (Public Housing Departments)	Eligibility • Same as that for Public Housing for Sale Scheme Modes of Subsidy • Subsidized interest rate • Limit on the maximum floor area that can be purchased Output • 117,110 loans from 1990 to 1999

Source: Yip and Chang (2003)

6.3.1.1 Settlement of Military Dependents' Villages

The government and millions of military forces and people moved to Taiwan from China in 1949, and the population increased rapidly and significantly; it was not possible to immediately build a large amount of housing for these people; thus, Taiwan was flooded with buildings constructed without licenses. Furthermore, other public constructions were not ready and land use was inefficient; hence, Taiwan had a serious post-war housing problem. However, the government was eager to stabilize military and domestic affairs and was too preoccupied to deal with the housing problem (Chang 1990).

In 1946, Taiwan's population was approximately 6.1 million and suddenly increased to 7.45 million; most of that increase was due to new residents coming from China. To solve the housing problem for these 1.5 million people, the government began to build houses or arrange dormitories; the government also made these people live together according to their armed service types and occupations in so-called "military dependents' villages". The statistics of the National Women's League of the R.O.C. of 1982 indicated that there were a total of 879 military dependents' villages and 98,535 households, not including buildings constructed without licenses.

In earlier times, most of the land used for building these villages was that of Japanese immigrants' villages from the period of Japanese Rule, and most of the houses were built after the war, except for some old buildings. In 1950, the common simple houses had a straw roof and bamboo-mud wall. There were four size types of these houses: (A) 41 square meters, (B) 33 square meters, (C) 28 square meters, and (D) 25 square meters; however, not every village had houses of all four types. The houses were distributed according to their official ranking via lottery drawing in which military servicemen, civil servants, teachers and congressmen participated; the residents had no property rights. From 1960 to 1970, the main parts of these houses were made of bricks and included facilities such as a household toilet, bathroom, kitchen, primary beam, tile and electric wire after the military repaired and built the houses.

6.3.1.2 Post-disaster Settlement

Taiwan is often afflicted by typhoons and earthquakes. In earlier times, house structures were not very solid and concepts such as urban disaster prevention systems and land capacities were not popular; thus, natural disasters always caused great losses of people's lives and properties, and the government embarked on a strategy of post-disaster settlements through temporary shelters. For example, a typhoon hit Taiwan's middle and southern parts on Aug. 7, 1959, and floods were caused by torrential rain. A total of 667 people died, 27,466 houses collapsed completely, and 18,303 houses collapsed partially. The government resettled 300,000 victims; this typhoon was Taiwan's most serious disaster after the war. The government mobilized the military and called millions of civilians to assist with the rescue and reconstruction and also established temporary shelters at public sites, schools at higher terrains, and public buildings. Chiayi had an earthquake ML = 6.1 on Jan. 8, 1964; this earthquake caused 106 people to be declared dead or missing, the complete collapse of 10,502 houses, the partial collapse of 25,818 houses, and big fires in the city area; moreover, 174 houses burned down. The government set up temporary shelters to settle the victims.

There was no public housing policy in the early period of the KMT's takeover. Nevertheless, the KMT government still put some efforts into public housing projects such as the "Settlement of military dependents' village", the "post-disaster settlement project" and the "public housing loan". Such policies were passively implemented by the government due to the events of emergent disasters and pressure from the U.S. government; to consolidate the regime, the KMT started to passively and temporarily enforce a public housing policy.

6.3.2 From the Enforcement of the Public Housing Act to the Presidential Direct Election, 1970s–1990s

In 1975, the government published the "Public Housing Act" and claimed that the policy could help achieve multiple purposes. First, this act could be the indicator of economic development. The policy was swiftly adopted into national economic development projects as the "6-year public housing construction project", and it was estimated that 100,000 units could be built from 1976 to 1981. This policy would imply 12 major construction projects, and it was estimated that 600,000 units could be built from 1980 to 1989. Second, this act could help reach the goal of "home ownership", the principle of people's livelihood. Furthermore, the act could counteract the speculative real estate business; the government could build a large amount of cheap public housing to take care of people with low or medium incomes. Third, these public houses could be the "model house", remove the image of low quality of public housing and enhance people's living and environmental quality. The government pacified people's feelings, improved the country's ability and image, intended to suppress the real estate market and supported economic development by promoting the public housing policy.

The implementation results differed greatly from the stated objectives for the following reasons: First, the progress of this project was slow. The public housing department was not well organized, and manpower and funds were not yet ready; moreover, land was not easy to obtain[3] (Mi 1988; Yip and Chang 2003) and therefore only 68,347 units were constructed through the end of 1985 (Table 6.2). Second, there were not many units that were allocated and open for civilians to buy. The distribution and selling processes were not open; households of military dependents and households relocated due to demolition often had first priority, and others had to line up and draw lots.

Third, the percentage increase in the provision of loans was lower than the rise in prices; thus, low- or middle-income households could not afford to buy houses.

[3] Taiwan used an ownership system for lands, most of which were owned by civilians, and public lands were limited. It was difficult to expropriate lands.

Table 6.2 Public housing directly constructed by Government in Taiwan

	Dwelling units		Dwelling units
1976–1981	68,347	1992	8,208
1982–1985	26,472	1993	2,862
1986	1,830	1994	6,010
1987	60	1995	11,092
1988	818	1996	9,478
1989	500	1997	6,035
1990	14,097	1998	6,043
1991	3,605	1999	88

Source: Construction and Planning Agency Ministry of the Interior, Executive Yuan

When Taiwan's economy boomed from 1978 to 1980, house prices also rose gradually. Take the prices of public housing and the provided loans in 1980 as an example: the selling price was NT 700,000–800,000, which was more than a million NT less than the prices of housing units in nearby private market neighborhood; however, people could only obtain a loan of 30 % of the housing price, and this low number was set according to applicants' economic conditions. Nevertheless, the government failed to consider that low- or middle-income households could not afford to pay the remainder. Hence, those people who finally bought public houses were not the ones that the government originally intended to take care of.

Fourth, the planning, design and construction quality of public housing, as one project of public construction, was of low quality because of the corruption and fraud of some local politicians or factions. Following a decade of severe recession in the real estate market, the situation of excess supply of public housing deteriorated. The program gradually slowed down after 1985. However, a short boom in 1987 increased the housing demand and accelerated public housing construction (Grange et al. 2006).

The public housing policy could not produce the effects that the government promised. Not only were minority groups and low- or middle-income households unable to afford to buy houses, but the ever-increasing house prices also became a serious social problem that led to the "homeless campaign" on Aug. 26, 1989. People who were not able to afford to buy houses established the "United association of the homeless" and slept on the Zhong-Xiao East Road, a street in the Taipei metropolitan area, to protest against skyrocketing house prices and unsound housing policies. Tens of thousands of people covered themselves with quilts and were lying shoulder to shoulder on Taipei's most expensive central land; they called for reasonable house prices and protested against the rocketing real estate prices due to the housing speculation of conglomerates.

The "Homeless campaign" received attention from the government and the mass media, and the government evaluated the feasibility of "rental and price control"; however, as the news faded, the government did not provide any policy to address the skyrocketing house prices.

6.3.3 *From the Direct Presidential Election Until Now, 1990s–Now*

During this period, Taiwan faced the problems of political wrangling between the KMT and the DPP,[4] economic stagnation and the decline of the GDP growth rate, a recession of the real estate market, and high business risks for real estate developers. Meanwhile, the government had failed to provide a large amount of public housing. Therefore, the government decided to postpone building public houses and return to a policy of considering housing needs. Consequently, the government pursued a public housing policy of mortgage interest-rate subsidies and tax reform. The policy of mortgage interest-rate subsidies was important during this period.

For the mortgage interest-rate subsidies, the government would subsidize interest rates to assist people to buy houses. For the public, the government allotted a total of NT$ 1,080 billion (US$ 36 billion) for this policy. House buyers older than 20 years, regardless of the purchasing purpose or type of house, could apply for a mortgage, and the limit was NT$ 2 to 2.5 million per household. Regarding the interest rate subsidy, in the overall subsidy provided to the public, for the first NT$ 400 billion, the yearly interest rate was fixed at 0.85 %; for the next NT$ 200 billion, the yearly interest rate was fixed at 0.425 %; and for the remaining subsidy, the interest rate was 0.25 %. In addition, there were other mortgage interest-rate subsidy plans for laborers, public servants and teachers, which were also subsidized interest rates; however, the maximum credit line and interest rate were different.

The mortgage interest-rate subsidy policy undoubtedly increased the short-term demand for housing and stimulated the real estate market. House prices and quantity reduced the business risks of real estate developers; furthermore, for 1 year in 1999, the government subsidized the interest rate for those buying the real estate developers' inventory of new buildings. At the beginning of the enforcement, the real estate market had boomed slightly; however, the effect of this policy later diminished because the overall interest rate decreased to a level even lower than that of this policy.

This policy appeared to boost the economy and stimulate people to buy houses. The government claimed that this policy would lead to a decrease in the supply of public new houses and the vacancy rate, assist people in changing houses and enhance the living quality, boost the construction industry, assist households of lower income and youths with stable jobs in satisfying their wishes to buy houses, promote the safety of the financial system, and advance the development of middle and southern Taiwan's public constructions and industries.

[4] DPP is the abbreviation of Democratic Progressive Party. It was founded in 1986 in Taiwan to counter KMT. The first members of DPP related to outside-the-KMT movement. Most of them were political prisoners, defense lawyers of the political prisoners, and their families. Taiwanese sovereignty is the first and most prominent issue on the party's platform.

After the policy was enforced and the results were examined, it became clear that the results that the government claimed this policy could achieve had not been realized; thus, the government changed the claim in its policy propaganda and emphasized that the implementation costs of this policy were much lower than the costs of building public houses and moreover that real estate developers, house buyers and banks would benefit. This policy allowed the government to avoid inefficiency and waste in building public houses and to flexibly use funds to reduce the cost of policy implementation because the interest rate subsidy was more flexible and could be adjusted according to the interest rate. For those people receiving the subsidy, they could more easily afford housing and freely choose their living area and product. For the banks, the house prices reflected the value of guarantees, and the possibility of recognizing bad debts would be reduced because house prices would not be too low.

Nevertheless, what the government did not explain was that this policy increased the national poverty gap. First, this policy provided subsidies without selecting applicants; hence, better-off consumers would be subsidized and the poverty gap between people with real estate and people without real estate would thus be larger. Consequently, consumers who temporarily could not afford to buy houses did not really increase their wealth due to the appreciation of assets. The loose review standard allowed house buyers who did not need the subsidy to obtain it; the excessive provision of the subsidy indirectly reduced the provision of other mortgage interest-rate subsidy projects because the government's resources were limited. Second, the salary level of public servants and teachers was above the average in Taiwan (not people with low or middle income); however, the government provided these people with housing subsidies, which would seize the rights and interests of the relatively disadvantaged people. Moreover, officials with higher ranks obtained more subsidies, a situation that did not conform to the original intention of providing the subsidy. Third, the low-interest loans made households with low income or youths who could not afford to buy houses in advance worse off; their monthly payment increased their living burdens and excluded other consumptions, and their living quality decreased.

When the effects that the government claimed the policy could achieve and the results were examined, it became clear that the government appeared to choose and exaggerate the positive effects and hide the flaws of the policy implementation. The government provided low-interest-rate loans to allow people to buy houses and to uphold house prices. The government was even concerned that the house prices of real estate developers' remaining houses could not be upheld and that they might have tied-up risks; hence, at some point, the government provided interest rate subsidies for those buying the remaining houses. In fact, the greatest beneficiaries of this policy were real estate developers and banking institutions that provided their loans. The consumers receiving the subsidy indeed bought houses at low interest rates; however, they paid higher house prices. Among these consumers, low- or middle-income households and youths who had a lower income assumed that they were taken care of by the government that paid for lower interest rates to buy houses; however, the prices could actually have been lower. When these consumers received the subsidy and bought houses, the living costs would be higher than what they could afford and make them sacrifice their living quality and assist in upholding house prices; however, these consumers could not feel the actual losses. For the consumers who did not meet the subsidy qualifications, it was more difficult to buy houses because house prices should have declined but did not, which would enlarge the poverty gap.

The nature of public housing was for rental; however, the government ignored the rental housing market policy. Taiwan's rental market was not popular because house owners were unwilling to release their houses for rental due to low rental prices, incomplete regulations related to renting, and the difficulty of maintenance and management. Thus, housing demanders could only buy houses to obtain housing services. Nevertheless, facing a high vacancy rate in Taiwan's housing market, high house prices and low rents, the government should promote the house rental market and make house owners willing to release their vacant houses for rental through a system. In addition, the government should implement related measures such as establishing a rental management system or introducing the third sector to be the rental manager to allow those who could not afford to buy houses and those who had difficulty renting houses, such as some minority groups including the elderly and women who experienced domestic violence, to have a good living quality. The government should not let house demanders buy houses to obtain housing services due to an unsound rental market.

6.4 Current Public Housing Policy

In January 2012, Taiwan had a presidential election. The government administration of the KMT for the past 4 years did not lead to a rapid growth of Taiwan's economy; in contrast, people were deeply dissatisfied with the rising house prices in the Taipei metropolitan areas. Among people's top 10 complaints in a survey conducted by The Executive Yuan in 2010, "high house prices and that people couldn't afford to buy houses" was listed on top. The mortgage interest-rate subsidy policy was no longer a policy to win votes. A group of people who did not receive the mortgage subsidy and who could not afford to buy houses because of past incorrect housing policies on March 23, 2010, formed a homeless association[5] that protested against the overly high house prices and claimed that there was no justice. Furthermore, 12 social welfare groups established the "Social Housing Advocacy Consortium" in 2010 to protest against the fact that the government had been ignoring the minority groups' housing rights for a long time. Facing the pressure of the upcoming presidential election in Jan. 2012, the KMT government "efficiently" launched the public housing policy before the election to ease the pressure from people's dissatisfaction about the overly high house prices and the ignorance of social groups' housing rights.

[5] This association was different from previous homeless activity; in addition to the general public who could not afford to buy houses, other social groups and NGOs also joined in.

6.4.1 Affordable Housing

The "Affordable housing policy" was the government's immediate response to people's complaints about high house prices. In the year of the protest, the government swiftly planned to release public land around the airport and MRT stations that was not completely developed for real estate developers to bid and then build houses; the price would be set by the government. This policy regulated that buyers had to be low- or middle-income households with no house and that the selling price of real estate developers should be fixed at a level set by the government, which was approximately 70 % of the local market price. After the Executive Yuan examined and ratified the policy, the government sold four public plots in the suburbs of New Taipei City by open bidding in 2011, and the companies winning the bids constructed and sold these affordable housing units according to the construction standard and selling price regulated by the government. It was estimated that there were a total of 8,241 units in these 4 sites, of which 7,594 units were for sale and 647 units were for rental.

The affordable housing policy was exposed widely in the mass media before the election. Officials expressed concerns for the overly high house prices and indicated that the government had just initiated a trial and that later the government would develop a public housing policy to control the high house prices. Before the public learned about the content and actual progress of this policy, the public housing policy of the KMT government, which actively responded to people's complaints and took care of minority groups, had made some contributions to KMT's triumph in the presidential election. Nevertheless, although affordable housing is still under construction, the effects of implementing the policy have not been obvious. It is highly questionable whether this policy can achieve the effects of controlling housing prices and taking care of minority groups. First, the affordable housing project only provides 8,241 units, and in reality it is impossible to suppress house prices with this low quantity of housing supply. After the KMT's candidate was elected as president, the new minister of the Ministry of the Interior announced the suspension of the affordable housing policy. Second, this policy only released 647 units for rental to low- or middle-income households and will not be very helpful for the minority groups.

According to the statistics through July 2012, a total of 4,009 units were provided for distribution by drawing lots, and 25,000 consumers met the qualifications. The public was very excited about the prospects of obtaining cheap affordable houses; thus, the mass media and most of the public opinion did not focus on the high house prices. The serious problem, that low- or middle-income households could not buy houses, was ignored by the mass media and public opinion due to the launch and implementation of the affordable public housing policy. The KMT government was the greatest beneficiary of this policy; it quickly launched this policy before the election to shift the focus; people's complaints about the government's incompetence were relieved, and the KMT government also won a second appointment for the president.

6.4.2 Social Housing[6]

Groups of the socially and economically disadvantaged, suffering from high house prices, gathered in 2010 and formed the "Social Housing Advocacy Consortium" and asked the government to take the housing rights of minority groups seriously. The initiators included 12 groups related to the elderly, women's domestic violence, laborers, parents of the mentally retarded, and the disabled. These groups protested against the fact that the government's public housing policy was only provided for those who "could afford" to buy houses; minority groups could not afford to buy houses, and it is always very difficult for these groups to rent houses due to discrimination. The groups required the following: (1) The government should list "social housing" as a necessary and significant item in its housing policy and set 5 % of the total housing amount as a present goal. (2) Social housing should be considered a public investment in social welfare, and the government should not prioritize financial profit or the problem of whether there is private investment; therefore, the government should assume the responsibility of leading the promotion and construction of public housing. (3) Social housing is to satisfy the housing rights of the socially and economically disadvantaged; hence, the government should establish appropriate standards (such as the recognition of objects, rent standards and evaluations of continuous residence), combine care and the subsidy system of social welfare, and introduce the NGO to build a model of sustainable management. 4. The government should institutionalize a social housing policy and promote the legislation of the "Housing Act" and a local "Housing Autonomy Regulation" as soon as possible.

Facing the pressure of the presidential election of January 2012, the KMT government "highly efficiently" passed the "Housing Act" on Dec. 30, 2011. It was the first time that Taiwan protected the housing rights of minority groups through a housing policy and legislation and the government could provide more social welfare than just rent subsidies. The "Housing Act" required that social housing should be built by the government or that the government could encourage the private sector to build social housing; these houses were only for rental, and 10 % or more should be provided for persons with special circumstances or identities. The act also included "Anti-discrimination clauses" to ensure the fairness of housing rights, and people should not prevent housing users from doing necessary repairs (including public space), letting guide dogs get in and out, and using public space, facilities, equipment and related legal services.

By 2012, social housing had become an important housing policy in other advanced countries; in comparison, Taiwan's social housing units made up only 0.08 % (around 6,000 units) of the total housing stock, which was much lower than the demand of 330,000 units; 2.27 % of general public housing was provided for the residence of the economically disadvantaged (approximately 170,000 units). Compared to Taiwan, the

[6] Social housing refers to housing to be rented by social groups; affordable housing refers to housing sold to low- or middle-income households.

percentages of social housing of other countries were all far higher than Taiwan's 0.08 %: Netherlands 34 %, England 20 %, Denmark 19 %, Finland 18 %, Sweden 18 %, E.U. 14 % on average, the U.S. 6.2 %, Japan 6.06 %, Hong Kong 29 %, and Singapore 8.7 %. Even if the Housing Act was passed, Taiwan still has a long way to go to catch up with the social housing development of advanced countries.

6.5 Why So Few Public Housing Units in Taiwan?

Why is the stock of public housing so low? Why did the government not put much effort into improving the housing situation of disadvantaged households? We believe that the answer is related to the political system. After the KMT took over Taiwan in 1945, Taiwan was under an authoritarian rule, of which the suppression of civilians by the armed force in 1947 was the symbol.[7] Since the KMT retreated from China in 1949, it, on one hand, restricted the social activities by martial law and, on the other hand, started to enforce local autonomy and allowed limited democracy to lessen civil pressures. After 38 years of martial law, the Democratic Progressive Party (DPP) was established in 1986 and the KMT announced the abolishment of martial law in 1987, which signified the end of authoritarianism. Since then, Taiwan's democratic thoughts that were formerly restricted started to develop, and Taiwan gradually entered the democratic political system of alternation of the ruling party. Nevertheless, Taiwan's "public housing policy" has never been a public housing policy, but a tool used by the administrators to seize or distribute political interests in the development process of Taiwan's political systems.

From 1945 to 1975, the KMT ruled Taiwan based on authoritarianism.[8] In the beginning of its rule, all social resources were used in national defense and hence public housing only included dormitories for officials and their relatives and post-disaster settlement programs. In 1954, the KMT allowed the direct election of a province councilor, and the government allowed limited democracy and enforced local autonomy. To consolidate its regime, the KMT government developed clientelism and traded economic resources for the political loyalty of local factions; the KMT did not interfere with the graft and corruption of local factions

[7] On the evening of February 27, 1947, an agent from the Alcohol and Tobacco Monopoly Bureau struck and injured a woman illegally peddling tobacco on Yenping Road in Taipei City, which led to another member of the public being shot and killed. On February 28, citizens of Taipei protested at the relevant organizations but were met with machine-gun fire from the Governor's Office. The situation escalated and spread across the island because people rose up in every place and rioted all across Taiwan. The KMT government sent troops to Taiwan and began to quell the unrest; this event turned into a massacre and continued as what became known as "country sweeping", an island-wide program of arrest and slaughter. The elite of Taiwanese society was sacrificed almost in its entirety, and there were heavy civilian casualties, with a death toll between 10,000 and 20,000.

[8] Authoritarianism denotes any political system that concentrates power in the hands of a leader or small elite that is not constitutionally responsible to the body of the people; this concept was first introduced by Adorno et al. (1950).

and some local politicians and also used judicature as a tool to protect or punish them.

From 1975 to 1996, clientelism[9] became increasingly popular. In 1975, Taiwan started to enforce the Public Housing Act, and public housing units were built in all areas. On one hand, the government showed its concern for public housing quality; on the other hand, public housing, as one project of public constructions, also became a channel for graft for local factions and some local politicians. After Taiwan entered into a democratic political system in 1996, the public housing policy became a tool for political parties to win election votes and to provide favors to the real estate developers who greatly assisted them during the elections.[10]

Taiwan's public housing policy was captured. Taiwan was not a democratic country and had no control over interest groups' lobbying and political donations.[11] As one of the interest groups, real estate development associations related to the housing field continued to use their interpersonal networks and operating experiences accumulated from the clientelism period to "kidnap" the government. The enforcement of the public housing policy appeared to take care of disadvantaged nationals; however, the prerequisite of the government's administration was to satisfy the interests of those groups or at least to not conflict with them. The regulations thus serve the interests of the special interest groups instead of the public (Stigler 1971; Etzioni 2009).

However, instead of the political system, some suggest that the situation whereby there are few public housing units relates to the protection of property rights in the Constitution (Chen 1995; Grange et al. 2006). These authors believe that public housing provision problems relate to land acquisition and finance. Therefore, the government adopted short-term measures, such as loans for house purchases or enabling the private provision of public housing with state facilitation. Although land acquisition appeared to be a reason, we did not see an improvement in the housing situation of socially or economically disadvantaged individuals.

---

[9] Clientelism refers to exchanging finances or services for political support. In the exchange process, there are roles of "patron" and "client"; the patron obtains clients' political support through 3 mechanisms, including material, normative and coercive mechanisms. Material exchange is the most basic foundation of the alliance between a patron and a client (Lande 1977; Clapham 1982).

[10] Real estate developers financially aided candidates in elections. The real estate developers not only financially aided the candidates but also offered other resources. For instance, the KMT and DPP were provided with commercial buildings in Taipei metropolitan areas as campaign offices in the presidential election of 2012.

[11] A series of Acts related to the "Sunshine Law" were enforced one by one after 2000, including (1) the "Act on Recusal of Public Servants Due to Conflicts of Interest", effective on July 12th, 2000; (2) the "Political Donations Act", effective on March 31st, 2004; (3) the "Act on Property-Declaration by Public Servants", effective on October 1st, 2008; and (4) the "Lobbying Act", effective on August 8th, 2008.

6.6 Conclusions

This chapter introduces the public housing policy in Taiwan after the KMT retreated from China and took over Taiwan. The government did not put much thought into public housing policy. All these causes led to a serious public housing problem in Taiwan: the housing rights of low- or middle-income households and minority groups were not taken seriously by the government in Taiwan. Under the agenda of winning votes, these groups were ignored by the government.

We expect that the government can address Taiwan's current public housing problems and move the policy toward the following directions: (1) Strengthening the house rental market. According to the housing census of the Directorate-General of Budget, Accounting and Statistics, Executive Yuan in 2010, Taiwan's vacancy rate reached up to 19.4 %, equal to 1,560,000 units. These empty houses represent the mistakes of the past housing policy, which caused resource allocation errors and waste. Using these vacant houses for rental would be helpful to solve the problem whereby the economically disadvantaged cannot buy or rent houses. (2) Introducing the power of "The Third Sector", i.e., NGOs. Public housing should feature "rentals", and the power of "The Third Sector" should be introduced in the future to assist the government in managing public housing.

Biography: Dr. Chin-Oh Chang received his Architecture Master's degree at MIT (Massachusetts Institute of Technology) in 1980, and a City and Regional Planning PhD degree at the University of Pennsylvania in 1986. He was President of the Asian Real Estate Society (AsRES) in 1997–1998, and the President of Global Chinese Real Estate Congress (GCREC) in 2009–2010. His research is published in Urban Studies, Housing Studies, Journal of Property Research, Habitat International, International Real Estate Review, and several other journals. He has concentrated his research in areas related to housing and land policy, real estate investment, and financial analysis.

References

Adorno TW, Frenkel-Brunswik E, Levinson DJ, Sanford RN (1950) The authoritarian personality. Harper & Brothers, New York

Chang CO (1990) A research on housing problem and housing policy. Chinese Housing Studies Association, Taipei (in Chinese)

Chen DS (1995) A city of money and power: sociological analysis of local factions, conglomerates and development of Taipei metropolitan. Chuliu Publisher, Taipei (in Chinese)

Clapham CS (1982) Clientelism and the state. In: Clapham CS (ed) Private patronage and public power. St. Martin's Press, New York

Directorate General of Budget, Accounting and Statistics (2010) Population and housing census. Executive Yuan, Taipei

Etzioni A (2009) The capture theory of regulations—revisited. Symp: Public Dilemmas Revisited 46:319–323

Grange AL, Chang CO, Yip NM (2006) Commodification and urban development: a case study of Taiwan. Hous Stud 21(1):53–76

Lande CH (1977) Introduction: the dyadic basis of clientelism. In: Schmidt SW, Lande LGCH, Scott JC (eds) Friends, followers, and factions: a reader in political clientelism. University of California Press, Berkeley/Los Angeles

Mi FG (1988) Public housing policy in Taiwan. Taiwan: Radical Quart Soc Stud 1(2):97–147 (in Chinese)

Stigler G (1971) The theory of economics regulation. Bell J Econ 5(2):335–358

Yip NM, Chang CO (2003) Housing in Taiwan: state intervention in a market driven housing system. J Comp Asian Dev 2(1):93–113

Chapter 7
The Story of Singapore's Public Housing: From a Nation of Home-Seekers to a Nation of Homeowners

Yongheng Deng, Tien Foo Sing, and Chaoqun Ren

Abstract For many Asian countries facing rapid urbanization and land scarcity problems, providing large-scale affordable housing for urban poor is a challenging task. Singapore has turned itself against the odds since independence by transforming itself from a nation of home seeker to home owner. As in 2011, public housing constitutes 82.65 % of the total housing stocks, and nearly 90 % of Singapore's households own the houses they live in. The Singapore's success story of public housing is built on an efficient centralized planning system. The government assumes a wide range of public housing activities from alienating state lands, building flats, allocating tenure to eligible citizens and financing purchase, to enhancing asset wealth. Housing and Development Board (HDB) and CPF (Central Provident Fund) Board are two main public agencies that have been instrumental in implementing various public housing policies in the island state. This chapter documents key policies and strategies that have helped shaped Singapore's public housing landscape over the last 50 years.

Y. Deng (✉)
Institute of Real Estate Studies (IRES), Department of Real Estate, School of Design and Environment, NUS Business School, National University of Singapore, Singapore
e-mail: ydeng@nus.edu.sg

T.F. Sing
Institute of Real Estate Studies (IRES), Department of Real Estate, School of Design and Environment, National University of Singapore, Singapore
e-mail: rststf@nus.edu.sg

C. Ren
Institute of Real Estate Studies (IRES), National University of Singapore, Singapore
e-mail: irsrc@nus.edu.sg

J. Chen et al. (eds.), *The Future of Public Housing: Ongoing Trends in the East and the West*, DOI 10.1007/978-3-642-41622-4_7,

7.1 Overview

Singapore has a two-tier housing market comprising a private housing market and a public housing market. Private housing is built and sold by private developers to households at full market prices in a *laissez-faire* system. Public housing is not a social good in Singapore; it is, however, built by the government and allocated to eligible Singapore citizens at concessionary prices. The transfer of ownership rights outside this regulated segment of the market is allowed after a 5-year minimum occupation period (MOP) condition has been fulfilled. The secondary market, commonly referred to the resale market, helps to fill in the demand that is not served by the public housing market. The demand for resale public flats may come from Singapore citizens whose income exceeds the eligibility threshold, single Singapore citizens, Singapore permanent residents (SPR), Singapore citizens with a non-Singapore spouse or non-Singapore family members, and orphans of deceased Singapore citizens and SPRs.

Like in the private housing market, resale flat prices are unregulated and fully determined by open market forces. An efficient secondary market improves price discovery in the primary housing market,[1]where new housing prices are determined by the government by deducting an undisclosed sum of subsidies from the open market prices.[2] Price differentials between new sale markets and resale markets create housing wealth, which has helped many Singapore households realize their dream of upgrading to private housing units. The upward mobility of Singapore households fits into the liquidity constraint models of Stein (1995) and Ortalo-Magne and Rady (2006).

Public housing constitutes the largest stock of affordable housing units that meet the housing needs of 80 % of Singaporeans. Both landed and non-landed housing units in private markets are limited in supply, but they provide a variety of choice of unsubsidized housing units for middle- to high-income households. In a typical upward housing mobility process, households facing liquidity constraints start the housing ladder by buying public housing units at concessionary prices from the government. They accrue housing wealth through price appreciation and non-cash subsidies in the form of concessionary prices for new public housing purchases. After meeting the MOP requirement, they cash up the housing wealth by selling their public housing and upgrade to private apartments and condominiums. The upward mobility process continues from non-landed condominiums to landed houses. Detached houses in the land-scarce Singapore command significant price premiums.

Two key agencies in Singapore have played pivotal roles in creating the success story of providing affordable public housing for the nation. The first is the Housing & Development Board (HDB), which was established on 1 February 1960 to assumes the responsibility of public housing developers in the country. The second is the Central Provident Fund (CPF) Board, which was formed on 1 July 1955 after the enactment of the CPF ordinance in 1953 to implement a compulsory savings scheme for working

[1] See Ong and Sing (2002), Sing et al. (2007).

[2] Since 2001, the government has shifted from cost-based pricing to market-based pricing. The new approach uses open market resale flat prices in the same neighborhood as comparable to set the base price, and deducts housing subsidies from it to derive the new flat price.

Singapore citizens and SPRs. Its role has been expanded to include meeting its members' financing needs in public and private housing purchases. This chapter aims to document key HDB public housing policies and CPF housing financing schemes underpinning the transformation of Singapore into a nation with a high ownership rate.

7.2 History of Public Housing

The formation of HDB led to the dissolution of the Singapore Improvement Trust, an agency set up by the British colonial administration during the post-war periods. It took over the role as the nation's public housing authority entrusted with the responsibility of solving the housing shortage problem in the post-independent period. It oversees the full cycle of public housing programs, starting from land assembly and acquisition, resettlement, town planning, architectural design, engineering work, and building-material production to the allocation, management, and maintenance of completed housing units. The total approach to the housing program gives HDB flexibility and autonomy in public housing planning, such that amenities like commercial, industry, and institutional uses and recreational facilities are seamlessly integrated into each public housing estate.

In 1964, the government made the Home Ownership for the People Scheme a national agenda by encouraging Singapore citizens to have a roof over their heads. Owning a home in the country offers not just financial security; it also helps Singapore citizens sink their roots in the country, which is believed by the political leaders to be an essential strategy to achieve overall stability economically, socially, and politically for the country. Mr. Lee Kuan Yew, the former Prime Minister and the former Minister Mentor of Singapore, wrote in his memoirs[3]:

> I wanted a home-owning society. I had seen the contrast between the blocks of low-cost rental flats, badly misused and poorly maintained, and those of house-proud owners, and was convinced that if every family owned its home, the country would be more stable....
>
> ... After independence in 1965, I was troubled by Singapore's completely urban electorate. I had seen how voters in capital cities always tended to vote against the government of the day and was determined that our householders should become home owners, otherwise we would not have political stability. My other important motive was to give all parents whose sons would have to do national service a stake in the Singapore their sons had to defend. If the soldier's family did not own their home, he would soon conclude he would be fighting to protect the properties of the wealthy. I believed this sense of ownership was vital for our new society which had no deep roots in a common historical experience.

The strategy of HDB in its first 20 years of the public housing program was to ramp up new public housing units in the shortest possible time to alleviate the problems of over-crowding and poor hygiene in the post-independence periods (Wong and Yeh 1985). High-rise and high-density living has been adopted by HDB as a pragmatic way of housing a large number of families without depriving limited land resources for other economic activities. The design of the earlier public

[3] Lee (2000).

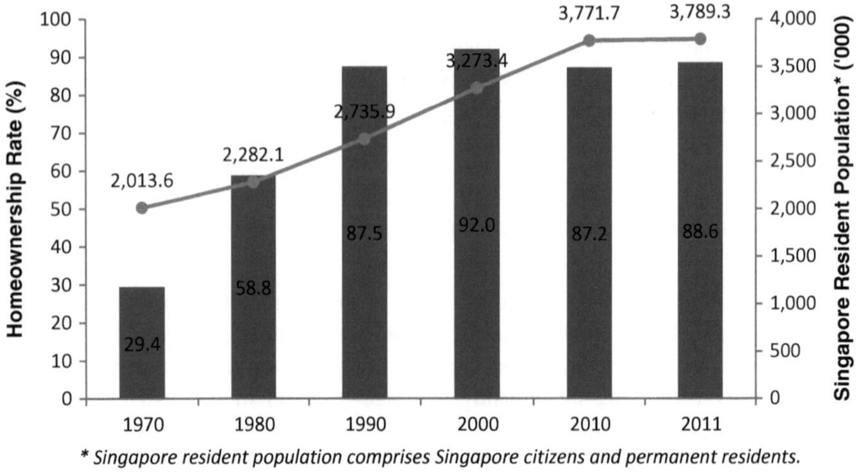

Fig. 7.1 Homeownership rate in Singapore (*Source*: Department of Statistics, Singapore)

housing was simple and utilitarian; it included typical slab blocks of 12 stories high with a common corridor connecting each lift landing floor. A void deck, which is an open space at the ground level, is a unique feature of a typical HDB housing block. It is used by residents for various social functions, which include wedding celebrations and funeral rites. Permanent community facilities like kindergarten, childcare centers, senior citizen corners, etc., have also been housed in some void decks.

After two decades of intense building programs, HDB completed 324,000 dwelling units of various sizes, ranging from one-room to five-room and executive flats, providing housing for 68.54 % of Singapore's population in 1980 (Fig. 7.1), which was a huge jump from the 9 % in 1960. The public housing dwelling stocks reached 85.64 % in 1990 before reaching the peak of 88.07 % in 1995. In December 2010, HDB marked a milestone in its 50 years of public housing history with the completion of one million flats at the Treelodge@Punggol, a new housing precinct located in the North-Eastern part of the island.

The homeownership program has been successful in transforming Singapore into a home-owning nation, with 92 % of the population owning a home in 1990. After the basic housing needs had been largely met, HDB slowed down its housing program in the late 1990s to give room for private developers to step up the supply of private housing to meet the rising aspirations of the population.

7.3 Meeting the Housing Needs: Diversity and Balance

7.3.1 HDB Flat Types

HDB flats come in different forms and sizes to cater to different needs of households. Flats consisting of one to three rooms were the basic flat types built by HDB in the 1960s. The smaller flats were replaced by bigger four- and five-room flats to keep pace with progress in the economic and social environments. The four- and five-room flats had areas of 90 sqm and 110 sqm, respectively. Large executive apartments/maisonettes with an average floor space of 150 sqm were discontinued in 1995. Studio apartments of 35–45 sqm were introduced in 1998 to cater to the housing needs of older citizens 55 years and above. They are sold with shorter leases of 30 years.

Private developers were brought in to inject variety into the design and construction of public housing flats in 1995. HDB sold lands by tenders for private developers to build executive condominiums (EC) with design and facilities that are comparable with private condominiums. The involvement of private developers was expanded in March 2005 to include public housing flats without condominium facilities under the "Design, Build, and Sell Scheme" (DBSS). The Premiere@-Tampines was the first DBSS project launched in 2006. A total of 13 sites across Singapore have to date been sold to private developers by tender for DBSS projects.[4]

DBSS flats and ECs are public housing projects[5] designed, built, and sold by private developers at open market prices. These two types of premium public housing appeal to the "sandwiched" class of families who do not meet the income ceiling criteria imposed on new HDB flats. The government provides housing grants to subsidize purchases by these households.

7.3.2 *Managing Supply and Inventory of HDB Flats*

Matching supply to demand is challenging for HDB. Adopting a supply strategy that is perfectly responsive to the demand is difficult because of the "stickiness" in housing production. A responsive supply system is the most cost-effective inventory control model in achieving the target service level. As public housing is a subsidized good, attaining the highest service level for the customers at the expense of high inventory costs is not socially desirable. While a price-based allocation system adopted by private developers in the sales of DBSS and EC projects is efficient, it causes price volatility and crowding-out effects on low-income households. HDB adopts a balanced and socially equitable approach through a ballot system and a queue system in allocating new flats.[6]

---

[4] The sales of DBSS sites have been suspended by the government since 2011. Source: Lim, Linette, "DBSS land sales halted," *Channel News Asia*, 4 July 2011.

[5] These two housing types are subjected to the same eligibility rules and resale restrictions imposed on public housing built by HDB.

[6] Mah, Bow Tan, Minister for National Development, "Housing Supply: Allocating Scarce Resources," TODAY, 1 October 2010, pB7.

Prior to October 1994, the demand for new HDB flats significantly outnumbered the supply, and the allocation of flats to eligible applicants was by "lottery" in a **balloting system**. "Winning" a flat "lottery" was highly uncertain. Moreover, successful applicants would face a long waiting time, in some cases as long as 7 years, for the keys to their flats.[7] In a system where the outcome is purely determined by chance, unsuccessful applicants are disappointed and frustrated when applicants who join the ballot late get flats ahead of them.[8] In 1994 the balloting system was replaced by a **queuing system**, known as the **Registration of Flat System** (RFS), to allay the anxiety of unsuccessful applicants who had failed repeatedly in their past ballots. Under the RFS, every applicant was assigned a queue number based on his/her choice of location of new flats, which were categorized into three zones: North, Northeast, and West. Of the new supply of flats in each batch, 15 % of the new flat supply in each batch would be allocated to those in the priority schemes, such as the Multi-Tier Family Scheme, the Join Selection Scheme, and the Third Child Priority Scheme. 60 % of the remaining supply was allocated to first-time applicants, and the balance would go to upgraders, who intend to change to bigger flats. The system followed the first-come first-served principle to ensure that everyone down to the last person in the queue would have a chance to choose his/her flat.

At the peak of the property market cycle in April 1997, there were 146,000 applicants in the RFS queue system, which far exceeded the annual supply of 30,000 new flats by HDB. Based on the statistics, it would take about 4.8 years on average to clear the demand (queue), even if the queue number were constant. However, the Asia Financial Crisis in 1997 caused an abrupt turn in the demand with many applicants voluntarily opting out of the RFS queue. The RFS pool shrank to 8,800 in 2002, and the unsold HDB flat inventory swelled to 17,000 as of May 2002. With the intention of clearing the stocks, HDB allowed new and existing RFS applicants to choose completed and unsold flats in its inventory under the **Walk-In-Selection (WIS)** scheme in April 2002. It scrapped and replaced the RFS with the new **Build-to-Order (BTO)** system in 2002.

Under the BTO system, new flats are built only on demand, after at least 70 % of flats in a new project have been booked. The BTO system gives applicants the flexibility to apply for new flats in their preferred location when new projects are launched. It is a demand-supply inventory system that could extend the lead time in delivery. In a weak market, a shortage in demand will delay a building program. When the demand is strong, the success rate in balloting for new flats declines when the number of applicants exceeds supply. Unsuccessful applicants will have to wait for the launch of the next BTO to put in new applications.

The BTO system and the scaling down in the building program in 2002 resulted in strong pent-up demand when the market observed an upturn in 2005–2006. The supply-demand imbalance in the market drove up resale HDB flat prices rapidly.

---

[7] Ditto.

[8] Lim, Allison, "First applicants to pick flats under queuing system are all praise," Straits Times, 19 July 1995.

In May 2011, the Minister for National Development, Mr. Khaw Boon Wan, called for HDB to step up the supply and "**build ahead of demand**" by removing the 70 % minimum order requirement in the BTO system.[9] He also gave priority in the flat selection to first timers (new applicants) to ensure that young couples would be able to buy their first homes via the BTO.

The HDB also carries out regular **Sales of Balance Flats** (SBF) exercises by offering unsold inventory accumulated from previous BTOs, excess replacement flats allocated for the Selective En-bloc Redevelopment Scheme (SERS),[10] and repurchased flats to potential buyers. The SBF allows buyers to choose from a wide range of flats either under construction or near completion. The SBF usually attracts strong interest, and separate ballots are conducted to match the stocks (supply) with the demand.

7.4 Public Housing for the Masses

In Singapore, the concept of ownership of public housing is referred to 99-year leasehold interests transferred to flat owners. 88.6 % of the HDB dwellers in Singapore own their flats as of 2012. As new HDB flats are subsidized, eligibility criteria are used to ensure that public housing flats are allocated only to Singapore citizens for occupation needs (see Table 7.1). Forming a family nucleus with at least one Singapore citizen is a key requirement to qualify for public housing flats. The family nucleus may fall within one of the three schemes, which are public, fiancé/fiancée, and orphan schemes.

As public housing caters mainly to low- and medium-income families, income ceilings are set based on a gross monthly household income of S$10,000,[11] which has been raised from the previous ceiling of S$8,000 with effect from 15 August 2011. If applicants plan to buy flats to live with members of an extended family, which include parents and children (married/single), the average gross monthly household income must not exceed S$15,000. The smaller flat types such as two-room flats in mature towns/estates and three-room flats in non-mature towns/estates are strictly reserved for families with income below S$5,000. Only low-income families with income below S$2,000 are eligible to buy two-room flats in non-mature estates/towns. The income ceiling for premium DBSS flats was

[9] "Khaw tells HDB to build ahead of demand", Channelnewsasia.com, 27 May 2011.

[10] Launched in August 1995, SERS is an estate renewal program involving the demolition and redevelopment of older flats in selected precincts. Displaced residents are compensated financially and given priority to buy new replacement flats in nearby locations or other locations at subsidized prices.

[11] All the value terms in the paper are quoted in Singapore dollar term

Table 7.1 Eligibility criteria for public housing by HDB and private developers

Housing type	New HDB flat	Design, Build and Sell Scheme (DBSS) flat	Executive Condominium (EC)
Citizenship	Singapore Citizen, or Family nucleus must comprise at least another Singapore Citizen (SC) or Singapore Permanent Resident (SPR)		
Age	At least 21 years old		At least 21 years old, or at least 35 years old under the Joint Singles Scheme
Family nucleus	(a) Public scheme:	Applicant + spouse + children (if any) Applicant + parents + siblings (if any) Applicant + children under legal custody, care and control (for widowed/divorced)	
	(b) Fiancé/ Fiancée Scheme:	Applicant + fiancé/fiancée	
	(c) Orphan Scheme:	Applicant + unmarried siblings	
			(d) Join Singles Scheme: Applicant + another single
Income Ceiling (gross monthly household)	S$10,000[a, c] S$5,000[d] S$2,000[e]	S$10,000[b, f]	S$12,000[g]
Restriction on concurrent ownership within MOP	Applicant, his/her spouse, family members and their spouses must not own, or dispose, or have an estate or interest in any other flat, house, building or land that include but not limited to HUDC flats (privatized and non-privatized), properties acquired by gift, properties inherited as beneficiaries under a will or as a result of the Intestate Succession Act, private properties, or properties owned/ acquired/disposed through nominees regardless of properties location Within 30 months before the date of application, and between the application date and the date of taking possession of the flat		
Maximum ownership rights	Eligible Singaporean household can only buy the following housing unit only twice: a flat from the HDB, a resale flat with CPF Housing Grant, a DBSS flat from developer, or an EC unit from developer		

Source: HDB and the Authors

[a]The revised income ceiling for an extended family is $15,000

[b]The revised income ceiling for extended family is $12,000

[c]Revised on 15 August 2011 applicable for 3 room (mature town/estate), 3 room (premium), 4 room and bigger flat

[d]Applicable for 3 room (non-mature town/estate) or a 2 room (mature town/estate)

[e]Applicable for 2 room (non-mature town/estate)

[f]Revised on 30 August 2010

[g]Revised on 15 August 2011

raised from S$8,000 to S$10,000 with effect from 30 August 2010. Households with gross monthly income of between S$10,001 and S$12,000 are eligible to purchase ECs built by private developers.[12]

[12] The previous income ceiling for EC was S$10,000 before 15 August 2011.

On 29 August 2010, several measures were introduced to dampen speculative demand in the public housing market.[13] One of the measures restricts concurrent ownership of HDB flats and private residential properties by HDB owners, who have not fulfilled the 5-year MOP requirement. Private property owners are barred from buying new HDB flats, unless they sell their private properties within 30 months, either before the application or between the application date and the date of taking possession of flats. As new HDB flats are sold with subsidies, households will not be eligible if they have already enjoyed "two bites of cherry" either in the form of buying a new flat from HDB or receiving government subsidies (CPF Housing Grant) in purchasing a resale flat, a DBSS flat, or an EC.

Since 2011, HDB and private developers have set aside a higher allocation of new flats to first timers to increase their chances of buying BTO projects. First-timer applicants include those who have not owned a HDB flat, a DBSS flat, or an EC; or who have not a received a CPF Housing Grant for the purchase of a HDB resale flat, a DBSS flat, or an EC; or who have not enjoyed other forms of housing subsidy.

Various priority schemes have been put in place to promote specific social objectives, such as to allow families of different generations to live close to each other, to promote mutual care and support between married children and their parents, to encourage families to have more than two children, to assist families in rental flats to own their flats, and to support aging-in-place.

The Ethnic Integration Policy (EIP) has been implemented since 1989 to foster harmonious living among ethnic communities by maintaining a balanced mix of different ethnic groups across HDB neighborhoods and within HDB flat blocks. The allocation of new HDB flats and sales of private developers' DBSS will strictly adhere to the neighborhood and block quotas set for each ethnic group. The EIP will also apply to resale flats and rental flats by HDB. During the selection of new flats, buyers of a selected ethnic group will not be allowed to book a flat if the maximum limit of the ethnic group has been reached. As the largest ethnic group in the country, the Chinese ethnic limit is set at 84 % and 87 % at the neighborhood and block levels, respectively. The Malay ethnic enclave must not exceed 22 % and 25 % at the neighborhood and the block levels, respectively. With effect from 5 March 2010, HDB increased the Indian/Other ethnic group limits from 10 to 12 % at the neighborhood level and from 13 to 15 % at the block level.

7.5 The Role of HDB as Financier for Public Housing

The financier role of HDB in offering concessionary loans is another cornerstone feature that has made public housing affordable to the masses in Singapore. A typical buyer will rely on three sources of funding, namely, personal equity (cash), mortgage loan, and accumulated CPF savings (including CPF Housing Grants), to finance his/her purchase of public housing.

[13] The measures were announced by the Prime Minister Lee Hsien Loong during the National Day Rally on 29 August 2011.

7.5.1 HDB Concessionary Rate Loans

HDB provides concessionary rate loans (CRL) to buyers of HDB flats and DBSS flats who meet the HDB's credit assessment and loan eligibility criteria. The concessionary interest rate is pegged at 0.1 % above the interest rate for the CPF Ordinary Account. The CRL interest rate is revised quarterly in January, April, July, and October each year in line with the revision of the CPF interest rate, but the current 2.60 % per annum CRL interest rate has not changed since July 1993. Prior to 1 January 2003, HDB also offered market rate loans for HDB and DBSS flat buyers, who were not eligible for CRLs.

The HDB CRLs provide low interest rate housing loans only to Singapore citizens who meet the eligibility criteria. Eligible HDB buyers are allowed to enjoy no more than two CRLs. If buyers have previously taken one CRL and one housing subsidy, they can have the *second bite on the cherry* in CRL if they plan to upgrade to a bigger flat. With effect from 6 March 2010, the second HDB CRL is made available to buyers who downsize or move to a flat of the same size as the first flat.[14] The policy encourages buyers to exercise more prudence in right-sizing their flats rather than being motivated by the second CRL rule to buy bigger flats.

HDB CRLs have the following characteristics:

1. The maximum loan term is set at 30 years or up to the age of 65 years of the borrower, whichever is earlier;
2. The HDB CRL interest rate is a monthly compounding rate pegged at 0.1 % above the CPF ordinary account interest rates;
3. The monthly installment is capped at 40 % of the gross monthly income of borrowers;
4. The loan ceiling is imposed at 90 % of the valuation/purchase price of the HDB flat (For flats purchased before 19 July 2005, the loan ceiling was set at 80 %.).

7.5.2 Upfront Cash Payments

After a HDB buyer has booked a BTO/SBF flat, he/she pays an option fee ranging from S$500 for a studio apartment to S$2000 for a four-room/five-room/executive flat by cash. For DBSS and EC projects, the option fee is typically 5 % of the purchase price, payable by cash. Upon exercising the option to purchase and signing of the Sales Agreement, the buyer pays the downpayment, stamp duty, and legal fees either using cash or CPF savings or a combination of both. For a buyer who is eligible to take HDB concessionary loans, he/she pays a 10 % downpayment, which is disbursed in two stages: 5 % upon the signing of the Sales Agreement and the balance 5 % at the key collection stage. If the buyer's

[14] Shankari, Uma, "HDB revises policies to stamp out speculation," *The Business Times*, March 6, 2010.

Table 7.2 LTV caps and down-payment requirements for individual buyers taking commercial loans

	Before 20 February 2010	30 August 2010		14 January 2011		06 October 2012		
Loan Characteristics[a]:								
Outstanding loan?	N.A.	No	Yes	No	Yes	No	No	Yes
Loan tenure > 30 year or 65 years?	N.A.	N.A.	N.A.	N.A.	N.A.	No	Yes	Yes
Maximum LTV	80 %	80 %	70 %	80 %	60 %	80 %	60 %	40 %
Total Downpayment	10 %	20 %	30 %	20 %	40 %	20 %	40 %	60 %
Modes of Payments:								
(a) *Signing of Sales Agreement stage*								
(i) by Cash	5 %	5 %	10 %	5 %	10 %	5 %	10 %	10 %
(ii) by CPF savings, CPF housing grants and cash		5 %		5 %		5 %		
(b) *Key Collection Stage*								
(i) by CPF savings, CPF housing grants and cash	5 %	10 %	20 %	10 %	30 %	10 %	30 %	50 %

Source: HDB, Monetary Authority of Singapore (MAS) and the Authors
[a]For individual borrowers only

CPF savings and CPF Housing Grant (if eligible) are sufficient, the buyer will not need to fork out any cash for the 10 % downpayment.

For buyers who take commercial bank loans to finance the purchase of new HDB flats, DBSS flats, or ECs, the downpayment requirements are affected by the two rounds of the government's macro-prudential measures in 2010 and 2012 aimed at stabilizing the overheating property markets. The new rules significantly lower the loan to value (LTV) ratio granted by commercial banks on property purchases (Table 7.2). With effect from 6 October 2012, individual borrowers who take commercial loans with a term of either more than 30 years, or extended beyond the age of 65 years, are required to fork out between 40 and 60 % equity. Ten percent of the equity must be paid by cash at the Sales Agreement signing stage, and the balance of the equity can be paid using their CPF savings, CPF Housing Grant, and cash upon completion of the projects.

7.6 Beyond Retirement to Housing Financing: Central Provident Fund

7.6.1 CPF Accounts and Contributions

The CPF is a compulsory saving scheme that helps working Singapore citizens (SC) and SPRs build up wealth for retirement needs. The CPF scheme has gradually

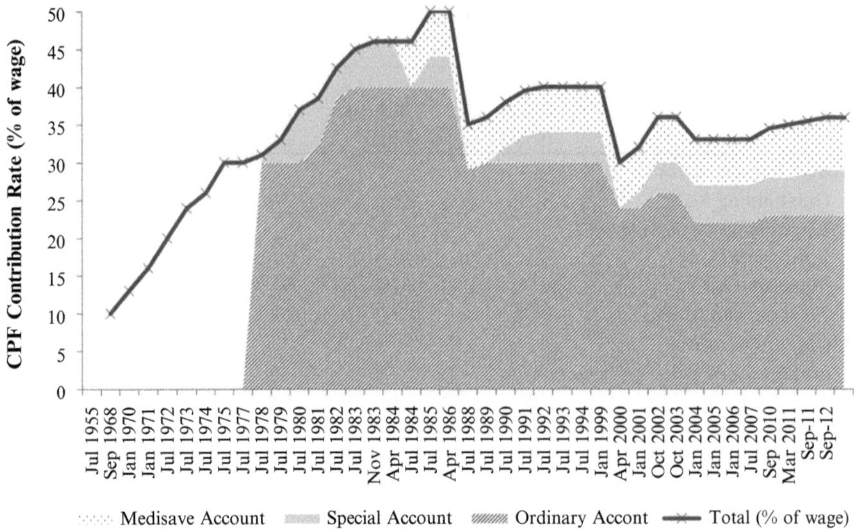

Fig. 7.2 Monthly CPF contribution rates and allocation to CPF accounts (*Source*: CPF, the authors)

been expanded into a multi-facetted social security plan that covers health care, housing, family protection, and investments. Under the CPF scheme, working SCs and SPRs and their employers contribute a fraction of their gross monthly wages into their CPF accounts. The monthly contribution rates vary by age and income of the members. The contributions by both employees and employers are capped by a monthly wage ceiling of S$5,000. The monthly contributions will be allocated into three different accounts, namely, an Ordinary Account (OA), a Special Account (SA) and a Medisave Account (MA), to serve different needs of the members. The contribution rates and the allocation of the contributions to the three different CPF accounts were adjusted over the years (Fig. 7.2).

Up to 1976, monthly contributions of CPF members were deposited into a single account, and the savings in the accounts could be withdrawn for various uses, such as home purchases, buying insurance, investments, and paying for education. As more savings were withdrawn over the years by the members for housing financing, a new account known as a "Special Account" designated specifically for retirement purposes was created in 1977. Withdrawals from this account are only allowed on the condition that members must reach the age of 55 years and above, and they must have set aside a minimum sum of S$113,000 (in 2003 dollar terms) as of 1 July 2012. The final Minimum Sum will be raised to S$120,000 (in 2003 dollar terms) on 1 July 2015. With effect from 1 January 2013, CPF members are also required to set aside a Medisave Minimum Sum of S$25,000.

The Medisave Account (MA) was set up in 1984 to provide for the healthcare needs of members and their dependents, especially during retirement. The savings can be used to cover hospitalization expenses and to pay for premiums of approved medical insurance.

As of 2012, the savings in OA earn a risk-free interest rate of 2.5 % per annum guaranteed by the government. Savings in the SA, MA, and Retirement Account earn a guaranteed return of 4 % per annum. An extra 1 % interest rate is also given to the first S$60,000 savings in the cumulated CPF balances, which include not more than S$20,000 in the OA.

7.6.2 *Public Housing Scheme*

In 1968, the government introduced the Public Housing Scheme (PHS) to allow Singaporeans to use their CPF savings to buy HDB flats. In 1981, CPF members were allowed to use their savings to purchase private residential property under the Approved Residential Properties (ARP) Scheme. These two Home ownership schemes (HOS) are important in helping residents own their homes.

Under the PHS, CPF members can use savings in the OA for downpayment and partial/full payments of purchase prices. Expenses on stamp duty, legal fees, and other related costs incurred in the purchase of public housing can be paid from OA savings. CPF members who take HDB concessionary loans in purchasing new HDB flats do not need to fork out any cash if their CPF OA savings are enough to pay for the downpayment. After paying the downpayment, they are required to use the balance in their CPF OA as upfront payments, and the shortfalls will then be financed by HCLs. They can still draw down their future monthly contributions to pay for monthly debt services of HCLs.

However, the use of PHS is subject to two withdrawal limits: the valuation limit (VL) and the CPF Withdrawal Limit (WL) (Table 7.3). The VL is defined as the lower of the purchase price or the valuation of the flat at the time of purchase. After reaching the VL, members can continue to draw down the CPF accounts under the WL up to 120 % of the valuation of the flat. If a member is above 55 years old when the VL is reached, the WL is allowed subject to meeting the cash component of the Minimum Sum Scheme (MSS). After the WL is reached, the member will need to use cash to make payments for the balance of the loan.

As of September 2012, the total contributions to CPF accounts amounted to S $1.859 billion, of which S$708 million has been withdrawn by members to finance purchases of both public housing (S$494 million) and private housing (S$215 million). Figure 7.3 shows the ratios of fund flows into and out of the CPF member accounts (dark line) and the ratio of withdrawals for private housing purchases over withdrawals for public housing purchase (dashed line) for the periods from July 1981 to September 2012. On average, CPF members use 41.8 % of the total CPF contributions to finance housing purchases, and the ratio of funds used for private housing financing over public housing financing is 58.64 %. The high outflows of CPF funds into the private residential market occurred during the housing boom periods from 1992 to 1996. However, in the recent housing booms from 2008 to 2012, the ratio of CPF withdrawals for private housing purchases over the public housing purchases was estimated at 27.73 % on average.

Table 7.3 Valuation limits and withdrawal limits for CPF public housing financing scheme

Flat type:	New HDB flat		Resale HDB flat	
Age of borrower:	<55 years	≥55 year	<55 years	≥55 years
(A) HDB concessionary loan:				
Valuation Limit (VL)	N.A.	N.A.	Yes	Yes
CPF Withdrawal Limit (WL)[c]	N.A.	N.A.	No[a]	No[b]
(B) Commercial bank loan:				
Valuation Limit (VL)	Yes	Yes	Yes	Yes
CPF Withdrawal Limit (WL)[c]	Yes[a]	Yes[b]	Yes[a]	Yes[b]

Note: *N.A.* Not applicable

[a]Subject to meeting the minimum sum cash component requirement

[b]Subject to meeting the minimum sum requirement

[c]The Housing Withdrawal Limit is as follows:

Effective date[d]	Housing withdrawal limit
1 Jan 2003 – 31 Dec 2003	150 % of VL
1 Jan 2004 – 31 Dec 2004	144 % of VL
1 Jan 2005 – 31 Dec 2005	138 % of VL
1 Jan 2006 – 31 Dec 2006	132 % of VL
1 Jan 2007 – 31 Dec 2007	126 % of VL
1 Jan 2008 onwards	120 % of VL

[d]For resale flats, it refers to the date of application received by HDB. For new flats, it refers to the date of booking

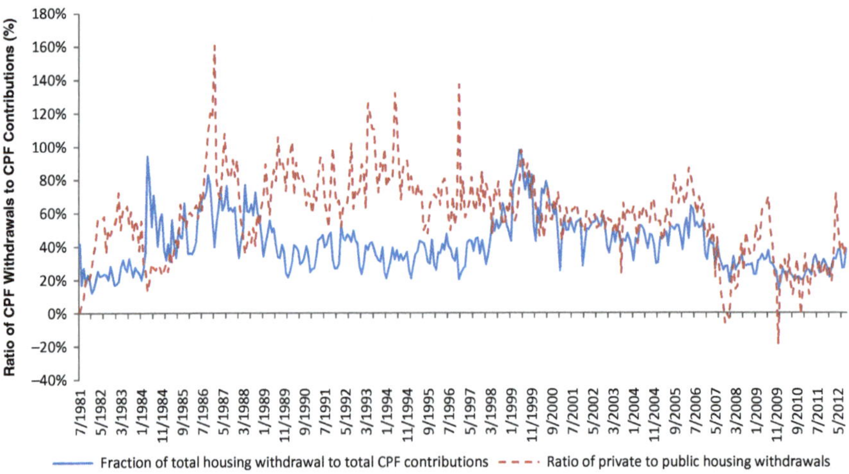

Fig. 7.3 CPF withdrawals for private and public housing financing (*Source*: Department of Statistics and the Authors)

Table 7.4 CPF housing grant for families and singles

	CPF housing grant for family			
	SC/SC household	SC/SPR household	Half family housing grant[a]	Singles grant
(A) DBSS Flat Buyer				
Average gross monthly household income up to S$8,000	S$30,000	S$20,000[b]	S$15,000	S$11,000[c]
Average gross monthly household income up to S$8,000 + living near parents/married child[d]	S$40,000	S$30,000[b]	S$20,000	S$20,000[d,e]
Average gross monthly household income from S$8,001 to S $10,000[f]	S$30,000	S$20,000[e]	S$15,000	
(B) EC buyer				
Average gross monthly household income up to S$10,000	S$30,000	S$20,000[b]	S$15,000	
Average gross monthly household income from S$10,001 to S $11,000[g]	S$20,000	S$10,000[b]	S$10,000	
Average gross monthly household income from S$11,001 to S $12,000[g]	S$10,000	S$0[b]	S$5,000	

Source: HDB and the authors

[a]Half Housing Grant is applicable, if you are a first-timer citizen and your spouse has previously enjoyed a housing subsidy

[b]If you are from an SC/SPR household, you can enjoy the full housing subsidy by applying for the Citizen Top-Up when your SPR family takes up Singapore Citizenship or when you have an SC child

[c]You are applying with your unmarried sibling (s) under the Orphans Scheme

[d]Your parents are staying with you in the flat; or at least one of the parents must be a Singapore Permanent Resident or Singapore Citizen

[e]Not applicable for DBSS buyers with average gross monthly household income above S$8,000 from Yishun PH1 and Tampines PH2 onwards

[f]This revision is only applicable to DBSS projects launched for public sale after 30 Aug 2010

[g]This revision is only applicable to EC projects launched for public sale on or after 15 Aug 2011

7.6.3 CPF Housing Grants

The government provides housing subsidies in the form of CPF Housing Grants to assist first-timer Singapore citizens to buy resale flats, or DBSS flats and ECs. The CPF Housing Grants partially subsidize eligible first-timer families for differences between new HDB flats and flats sold in the open market, which include resale flats, DBSS flats, and ECs. The housing grants are used to make initial payments for flats. However, these grants are not used to pay the "cash over valuation," defined as the difference between the price demanded by sellers and the valuation of a resale flat.

The government currently provides two types of CPF housing grants: the CPF Housing Grant for Family and the CPF Housing Grant for Singles. SCs and/or SPRs with a family nucleus can apply for the CPF Housing Grant for Family subject to meeting the income and age criteria (Table 7.4). They will receive a one-off grant of S$30,000, if the buyers are SC, and S$20,000, if one of the buyers is SPR. If they buy a resale flat or a DBSS flat near either their parents' or married child's house, which is either a HDB flat or an owner-occupied private house, SC and SPR families are entitled to the higher-tiered grants of S$40,000 and S$30,000, respectively. Singles of 35 years and above are eligible to apply for the CPF Housing Grant for Singles if they buy a resale flat or a DBSS flat with an unmarried sibling under the Orphan Scheme, on the condition that their combined income is below S $8,000 per month. They are given a grant of S$11,000. If the purchased flat is located near occupied houses of their parent or married child, S$20,000 is given under the higher-tiered CPF Grant for Singles Scheme.

SC and SPR families that have received the CPF Housing Grant for Family can apply for the CPF Housing Top-up Grant, if the non-citizen spouse or child has subsequently become a Singapore citizen. Grant recipients who are single but subsequently marry a first-timer Singapore citizen can apply for a top-up grant for their spouses who are non-grant recipients subject to meeting the eligibility criteria. If a single grant recipient marries a Singapore citizen, he/she is eligible for the Half CPF Housing Grant for Family, when he/she buys a resale flat, a DBSS flat, or an EC.

The above CPF Housing Grants are not applicable for singles and/or families whose essential family members belong to one of the following categories:

- They are the owners of a flat bought direct from HDB, a DBSS flat, or an EC bought from the developer.
- They have sold a flat that was previously bought from HDB, or a DBSS flat or an EC bought from the developer.
- They have already received the CPF Housing Grant for the purchase of an HDB resale flat.
- They have enjoyed other forms of housing subsidy previously, such as benefits under the Selective En bloc Redevelopment Scheme (SERS, or privatization of HUDC estate.[15]

7.6.4 Subsidies for Lower-Income Families

On 3 March 2006, the government introduced the Additional CPF Housing Grant (AHG) scheme to help low-income families with a monthly household income of not more than S$4,000 buy their first house. An AHG ranging between S$5,000 and

[15] The Housing & Urban Development Company Pte Ltd (HUDC) was set up in 1974 to build affordable "condominium" styled public housing for middle-income households, but the HUDC scheme was terminated in 1987. In 1995, the privatization of HUDC estates was introduced in phases to transfer the ownership rights (strata-titles) of HUDC units to residents. Chin, Daryl, "12 of 18 HUDC estates already privatized - 5 more in the process of privatisation," *The Straits Times*, September 17, 2012.

S$30,000 is given to eligible households to make an initial payment when they purchase a new HDB flat, a resale HDB flat, or a DBSS flat. The AHG scheme was enhanced on 24 August 2007. The Enhanced AHG (EAHG) raises the income ceiling of the AHG from S$4,000 to S$5,000 and increases the maximum grant sum from S$30,000 to S$40,000.

A new Special CPF Housing Grant (SHG) scheme was announced by the government on 3 March 2011 to further ease the financial burden of first-timer families with a monthly income below S$2,250. The new SHG ranging between S$5,000 and S$20,000 is given on top of the EAHG, but the grant is only applicable for the purchase of a smaller two-room or three-room standard flat in non-mature HDB estates. A typical family with a monthly income lower than S$1,500 will receive a total grant of up to S$60,000 (S$40,000 EAHG and S$20,000 SHG), whereas for a family earning S$2,001 to S$2,250, the grant sum could add up to S$35,000, when they buy a three-room HDB flat in a non-mature estate.

7.7 Moving Up the Housing Ladder

The public housing stocks constitute about half of the gross housing wealth in the country (Phang 2001). Homeowners can cash out their housing wealth in an active secondary (resale) public housing market that has been established since 1971. Resale activities help ease the liquidity constraints of households and facilitate upward mobility in the housing ladder. Homeowners can sell their flats in the resale market to eligible buyers at a mutually agreed upon price (open market price). Eligible buyers are required to meet the quotas set under the Ethnic Integration Policy (EIP).[16] Before selling the HDB flats, DBSS flats and resale flats, owners must meet the MOP of 5 years.

Since April 1997, each eligible family is limited to "two bites of a cherry" that is they can only enjoy a maximum of two housing subsidies either through buying a new flat directly from HDB or receiving the CPF Housing Grant in purchasing a resale flat or a DBSS flat. A resale levy is imposed on a second timer when he/she buys a second subsidized HDB flat. However, the resale levy is waived if he/she sells a resale flat that was previously bought without the CPF Housing Grant, or if he/she upgrades to a private property. Under the old system adopted in 1982, the resale levy increased with room size following a graduated scale ranging between 15 % for a three-room resale flat and 30 % for an HUDC. A new resale levy structure was introduced on 3 March 2006, where a fixed lump sum amount ranging between S$15,000 and S$50,000 is levied according to the first subsidized flat type.

Upon the sale of flats, HDB flat owners with an outstanding HCL loan will apportion their sale proceeds in the following order: (1) outstanding HDB loan/bank

[16] A new SPR quota capping non-Malaysian PR at 5 % and 8 % at the neighborhood and block levels, respectively, was introduced with effect from 5 March 2010.

loan, (2) HDB resale levy (if applicable), (3) CPF refund. For HDB flats bought with commercial bank loans, the sale proceeds will be used to pay off the outstanding bank loan, CPF refund, and HDB resale levy (if applicable), in descending order. In the sale of flats with negative equity, owners will need to pay the shortfalls between sale proceeds and outstanding loan balance by cash to either the HDB or banks depending on the loan type.

If a seller is below 55 years old, he/she will have to refund both principal withdrawn and interest accrued back into his/her CPF account. If a seller is 55 years and above, a partial refund is required, which is the lowest of the Minimum Sum Deficiency (MSD)[17] or the sum of principal withdrawn and accrued interest. The refund is credited directly into the Retirement Account (RA).[18] If the refund falls short of the MSD requirement, the seller is required to top up the RA in cash. The cash top-up is waived if the flat is sold at market value. If the MSD is pledged by a second property of the seller, which is also financed with CPF savings, the MSD top-up is required when the second property is sold.

7.8 Conclusion

Public housing is an important channel through which transfers of wealth to middle- and lower-income Singaporean households are facilitated. The government's dual roles as a housing developer and a financer in the HDB-CPF system have been instrumental in transforming Singapore from a nation of home seekers to a nation of homeowners in the past 50 years. The housing system has attained the objective of providing affordable housing to the masses. At the same time, it helps promote social compact by creating asset wealth to the people.[19]

The HDB-CPF system has a proven track record of delivering desirable housing welfare to Singapore citizens (Phang 2007). Many countries have been attempting to emulate Singapore's success story in housing but with different degrees of success. As a part of the unique institutional structure of Singapore, HDB and CPF play instrumental roles in translating the government's public housing vision into reality. This institutional structure is characterized by a dominant ruling political party and a network of competent civil service capability, and supplemented by strong governance and a fair distribution structure.

---

[17] The Minimum Sum Deficiency is the Minimum Sum applicable when a member turns 55 less the balance in his/her Retirement Account (excluding interest earned).

[18] A Retirement Account (RA) is set up when CPF members reach the age of 55 years. The Minimum Sum (MS) set aside in the RA can be made up of savings in OAs and SAs and/or property pledge of up to 50 % of the MS. For members who are unable to set aside the full MS in cash, their property bought with their CPF savings will be automatically pledged, for up to half of their MS.

[19] "Something for Everyone," *The Straits Times*, 19 February 2005.

There are two challenges facing the public housing system in Singapore. First, it is challenging to balance the pricing dynamics between a regulated primary market and a decentralized *lazier-faire* secondary market. On the one hand, HDB needs to ensure that new flats are priced at a level that is affordable to the masses; on the other hand, it needs to protect the housing wealth of existing homeowners by minimizing distortions in the secondary market pricing mechanism. The recent steep increases in resale HDB price fueled by private housing price increases coupled with rising costs of lands and other inputs (material and labor) have imposed great pressure on HDB in reining price increases in new flats.[20] Second, HDB has stepped up efforts to improve the design and quality of new generations of public housing flats to meet the rising aspirations of Singaporean families. Its quality strategy is an expensive public policy, which can only be made possible by increasing public housing funding.

References

Deng Y, McMillen DP, Sing TF (2012) Private residential price indices in Singapore: a matching approach. Reg Sci Urban Econ 42(3):485–494

Lee KY (2000) The Singapore story: memoirs of Lee Kuan Yew, vol 2, From third world to first, 1965–2000. Time Media Private Limited, Singapore

Ong SE, Sing TF (2002) Price discovery between private and public housing markets. Urban Stud 39:57–67

Ortalo-Magne F, Rady S (2006) Housing market dynamics: on the contribution of income shocks and credit constraints. Rev Econ Stud 73:459–485

Phang SY (2001) Housing policy, wealth formation and the Singapore economy. Hous Stud 16 (4):443–459

Phang SY (2007) The Singapore model of housing and the welfare state. In: Groves R, Murie A, Watson C (eds) Housing and the new welfare state: perspectives from East Asia and Europe. Ashgate, Aldershot

Sing TF, Tsai IC, Chen MC (2007) Price dynamics in public and private housing markets in Singapore. J Hous Econ 15(4):305–320

Stein JC (1995) Prices and trading volume in the housing market: a model with down-payment effects. Q J Econ 110:379–406

Wong A, Yeh S (eds) (1985) Housing a nation: 25 years of public housing in Singapore. Housing and Development Board, Singapore

[20] See Deng et al. (2012) for a discussion on the rising of private residential housing prices in recent years in Singapore.

Chapter 8
New Experiments in Public Housing Supply in Seoul, South Korea: The Possibilities and Limits

Yeong-Hee Jang and Soo-Hyun Kim

Abstract South Korea began supplying public housing relatively late considering its economic development and severe housing shortage. Since 1990, however, the Korean government has rapidly expanded public housing to approximately 5 % of households. Moreover, each of Korea's political parties is in competition to supply as many public housing units as possible. The Korean government has set the goal of expanding public housing to 12 % of all households by 2018.

The Seoul city government's target is to supply 80,000 public housing units in 4 years (2011–2015), which will effectively increase the stock to 7 % of households. However, the city government has struggled to acquire enough land to build public housing. For this reason, it is introducing new methods to supply public housing, such as purchasing existing private houses, acquiring public housing units in redevelopment projects, and encouraging small-scale developments, among others.

These experiments are beneficial to finding practical ways to increase the public housing supply in countries of high population concentration with less available land and in countries that belatedly began their public housing programs.

8.1 Introduction

Over the last 10 years, public housing policy has undergone significant shifts in European countries with long histories of public housing. Housing ownership is encouraged, and consequently, the supply of public housing has decreased. However, an increase in housing prices and private housing rent has led to a high

Y.-H. Jang (✉)
Vice President, The Seoul Institute, Seoul, South Korea
e-mail: yhjang@si.re.kr

S.-H. Kim
Graduate School of Urban and Real Estate Studies, Sejong University, Seoul, South Korea
e-mail: shkimsdi@sejong.ac.kr

J. Chen et al. (eds.), *The Future of Public Housing: Ongoing Trends in the East and the West*, DOI 10.1007/978-3-642-41622-4_8,

concentration of low-income households in public housing. Spatial separation has also continued. In public housing, spatial separation problems have led to policy changes, mitigating eligibility for public housing and expanding the housing subsidy program. Public and private market integration has been another approach to cope with the increased demand for public housing. In contrast to Europe, East Asian countries have developed different policies to cope with the financial burdens of public housing. Major cities in South Korea, Japan, and China are in a state of high residential density and growth.

Public housing policy had a relatively late start in Korea but has received greater attention due to the rise in housing prices and demolition of low-cost housing. Homeownership policies have exacerbated household debt. The problem has continued to magnify and is now a national concern in Korea. Public housing has become an important policy agenda, but the shortage of land is an obstruction to resolving the issue.

The Korean government began building public housing in 1989, which is relatively late in comparison to European countries. Since that time, Korea has steadily supplied public housing, and the supply rate to total stock has modestly increased to 2.0 % in 1995, 2.5 % in 2000, and 5 % in 2010. This increase will continue to carry forward because the government has targeted a public housing rate of approximately 10 % of households in 2022 (KRIHS 2013). Both conservative and progressive Korean politicians agree that an increase in public housing is necessary. Korea's public housing policy has been regarded as having a late start, but it is considered to have developed considerably within a short period (Kim 2011).

The current mayor of Seoul, Park Won-Soon, is one of the most active politicians in terms of expanding the public housing stock. He pledged to supply 80,000 public housing units by 2015, which would increase the stock to 7 % of households (SMG 2012a). The former mayor, Oh Se-Hoon, also made efforts to expand public housing to include the middle-income class through *shift housing*, a new public housing program, which would become his political symbol. However, the city government has struggled to acquire enough land to build public housing. Seoul has virtually no vacant land. Hence, the city government has adopted the FAR (Floor Area Ratio) as an incentive to secure public housing in large-scale redevelopment projects. However, the supply was disrupted because of the 2008 financial crisis and housing recession, which led to the delay of large-scale new development and redevelopment projects.

The city government is now attempting to introduce new public housing supply methods, such as purchasing existing or newly built private houses, contracting private landlords to use their existing houses for public purposes, and building cooperative housing with nonprofit investment on public land. Most of these methods utilize the private sectors.

These experiments are beneficial to finding practical methods to increase the public housing supply in countries of high population concentration with less available land and in countries that belatedly began public housing programs. This paper explains these new methods and backgrounds and investigates the possibilities and limitations of each method. It also attempts to compare these methods to other programs that utilize the private sectors to provide public housing in other countries.

8.2 History and Issues of Public Housing in Korea

8.2.1 History of Public Housing

The first public housing units in Korea that can be labeled as such based on international criteria emerged in 1989. Surging rental costs in the private sector led the government to initiate 190,000 units of permanent public housing for the lowest-income households, which roughly equal the number of families on livelihood assistance.

In 1990, permanent public housing was expanded through redevelopment projects in response to the serious social conflicts deriving from tenants residing in project areas. Redevelopment public housing, which made up 17 % of newly built houses, was supplied as alternative housing for tenant families in redevelopment projects. This continues to be a condition for urban redevelopment projects.

In 1993, the permanent public housing program was changed to 50-year public housing, and the target population shifted from families receiving welfare to those earning below 70 % of the average income. A supply target of 100,000 houses over the next 5 years was set. In 1998, the public housing program was changed again, this time into national public housing as part of the effort to protect people's living standards following the Asian financial crisis. The goal was to increase the housing stock to one million homes over the span of 10 years until 2010. In 2003, the central government initiated a plan to produce one million rental housing units by 2010; it was able to produce roughly 750,000 units by enacting a special law on national public housing in 2003 and by instituting other methods, such as purchasing existing housing (purchased public housing) and leasing existing housing (leased public housing).

Since 2008, however, the national public housing supply has decreased, with the new government administration increasing housing for sale rather than the public housing supply. Meanwhile, in 2007, the Seoul city government began to supply *shift housing* to accommodate the middle-income class. The purpose was to encourage the middle class to live in *shift housing* rather than purchase a home, by changing the perception that public housing residences are only for low-income groups.

The public housing inventory reached approximately 730,000 houses nationally, which roughly equaled 4.4 % of all families in 2010. During that same period, 165,000 units were supplied, which was equivalent to 4.6 % of all households in Seoul (Fig. 8.1).

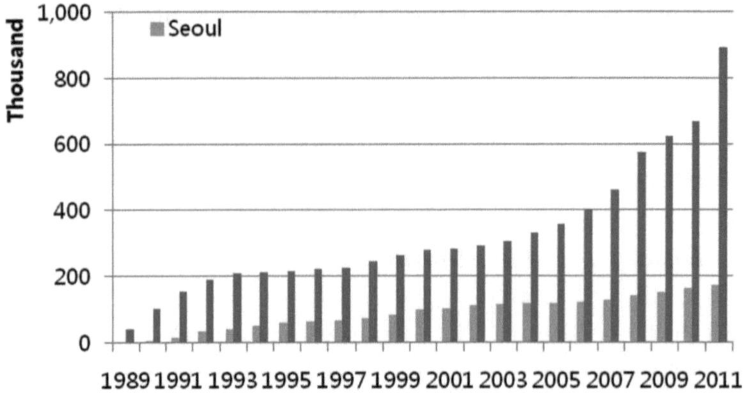

Fig. 8.1 Cumulative public housing stock increase (Source: Data from Land & Housing Corporation (LH), Ministry of Land, Transportation and Maritime Affairs (MLTM), Seoul Housing Corporation (SH); modified by the author)

8.2.2 Public Housing Programs

Various types of public housing have been developed in Korea over the past 20 years. Korean public housing can be divided into permanent rental, purchased and leased housing for the lowest income tier, national rental housing for those earning below 50 % of the average income, redevelopment rental housing for tenants of redevelopment projects, and *shift housing* for the middle-income class. Redevelopment rental housing and *shift housing* were originally initiated by the Seoul city government and then expanded by the central government. Public housing programs can be delineated by tenant income and payable rent capacities (Table 8.1). Rent is determined based on production costs, which make public housing rents much lower than the market rates. The question of whether public housing should be limited to low-income brackets or expanded to the middle class is one of the most important issues surrounding public housing in Korea.

Public housing programs can be simplified into three classifications based on tenant income qualifications. Type 1 is targeted at the lowest income level, which is less than 50 % of the average monthly income, and includes permanent public housing and purchased public housing. Type 2 is targeted at income groups below 70 % of the monthly average and includes redevelopment public housing and national public housing. Type 3 is *shift housing*, which is available to those earning up to 180 % of the average monthly income. Types 1, 2, and 3, respectively, make up 36.4 %, 52.7 %, and 10.9 % of the total public housing stock in Seoul and 31.7 %, 66.1 %, 2.2 % of the national total. Figure 8.2 shows the cumulative stock types in Seoul.

Table 8.1 Qualification of public housing program

Program	Supply period	Qualification	Rent levels compared to market rent
Permanent public housing	1989–1995	Less than 50 % of the average income	10–20 %
50-Year Public Housing	1993–1997	Less than 70 % of the average income	50–70 %
Redevelopment Public Housing	1992–Present	Redevelopment area tenant residents, Housing savings account subscribers	50–70 %
National public housing	1998–Present	Less than 50 m^2: Less than 70 % of the Average Income (priority to monthly income of less than 50 %) Less than 60 m^2: Less than 70 % of the Average Income Greater than 60 m^2: Less than the Average Income	70–80 %
Purchased & leased Public housing	2002-Present	Less than 50 % of the average income (Note: Disabled – less than 100 %)	10–20 %
Shift housing	2007–Present	Less than 60 m^2: Less than 70%of the average income Less than 85 m^2: less than 150 % of the average income Greater than 85 m^2: Less than 180 % of the average income	More than 80 %

Sources: Easy Finding Life Statute (http://onclick.law.go.kr), Homepage of SH Corporation (http://www.shift.or.kr/), Sale and Rent Application System by LH Corporation (http://myhome.lh.or.kr/rent/)

8.2.3 Issues and Major Challenges

8.2.3.1 Issues in Public Housing Policy

Public housing began during Korea's economic development phase, which is late compared to other developed welfare states. Still, the quantity of public housing has steadily increased. Moreover, each of Korea's political groups agrees that the stock must be further increased to at least 10 % of all households. Despite its accomplishments in public housing, however, Korea still faces many challenges.

First, the number of public housing units remains insufficient. Public housing has yet to reach 5 % of households and therefore does not meet the needs of the lower class. This insufficiency is regarded as one of the reasons why the rent in the private rental market has continued to increase since 2009. According to a survey of housing experts in Korea, "if the public housing stock increases to 10 %, it will be possible to stabilize the private rental market" (Lim 2010).

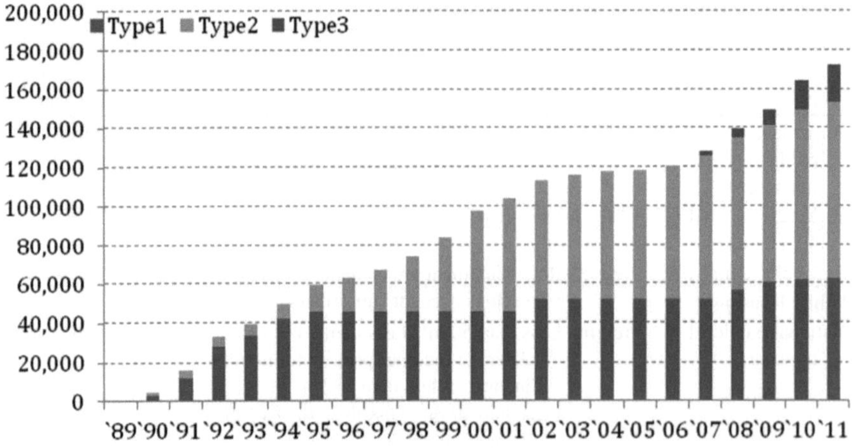

Fig. 8.2 Public housing increases by type in Seoul (Note: Type 1 permanent, purchased and leased public housing; Type 2 national, 50-year, and redevelopment public housing; Type 3 Shift housing) (Source: Data from Seoul Metropolitan Government, Housing Policy Bureau)

Second, the physical location of public housing is too far from the existing urban areas. Finding suitable land within cities has been difficult because Korea had already reached 90 % urbanization when the public housing supply was initiated; by the early 2000s, Korea's urbanization was fully mature. During the Roh Moo-hyun administration (2002–2007) in particular, the launch of large-scale housing projects in peripheral regions was inevitable because the government was rushing to develop 100,000 houses per year. During this process, rental housing was constructed in places such as greenbelt-lifted areas, where public transportation was inconvenient. Such large-scale developments on city outskirts triggered purchased and leased public housing programs in existing urban areas.

Third, permanent public housing, an early public housing complex, is severely isolated from society and is in close quarters with the economically disadvantaged. From the beginning, permanent public housing was designed to accommodate Korea's lowest-income group; 85 % of residents have been livelihood assistance recipients (MOCT 2005). National public housing areas that were constructed more recently are less saturated with the economically disadvantaged, but the areas are still isolated because they were designed as large-scale complexes of 500–2,000 households.

Fourth, the present financing mechanism for public housing construction appears difficult to sustain. This is because large amounts of public housing funding unusually depend on the LH's (Land and Housing Corporation, previously known as the Korea National Housing Corporation) finances rather than on the government's. The LH utilizes revenues from sales of residential and land development projects to fund public housing. Only about 10–20 % of public housing construction funds are from government finances; 30 % is from the National Housing Fund and 20–30 % is self-financed by the LH. However, this process has become infeasible due to the downturn in the real estate market following the financial crisis of 2008. The LH's debt has grown to more than one hundred trillion won ($900 million), making the resolution of this debt a national agenda. In addition, loans from the National Housing Fund (NHF), which is a government-operated housing fund for low-income households, has approached its limit because funding has been restrained due to the housing recession. The funds of the NHF largely consist of savings from the housing subscription accounts for new homes and the housing bonds that all new home buyers are obligated to purchase.

Fifth, although the rent levels are generally 10–70 % of the market price (the permanent public housing rate is only 10–20 % of the market price), there is no differentiation according to income level. Currently, public housing rents are determined based on production costs.

Sixth, the local government's role in management and operation is restricted. In Korea, 80 % of public housing is owned, managed, and operated by the LH, which is a central government-affiliated organization; the rest is owned by the SH (Seoul Housing Corporation), a Seoul government-affiliated organization. Although public housing has strong local features, the selection of tenants, management, and operation are assigned to the central organization. This structure was influenced by Korea's strongly centralized administrative and financial systems. Housing policies are regarded as the responsibility of the central government rather than of local governments. However, local government participation in the management of public housing has increasingly become more necessary to fulfill the needs of localities.

Lastly, the deterioration of public housing is another serious problem because budgets for repairs and management are not properly appropriated. Low rents and management fees make adequate management difficult. Permanent public housing, which began to be supplied only 20 years ago, suffers from severe deterioration due to lack of management. Reconstruction or remodeling is now being considered (MOCT 2005).

8.2.3.2 Major Challenges of Public Housing

Six tasks, mostly related to each other, are largely considered to be important challenges for public housing policies in Korea.

The first is the goal of ensuring future public housing supply. Political and civic groups in Korea have set high public housing goals. However, experts have predicted that increasing the public housing stock to more than 10 % of households is difficult to achieve. Due to the late start of Korea's public housing program, obtaining suitable land located within urban areas is challenging. In addition, private rental housing has already taken on a significant role in the housing market. Other methods of increasing public housing through partnerships with the private sector have been discussed. This will be presented in Chap. 4 as part of Seoul's new experiment.

The second issue relates to securing lands for public housing. Whereas the traditional method involved locating new housing units on city outskirts or greenbelt-lifted areas, the present challenge is to secure spaces within existing areas. This discussion is relevant to the issue of whether all public housing should be newly built. New developments are no longer relevant because the number of houses has already exceeded the number of households. Consequently, alternative methods, such as purchasing existing houses or utilizing private housing as public housing, are being considered more actively.

The third issue is about the integration of public housing in society. It is necessary to commingle tenants regardless of income class by reducing the size of public housing complexes. Adjusting rents by income levels is essential to allow tenants who cannot afford rents to mix with other groups (LH 2009). However, integration will need further efforts because public housing tenants largely consist of poor households, which makes them less likely to participate in community activities within the complex.

The fourth issue relates to financing methods. As described above, Korea's public housing is in an unusual and unsustainable state in which the government's finances are rather limited. Different methods for financing should thus be discussed. It is necessary to examine whether the government budget should cover the costs, whether the LH should cover most of the costs as it has previously done, or whether another funding source should be obtained, such as the national pension fund.

The fifth issue involves the rent determination mechanism. Rents are currently uniformly determined based on production costs rather than on household income. It is appropriate to consider each household's ability to pay and operate a rent supplement program according to the household's features. However, it is uncertain whether a rent supplement program based on income would be successful because income verification methods for low-income groups are still underdeveloped (MLTM 2011).

The sixth issue is about deciding on which groups should be selected as main or preferential target tenants when public housing is expanded. Permanent public housing targets the poorest groups, whereas national public housing targets those in the 3rd to the 4th deciles. On the other hand, *shift housing* targets the 4th to the 6th deciles. Therefore, it should be determined whether to expand housing to the middle-income class or continue to limit it to low-income households.

8.3 The Housing Market and the Demand for Public Housing in Seoul

8.3.1 Housing Market Trends

8.3.1.1 High Burden Due to Housing Prices and Rents

Seoul, the capital of Korea, represents only 0.6 % of the surface area of the country but accounts for 22 % of the country's entire population, or roughly 10 million people. Naturally, housing prices and rents are the highest in Seoul. A typical 85 m^2 apartment costs approximately 460 million won (US $400,000), which is at the

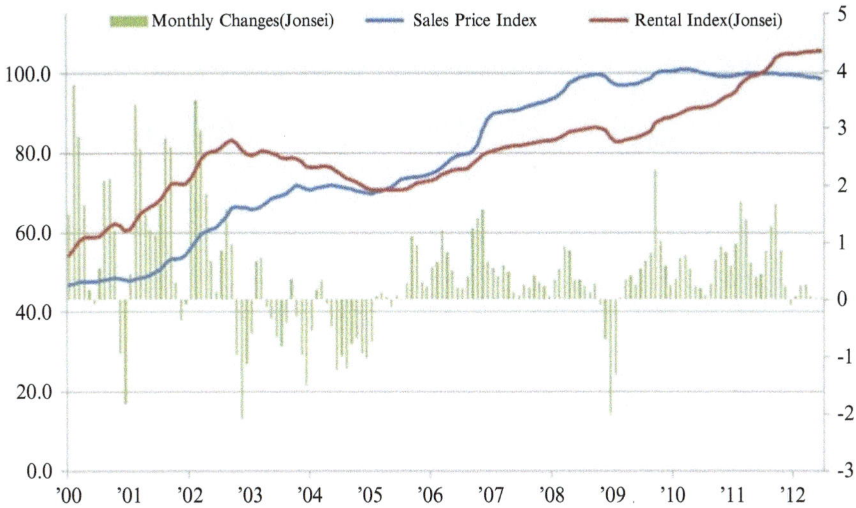

Fig. 8.3 Housing sales price and rent fluctuations in Seoul (Source: Housing and Rent Price Index from Kukmin Bank, 2012. 6)

upper end of the global cost spectrum (SMG 2012b). Seoul's 2010 PIR (price-to-income ratio) index is 9.9, which is low in comparison to the PIR indexes of comparable Asian cities, such as Beijing, Shanghai, or Hong Kong, but still very high compared to those of cities in Western Europe.[1]

Over the past 10 years, the housing stock has increased by 1.4 million units, but the percentage of homeowners has been held to approximately 40 % due to increased housing prices. Although the percentage of homeowners slightly increased during the housing market boom between 2000 and 2005, it again decreased during the housing market downturn between 2005 and 2010. The actual percentage of homeowners in Seoul is 51.3 %; homeowners that do not reside in their homes account for the 10 % discrepancy. These people are most likely those who purchased housing during the housing boom and now plan to sell due to the heavy burden of loan repayments (Lee 2012) (Figs. 8.3 and 8.4).

[1] Ratio of house price to annual household income: Hong Kong, 12.6; New York, 6.2; London, 6.9 (the above are based on the median income and median house price); Singapore, 4.4; Tokyo, 10.0; Shanghai, 15.9; Beijing, 22.3 (the above are calculated based on the price of a 70-sq. meter home divided by the average annual pretax household income). Sources: CEIC Data, 8th Annual Demographia International Housing Affordability Survey, national statistical offices, and IMF staff estimates.

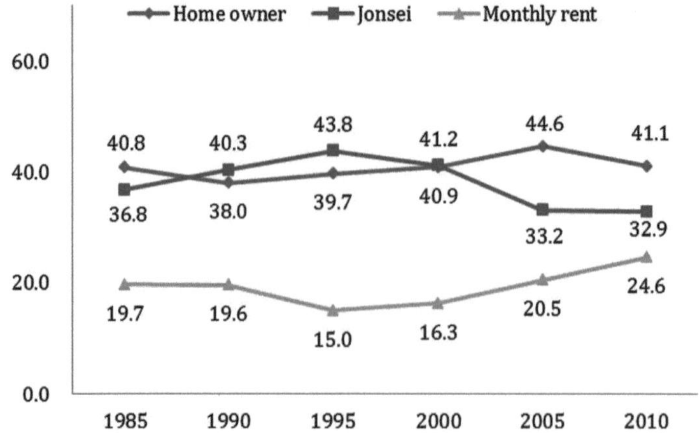

Fig. 8.4 Housing tenure changes in Seoul (Source: Statistics Korea, National population and housing census http://kosis.kr; The Seoul Metropolitan Government (Statistics Office) http://stat.seoul.go.kr)

8.3.1.2 Tenure Changes: Reduction in Jeonse Rentals, Increase in Monthly Rentals

Like its PIR, Seoul's RIR (rent-to-income ratio) is 23.3, which is considered high from a global perspective.[2] This is due to Korea's unique *Jeonse* or high-deposit rent system. The *Jeonse* system requires the renter to make an upfront deposit equivalent to half the value of the home at the beginning of the lease period. That deposit is returned in full at the end of the lease period. From the landlord's position, he/she can utilize the deposit because it is essentially an interest-free loan. From the tenant's position, he/she has the benefit of zero monthly rent payment. The *Jeonse* system has helped give tenants stability by providing them with an opportunity to reside in homes comparable to those of homeowners at half the cost.

However, the *Jeonse* system has been in decline as a result of the housing recession. As home values decrease and with no foreseeable house price margin, the deposit alone has no practical benefit because it is far below the value of the home. Over the past few years, a continuous rise in rent deposits has been followed by an increase in household borrowing; this is thought to be a direct outcome of the downturn in housing prices. The increases in household loans and in the interest payments on those loans is essentially equivalent to monthly rent payment. Accordingly, monthly rent payment tenancy is on the rise and expected to increase further in the future.

[2] Rent-to-income ratio: Seoul, 23.3 (based on median) and 30.3 (based on average); Hong Kong, 18.0 (based on median). Sources: 2010 Housing Survey, KRIHS 2011, Hong Kong Population and Housing Census 2011.

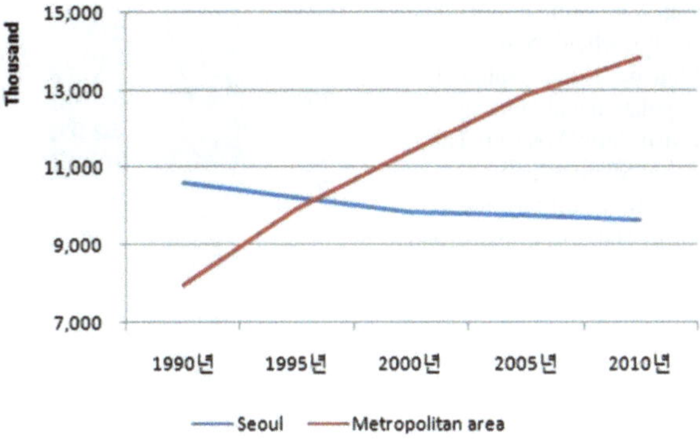

Fig. 8.5 Changes in population 1990–2010 (Source: Statistics Korea, National population and housing census http://kosis.kr; The Seoul Metropolitan Government (Statistics Office) http://stat.seoul.go.kr)

8.3.1.3 Increased Dependency on the Private Rental Market

In 2010, 41.1 % of the 3.5 million households in Seoul were owner-occupied, and 57.5 % were renter-occupied. Among the renters, only 8.3 % resided in public housing. According to the 2010 national population and housing census, owner-occupied households had decreased by 3.5 % (120,000 households) from 44.6 % in 2005 to 41.1 % in 2010. During the 5-year interval, the supply of public housing increased by only 46,000 units, which consequently increased the dependency on private rental housing.

8.3.2 Socioeconomic Changes

8.3.2.1 Changes in the Population Structure

Seoul's housing market has undergone structural changes in accordance with the population it serves. First, the population has steadily decreased from 10.6 million in 1990 to 9.6 million in 2010. On the other hand, the population in the capital region surrounding Seoul has steadily increased from 8.0 million in 1995 to 13.8 million in 2010. This is because of the steady development of new towns surrounding Seoul. The consistent development of new towns has helped provide quality housing at an affordable price, therefore attracting the middle class to move to suburban areas. The new towns have also attracted tenants who are unable to find adequate *Jeonse* housing within Seoul (Fig. 8.5).

Second, changes in household size and age groups are also important factors that influence Seoul's housing market. The increase in single-family households and the decrease in 4-member family households are especially notable. Also, the impact of low birth rates has led to a decrease in the population under the age of 40 years; conversely, the percentage of the population over the age of 40 is increasing (Fig. 8.6 and 8.7).

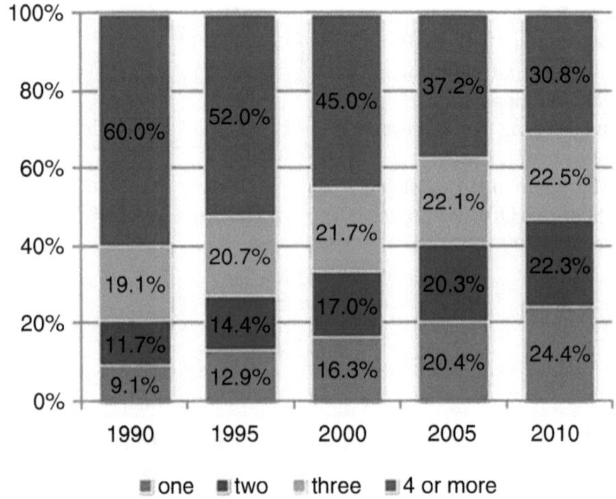

Fig. 8.6 Number of people per household (Source: Statistics Korea, National population and housing census http://kosis.kr; The Seoul Metropolitan Government (Statistics Office) http://stat.seoul.go.kr)

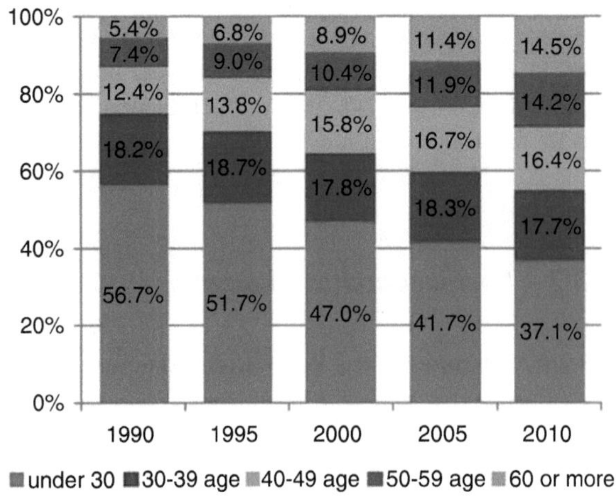

Fig. 8.7 Population ratio by age (Source: Statistics Korea, National population and housing census http://kosis.kr; The Seoul Metropolitan Government (Statistics Office) http://stat.seoul.go.kr)

8.3.2.2 Housing Instability Among the Younger Generation

Lastly, instability in employment among the younger class makes it difficult for this group to enter the housing market. The likelihood of becoming homeowners among the younger class is very low because of occupational instability and lower income. *Gosiwon* housing, a cheap one-room monthly rental unit, has become a popular residence for this group. The *Gosiwon* is a typical example of poor housing conditions; the unit is approximately 3 m^2 in size, created by subdividing the floor of a commercial building into small rooms. In Seoul alone, approximately 150,000 people reside in this housing type. The increase in the members of this younger generation residing in *Gosiwon* and in elders residing in *Jjokbang* (1-room shanty housing) presents a new challenge to public housing policy (Fig. 8.8).

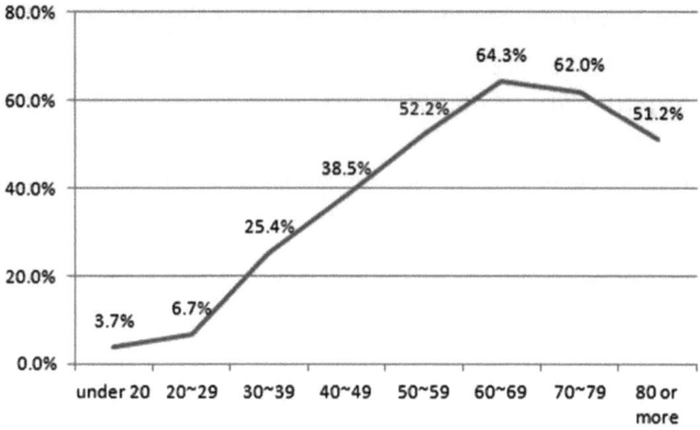

Fig. 8.8 Homeownership rate by age (Source: Statistics Korea, National population and housing census http://kosis.kr; The Seoul Metropolitan Government (Statistics Office) http://stat.seoul.go.kr)

8.3.3 Demand for Public Housing

As previously mentioned, Seoul's housing market has experienced great changes since the financial crisis of 2008. The continuing low birth rate and the aging population have resulted in a decrease in the number of people per household. Changes in the economic structure negatively influence homeownership, especially among younger groups. As a result, the number of households in private rental housing has continued to increase. In addition, the tenure type in the rental market is changing, with decreases in traditional *Jeonse* rent types and increases in monthly rent types.

The 2011 Housing Survey on Rental Households shows that the RIR (rent-to-income ratio) of those in the 1st and 2nd income deciles residing in private rental housing is 41.7 %. On the other hand, the RIR in public housing households is 25.1 %, which is much lower than that in private rental households (MLTM 2012). Accordingly, housing welfare support, such as public housing or rent subsidies, is an imperative policy agenda for low-income households residing in private rental housing.

The fact that 20,000 households are on the waiting list for permanent rental housing in Seoul is another reason to increase the supply of public housing (internal data from the city of Seoul 2012). The high competition for public housing is further evidence of the high demand for public housing.

In addition, public housing ranked 1st in a citizen survey on policy preferences conducted under Mayor Park Won-Soon in 2012; *shift housing* had ranked 1st during the previous administration (SMG 2012a). All of these facts strongly support the high demand for public housing in Seoul and Korea.

8.4 New Experiments on Public Housing Supply in Seoul

8.4.1 *Supply Plan of 80,000 Units*

The expansion of public housing again became an important pledge during the 2011 mayoral election. This was because most citizens were in favor of increasing the number of public housing units (SMG 2012a). Thus, the supply of 80,000 units became a major policy agenda for the new mayor of Seoul, and a special plan of action was developed to achieve this goal.

According to the plan, 45.5 % of the 80,000 units will be supplied through large-scale land development projects, approximately 33.6 % through redevelopment projects in existing areas and approximately 12 % through the purchase of private housing among existing homes. In the redevelopment projects, 20 % of the supply will be utilized as public rental housing by the government, which will purchase the housing units for tenants who would like to stay in local residences.

The Seoul city government plans to supply approximately 10 % of public housing through a number of new measures (i.e., small-sized and low-rise developments, public-private partnerships, etc.). Given the challenging task of providing affordable housing in existing areas, the city government has engaged in a variety of experiments to secure public housing. Customized public housing using neglected small-sized land targets groups that until now were estranged from public housing policy (i.e., newlyweds, college students, single youth, etc.). Meanwhile, constructing mid- or low-rise buildings has the advantage of shorter construction times of approximately 6 months (Table 8.2).

8.4.2 *Supply Mechanisms*

8.4.2.1 Supply Through Large-Scale Land Development

Public housing has mainly been supplied through large-scale housing development, which is the most efficient method of addressing a housing shortage problem. Large, new town developments on the outskirts of Seoul have also become an effective form of housing supply; 56.0 % of the public housing in Seoul was constructed in this manner, and 45.5 % of the 80,000 units are planned to be accomplished in the same manner. Nationally, nearly 90 % of the volume was supplied through this method.

Table 8.2 The supply of 80,000 public housing units by supply method

Large scale land development (Apartment type)	Redevelopment project (Apartment type)	Purchasing existing housing (low-rise multi-family housing type)	Small-scale development, public -private cooperation (low-rise multi-family housing type)
45.5 %	33.6 %	12.0 %	10.0 %

Source: The Seoul Metropolitan Government (2012a, b)

However, the problem with outskirt locations is that they are far from areas of commerce so other methods have been discussed to avoid this issue.

8.4.2.2 Supply Through Urban Redevelopment Projects

The difference between the Seoul city government's public housing plan and that of the central government is the utilization of redevelopment projects. Urban redevelopment projects are a key source of public housing supply in Seoul. The city has supplied public housing to tenants who reside in these areas, and this system continues to this day, with 54,000 units built thus far. Currently, 20 % of the newly built units are required to be supplied as public housing. Using its own funds, the Seoul city government purchases all public housing developed at the construction cost. The land cost is replaced with floor area ratio incentives. A crucial issue in this approach is that redevelopment and reconstruction projects are sensitive to real estate business fluctuations. Beginning in 2011, there has been a sharp drop in the volume of approved business due to the housing market recession. Accordingly, delays in the activation of redevelopment and reconstruction projects are expected for some time.

8.4.2.3 Supply Through the Purchase of Existing Housing Units

Purchasing multifamily homes for public housing use began in 2003. To promote the public housing plan of one million units, large amounts of public housing were built in new towns located in outer regions. Such public housing units received criticism for their remoteness, and a new program to purchase multifamily houses in existing areas was thus started (Yoon 2006). However, the purchase cost of one unit is approximately 160 million won (US $150,000), which is almost equal to the cost of construction. This means that the old unit would be more costly than the new one because of the repair expenses it would require. Also, difficulty in managing the units would be an additional problem because of the scattered locations of the units.

However, public housing in existing areas has been very popular among residents, which are largely made up of very low-income households. This is because such housing units are located in existing residential areas with low rents and no indications of public housing. Also, the small-scale and scattered locations make social contact more accessible. Social welfare agencies sometimes use multifamily public housing as homes for the elderly and for persons with disabilities. The number of purchased public housing units in existing areas in Seoul increased by 25,000 in 2011.

8.4.2.4 Supply Utilizing Small-Scale City Land

Recently, the use of small-sized city-owned land and unused urban planning lots, such as schools and parking lots, for public housing development has been actively reviewed. Among these, parking lots have the most potential. A mixed-use model has been examined as a possible way to secure parking spaces as well as public housing by adjusting the floor area ratio. Securing public housing while maintaining the existing streets and houses is beneficial in the use of small-sized land. Lots from 400 to 1,500 m^2 in size are being actively examined as a potential source of small-sized housing units of 15–50 m^2. Additionally, small-scale public housing can supply public services through the provision of shared facilities, such as guesthouses, study rooms, and child care services for the neighborhood communities.

8.4.2.5 Public Studio Projects for Single Youths, the Hope Housing Project for College Students

Massive demolitions of small-size low-cost housing through redevelopment projects impelled the city government to adopt the "Urban-Life Housing" program in 2007. As redevelopment projects centered near university and downtown areas have progressed, the housing conditions for low-income households and college students have worsened, eventually becoming an important social issue. The shortage of low-cost housing brought forth the "Urban-Life Housing" program. Due to the high land costs in Seoul, this program focused primarily on super-small studios. Such studios have contributed to meeting the residential demands of one-person households, such as students and workers who require relatively low rent. "Urban-Life Housing" was well received because it significantly loosened the parking provision requirement. Parking requirements have been a major obstacle to increasing affordable multifamily housing in Seoul because of the high land costs. Although the college authorities are mainly responsible for resolving the housing problems of students, the city government has created a city-level response through the "Hope Housing Project," which provides spaces for college students. A total of 25,000 rooms is to be supplied at 20–30 % of the market price by 2020.

8.5 New Experiments in Public-Private Cooperation

The Seoul city government is driving a new and distinctive method to fulfill the 80,000-unit supply plan. This plan calls for making use of private land and capital and adopting a cooperative approach. Countries that have suffered from lack of land and shortage of finances have attempted various methods to provide public housing. These include "private land-public housing" (a public institution borrows private land and constructs public housing), "public land-private housing" (a private entity borrows public land and constructs public housing), and "combined development of public and private housing and private offices on public land." Although there are slight differences in their methods, many countries have used private capital to supply public housing and redevelop old public housing complexes (Lee 2011).

8.5.1 Experiment 1: Remodeling Shanty Pocket Rooms – Support for Private Housing

Approximately 3,000 shanty pocket rooms exist in Seoul. These are located near rundown urban areas and charge daily rent. The rooms are used by people who are practically homeless. Shanty pocket rooms offer extremely poor living conditions and are highly vulnerable to fire. To improve residential stability, a remodeling program for these communities was initiated in 2012. However, when the government supports the remodeling of privately owned shanty pocket rooms, tenants become vulnerable to rent increases because limiting rent increases is a complex issue in Seoul, where the housing demand is greater than the supply.

To cope with this problem, the city government supports the remodeling costs under the condition of a 6-year rent freeze. However, this may be a difficult condition to meet in Seoul given the insufficient supply of affordable rental housing. Nevertheless, due to the difficulties in securing land and financing land purchases, using private resources at a reasonable price is expected to be one of the alternatives to provide public housing.

8.5.2 Experiment 2: Cooperative-Type Housing

The purpose of cooperative housing is to encourage the formation of an autonomous residential community through resident participation and community activation. Such housing aims to achieve a stable living environment through voluntary construction and community management. Although ideal, cooperative housing is a difficult task in Seoul because land is scarce and costs are high. The first experiment in cooperative public housing is currently being undertaken with the common aim of child care; the city will select a project coordinator and recruit members to participate in a child-care community housing cooperative. The selected residents will begin participating in the cooperative housing from the construction stage. If the community activation is considered successful, the Seoul city government's experiment will suggest a new model for public housing.

8.5.3 Experiment 3: Supply of Public Housing on Private Land

Providing public housing on private land leased out for over a 20-year period is also being pursued. This method pays land rent to a landlord and makes use of the public housing over a 20-year period. The city government expects to pay loan interest rates as land rent for a 20-year term. Therefore, finding a private owner who will lease the land for that period of time is a requisite condition.

Japan has been operating a public housing program on leased land since 1983. Japan's UR (Urban Renaissance Agency) constructs public housing and shopping properties and then transfers these properties to the landowner under favorable payment terms. The UR also pays rent to the owner until the end of the term. These properties operate as UR public housing at 70–80 % of market costs.

8.5.4 Experiment 4: Supply of Public Housing Using Private Capital

The Seoul city government is investigating new ways to supply public housing constructed with the use of long-term private capital. By using open facilities, such as parking lots and underutilized public facilities, it attempts to create complex developments, including private and public housing, offices, etc. The method operates under the same terms and conditions as public housing while the developer makes up for the investment expenses and rental management fees with the profits from other private facilities. Still, the feasibility of mixed development is questioned because it partially overlaps with the role of public corporations, such as the SH and the LH. Even if private capital is successfully raised, controversy over preferential treatment is anticipated because of the behavior of private capital in other SOC projects.

Since 1999, Japan has promoted the use of private capital through a measure called the Private Finance Initiative (PFI) (Miyashita 2003). The PFI pushes the right of private operators to lease public land and build public housing and of municipalities to lease or buy the public housing units back. The PFI method has often been adopted to remodel aged large-scale public housing complexes, and its use continues to increase (Miyoshi and Abe 2008). Although the public sector provides quality residential services and the private sector creates new business opportunities, public-private partnerships are expected to eventually increase the rent due to project development costs, which will eventually lead to the heightening of tenant qualifications. In the US and the UK, the rent levels of public housing supplied by private funding have already been reported to be higher (Gibb 2002; Fraser and Kick 2007; Murillo 2001).

8.6 Conclusion

The Seoul city government's efforts to increase public housing despite difficult conditions are highly regarded in Korea. Small-scale developments and public-private partnerships are pursued to achieve social diversity, alleviate land shortage problems, and lessen the government's financial burdens in Seoul. Resistance to public housing is also an additional driver of public-private partnerships in this area. However, these partnerships are likely to have limited effects in securing public housing for low-income households because adequate profits need to be secured for the private participants.

To achieve the goal of securing public housing equivalent to 10 % of the total stock, the development of diverse methods of reusing existing land is necessary. Experiments utilizing private resources for public housing will continue in the future, with public housing complexes more than 20 years of age and underutilized public facilities likely to be among the first subjects. Although public-private partnerships alleviate the problem of land shortage and financial burden in many countries, they present a more effective mechanism for securing affordable housing than low-income housing. For this reason, continued discussion is necessary on the role of public-private partnerships in ensuring future public housing supply.

Although large-scale housing rental supply through new development or redevelopment projects is expected to continue in the future, a massive increase in public housing can no longer be expected. This is because large-scale development on the outskirts of Seoul is no longer as effective or as preferred as it once was.

An innovative endeavor is necessary in the Seoul city government's efforts to supply public housing within existing urban areas because the supply mechanism is changing from large-scale complexes to small-scale developments. Small lots in existing urban areas require a new design and development method to supply public housing. The provision of a community space that integrates tenants and community residents is also another experiment. This model is related to community activation, which has recently become a major policy agenda of the Seoul city government. Although this method requires far more effort, it is expected to increase the satisfaction of residents in public housing in the long run.

References

Fraser J, Kick E (2007) The role of public, private, non-profit and community sectors in shaping mixed-income housing outcomes in the US. Urban Stud 44(12):2357–2377

Gibb K (2002) Trends and changes in social housing finance and provision within the European union. Hous Stud 17(2):325–336

Kim S-H (2011) Belated, but Grand? – The future of public housing in Korea. Paper for the Public Housing Future Symposium in Hong Kong (Sept 2011)

Korea Research Institute for Human Settlement (KRIHS) (2013) Study on comprehensive long term housing plan (2013–2022), A project report

Lee D-H (2011) Supply strategy for the public rental housing through small-scale development in deteriorated areas. 2011 Research report. Seoul Development Institute, pp 44–51

Lee C (2012) Prospects of changes in the housing market and the direction of housing policy in Korea. Real Estate Focus 55:16–30, Korea Appraisal Board

LH Corporation (2009) A study on the improvement of quality of life in long-term public rental housing. Research report

Lim S (2010) Study of the effects of long-term rental housing. PhD dissertation, University of Seoul

Metropolitan Government (SMG) (2012a) Seoul Municipal Government Operation Plan, An internal report

Ministry of Construction and Transportation (MOCT) (2005) A survey of permanent rental gousing. Research report

Ministry of Land, Transportation and Maritime Affairs (MLTM) (2011) An examination of purchased rental housing and leased rental housing. Research report

Ministry of Land, Transportation and Maritime Affairs (MLTM) (2012) Housing survey of households living in rental housing. Press release

Miyashita N (2003) Structure of urban regeneration. J Jpn Railr, January

Miyoshi F, Abe H (2008) Survey report on public housing redevelopment and application of PFI program. Osaka University

Murillo F (2001) Public-private partnership, the compact city, and social housing: best practice for whom? Dev Pract 11(2&3):336–343

Seoul Metropolitan Government (Statistics Office). http://stat.seoul.go.kr

Seoul Metropolitan Government (SMG) (2012a) Seoul Municipal Government Operation Plan

Seoul Metropolitan Government (SMG) (2012b) Seoul life hope index. http://performance.seoul.go.kr

SH Corporation. http://www.i-sh.co.kr

Statistics Korea (2012) National population and housing census. http://kosis.kr

Urban Renaissance Agency http://www.ur-net.go.jp

Yoon J-H (2006) Evaluation on national public housing. National Public Housing White Paper. Land and Housing Research Institute

Chapter 9
Public Housing and Neoliberal Policy in Japan

Yosuke Hirayama

9.1 Introduction

In many developed countries, postwar housing systems have included measures to provide social rented housing, playing an important role in improving the housing conditions of low-income groups. Over the past three decades, however, within the context of pervasive neoliberalism, governments have increasingly reoriented housing policies towards facilitating the production and consumption of market-based housing. This has led to the expansion of home ownership with reductions in the availability of social rented housing. Various societies are now beginning to experience new phases of housing situations with a decline in low-income housing.

This chapter looks at the case of Japan in regard to transformations in social housing systems. Neoliberal prescriptions do not necessarily produce equivalent outcomes because they are mediated by the indigenous social, economic, political, and institutional contexts of particular countries and thus have diverging effects on housing processes (Forrest and Hirayama 2009). In this regard, Japan serves as a vivid exemplar in terms of how neoliberal policy has affected low-income housing. Since the immediate postwar period, Japan's housing policy has been focused on the promotion of middle-class home ownership, while the direct provision of public rented housing for low-income households has been significantly residualized (Harada 1985; Hayakawa 2002; Hirayama 2003, 2007; Ohmoto 1985, 1996). In Japan, therefore, neoliberal prescriptions have effectively combined with a traditionally residualized public housing policy to erode the low-income housing system. Within the context of marginalized public housing, corporate-based employee housing and low-rent private rented housing have played a role in supplementing the low-income housing sector. However, the ascendance of neoliberal policy has begun to disintegrate the overall system of providing low-rent housing.

Y. Hirayama (✉)
Graduate School of Human Development
and Environment, Kobe University, Kobe, Japan
e-mail: yosukeh@kobe-u.ac.jp

J. Chen et al. (eds.), *The Future of Public Housing: Ongoing Trends in the East and the West*, DOI 10.1007/978-3-642-41622-4_9,

Moreover, Japan's long-standing economic stagnation has progressively undermined housing security, which raises questions as to the extent to which neoliberal policy is practical in providing low-income people with adequate, affordable housing. Immediately after the bubble economy collapsed at the beginning of the 1990s, Japan entered a noticeably prolonged period of recession accompanied by minimal or negative real growth in GDP, rising unemployment rates, and reduced real incomes. Although the Japanese economy eventually began to recover in 2002, the economic upturn did not translate into an improved household economy. Furthermore, Japan reentered an enduring recession in 2008 after becoming entangled in the global financial crisis triggered by the U.S. subprime mortgage meltdown. An additional strong blow to the nation's weakened economy was the onset of the major earthquake in Tohoku in 2011. Within the context of the post-bubble stagnation, the introduction of neoliberal policy was expected to stimulate economic recovery, and a shift in housing policy towards market-based provision was assumed to improve housing conditions. Nevertheless, the economy has continued to decline, while the marginalization of low-income housing has further increased insecurity with housing. This chapter explores transformations in the Japanese public housing system, focusing on the impact of neoliberal policy on housing circumstances surrounding low-income people. It begins by investigating the context in which Japan's public housing has been developed, placing particular emphasis on its traditionally residual nature and the more recent adoption of neoliberal prescriptions. This will be followed by analyses pertaining to transformations in housing conditions as a consequence of neoliberal policy.

9.2 Postwar Reconstruction and the Housing System

Governments in many countries, including Japan, have redirected housing policies towards a more neoliberal model, leading to a decline in social housing sectors. However, housing systems have assumed a path-dependent nature, and therefore, the diffusion of neoliberalism has interacted with the local housing contexts of particular societies to result in the diversification of housing transformations. This and the following sections highlight the historical trajectories of Japan's housing system as a case in which neoliberal policy has further marginalized public housing, which has traditionally been residualized.

After the end of the Second World War, the Japanese government took the initiative in establishing a postwar housing system that was oriented towards middle-class home ownership (Hirayama 2007; Hirayama and Ronald 2007). The Government Housing Loan Corporation (GHLC), which was founded as a state agency in 1950, provided many households with low-interest mortgages to acquire or construct their own homes. Of the various measures available through housing policy, the supply of GHLC loans was especially emphasized as a means to promote home ownership. Private rented dwellings dominated the prewar housing market, accounting for approximately 80 % of all housing in prewar urban areas. Wartime rent controls were not abolished in the immediate postwar period, and there was a decrease in the number of modest-to-middle-income households that were able to pay considerable rents. This resulted in a decline in investment in private rented housing and a counter increase in the building of owner-occupied housing. There were also a number of conversions from private rented dwellings to owner-occupied dwellings. The rate of home ownership rose dramatically to 58 % in 1953 and to 71 % in 1958. The figure then fell in the 1960s, mostly due to high-speed urbanization, which is typically accompanied by an increase in rented dwellings. Since the late 1960s, however, despite rapid urbanization, with the provision of GHLC loans aimed at encouraging home ownership, the rate of owner-occupied housing has been maintained at around 60 %, making it the dominant housing tenure.

In terms of creating a postwar housing system, government policy was directed at the formation of a social mainstream (Hirayama 2003, 2007). There was an overwhelming housing shortage when the war ended. The Department of Post-War Reconstruction estimated the housing shortage immediately after the war to be as many as 4.2 million dwellings, which was more than one fifth of the total number of existing dwellings in Japan at that time. Housing was in particularly short supply in urban areas that had been most devastated by intensive air raids. Government housing policy was thus expected to wrestle with the housing shortage situation. However, the objectives of Japan's housing system went beyond shelter issues (Hirayama 2003). Japan began to address fundamental reforms centering on demilitarization and democratization under orders of the US General HQ. Industry and the economy had completely collapsed, and most people were living in extreme poverty. The housing system was thus expected to play a role not only in addressing housing shortages but also in strengthening the foundation of Japan's overall reconstruction. In line with this, the framework of postwar housing policy was designed to enhance mainstream society. Support for people assumed to form the core of society was given priority under housing policies in order to construct a new state and to encourage the rebuilding of industry and the economy. This is what drove the orientation of the housing system towards home ownership.

The postwar Japanese government also began to implement public housing policy. The Public Housing Act and the Japan Housing Corporation (JHC) Act were enacted in 1951 and 1955, respectively. Public housing, which is subsidized by the national government and constructed, owned, and managed by local governments, is allocated to low-income households at subsidized rents. The JHC was founded as a national-level public corporation to develop multifamily housing estates for both rent and sale for urban middle-income groups. There have also been local-level public corporations that construct multifamily housing for rent and sale. However, the government did not seek to expand the social housing sector, and the direct provision of public housing was positioned as a residual measure. The rates of low-income public rented housing and public-corporation rented housing have been low, corresponding to approximately 5 % and 2 %, respectively.

It is also important to carefully look at the composition of the low-rent housing sector in understanding the structure of Japan's housing system. There is a tacit assumption that affordable housing for low-income households is provided almost exclusively in the form of "decommodified" social housing outside the market sphere. In reality, however, decommodified housing is not necessarily limited to social housing, and low-rent housing may be supplied within the market domain. Particularly in countries like Japan, where social housing is extremely residual, some other types of housing have been assumed to supplement the supply of low-income housing. In this sense, the concept of a low-rent housing sector is worth reexamining, and it is necessary to reexplore elements that make up the area of low-rent housing to understand how housing is provided to low-income households. In the case of Japan, public housing has indeed been marginalized, but corporate-based employee housing has supplemented the decommodified housing sector, and some low-rent housing has been supplied within the sphere of the private market. Critically, the provision of corporate-based housing and low-rent private housing has been effective in enabling the government sector to avoid having to construct public housing that is sufficient to meet the housing needs of low-income groups.

Japan's postwar reconstruction was intertwined with the development of a "company society" in which the government supported the security of employment and the provision of corporate-based welfare with regulatory measures and tax incentives (Fujita and Shionoya 1997). Many companies adopted a lifelong employment system and a seniority system for wages and promotion, which provided a model of the "company as a family." Within the framework of the "company society" system, the corporate sector has provided employees with a variety of occupational welfare services, including housing welfare (Ohmoto 1996; Sato 2007). Major corporations have implemented in-house systems to support their young employees in securing housing, including low-rent dormitories for single employees and low-rent employee housing for married employees and their household members. From the 1950s to the 1970s, the rate of employee housing was approximately 5–8 %, which was comparable with the rate of public rented housing. Corporate-based housing welfare, which is targeted at specific corporation members, cannot be considered to compose a "social" housing sector. However, employee housing, along with public housing, has constituted a "decommodified" housing sector, supplementing the system of providing low-rent housing.

Private rented housing in Japan has the second highest rate, just after owner-occupied housing, and represents approximately one quarter of all housing. The government has not supported the supply of private rented housing. There has been little assistance given for the construction of private rented housing and absolutely no provision of rental allowances. However, the private rented housing sector has included a considerable amount of low-rent housing, serving as a substitute for expanding public rented housing. In Japan's private rented housing market, many "nonprofessional" property owners have characteristically managed low-rent dwellings. Although providing private rented housing has not been particularly profitable, many individuals or families who hold land have constructed rented housing as a sideline without having to invest in site acquisition (Morimoto 1994). This has made the supply of low-rent housing possible. The rents for multifamily dwellings of wooden structures have been set at particularly low levels. While dwellings of this type have mostly been substandard in terms of floor area and amenities, they have functioned as low-cost shelters for low-income renters to live in. Thus, within the context of residualized public housing, the low-rent private housing sector, in addition to the corporate sector, has constituted the Japanese low-income housing sector.

9.3 Developmental State Policy and Public Housing

The Japanese state, which has often been described as a "developmental state," has prioritized and orchestrated economic expansion to legitimize itself and sustain social stability (Fukui 1992; Machimura 2004; Murakami 1992). In line with this, housing policy oriented towards middle-class home ownership not only provided housing but was also firmly embedded within the framework of economic development. The Economic White Paper in 1956 declared that the era of postwar confusion had come to an end, and, indeed, industry and the economy began to develop at a striking pace. From the mid-1950s to the early 1970s, the average annual GDP growth was as high as 10 %. The Liberal Democratic Party (LDP), a party of establishment conservatives, held power almost exclusively since it was founded in 1955, while the Democratic Party of Japan (DPJ) was in office during a relatively short period from 2009 to 2012. The conservatives, backed by strong connections in business circles, took a clear line oriented towards economic development, and successive LDP governments were consistently inclined towards encouraging the mass construction of owner-occupied housing as a key engine for accelerating economic expansion (Oizumi 2007). In 1966, with the enactment of the Housing Construction Plan Law, Five-Year Housing Construction Plans began to be drawn up periodically as a foundation for housing policy. Under these plans, the majority of subsidies or public funding for housing construction mostly took the form of GHLC loans. The government's concern was focused on stimulating the mass production of housing, especially owner-occupied housing, by setting a targeted amount of housing construction. There was a cycle in which economic development brought about an increase in the number of middle-class households that could purchase a house, and the expansion of the acquisition of owner-occupied homes further accelerated economic growth.

The first oil crisis of 1973 marked a turning point in housing policy, and state intervention in the housing market expanded. Although the business climate recovered after a short recession caused by the crisis, the era of high-speed economic growth came to an end, and a period of low growth began. The government further geared housing policy towards the mass construction of owner-occupied housing to revitalize the economy, putting more stress on encouraging people to acquire their own houses with a mortgage provided by the GHLC.

In accordance with developmental state housing policy, which emphasized the importance of expanding middle-class home ownership, public housing was further

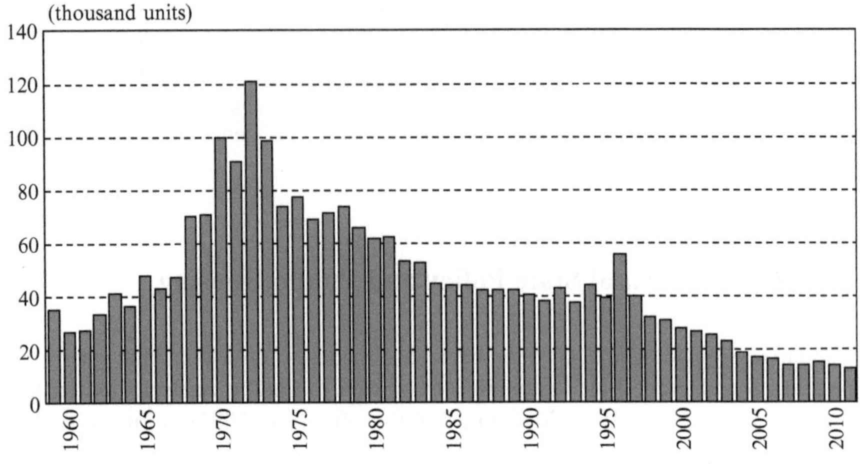

Fig. 9.1 New starts of public housing (Source: Ministry of Land, Infrastructure and Transport and Tourism)

residualized. New starts of public housing, which had increased until the end of the 1960s, began to decrease in the early 1970s (see Fig. 9.1). To residualize public housing systematically, the income criteria for moving into public housing were progressively narrowed (Hirayama 2007). At the time of the 1951 Act, the majority of households, or the lowest 80 % of all income groups, qualified for public housing. However, this percentage dropped to 40 % in 1968, to 33 % in 1973, and then to 25 % after the amendment of the Act in 1996. In addition, a series of discriminatory measures were developed in relation to households whose incomes increased after moving into public housing. The 1959 amendment established a system in which a household whose income exceeded a certain amount was required to make an effort to move out, and the 1969 amendment made it possible for local governments to formally request those with higher incomes to move out. Although the system of rent calculation was originally based on the cost of building construction and site acquisition, the 1996 amendment introduced a new system of rent calculation based on a set of factors that included tenants' incomes. As a result, residents with improved incomes have increasingly been pressured to move out of public housing because they have been required to pay market-level rents and have lost any economic advantages of living in public housing. Furthermore, "welfare categories" have been introduced in terms of more restrictive criteria and necessary qualifications to move into public housing. Although overall public housing provision has been reduced, special public housing provision, exclusively for elderly people, those with disabilities, and single-parent households, has been increased. Public housing is now for the "deserving poor" and has been justified for as long as it has been residualized. It has become increasingly difficult to be regarded as worthy of the title "the deserving poor" simply by being a low-income earner.

Within the framework of Japan's postwar home-ownership-oriented housing policy, many people have ascended the housing ladder from rented to owner-occupied housing, which has expanded the mainstream society (Hirayama 2003, 2007). Until the 1960s, public housing was aimed at young households with lower incomes, and they were expected to move out of public housing after a short period and acquire their own housing as their incomes increased. Within this context, public housing was a step on the housing ladder that eventually led to the social mainstream. Since the 1970s, however, the government has separated public housing from mainstream society. Thus, public housing, which has been removed from the housing ladder, has increasingly functioned as an isolated domain where the classes with the lowest income live indefinitely.

In the early postwar era, the Japan Housing Corporation was expected to play a key role in providing adequate dwellings to an increasing number of urban middle-income households. In large cities, such as Tokyo and Osaka, the JHC developed multifamily housing estates called *Danchi*, where concrete structures and open spaces were combined on a large scale to represent a postwar modern landscape (Hirayama 2003). New starts of JHC housing, however, began to decrease at the beginning of the 1970s. The difficulties the JHC was confronting in developing housing estates had grown by the 1970s. Within the context of a rapid increase in land prices, development sites became increasingly distant from city centers, rents rose sharply, and a large number of housing units became vacant. Local governments began refusing to give permission for developments by the JHC because they had neither the intent nor the ability to bear the responsibility for providing residents in JHC estates with road infrastructure, utilities, and schools.

Japan's developmental state policy corresponded with the formation of the "Japanese-style welfare society." From the late 1970s to the 1980s, a dispute emerged over whether or not European welfare state models should be applied in Japan, within the context of Japan's growing affluence, because a stark contrast between economic prosperity and poor public welfare provision had been developing (Hirayama 2007). With the beginning of a period of low growth in the 1970s, however, LDP politicians and government bureaucrats began to construct policy discourses that emphasized the necessity to develop a "Japanese-style welfare society" (Shinkawa 1993). The basic idea was to revitalize the traditional Japanese spirit and practice of mutual help and to characterize families, companies, and local communities as principal welfare providers. In particular, reciprocal family relations with residential property ownership were positioned as central pillars of Japan's welfare approach. In addition, the "company society" system was considered to be a key element in providing welfare. In the view presented by conservatives, Western welfare states failed to maintain vigorous economies due to increased dependence on public welfare, and traditional Japanese society and its value system were superior in sustaining the vitality of the nation. The LDP-run government carefully avoided using the term "welfare state" and instead sought to popularize the expression "welfare society," suggesting its intention to rationalize the limited expansion of state welfare. Within the framework of this "Japanese-style welfare society," the conservative administration preferred an owner-occupied housing sector to a rented housing sector and further marginalized the public housing system.

Thus, the shape of Japan's postwar housing policy became clearer in the 1970s, and this raised questions as to how it should be understood. In this respect, there have been various attempts to analyze the Japanese housing system in comparison with its Western counterparts and within the context of East Asia. Esping-Andersen (1997) drew on his own welfare-state typology (Esping-Andersen 1990) to suggest that Japan's case is a hybrid of liberal and conservative regimes, implying a lack of social democratic aspects in its welfare system. As Harada (1985) and Ohmoto (1985), among others, pointed out, the state of Japan, which has never set out to expand the social housing sector, has differed from the European welfare states in terms of formulating housing policy strategies. Holliday (2000) sought to situate social policies in East Asian nations, including Japan, within his conceptual framework of "productivist welfare capitalism," in which social policies were subordinated to the imperatives of economic development. According to Groves et al. (2007), the growth of home ownership has progressively played a more significant role in shaping "property-owning welfare states" in East Asian nations, including Japan, as well as some European countries (see also Malpass 2008; Ronald 2008). A complete consensus on the characteristics of Japan's housing policy has not yet been reached. However, there is likely to be agreement with regard to a low level of social housing and a high level of home ownership, along with public policy prioritizing economic development in the formation of the Japanese postwar housing system.

9.4 Neoliberalism and the Housing Safety Net

Since the mid-1990s, Japan's housing system has been radically reorganized to put it in line with neoliberal policy, expanding the market economy in providing housing and mortgages (Forrest and Hirayama 2009; Hirayama 2010a, b; Hirayama and Ronald 2007). Neoliberalism refers to a political-economic project involving reduced state intervention in social and economic affairs and the assertion of the superiority of market processes, proposing that human well-being can best be advanced by liberating individual entrepreneurial freedoms and skills within an institutional framework characterized by private property rights, free markets, and free trade (Harvey 2005). In Japan, as in many other advanced economies, the housing sphere has been the main target of liberalization. As Torgersen (1987) suggested, housing has been positioned as a "wobbly pillar" of social policy because compared with education, health care, and social security, housing is much more likely to be provided in the market domain. Housing systems have thus been particularly vulnerable to ideological transformations and have been at the forefront of policy shifts.

Compared to Western countries, particularly those that are Anglo-Saxon, the introduction of neoliberal policies in Japan has been especially slow (Forrest and Hirayama 2009). While the liberalization of policy in Britain and the U.S. started in the early 1980s, Japan's version of neoliberal policy did not begin to emerge until the mid-1990s. The LDP, along with government bureaucrats, had played a key role in controlling developmental state policy in Japan. Therefore, the radical adoption of neoliberal policy by the LDP might have meant an attack on itself, generating a contradiction within its political base. Moreover, unlike the economies of Western countries that had experienced prolonged recession since the oil crisis in the early 1970s, Japan's economy had maintained a relatively strong performance until the bubble burst. This accounted for the delay in reorganizing policy. With the long-standing stagnation after the bubble period, however, the perceived crisis in the developmental state began to fuel the reorientation of policy. In September 2009, the party in power changed from the LDP to the DPJ. The DPJ administration maintained the basic course of policy to liberalize the market economy that the LDP had adopted. Then, in December 2012, the LDP returned to power.

To adopt a neoliberal course, the Housing Construction Plan Law, which had provided a foundation for traditional housing policy, was discontinued in 2005. This was followed by the 2006 enactment of the Housing and Livelihood Basic Law, which reoriented the roles played by the government and private sector in operating a new housing system towards a more liberalized market economy. Within the framework of neoliberal policy, the government started to reduce the supply of GHLC loans in the mid-1990s and ultimately abolished the corporation in 2007. The dissolution of the state agency, which had constituted the core of the housing system, was an important watershed in the postwar history of Japan's housing policy. The large vacancy in the housing loan market created by the abolition of the GHLC was swiftly filled with the expansion of mortgages supplied by private banks. Moreover, the Housing and Urban Development Corporation, the successor to the Japan Housing Corporation, was reorganized into the Urban Development Corporation in 1999 and again into the Urban Renaissance Agency in 2004. The new agency reduced its commitment to public housing schemes substantially. In terms of low-income public housing, new starts, which had already been on the decrease, came to an almost complete halt. In addition, since the early 2000s, the reconstruction of public housing developments has tended to result in a decrease in the number of dwellings. This has led to a reduction in the overall stock of public housing.

Since the bubble burst, continued economic decline has undermined the security of housing, and the government has thus been pressed to form a housing safety net system for those who cannot access adequate, affordable housing in the competitive sphere of the market. This led to the 2007 enactment of the Housing Safety Net Law. However, the adoption of a neoliberal course in formulating policy meant that the government has sought to construct only a minimal housing safety net (Hirayama 2010a). The principal measure for forming a housing safety net is to provide low-income public housing. However, the number of available public rented dwellings has been significantly limited. The government has sought to reinforce the housing safety net by implementing new housing programmes that reach beyond the supply of low-income public housing, which has, for example, encouraged owners of private rental properties to accept older people with low incomes as tenants. Nonetheless, the scale of these new programmes has been very small. Essentially, housing policies have been contradictory; the government has had no choice but to construct a housing safety net for those who are not able to enter the housing market, but at the same time, it has restricted the coverage of the housing safety net to expand market-based housing.

Since the mid-1990s, with the introduction of neoliberal policy, public housing has become more clearly characterized as "welfare housing." Neoliberal policy has focused on labour market participation rather than public assistance in addressing social issues pertaining to the economic conditions of low-income people (Saunders 2005). In line with this, the Japanese housing safety net system has targeted a limited number of those regarded as unable to enter the labour force. This has been based on the assumption that employable people can and should secure housing within the framework of the market economy. Therefore, the government has reinforced the tendency of public housing to more narrowly target specific groups that coincide with "welfare categories." Elderly people and single parents, among others, are disadvantaged when it comes to entering the labour market and thus are seen as more qualified for public housing. Households that do not fit into the "welfare categories" are seen as employable and expected to find housing in the market. The 2007 Housing Safety Net Law defined low-income groups, including homeless people, disaster victims, single-parent households, and the elderly, as well as households rearing children, as "people qualified for public support in securing housing." Most of these groups have been positioned as targets of the housing safety net system because they are not easily employable. Households raising children do not necessarily have low employability, but in the context of declining fertility, the housing security of these households has become a policy priority. After the 1996 amendment of the Public Housing Act, it became possible for local governments to relax the income level limits related to moving into public housing for the elderly and some other "welfare category" households.

Many developed countries have reshaped their housing systems by reducing government assistance for social rented housing sectors (Fitzpatrick and Stephens 2008; Whitehead 2003). However, the impact of neoliberalization on housing conditions has differed according to the policy trajectory of each particular country. Even if new construction of low-income housing is reduced, the supply of social rented housing built in the past plays a significant role in providing housing opportunities for low-income people in the present and the future. Up until the 1960s, many European countries built a large number of social rented housing units consisting not only of public housing owned by the government sector but also of low-rent housing provided by nonprofit organizations and subsidized private rental housing (Balchin 1996). Despite neoliberalization, these countries still maintain a considerable quantity of social rented housing. According to data released in the early 2000s, the rate of social rented housing was 35 % in the Netherlands, 21 % in Britain, 18 % in Sweden, and 17 % in France (Kemp 2007). In contrast, neoliberal policy has further residualized the social rented housing sector in Japan, which had consisted almost exclusively of housing owned by the public sector and had been historically marginalized.

As has been discussed, corporate-based employee housing and low-rent private rented housing, in addition to public rented housing, have constituted the low-income housing sector in Japan. However, neoliberal prescriptions, along with the post-bubble economic decline, have begun to unravel the overall mechanisms for providing low-rent housing. After the bubble burst, the deep recession began to erode the economic foundations of the "company society" system, resulting in a decrease in the supply of employee housing. Moreover, neoliberal policy has led to the "casualization" of the labour market. With the prolonged recession, increasing numbers of corporations began abandoning the system of lifelong employment and introduced a performance-based system to replace the seniority system. In addition, along with the deregulation of employment practices, the labour market has been reoriented around declining stability in employment, with associated sharp increases in the number of short-term contracts, part-time workers, and temporary employees. The provision of employee housing, which was instrumental in recruiting young people as longtime employees, corresponded to the lifetime employment system. Conversely, this "casualization" of employment practices has implied the decreased necessity for corporations to provide housing welfare.

In terms of the private rented housing market, the number of existing low-rent dwellings has been decreasing due to structural ageing or dilapidation. Most owners of low-rent properties had neither the financial ability nor intention to invest in material maintenance or improvements because of low profitability. This accelerated the decrease in low-rent properties. Furthermore, the government began to restructure the private rented housing market in alignment with neoliberal policy in the late 1990s. The intention was to "modernize" the system of providing and financing rental housing while establishing a more "professional" and profitable market for investments in private rented housing. This led to major amendments to the Housing Lease Act in 1999. Before this amendment, tenants' security of tenure was protected; thus, landlords could not easily evict them. However, with this amendment, it is now possible for owners to rent their houses for more limited periods and thus more accurately calculate their prospects of making profits. The government has also sought to establish a rental property security market, which requires yields from security investments to be more predictable. As a consequence of the new policy to modernize the private rented housing sector, low-rent dwellings provided by nonprofessional landlords are declining, while higher-rent dwellings financed by more professional investors are on the increase.

9.5 Regional Devolution and Public Housing

The neoliberal policy that the Japanese government has adopted not only expands the supply of market-based housing but also encourages the decentralization of housing policy jurisdiction (Hirayama 2010a). Since the mid-1990s, a decline in the allocation of national subsidies has increasingly forced local governments to become economically independent and to participate in interregional economic competition. This has been reflected in housing policy transformations and in other policies. This section looks at the impact that decentralization has had on the public housing system.

The regional devolution of housing policy has led local governments to devise creative measures to cope with local housing issues. It has become both possible and necessary for many municipalities to not simply accept policies of the central government but to experiment with their own ideas on housing issues. In the area of community development, collaboration between local governments, citizen groups, nonprofit organizations, and specialist groups has grown, leading to new housing programmes. The various new plans that have been germinating involve rehabilitating existing housing, exploiting local architectural materials, and designing housing estates that are harmonious with the local landscape.

However, it is both theoretically and practically impossible for local initiatives alone to expand the housing safety net system (Abe 2001). The large majority of local governments cannot be proactive in providing low-income public housing. The financial burden imposed on local governments by constructing and maintaining public housing is too heavy. Because public housing absorbs low-income people, it does not strengthen local tax bases but instead makes it necessary for local governments to increase welfare-related expenditures. If the financial burdens that local governments bear for low-income people become too heavy, middle-class voters will increasingly become dissatisfied with local policies. With neoliberal policy, public housing has been converted into "welfare housing," which has resulted in a decrease in rent revenues and an increase in rent arrears. A system aimed at reducing or even waiving rent for households whose incomes have fallen due to job loss or illness does exist. However, this system is not accompanied by subsidies from the central government and thus requires local governments to bear the full financial burden.

Before the adoption of neoliberal policy, the national government had practiced a top-down approach to encouraging local governments to construct and manage low-income public housing. The Housing Construction Plan Law, which was active from 1966 to 2005, involved allocating quotas related to the construction of public housing to local governments. This suggests that, without instruction and financial assistance from the central government, local governments would be reluctant to provide low-income housing.

Along with the expansion of the market economy and the emergence of interregional economic competition, local governments have begun to establish policies to strengthen their competitiveness. Simultaneously, the view that housing measures aimed at low-income people do not enhance local competitiveness but rather impede it has become more widespread. According to *The Asahi Shimbun*'s research in 2010 on the future plans of 47 prefectural governments and 19 large city governments regarding the quantity of low-income public housing, 16 prefectures and four cities said that they would reduce public housing properties, while only one prefecture and one city indicated that they would increase them (28 prefectures and 12 cities said they would maintain the current quantity, and two prefectures had no plans related to the future amount of public housing).

Within the context of decentralized housing policy and increased economic competition, local governments have tended to favour housing measures that expand the middle-class housing market to increase the number of middle-class taxpayers and consumers. While the central government has not yet developed a rent allowance system, some local governments in large cities have implemented their own such programmes. However, typical local rent allowance programmes are not aimed at low-income people but are focused on newly married young couples. This is based on the assumption that young couples will increase their income in the future and help bolster the local government's capital. These rental subsidy programmes are not only housing policy measures but also local economic strategies. According to 2009 data provided by the government, 75 municipalities implemented 120 local programmes pertaining to rental allowance. Young newly married couples accounted for 83 % of all households that benefitted from local rental subsidy programmes. The percentages of single-parent households and elderly households were very low at 5 % and 4 %, respectively.

The fiscal system has also been reorganized to align with neoliberal policy that promotes regional devolution of housing jurisdiction. This is best represented by the integration of various individual national subsidies, including those related to housing, into a "block grant" package whereby limits to local government's discretionary power regarding the formulation and implementation of local programmes are relaxed. The new fiscal system will undoubtedly lead local governments to adopt more competition-oriented strategies and to further residualize low-income housing policy. The 2005 Local Housing Special Law systematized a housing related block grant system. This was followed by the introduction of the Social Capital Block Grant in 2010, which integrated not only housing-related subsidies but also various individual subsidies for road construction, water supply, and community development, as well as other subsidies over which the MLIT had jurisdiction. Transformations in the fiscal system are providing the basis to further liberalize and decentralize housing policy and marginalize the housing safety net system.

9.6 Transformations in Housing Conditions

What then are the consequences of neoliberal policy in the area of low-income housing? This last section explores transformations in the housing conditions of low-income groups. In response to the post-bubble stagnation, neoliberal thought was introduced to formulate policy with expectations of stimulating economic recovery; accordingly, the reorientation of housing policy towards accentuating the role of the market in supplying and consuming housing was considered to be effective in improving the housing situation. However, Japan's economy has continued to decline, and it has been increasingly difficult for low-income households to secure housing. Moreover, in alignment with neoliberal policy, the government has only constructed a minimal housing safety net and has further marginalized the public housing system that had traditionally been residual. Consequently, there has been a serious decline in housing opportunities provided to low-income groups. Japan's housing situation is now revealing limitations imposed by neoliberal policy in terms of enhancing housing security for low-income people.

The continued implementation of neoliberal policy has led to a substantial decrease in the availability of low-rent dwellings (Hirayama 2010b). As has been discussed, new construction of public housing has almost stopped, and the reconstruction of public housing developments has resulted in a reduced number of dwellings. The Urban Renaissance Agency has also begun to dispose of a number of rental properties. Thus, the number of public rented dwellings, including both low-income public dwellings and public corporation dwellings, decreased from 3,120,000 in 2003 to 3,010,000 in 2008. As has been argued, corporate-based employee housing, along with public housing, has constituted the "decommodified" housing sector. With the weakening of the "company society" system, however, many corporations have begun to unload considerable numbers of properties previously used for employee housing. The amount of employee housing, which was 2,050,000 in 1993, decreased to 1,400,000 in 2008. Consequently, the availability of "decommodified" housing has been significantly reduced. The ratio of public rented housing plus employee housing against all rented housing dropped from 31 % in 1993 to 25 % in 2008. The number of low-rent properties in the private rental housing market has also been on the decrease. Private rented multifamily dwellings of wooden structures, which are of low quality but have low rents, accounted for 24 % of all rented housing in 1993. The figure had decreased to 13 % by 2008.

According to the National Survey of Family Income and Expenditure, changes in the economic conditions of renters have been exacerbated by a combination of decreased nominal incomes and increased nominal rents, which has increased the burden imposed by rent payments (Hirayama 2010b). Since the bubble burst, the stagnated economy has continued to be deflationary. This has been reflected in the fact that the average nominal annual income of renters decreased from 6.3 million yen in 1994 to 5.6 million yen in 2009. The average nominal monthly rent, which was 29,800 yen in 1989, rose to 50,500 yen in 2009. The deflationary economy and the associated decrease in incomes might have been expected to encourage a drop in market rents. Nevertheless, real rent levels have continued to rise. The main factor behind this is the reduced availability of low-rent housing. As a result, the average rent-to-income ratio continuously increased from 9.6 % in 1989 to 15.1 % in 2009.

Low-income public housing has played a central role in forming a housing safety net. As has been argued, however, the government has increasingly emphasized the marginal nature of the public housing system in accordance with a more neoliberal direction and has progressively limited its target recipients to the lowest-income groups. Public housing was often constructed on large-scale developments on the fringes of cities, where people with low incomes were housed together. This has

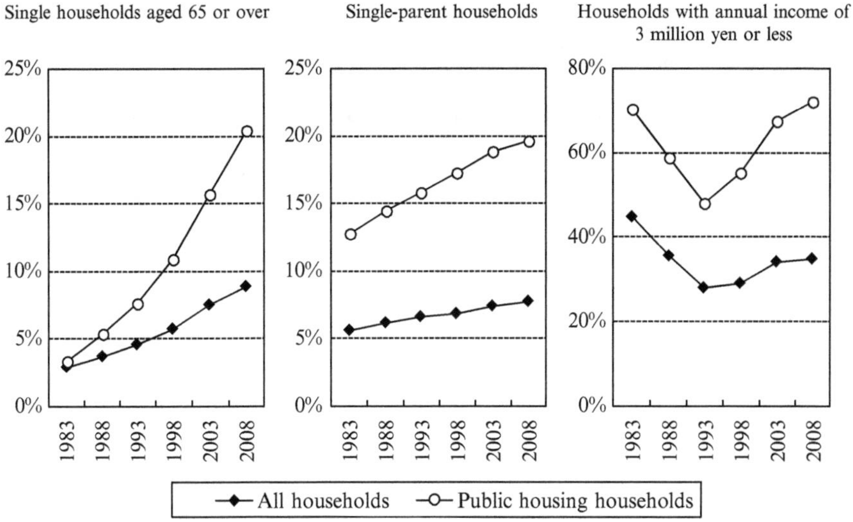

Fig. 9.2 Ratios of elderly single households, single-parent households and low-income households (Source: Housing Survey of Japan and Housing and Land Survey of Japan)

increasingly separated public housing estates from surrounding neighbourhoods both socially and spatially. As shown in Fig. 9.2, the differences between households in public housing and all other households have widened sharply in terms of the percentages of elderly single people, single-parent households, and low-income households. Public housing, where low-income households have lived for longer periods, has also been removed from the housing ladder. As Fig. 9.3 shows, there has been a decrease in households that have moved out of public housing, which indicates an increase in those who permanently remain in public housing.

Furthermore, the "casualization" of the labour market has combined with a decline in the availability of low-rent housing to create a new housing crisis characterized by an increase in the number of people who have lost both employment and housing (Hirayama 2010a). Particularly since the late 2000s, when Japan began to be affected by the global financial crisis, housing security among low-income people has been seriously undermined. Many manual workers who had lived in company dormitories were laid off, resulting in an increase in those who lost both jobs and dwellings simultaneously. Increasing numbers of renters in the private rental housing market have been unable to pay their rent, largely due to job losses. Consequently, the forcible eviction of renters who are in arrears by landlords and rent guarantor firms has generated a new social problem.

In response to the housing crisis, the government began to launch a series of emergency housing measures to cope with displaced workers in the late 2000s (Hirayama 2010a). This involved, for example, temporarily providing rental allowances and various loans to finance living expenses. These emergency housing measures, meant to benefit displaced workers for limited periods, were designed

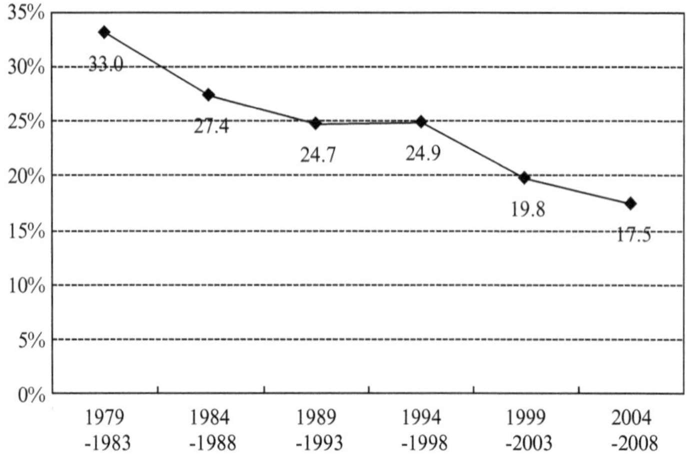

Fig. 9.3 Ratio of households who moved from public housing (Note: Ratio indicates percentage of households who moved from public housing during each period against all public housing households at the beginning of the period. Source: Housing Survey of Japan and Housing and Land Survey of Japan)

to encourage workers to return to the labour market and, subsequently, the housing market. This corresponded with the neoliberal principle accentuating the importance of participation in the labour market. The government has characterized the set of emergency housing programmes as a "trampoline-style second safety net." The concept was to build a "second safety net" that, added to the "first safety net" of the unemployment insurance system, would act as a "trampoline" by helping displaced workers bounce back into the labour market. Ideally, this would prevent workers from relying on public assistance as their "last safety net." With the spread of the housing crisis, the number of households wishing to move into public housing soared dramatically, but there were few public rental dwellings available. Thus, the "second safety net" was expected to help people return to the labour and then the housing market.

However, emergency housing measures have not been significantly effective in securing dwellings. The expansion of neoliberal policy has been accompanied by a cycle in which the liberalization of market forces has translated into a more precarious market. With the "casualization" of the labour force, laid-off workers cannot necessarily find new employment opportunities, and even if they do return to the labour market, they cannot necessarily earn sufficient wages to access the housing market. Moreover, as has been discussed, there has been a decrease in the supply of low-rent housing. Even when displaced workers do reenter the labour market, it has progressively become more difficult for them to secure affordable places to live in because of transformations in the housing market. The decline in the availability of low-rent housing has critically undermined the effectiveness of emergency housing measures.

9.7 Conclusion

In many developed countries, neoliberalism has been pervasive and even normative in shifting housing policies towards expanding market economies, resulting in a decline in social rented housing sectors. However, the impact of neoliberalization on housing processes has been strongly differentiated according to the housing situation at the time at which the policy shift took place. In many European countries, even after neoliberal policy began to affect the organization of housing systems, the large accumulated supply of social rented housing, along with the development of rent allowance systems, played a significant role in providing low-income people with housing. In contrast, Japan's postwar housing policy has consistently favoured the growth of middle-class home ownership, while the public rented housing sector has been residual, and rent subsidy systems have not existed. This deficiency has combined with neoliberal policy to even further marginalize low-income housing. In Japan, not only public housing but also employee housing and some private rented housing have made up the low-rent housing sector. Along with neoliberalization, however, the overall system of providing housing at low rents has progressively disintegrated. Among developed countries, Japan's housing safety net system has been particularly flimsy.

The experience of Japan suggests a new question with regard to whether or not the consequences of neoliberal policies will lead to reshaped housing systems. In Japan, neoliberal practices have been considered to facilitate economic recovery, and the expansion of market-based housing has been expected to improve housing conditions. However, along with prolonged economic stagnation, it has become progressively difficult for those on low incomes to find adequate housing in the sphere of the market. Moreover, a decline in public housing, as well as employee housing and low-rent private housing, has disintegrated the system of providing affordable housing to low-income groups. With the reduced availability of public and other low-rent housing, a new housing crisis has provoked a sharp increase in people who cannot secure dwellings. It is thus likely that the Japanese government will be pressed to reconsider the organization of housing policy and improve the conditions of low-income housing. At this point, it is not certain whether the Japanese government will undertake a substantial restructuring of housing policy beyond neoliberalism. What is certain is that the current, residualized low-income housing system will not be able to overcome the housing crisis.

References

Abe M (2001) Jutaku seisaku niokeru jichitai no yakuwari [The role of municipalities in housing policy]. In: Harada S (ed) Nihon no Toshi Hou vol. 2 [Japan's Urban Laws vol. 2]. Tokyo University Press, Tokyo, pp 299–320

Balchin P (ed) (1996) Housing policy in Europe. Routledge, London

Esping-Andersen G (1990) The three worlds of welfare capitalism. Polity Press, Cambridge

Esping-Andersen G (1997) Hybrid or unique?: the Japanese welfare state between Europe and America. J Eur Soc Policy 7(3):179–189
Fitzpatrick S, Stephens M (eds) (2008) The future of social housing. Shelter, London
Forrest R, Hirayama Y (2009) The uneven impact of neo-liberalism on housing opportunities. Int J Urban Reg Res 33(4):998–1013
Fujita Y, Shionoya Y (eds) (1997) Kigyo nai Fukushi to Shakai Hosho [Employee benefits and social security]. Tokyo University Press, Tokyo
Fukui H (1992) The Japanese state and economic development: a profile of a nationalist-paternalist capitalist state. In: Applebaum RP, Henderson J (eds) State and development in the Asian Pacific Rim. Sage, London
Groves R, Murie A, Watson C (eds) (2007) Housing and the new welfare state: perspectives from east Asia and Europe. Ashgate, Aldershot
Harada S (1985) Sengo jutaku housei no seiritsu katei [The establishment process of housing laws in post-war Japan]. In: Institute of Social Science, Tokyo University (ed) Fukushi Kokka vol. 6: Nihon no Shakai to Fukushi [The welfare state vol. 6: Japanese society and welfare]. Tokyo University Press, Tokyo, pp 317–396
Harvey D (2005) A short history of neoliberalism. Oxford University Press, Oxford
Hayakawa K (2002) Japan. In: Agus MA, Doling J, Lee D (eds) Housing policy systems in south and east Asia. Palgrave Macmillan, Houndmills, pp 20–37
Hirayama Y (2003) Housing and social inequality in Japan. In: Izuhara M (ed) Comparing social policies: exploring new perspectives in Britain and Japan. Polity Press, Bristol, pp 151–171
Hirayama Y (2007) Housing and state strategy in post-war Japan. In: Groves R, Murie A, Watson C (eds) Housing and the new welfare state: perspectives from east Asia and Europe. Ashgate, Aldershot, pp 101–126
Hirayama Y (2010a) Neoliberal policy and the housing safety net in Japan. City Cult Soc 1 (3):119–126
Hirayama Y (2010b) Housing pathway divergence in Japan's insecure economy. Hous Stud 25 (6):777–797
Hirayama Y, Ronald R (2007) Housing and social transition in Japan. Routledge, London
Holliday I (2000) Productivist welfare capitalism: social policy in east Asia. Political Stud 48:706–723
Kemp P (ed) (2007) Housing allowances in comparative perspective. Policy Press, Bristol
Machimura T (2004) Kaihatsushugi no shuen ka, atarashii kaihatsushugika [The end of developmetalizm or new developmentalizm]. In: Watanabe O (ed) Henbo Suru Kigyo Shakai Nihon [Transformations in Japan's company society]. Junpo Sha, Tokyo
Malpass P (2008) Housing and the new welfare state: wobbly pillar or cornerstone? Hous Stud 23 (1):1–19
Morimoto N (1994) Toshi Kyoju to Chintai Jutaku [Urban rental housing]. Gakugei Shuppan Sha, Kyoto
Murakami Y (1992) Han Koten no Seiji Keizai Gaku [Political economy of anti-classics]. Chuou Koron Sinsha, Tokyo
Ohmoto K (1985) Fukushi kokka to wagakuni jutaku seisaku no tenkai [The welfare state and housing policy in Japan]. In: Institute of Social Science, Tokyo University (ed) Fukushi Kokka vol. 6: Nihon no Shakai to Fukushi [The welfare state vol. 6: Japanese society and welfare]. Tokyo University Press, Tokyo, pp 397–452
Ohmoto K (1996) Kyoju seisaku no gendai shi [Modern history of housing policy]. In: Ohmoto K, Kaino M (eds) Gendai Kyoju: Rekishi to Shiso [Housing policy: history and ideology]. Tokyo University Press, Tokyo, pp 89–120
Oizumi E (2007) Transformations in housing construction and finance. In: Hirayama Y, Ronald R (eds) Housing and social transition in Japan. Routledge, London, pp 47–72
Ronald R (2008) The ideology of home ownership: homeowner societies and the role of housing. Palgrave Macmillan, Basingstoke

Sato I (2007) Welfare regime theories and the Japanese housing system. In: Hirayama Y, Ronald R (eds) Housing and social transition in Japan. Routledge, London, pp 73–93
Saunders P (2005) Welfare to work in practice: social security and participation in economic and social life. Ashgate, Aldershot
Shinkawa T (1993) Nihongata Fukushi no Seiji-Keizaigaku [Political economy of Japanese-style social welfare]. San-ichi Shobo, Tokyo
Torgersen U (1987) Housing: the wobbly pillar under the welfare state. In: Turner B, Kemeny J, Lundqvist L (eds) Between state and market: housing in the post-industrial era. Almqvist and Wiksell International, Stockholm, pp 116–126
Whitehead C (2003) Restructuring social housing systems. In: Forrest R, Lee J (eds) Housing and social change: east-west perspectives. Routledge, London, pp 46–68

Part II
Public Housing in the West

Chapter 10
Public Housing in Europe and North America

Alan Murie

10.1 Introduction

Public housing has featured in most countries in Europe and North America, emerging at different times, in response to various demands and with changing roles. In its earlier forms it was distinguished from private sector housing because it was built, owned and controlled by central or local government and decisions about who lived there and what rents were charged were bureaucratically rather than market determined. Variations from this model included construction by the private sector for government and the use of various arms length or other agencies to own or manage housing on behalf of government. By 2012, more than 100 years after the earliest experiments, this type of public housing is now unusual in Europe and North America with municipal housing companies in Sweden and local authority housing in the UK being the closest to this model. Much of the public housing from previous eras has transferred to private housing tenures – although it may retain distinctive roles in the market associated with history, reputation, built form and location. The general trend has been to reduce the size of the public sector and diminish its distinctiveness through changes in policy and financing. Public housing has matured and passed through various transitions associated with growth and decline, a changing political, economic and social environment and innovation in financial, organisational and governance arrangements. Rather than forming a radical, competitive alternative to private provision that appeals to a wide section of the population, it has tended to become a safety net catering for lower income and vulnerable households.

Because of the extensive changes to public housing it has become normal to discuss it as part of a wider social rented sector with a greater variety of forms than early public housing. The most significant players in this wider social rented sector

A. Murie (✉)
Centre for Urban and Regional Studies, School of Geography, Earth and Environmental Sciences, University of Birmingham, Birmingham, UK
e-mail: a.s.murie@bham.ac.uk

J. Chen et al. (eds.), *The Future of Public Housing: Ongoing Trends in the East and the West*, DOI 10.1007/978-3-642-41622-4_10,

in Europe and North America are not state controlled but have differing degrees of independence from the state. They contract many services from the private sector and their financing, rents and management are often indistinguishable from the private sector. In essence the social rented sector has become much more like the private sector than earlier forms of public housing. The category social housing embraces various organisational arrangements and approaches to property management and maintenance, finance and rent setting that have much in common with the private sector. This is not to deny that it provides an alternative to the pure private sector model. European and North American public and social rented sectors exist alongside and separate from the private sector. In some cases these alternatives to the private market are substantial and act to compete with and moderate the operation of the private housing market. How far they succeed in doing this, for whom, and with what impact on life chances varies between and within countries.

The terms public and social rented housing conjure up various images. These may be images of high quality architecture and neighbourhood planning and of highly desirable images, high quality dwellings that act as a platform for social mobility. Or they may be of run down, poorly maintained, disordered concrete jungles that are difficult to manage and to live in. Some represent improvements in living conditions and redistribution of opportunity; others suggest places that entrap vulnerable households and add to the problems they experience. Such images may be accurate in particular places and at particular times but they are entirely misleading as representations that hold true across public and social housing in Europe and North America. Neither public nor social rented housing refers to a well-defined, single, category, to a uniform commodity or service or to intrinsic and common characteristics. Consequently it is important to exercise caution in generalising about public housing within and between countries. It is unwise to make sweeping rhetorical assertions about the sector irrespective of context and more appropriate to refer to public housing in specific places and at particular times. Robust generalisations are circumspect and acknowledge that the nature and role of public housing differs and is shaped by developments in other parts of the housing system, by social, economic and demographic change as well as by policies and practices operating within the sector and determining access to it.

The Chapters that follow this one provide insights into individual countries and focus on recent developments and debates that highlight issues of variation and change. This Chapter introduces these accounts by referring in turn to perspectives and transitions that underpin variations across Europe and America and to themes that are strongly represented in the research based literature on these countries.

10.2 Perspectives on Public Housing

Governments in Europe and North America responded to political, social and economic demands for affordable housing to varying extents and in different ways. In one ideal type form public housing involved public agencies directly funding, building, acquiring, owning and managing dwellings. In practice more mixed models were more common with both local and central government operating directly or through other agencies and working with partners including voluntary and private sector organisations; and approaches changed over time with ownership and responsibility being transferred between agencies and with changes in financial arrangements, accountability and governance. Public housing in this perspective is about production, ownership and management and not the characteristics of consumers.

In some countries public housing was always reserved largely for disadvantaged households with strict rules governing both allocation and continuing occupation. But the more common approach was to provide housing for people who lacked adequate housing and to provide them with a secure home irrespective of subsequent changes in circumstances. Public housing has generally been distinguished from social housing because it was not aimed purely or even mainly at the poorest sections of the population. It reflected wider values and ambitions (see e.g. Danermark and Elander 1994: Harloe 1985). Nevertheless in contemporary debate and with the widespread restructuring of housing the terms public and social rented housing have come to be interchangeable and refer to housing provided by not-for-profit agencies operating parallel to the private sector although usually using private funds. In this parallel sector access and prices may be set directly by public authorities and investment may be strongly influenced by government.

Every country has a distinctive history in terms of when and why public housing was developed, what form it took and what agencies were used, how it operated and what its social role was. Countries have different legacies in terms of the proportion of the dwelling stock and the vintage and types of dwellings associated with public housing, their location and quality, how they are financed and managed and where accountability rests. And as time has passed from when housing was initially built or acquired by public sector bodies changes have occurred in maintenance and repair, the social economic and political context and in ownership and management. In many countries privatisation has been a major feature and what was public housing is now private or owned by hybrid successor organisations.

Some indications of the scale of social rented housing is provided in Table 10.1. This shows a range from zero in Greece to 35 % in the Netherlands. The Table also highlights problems in finding statistics referring to the same years as well as over definitions of tenures.

It is important to recognize that if, in the past, public and social rented housing always operated with rents that were below market levels the picture today is more complex. In some cases policy and regulation has pushed rents up to or close to market levels and there has been a shift towards subject rather than object subsidy systems; rather than setting rents below market rates and so subsidizing rents for all tenants the tendency has been to move towards market rents and to provide assistance with housing costs through the social security system usually based on individual tests of income.

These statistics refer to one point in time and present some challenges. In relation to public housing they refer to a remnant after privatisation and transfer

Table 10.1 All households by tenure: selected countries of Europe and North America (%)

Country	Social renting	Owner occupation	Private renting	Others	Year
USA	3	68	30	–	2002
Canada	6	66	28	–	2001
Greece	0	80	20	0	2001
Portugal	7	76	15	2	1999
Hungary	4	92	3	1	2003
Lithuania	4	84	5	7	2002
Slovenia	7	82	3	9	2002
Czech Republic	19	47	10	24	2001
Iceland	2	78	5	16	2003
Germany	6	41	49	5	2001
Belgium	7	74	16	3	1999
Finland	17	64	15	4	2001
France	17	56	21	6	2002
Denmark	19	53	18	9	1999
UK	20	70	10	–	2001/2002
Sweden	21	55	24	–	1997
Austria	23	57	17	3	2001
Netherlands	35	53	12	–	1998

Source: Scanlon and Whitehead (2004)
Notes: Co-operative tenure in Sweden treated as owner-occupation

of stock to other tenures and do not capture the extent to which public housing has contributed to the character of other tenures. The statistics also reflect the distinctive pathways taken by different countries with housing built with public subsidy appearing in various tenures including the cooperative and not for profit housing that reflects the rich variety of alternatives developed in addition to public and private ownership.

The statistics presented above are compatible with an initial identification of four broad traditions within Europe and North America in relation to public housing intervention. Variation within each of these groups is considerable but there is a clear distinction between three types with low rates of public or social rented housing and a fourth type where generally higher levels of public and social rented housing reflect strong interventionist traditions.

1. In North America public housing was promoted in wartime and in periods of economic crisis but never commanded sustained support that crossed political and interest group boundaries and the implementation of programmes often attracted local resistance (Fuerst 1974; Varady et al. 1998). Although there were stronger ambitions in some cities public housing nationally accounted for a small share of the market and was largely regarded as welfare housing. Privatisation and regeneration significantly changed the sector and further reduced its size.
2. The countries of Southern Europe never developed strong interventionist housing policies. Policies operated in the context of family and community

based self-provision and self-promotion and state housing developments were generally limited. Where they did emerge some were sold to occupiers at the outset and the continuing role of the state in management and ownership remained small. Some privately owned estates have always been seen as public housing and these included poorer quality developments designed for particular groups (Allen et al. 2004; Hall et al. 2005).

3. Although Central and Eastern European countries now have very low levels of public housing, this is a consequence of sharp breaks in policy associated with political and economic changes (Hegedus 2007). The state, especially in the three decades from the 1950s dominated housing construction. Within centrally planned economies the role of state building companies and factory built housing was critical and the mass form of construction reflected the products and economics of this sector. Other policies had resulted in generally high levels of requisition or nationalization of the dwelling stock (especially in urban areas). Public housing, consequently, accounted for very significant shares of housing provision. Policies to sell dwellings especially to sitting tenants were often well developed before the political changes at the end of the 1980s introduced a variety of more active privatization and, in some cases, the restitution of properties to original owners. By 2010 these high interventionist countries mostly had very small remnant public housing sectors. Privatised estates nevertheless reflected the history of production, management and occupation and the differences in location and desirability that had affected the operation of the public sector. As Hegedus indicates (below) the systems emerging after privatization involved a variety of pragmatic adjustments rather than a common approach.

The fourth group includes countries in North and West Europe and includes countries with the longest traditions (Pooley 1992) and the largest continuing influence of public housing as well as remnant sectors. These countries generally developed public housing as a response to more pluralistic and democratic pressures than applied in central and Eastern Europe and even parts of Southern Europe. Consequently there are considerable variations in the share of publicly subsidised housing, its organization and character (Donner 2000; Lujanen 2004). Although the share of public and social rented housing has generally declined as a result of privatization, regeneration and recent patterns of new building the impact has not been as dramatic as in Eastern and Central Europe. In Sweden and Norway the strong co-operative housing tradition continued to shape a different pattern of housing. In Germany (see Knorr-Siedow below) a distinctive approach to subsidy supported a wide range of providers, including co-operatives, municipal and state-owned housing companies, larger institutional and small-scale private landlords. It also generated an automatic restructuring with the passage of time and a dramatic and continuing 'melting away' of social housing. In the UK and Ireland privatization through sales to individual sitting tenants dramatically reduced the municipal sector. This pattern has been repeated later and less dramatically elsewhere with France, the Netherlands and Sweden all adopting policies to sell dwellings.

Demunicipalization involving large scale transfers of stock to new landlords occurred at an earlier stage in the Netherlands than in the UK or Germany but in each of these cases the emerging system included robust housing associations with considerable independence from the state and a capacity to choose how far they adopted an approach similar to private landlords or adopted different principles and practices. Rents have moved closer to market levels but some are determined by considerations other than profit; lettings and management of tenancies gives some attention to housing and other dimensions of need and vulnerability and some elements of government regulation and public accountability exist. The debate about whether reorganizations represent privatization relates to the extent to which agencies adopt different policies and practices than the private sector (see Boelhouwer below and Malpass 2000; McDermont 2010).

In these countries public housing was generally built for households irrespective of their occupation and, with some exceptions in Central and Eastern Europe, few countries adopted practices similar to the Chinese tradition of building by state owned enterprises exclusively for their own workers. Nevertheless, some developments, because of location near particular places of employment, housed disproportionate numbers of people who worked together. Some state housing was always associated with higher standards or status and stratification within the public sector has been a constant feature. The competition for the most attractive public housing was always greater than for other estates and dwellings and the evidence suggests that what housing people accessed within the public sector was affected by bargaining power associated with ability to wait or occupational status. Households in the most desperate need were more likely to accept the least attractive dwellings and estates while others could hold on for something better. In all countries with significant public or not-for-profit housing, some neighbourhoods built by the state to house affluent working-class groups or a mix of income groups have become less attractive to middle-income groups. Social stratification between estates within state housing was normal in Central and Eastern European countries (Szelenyi 1983) and is evident in all state housing systems. As social and economic inequality has increased the least reputable and attractive estates have become more associated with lower income, unemployed and benefit dependent households and the concentration of deprivation in these neighbourhoods has come to be seen as an emerging problem for public policy. The different vintages designs and types of public housing are associated with stratification between more and less affluent working class households. The public sector reflected inequalities in a similar manner to the private sector: access to the best housing was achieved by households with most bargaining power and often higher incomes.

10.3 Explanations

Debates about why some countries have had more interventionist traditions than others form an important part of explanations related to public housing. Although every country in Europe and North America has a distinctive story, public housing was a common response to urbanization and the urban housing problem. There have been various attempts to identify groups of countries with broadly similar approaches (see e.g. Donnison 1967; Doling 1997). Assumptions that the extent or form of state intervention in housing, or the welfare state more generally is associated with industrialisation, stage of economic development or some other universal determinant have not stood up to critical analysis. Alternative approaches to explanation of similarities and differences between countries have tended to start with typologies of welfare states and assume that patterns of housing intervention are symmetrical with these. However this is unsatisfactory for various reasons. The most common starting point for this approach has been Esping-Andersen's (1990) identification of types of welfare state regime. Esping-Andersen emphasised decommodification and the importance in the welfare state of citizenship rights, rather than income, in determining access to services. Decommodifcation occurs 'when a service is rendered as a matter of right and when a person can maintain a livelihood without reliance on the market' (page 22). Esping-Andersen's conceptual framework and account of path dependency and political coalitions underpinning welfare systems is persuasive but in order to operationalise this in a manageable way he used a subset of measures of welfare state activity. He 'measured' the extent of decommodification by referring to the eligibility rules, levels of income replacement and entitlements offered by different countries' arrangements for old age or retirement pensions, sickness benefits and unemployment insurance. In effect this assessed selected dimensions of welfare state activity rather than the full extent of decommodification. He assessed how generous, universal and redistributive pensions, sickness and unemployment insurance systems were and provided a separate decommodification score for each of these three areas and a combined decommodification score (p. 52). It is this combined score that has attracted most attention and commonly been used to label welfare regimes as liberal, corporate or social democratic.

The operationalisation through a limited number of social security benefits neglects other social security and fiscal measures as well as education, health, housing and other services and interventions. Because social security measures are designed to complement and integrate with one another and with other measures reference to a selected subset provides a distorted view. There is also a concern that the particular time period selected influences the results and that there is a neglect of the role of other institutions such as the family, not for profit organisations and occupational welfare.

All of these considerations are very relevant to housing. The outputs from Esping-Andersen's quantitative analysis do not take account of the decommodification of housing, and the extent to which people are able to continue to live in housing even when they are unable to afford the market price for it. One potential indicator of this is the size of the public and not-for-profit sector in different countries. In practice the fit between Esping-Andersen's regime types and the share of housing in public and not-for-profit housing sectors is not a very good one. A country such as Belgium which has a very high decommodification score in Esping-Andersen's analysis has a very small public and not-for-profit housing sector. Switzerland which has a relatively high decommodification score similarly has a very small decommodified housing sector. In contrast, the United Kingdom in 1980 had a very large decommodified housing sector, (1 in 3 of all properties). Ireland has a very small decommodified housing sector and this fits with the decommodification score in Esping-Andersen. However a larger part of the housing stock of Ireland or the UK was built by the state and privatisation has involved subsidised rather than market sale. Consequently, the current housing structure obscures a much more substantial decommodified housing programme. In addition to these issues systems of housing allowances differ between countries and again affect the extent of decommodification.

The conclusion from this is that the nature of differences between housing systems can not be read off from the welfare regimes presented by Esping-Andersen. The processes that he argued have determined the welfare state also determine housing arrangements; but the complexity of these local and national processes means that the regime types identified by Esping-Andersen do not determine or correlate with structures of housing provision. Social security systems have developed in the context of patterns of housing provision and subsidy but Esping-Andersen's discussion of the politics of welfare states largely neglected housing and his quantitative analysis relies on national level data related to some social security benefits. This neglects the extent of payments in kind or, in the case of housing, the pattern of housing costs, specific housing subsidies and rights related to security of tenure. Housing provision and subsidy often varied considerably within countries as products of the local rather than national welfare state. Countries where specific housing subsidies and interventions through rent regulation and control or public housing provision were limited often set social security benefits at higher levels relative to income because housing costs were high and other policies to render housing secure and affordable were not so well developed. Some of these less interventionist countries appear, from Esping-Andersen's analysis, as having more generous and more redistributive regimes. Where complex, locally specific rent controls and housing subsidies (including object subsidies) have a greater impact on household budgets (and social security systems) this is insufficiently taken into account in the analysis and the tendency is for these countries to be categorised further towards the 'liberal' end of the spectrum than might otherwise be the case. Countries with less local and interventionist housing traditions are more easily subjected to Esping-Andersen's method which struggles to account for more complex policy and practice related to housing (and other payments in kind). The weaknesses of this approach are most apparent where highly interventionist public housing traditions operate within (and perhaps partly explain) less generous welfare states (Groves et al. 2007; Murie 2009). Allen et al. (2004) observe that 'large-scale quantitative studies…are institutionally thin, unable to describe particular societies in any depth. Comparison is bought at the expense of understanding how institutions are articulated within specific societies'. (p. 94).

Public housing gained governmental support because of political pressure to moderate market patterns: to build more (high quality) housing, replace slum housing, meet the demands and aspirations of ordinary working families and provide a steady investment to support economic growth. Much of the literature argues that working class pressure and threats to political order were key factors explaining the development of housing and wider welfare state arrangements, especially in Europe (Harloe 1985). The historical accounts of different countries demonstrate that even where there were similar pressures the timing and nature of responses varied. Different systems for housing production, ownership and management reflected various influences and compromises.

In addition to accounts of the origins of public and social rented housing and explanations for different starting points and foundations in terms of finance and organization there are alternative views of patterns of development over time. Accepting initial differences there has been a debate about whether housing policy systems are diverging or converging (e.g. Doling 1997; Malpass 2008). Some of this involves empirical observation about similar policies and actions (including privatization) but a more complex debate is about whether apparently similar trends occur as a response to common factors or occur for different reasons. In either case the outcomes of similar processes applied to different systems may not be the same.

When it comes to explaining why public sector and social rented housing expanded further, or declined or why its role and reputation changed there is some confusion. Some accounts (Power 1987, 1993) tend to look inwards and seek to explain these later changes by referring to policies applied to public housing: rents, allocation policies and housing management. Such inward looking explanations tend to explain change by referring to the landlord, the management regime, the financing of the sector or other housing policy factors. However, the importance of these elements needs to be balanced by reference to wider external influences: urban political pressures, changing demography, economic environment, professional and technical advocacy and changes in other tenures. Arguably, these factors are more important than the internal changes to social housing. This argument links with a broader perspective that the most powerful drivers of change in social housing are found in the housing market, society and the economy. The common transitions experienced across the very different public housing sectors in Europe and North America are attributable to these external drivers rather than common operation of the public sector itself.

10.4 Transitions

Explanations for different traditions in housing and public housing have tended also to emphasise path dependency and continuities associated with stable political coalitions. The largest, best-resourced public housing sectors emerged in the Netherlands, Sweden, Denmark, Finland, Austria and the UK where political coalitions had the strongest social and economic base and were sustained over time. Germany might also be included in this list although, as is explained below, it explicitly adopted an approach under which public housing melted away with the passage of time. Earlier policy actions affect the options available at later stages and path dependency is important in accounting for distinctive approaches to housing provision. As organisational arrangements and practices matured they themselves generated capacity, competence and further political support. The expertise in housing development and management expanded in these organisations and became a resource for governments seeking to address housing and economic problems.

While path dependency provides one important insight into public housing systems it is also essential to engage with a reality of significant change even where there have not been dramatic breaks in continuity associated with war or dramatic political and economic changes. Public housing systems have undergone a number of transitions which add further levels of complexity and difference to those associated with their origins. Path dependency is not the same as path determination. Some options are not available if there is no legacy to work with, but significant changes in policy direction do occur even where strong legacies exist. In this sense the breaks in continuity in Central and Eastern European systems and those associated with transfers of ownership, privatisation and regeneration elsewhere are important transitions and can be briefly considered alongside others associated with the passage of time:

- Demographic transitions. The populations living in public housing have changed with the demographic structure of populations. More older households, single person households and smaller families are also associated with cohort effects. New tenants have tended to be younger and in early stages of their housing career but cohorts ageing in place change the characteristics and needs of residents over time.
- A relatively uniform sector develops new fault lines with new construction that reflects the changing designs, materials, economics and technologies dominating construction and with new development is in different locations within the city region.
- Physical and social obsolescence. Over time some elements of dwellings prove unsuitable, deteriorate physically or are regarded as unattractive. Some designs, construction types and energy technologies do not stand the test of time and are rejected by households able to exercise choice.
- Economic transitions. Some public housing that attracted middle and higher income groups and occupational categories, because its design, facilities and location was superior to much of what was available in other tenures lost its comparative advantage as other tenures offered new choices. Changes in the occupational and class structure and changes in local economies and commuting patterns have added a further layer of change.
- Tenure transitions. As older privately rented housing declined the lower income groups that had continued to live in this tenure as public housing developed increasingly sought housing in the public sector. Private renting also ceased to be the main alternative to public housing for other income groups. At the same time the promotion and privileging of home ownership, through various public policies and market developments, changed the availability of accessible new housing in other tenures and locations and perceptions of public housing.

- The dominant policy approaches associated with the establishment and construction of public housing generally included significant initial subsidy that would diminish over time. New subsidy was needed for further new building or acquisition but over time the historic debts associated with any development would decline in real terms. It has been argued that this financial maturation would enable public housing to become self sustaining over time and to be able to operate with rents below market levels without requiring the levels of social security support that market priced renting would. In practice the orthodoxies in favour of setting rents at or approaching market levels, adopting subject rather than object subsidies and dismantling public housing through privatisations (at heavily discounted prices) have altered the financial model and its effectiveness.

Andersson (below) refers to different stages in the development of housing provision in the five Nordic countries. Similar phases could be identified elsewhere. The transitions referred to above mean that public housing is not a fixed commodity but its status and role is constantly revised. All countries in Europe and North America have long passed beyond the establishment and expansion phases associated with early urbanization. All of them have encouraged an individualised home ownership sector associated with asset building by households and this has changed what is generally perceived as the main alternative to public housing. When the alternative was private renting the competitive advantages of public housing were more categorical. As governments have favoured home ownership they have also reduced investment and state engagement in public housing. The political and ideological debate has shifted with the advantages of home ownership being overstated and the intrinsic weakness of public housing being asserted. Where in practice the maturation of public housing left it as a sustainable alternative to private housing the dismantling of public housing through privatization has further shifted the balance of advantage away from public housing.

10.5 Privatisation

There is a very substantial research based literature referring to the privatisation of public housing (Jones and Murie 2006). This key transition has affected each of the groups of countries identified above but naturally has been most significant where public housing had been most strongly represented. Some countries had sold housing built by the state or with public funds as soon as it was built or shortly after. In other cases there are repeated examples of small numbers of properties being sold to sitting tenants. Larger scale stock transfers from municipal to other landlords also occurred in the Netherlands and elsewhere. The most controversial and radical changes however are associated with mass sales to home ownership in the 1970s and later. In the UK individual municipalities pioneered council house sales before there was a Right to Buy (Murie 1975) and similar policies were adopted elsewhere.

So, for example, Hungary or Bulgaria had expanded home ownership through sales of public housing before the political and economic changes of 1989.

The scale of privatisation through sales of public housing to sitting tenants expanded dramatically in the UK as a result of legislation in 1980. This gave almost all sitting tenants the Right to Buy the property they lived in with very generous discounts that reduced the prices paid well below market levels. This policy attracted wide interest and in subsequent decades all public housing regimes have adopted some similar approach to privatisation. Some, especially in Central and Eastern Europe provided even more generous discounts on market prices; others (e.g. in France, Sweden and the Netherlands) were initially more limited in application or remained discretionary.

The dominant debates about the impact of privatisation across Europe and North America refer to the growth of home ownership. Opportunities to buy were not taken up by all tenants and even in the Central and Eastern European countries, where purchase was most common, it was lowest income and older households and those in the least attractive properties who did not buy. In the UK, for example, purchasers were typically more affluent, middle-aged tenants living in attractive properties. Most tenants bought with no intention of moving or making a speculative gain and if they purchased with a mortgage it was low relative to property value (because of discounts). The best properties in the best locations sold most and this pattern along with the lack of new council building reconcentrated council housing in less attractive urban estates, flats and non-traditional dwellings (Forrest and Murie 1990). Sales benefitted the existing generation, which had graduated to valuable locations and properties at the expense of households awaiting the opportunity to succeed them as tenants. The receipts from sales were rarely used for housing related activities.

If we move beyond the generation directly affected by privatisation the complexity increases. For example in England some of the growth in home ownership proved temporary as some sold council houses were resold to private renting (with fewer to social renting). The proportions involved vary between places: in parts of London around 25 % had become private rented by 2002 (Jones and Murie 2006) and on large council estates in Birmingham up to 40 % of growth in private ownership was private renting (Murie 2008). In Germany the process of privatisation meant that some transfers were direct to private landlords and there is every reason to believe that the English experience will not prove an exception and will be mirrored elsewhere. One perspective is that subsidies in the form of discounted prices temporarily inflate the level of home ownership. In subsequent transactions, at market prices, putative owner-occupiers had no equivalent subsidy and buy to let purchasers could pay more. What purported to be a populist response to the demand for home ownership became a two-stage transfer. Initial privatisation was a state subsidised transfer from collective to individual ownership. In the subsequent commodification stage transfers to a deregulated private rented sector neither matched household aspirations nor politicians' commitments to home ownership and responsible renting. The assumption that privatisation of public housing would leave an uncomplicated legacy of expanded home ownership needs modification in view of subsequent sales to private landlords.

10.6 Residualisation

Privatisation policies changed the size of the public sector, further narrowed its social base and speeded the transition towards a more residual or welfare service targeted on the poorest and most vulnerable households rather than on a wider mix of households. However it is important to recognise that residualisation of public housing is not simply a consequence of privatisation. This has been most fully discussed in relation to the UK where residualisation (Forrest and Murie 1983) reflected various factors including demographic and economic changes that contributed to increased income and social inequality. Private rented housing had provided the main housing opportunities for the poorest, especially where rents and standards were low and as this sector declined the poorest households were increasingly dependent on public housing. At the same time the expansion of access to home ownership and the advantages associated with it drew demand from younger, affluent working class households away from public housing. This change in the pool of demand for public housing led to changes in the social and economic profile of public sector tenants irrespective of what allocation policies were adopted and it is misleading to attribute residualisation to changes in rationing processes. Similarly changes in housing subsidy (from object to subject subsidies) and privatisation speeded and deepened residualisation but did not explain it.

Although some commentators suggested that residualisation was an aspect of UK exceptionalism it is now evident that it is the common experience across Europe. Residualisation of public housing is commonly referred to wherever significant, socially mixed public sector housing existed in the past. The attractions of home ownership, greater inequality and changes in the structure of the housing market have had similar effects everywhere.

10.7 Legacies

Public housing in Europe and North America leaves a number of legacies – most obviously in dwellings that provide homes for people in different tenures. The collective public sector housing legacy includes dwellings generally attracting high demand and high satisfaction and others that are much more difficult to live in. The evaluation of what public housing has contributed involves more than reference to the remnant residualised and stigmatised sectors that still form public sector housing. In order to explain the legacies that exist we need to adopt layered explanations that embrace different origins, continuing political debates and important transitions. Such layered explanations will include similar processes and drivers but generate different outcomes. How, why, when and where processes take place and what outputs emerge accounts for differences between and within countries.

Residualisation and the transfer of some of the best public housing to the private sector altered the perception and reality of public housing. Some commentaries suggest that newly acquired characteristics and those arising from complex external factors were intrinsic attributes associated with municipal ownership, bureaucratic processes, absence of choice, security of tenure and subsidy systems. While such views are easily contested they resonate with neo-conservative views of family, faith and home and neo-liberal views related to the superiority of markets. Public housing had for various reasons lost the political, social and economic support that had contributed to its growth and the actions taken following this made it more exposed to agendas for 'reform'.

In this context a smaller public housing sector is more targeted and the fit between public housing and income, employment status, and occupation is strengthened. The combination of shrinking and targeting has dismantled the earlier vision of a classless or socially mixed tenure. And in some cases the safety net role also implies stronger links with migrant groups, ethnic and gender differences. The relabeling of public sector housing as social housing has partly reflected a clearer, narrower social role.

This legacy would only prove temporary if there was a prospect of rebuilding the share and reach of public sector housing. But such a prospect is difficult to imagine in view of the discourses around housing and public expenditure and the erosion of the asset base that could have cross subsidised growth and provided a platform for its expansion. The political debate across Europe and North America means that there is unlikely to be any going back on the developments of recent decades. Once transferred out former public sector dwellings are too expensive to buy back. The financing of expansion through acquisition or new construction would require new subsidy up front or continuing subsidy to assist with the higher rents needed to cover costs. Nevertheless social rented housing remains a better way of providing affordable housing than higher rent private provision. Where housing associations are robust and well resourced they have continuing capacity to invest and provide an alternative to private housing. In this sense their role and capacity is an important legacy.

10.8 Conclusions

This Chapter has outlined some of the debates that surround the role of public housing in Europe and North America. It has emphasised variation over time and between as well as within countries. It has argued that when seeking to explain aspects of public housing it is important to specify time and place and adopt a layered approach referring to contextual factors and transitions that have reshaped public housing. It is best to avoid grand generalisations about public housing and assertions that change is simply explained by the intrinsic nature of public housing and policies adopted towards it. Public housing has been and continues to be shaped by patterns and discourses related to inequality and social class. It has been and often still is a key resource for low income households, migrants irrespective of ethnicity and for ethnic minorities especially in urban areas. This role remains and may grow rather than diminish in the future through further residualisation or other developments.

Public and social rented housing in Europe and North America account for a much smaller share of the market than in the past but the legacy is larger than this suggests. In some cases the remnant sector may continue to decline. Hegedus' account of experience in Hungary applies to differing extents elsewhere. Privatization has left a low-quality public and social rented housing stock, concentrated in the worst parts of the city, needing rehabilitation and with tenant households experiencing multiple social problems. The costs and difficulties of management make further privatization attractive and further shrinkage is likely to exacerbate residualisation and segregation.

The remnant public sector will continue to be reshaped by political pressures reflecting different ideological positions. But it will also be reshaped by changes in affluence and inequality, changing employment, life styles and expectations and by how other tenures develop in the future. Public housing, looking forwards, is likely to undergo new transitions. These may, for example, arise because housing systems have become more dominated by the private sector and impose market costs and because there are greater differentials in earnings and higher levels of poverty. In this context, the private sector is unlikely to eliminate housing shortages. Trickle down or filtering does not deliver good quality housing to everyone and the market is less effective, than public housing, in providing high quality housing for the lowest income groups. In the new market dominated environment insecure, sub-standard housing is likely to remain or expand and lower income groups, newly forming households and migrants are likely to have limited choice and experience high housing costs. Government either accepts reduced housing standards for some citizens or higher social security costs or both. Middle income households are also affected by inflated housing costs and housing shortages and any squeeze on access to home ownership. Households whose circumstances change with age or loss of employment and income may also find the private market unsupportive. It may be that, in the future, neither home ownership nor private renting will provide sufficiently secure havens.

In this context the reliability, respect for housing rights and accountability of not for profit housing associations and the quality of their stock may make them attractive. Higher standards of maintenance and active regeneration may mean that social landlords offer better housing opportunities than private landlords. The extent to which social landlords provide a more attractive offer will depend upon the policies these organisations pursue – partly but not solely determined by their financing and regulation and by practices in the private sector. The next transition may involve some revalorisation of this remnant of public housing and put it in a position to command political support, investment capacity and a new phase of growth. The future of the sector will continue to reflect the wider environment in which it operates and the nature of alternatives to it.

References

Allen J, Barlow J, Leal J, Maloutas T, Padovani L (2004) Housing and welfare in Southern Europe. Blackwell, Oxford

Danermark B, Elander I (1994) Social rented housing in Europe: policy, tenure and design. Delft University Press, Delft

Doling J (1997) Comparative housing policy. Macmillan, London

Donner C (2000) Housing policies in the European Union. Christian Donner, Vienna

Donnison D (1967) The government of housing. Penguin, Harmondsworth

Esping-Andersen G (1990) The three worlds of welfare capitalism. Polity Press, Cambridge

Forrest R, Murie A (1983) Residualisation and council housing: aspects of the changing social relations of housing tenure. J Soc Policy 12(4):453–468

Forrest R, Murie A (1990) Selling the welfare state, 2nd edn. Routledge, London

Fuerst JS (1974) Public housing in Europe and America. Croom Helm, London

Groves R, Murie A, Watson C (2007) Housing and the new welfare state: perspectives from east Asia and Europe. Ashgate, Aldershot

Hall SG, Van Kempen R, Dekker K, Tosics I (eds) (2005) Restructuring large-scale housing estates in European cities: good practices and new visions for sustainable neighbourhoods and cities. Policy Press, Bristol

Harloe M (1985) The people's home: social rented housing in Europe and America. Blackwell, Oxford

Hegedus J (2007) Social housing in transition countries. In: Whitehead C, Scanlon K (eds) Social housing in Europe. LSE, London, pp 165–177

Jones C, Murie A (2006) The right to buy: analysis and evaluation of a housing policy. Blackwell, Oxford

Lujanen M (2004) Housing and housing policy in the Nordic countries. Nordic Council of Ministers, Copenhagen

Malpass P (2000) Housing associations and housing policy: a historical perspective. Macmillan, Basingstoke

Malpass P (2008) Histories of social housing: a comparative approach. In: Scanlon K, Whitehead C (eds) Social housing in Europe II. LSE, London

McDermont M (2010) Governing independence and expertise: the business of housing associations. Hart Publishing, Oxford

Murie A (1975) The sale of council houses: a study in social policy. Occasional paper, 35. CURS, University of Birmingham, Birmingham

Murie A (2008) Social housing privatisation in England. In: Scanlon K, Whitehead C (eds) Social housing in Europe II. LSE, London, pp 241–260

Murie A (2009) The modernisation of housing in England. Tijdschr Econ Soc Geogr 100 (4):535–548

Pooley CG (ed) (1992) Housing strategies in Europe, 1880–1930. Leicester University Press, Leicester

Power A (1987) Property before people. Allen & Unwin, London

Power A (1993) Hovels to high rise: state housing in Europe since 1850. Routledge, London

Scanlon K, Whitehead C (2004) International trends in housing tenure and mortgage finance. CML, London

Szelenyi I (1983) Urban inequalities under state socialism. Oxford University Press, Oxford

Varady DP, Preiser WE, Russell FP (1998) New directions in urban public housing. CUPR Press Rutgers, New Brunswick

Chapter 11
From Public Housing to Joint Ventures: Lessons from the U.S. Housing Policy Development

Lan Deng and Zhu Xiaodi

Abstract Almost eight decades have passed since the U.S. government first established its role in helping low-income families' housing consumption. The government efforts began with the public housing program, created in response to the housing austerity caused by the Great Depression. However, over the years the U.S. government has moved away from the public housing model. Instead, it has established a housing policy framework that features the participation of the private sector in affordable housing production, albeit with significant public assistance. Meanwhile, a greater emphasis has been placed on providing quality neighborhoods and expanding socioeconomic opportunities to low-income families. By examining the successes and failures in U.S. housing policy development, this paper will offer suggestions on what emerging economies like China can learn from the U.S. experience, given their ambitious efforts in expanding affordable housing provision to low-income families.

11.1 Introduction

Scholars have often argued that for both efficiency and equity reasons, government action is required in the production, distribution, and consumption of housing goods (Rosen 1985). Therefore, a variety of housing policies have been adopted across different nations, regardless of their orientation towards free markets or central planning (Hårsman and Quigley 1991). In the United States, the Housing Act of 1949 states that every American deserves to have a "decent home in a suitable

L. Deng (✉)
Urban and Regional Planning, University of Michigan, Ann Arbor, MI, USA
e-mail: landeng@umich.edu

Z. Xiaodi
The DC Office, The Ameson Education and Cultural Exchange Foundation, Washington, DC, USA
e-mail: zhuxiaodi@ameson.org

J. Chen et al. (eds.), *The Future of Public Housing: Ongoing Trends in the East and the West*, DOI 10.1007/978-3-642-41622-4_11,

living environment." Motivated by this ambition, the United States has developed a complicated housing system that consists of a mind-boggling array of interventions by various levels of governments.

One important function of this system is to boost families' housing consumption through various government subsidy programs. For example, certain provisions of the federal income tax code, including the mortgage interest deduction and the deferred capital gains tax, have significantly reduced the homeownership cost for middle and upper income classes. The mortgage interest deduction policy alone is estimated to cost the U.S. government about $100 billion annually in terms of tax revenue loss (Landis and McClure 2010). However, these benefits are not available to low-income families who have to rent. For those families, additional resources are allocated to help them.

Unlike the tax benefits for homeowners, the housing assistance provided to low-income renters is not an entitlement in the United States. Thus, the U.S. government has spent far less resources for this purpose. Only about one third of the eligible renter households have received such assistance (U.S. General Accounting Office 2002). In 2010, about 6.6 million low-income renters received various forms of rental housing assistance from the federal government, costing $44 billion in total (U.S. Department of Housing and Urban Development (HUD) 2011, 2012a, b, c; National Council of State Housing Agencies 2011).

How has this limited housing subsidy been delivered? Starting with its first involvement in the housing market by building housing for war workers during World War I, the U.S. government has implemented various low-income housing programs. As Olsen (2003) summarized, these programs, despite their variations, can be generalized into three basic approaches. The first and oldest approach is the public housing model, characterized by the government ownership and operation of housing built for occupancy by low-income households. The U.S. government created the public housing program in the 1930s in response to the housing austerity caused by the Great Depression. The second approach is for the government to contract with private parties to build (or substantially rehabilitate) and operate housing for these households. The project-based Section 8 program created in the 1970s and the Low Income Housing Tax Credit (LIHTC) Program established in the 1980s are such examples. The third approach operates by issuing rental assistance to help eligible households rent housing from the existing housing market. The tenant-based Section 8 program, created in the 1970s and later renamed as the Housing Choice Voucher Program, represents such efforts.

All three approaches share the same goal of providing quality housing to low-income families. The first two involve active intervention in the housing production process and are also called supply-based approaches. The voucher approach encourages families to become more effective housing consumers and is called a demand-based approach (Olsen 2003). Over the years, the U.S. government has moved away from the public housing approach. Instead, it has established a housing policy framework that emphasizes the participation of the private sector, either through production subsidies or demand subsidies. Moreover, as the U.S. housing policy evolves, a greater emphasis has been placed on providing quality neighborhoods and expanding socioeconomic opportunities for low-income families. This paper reviews the history of U.S. housing policy development and documents the critical changes that have taken place. In particular, it examines the experience of the public housing program and how it has been replaced by other programs, such as the voucher and the LIHTC programs. By examining the successes and failures in U.S. housing policy development, this paper offers suggestions on what China can learn from the U.S. experience, given China's ambitious efforts to expand its housing assistance to low-income families.

11.2 The History of the Public Housing Program in the United States

The history of the public housing program has been well documented in the U.S. literature. Hays (1995), for example, conducted an insightful analysis of how the ideological disagreement between the liberals and the conservatives has shaped the experience of the public housing program. Schwartz (2010), on the other hand, offered a comprehensive review of the program's recent status, including who live in public housing projects, where the projects are located, and what challenges the program faces today. This section will briefly summarize the work in this area by documenting the rise and fall of the public housing program.

As in many other countries, public housing in the United States first emerged as a response to the housing problems that the nation experienced due to industrialization. As early as the 1840s, when slums spread across cities, housing reformers believed that poor housing conditions not only ruined residents' health but were also the root of many social problems (Zhu et al. 2009). Throughout the late nineteenth and early twentieth centuries, these reformers successfully advocated for the establishment of building and sanitary regulations. To encourage private developers and landlords to provide better housing for the poor, reformers even assisted in developing model housing projects (Von Hoffman 2000).

Despite the reformers' efforts, the federal government chose to stay out of the private housing market and left the industry alone (Zhu et al. 2009). The outbreak of World War I, however, forced the federal government to address the housing shortage problem. In 1918, Congress appropriated $110 million to start two separate programs to house war workers. Nevertheless, the initial federal involvement was neither the result of a conscious effort to help the poor nor the effect of an increased reform spirit but an exercise of war power (Jackson 1985). When the war ended, Congress returned to its previous preference for individualism. The wartime public housing programs did not lead to permanent federal involvement (Szylvian 1999).

The Great Depression fundamentally changed the role of the government in the housing sector. Between 1928 and 1933, housing construction had fallen by 95 %. Half of the home mortgages in the United States were technically in default by 1933

(Jackson 1985). It was not a time for the laissez fair approach. Instead, bold government actions were taken to address the crisis. The National Housing Act of 1934 was passed to help revitalize the housing industry and generate jobs to boost the economy. The Federal Housing Administration (FHA) was also established to provide insurance for private residential mortgages and home improvements. This was followed by the founding of the Federal National Mortgage Association (now known as Fannie Mae) in 1938, which created a secondary market for loans insured by the FHA (Von Hoffman 2000). The long-term effects of these approaches on boosting homeownership have been highly positive. As a result, the homeownership rate in the United States rose from just over 40 % in the early 1940s to 62 % in 1960 (Van Order 2000).

Almost as a sideline, the Housing Act of 1937 authorized the federal government to directly build some rental housing for low-income families, which marked the beginning of the public housing program in the United States. Taken together, the efforts to address the housing austerity caused by the Great Depression created a two-tiered federal housing policy, with one boosting homeownership for the middle and upper classes and the other helping low-income families' housing consumption. This two-tiered system, with one dominating the other, profoundly influenced the outcomes of the U.S. housing policy. As the following discussion shows, the successful efforts to improve affordability for homeownership have partially accounted for the failure of the development of government-assisted housing for the less fortunate. The more successful the first tier was, the less public support remained for the second tier (Zhu et al. 2009).

From its beginning, the public housing program in the United States encountered strong political difficulties due to the suspicion that public housing would compete with private market housing. Conservative politicians also argued that the program would foster dependency among the poor (Zhu et al. 2009). Between 1938 and 1942, Congress cut off funding for the public housing program. During World War II, it funded housing for defense-related reasons but banned funding for low-income households. Congress did not authorize any more public housing until the passage of the Housing Act of 1949.

The landmark Housing Act of 1949 is remembered more for its ambitious goal than for what it actually delivered. The Act states that every American deserves to have a "decent home in a suitable living environment." As a first step, it set up a plan to build 135,000 public housing units annually. However, due to the outbreak of the Korean War, the plan was soon downsized and was never revived after the war ended. Under the sway of political fights between Republicans and Democrats, the public housing program in the United States was never funded as promised by the 1949 Housing Act. The program's beneficiaries also changed over time. While it was first developed to serve middle- or moderate-income families that were temporally poor due to economic recession, changes in the program rules strictly limited public housing units to the very poor. On the other hand, thanks to the postwar prosperity, more and more middle- and moderate-income families became homeowners. Many of them joined the group of conservative politicians and private developers to fight against public housing projects in their neighborhoods due to the concern that those projects may bring down their neighborhoods and housing investment (Zhu et al. 2009). The problems got even worse as the urban renewal program in the 1950s displaced many low-income families from their neighborhoods and forced them to crowd into public housing properties. The living conditions in those properties also deteriorated quickly.

Public housing was able to survive only because of the shift toward welfare capitalism in the 1960s (Zhu et al. 2009). The establishment of the Department of Housing and Urban Development (HUD) and the Housing and Urban Development Act in 1968 led to an expansion of public housing by over 200,000 units per year. However, public housing continued to be the last resort of the poor and minorities. The concentration of social and economic problems in some public housing properties made the program an easy target of blame in political fights. In 1973, President Nixon imposed a moratorium on future public housing construction.

Despite the highly visible problems associated with some public housing properties, it is not fair to claim that the public housing program is a complete failure in the United States. As Schwartz (2010) pointed out, public housing in the United States is very diverse. Most public housing units are in good shape and have been providing adequate housing for the nation's most vulnerable groups. The most troubled public housing properties are often found in distressed central city neighborhoods operated by large housing authorities, such as Chicago or St. Louis. Public housing sheltering the elderly and run by smaller housing authorizes tends to be in better conditions (Schwartz 2010). Still, to a large degree, and for too long, the public housing practice in the United States has failed the expectations of its supporters, and the negative image of public housing has continued to challenge the role of the government in managing the housing supply. Today about 1.1 million public housing units exist in the United States. In fiscal year 2010, the federal government spent $4.7 billion in operating fund and $2.5 billion in capital fund to manage these units (HUD 2012a, b).

11.3 The Shift from Production Subsidies to Demand Subsidies

After several decades of construction boom, it became clear in the 1970s that the nature of the housing problem had changed in the United States. As both the quantity and quality of housing stock improved consistently, the country no longer had a widespread housing shortage or the problem of living in substandard dwellings. Instead, many households experienced an affordability challenge, which means they were paying too large a percentage of their income for housing of adequate quality (Hayes 1995). Given this new problem, Congress passed the Housing and Community Development Act of 1974, which led to two important changes in U.S. housing policy development: the increasing importance of the private sector in providing affordable housing services and the shift from production subsidies to demand subsidies.

More specifically, the Housing Act of 1974 created the Section 8 program to provide both project-based and tenant-based rental assistance. Unlike public housing, where units are government-owned, both the project-based and the tenant-based Section 8 program offer housing subsidies for privately owned units. The program specified that 25 % of the household income (later increased to 30 %) is the reasonable rent burden for low-income households and that the federal government would pay the difference between this figure and a fair market rent, calculated based on comparable units in the local market. However, how subsidies were distributed differed between the project-based and the tenant-based Section 8 program.

Under the project-based Section 8 program, HUD would sign a long-term contract with private developers or landlords who would like to build or rehabilitate housing affordable to low-income households. The contract guarantees a stable flow of rent assistance to these developers or landlords during the specified period. The guarantee of a stable income, in combination with other financial subsidies, such as tax deductions or tax-exempt bonds, created the leverage for developers to attract private capital and promoted the production of assisted housing units (Zhu et al. 2009). The project-based Section 8 program is also known as the Section 8 New Construction and Substantial Rehabilitation program. In a much shorter time, it produced about the same number of housing units as the public housing program did. Although the program was popular with the development community, the long-term guarantee turned out to be very expensive for the federal government, especially in comparison to the tenant-based Section 8 component. The Republican administration began to curtail the project-based program in 1981 and eventually terminated it in 1983. Today there are about 1.1 million project-based Section 8 housing units under contract with HUD (HUD 2012c). In 2010 the federal government spent about $9 billion on this program (National Council of State Housing Agencies 2011).

The tenant-based Section 8 program, by contrast, offers housing assistance to individual households, not to particular projects. By issuing housing vouchers or housing certificates to individual households, the program subsidizes housing demand, not housing production. Qualified low-income households need to rent housing on their own from the private market. HUD will pay the difference between the fair market rent and the reasonable rent burden calculated based on household income. The tenant-based Section 8 program is also known as the Section 8 Existing Housing or the Section 8 Certificate and Voucher program, with some minor differences between vouchers and certificates. Viewed as a market-based solution, the tenant-based Section 8 program has been popular among both the liberals and the conservatives (Hayes 1995). Since households can move and take the subsidy with them, it is widely believed that the program's portability offers more opportunities for low-income families to live in better neighborhoods and have better access to socioeconomic opportunities (Deng 2007).

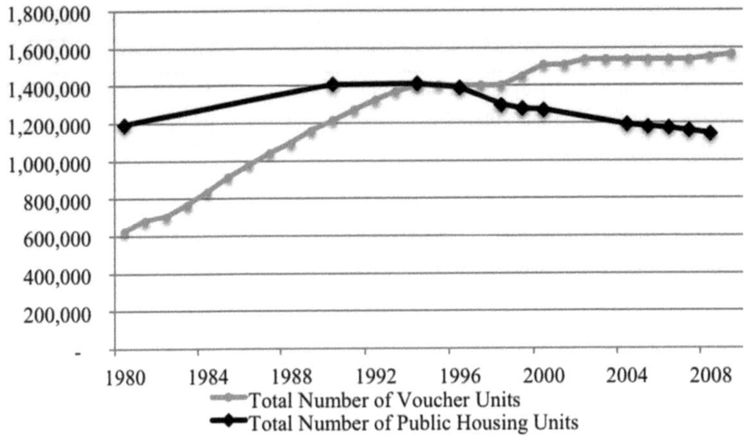

Fig. 11.1 Changes in housing units subsidized by vouchers versus public housing (Source: Compiled by the authors with data from Schwartz (2010))

The failure of the Democratic administration to deal with the unprecedented stagflation in the late 1970s eventually brought a conservative administration to power in the 1980 election. This "set the stage for a major shift in expenditures and in philosophy at the federal level, and housing programs could hardly avoid the effects of this shift" (Hayes 1995, p. 233). The dominant characteristic of the housing policy during the Reagan Administration was the extensive budget cuts in housing assistance, from $30 billion in the FY 1981 budget to $17.5 billion in the FY 1982 budget and $8.6 billion in the FY 1983 budget (Hayes 1995). In addition, the reduced Section 8 housing subsidy was only offered for the tenant-based program. Thus, since 1983, except for replacing existing units, the federal government has no longer built new housing projects through either the public housing program or the project-based Section 8 program. Instead, maintaining and operating their existing housing stock has become the main responsibility of both programs. Government-assisted new housing construction has been limited to the elderly and handicapped. By contrast, the tenant-based Section 8 program has grown rapidly. After some minor modification in program rules, the program was renamed as the Housing Choice Voucher program in 1998 and has now become the largest single program for low-income housing assistance in the United States.

Figure 11.1 describes the growth of the voucher program in contrast to the shrinking of the public housing stock in the last three decades. As Fig. 11.1 shows, after finishing its pipeline projects as well as some small additions of senior housing projects, public housing reached its peak of 1.4 million units in 1994. Since 1994, with little new construction coming and the demolition of distressed properties, the public housing stock has declined to about 1.1 million units in 2008. By contrast, the number of housing units subsidized by the voucher program has increased significantly, from about 624,604 units in 1980 to 1.55 million units in 2008. As the U.S. government continues to downsize the project-based assisted

Table 11.1 Fair market rents in the ten largest metropolitan areas in 2010 and 2013

Metropolitan areas	2010 FMR	2013 FMR
New York-Northern New Jersey-Long Island, NY-NJ-PA	$1,359	$1,474
Los Angeles-Long Beach-Santa Ana, CA	$1,420	$1,421
Chicago-Joliet-Naperville, IL-IN-WI	$1,015	$966
Dallas-Fort Worth-Arlington, TX	$894	$924
Houston-Sugar Land-Baytown, TX	$892	$945
Philadelphia-Camden-Wilmington, PA-NJ-DE-MD	$1,095	$1,119
Washington-Arlington-Alexandria, DC-VA-MD-WV	$1,494	$1,412
Miami-Fort Lauderdale-Pompano Beach, FL	$1,206	$1,122
Atlanta-Sandy Springs-Marietta, GA	$912	$874
Boston-Cambridge-Quincy, MA-NH	$1,357	$1,444

Source: Compiled by the authors with data from the U.S. Department of Housing and Urban Development (2012d)

Note: *FMR* fair market rent. Fair market rents listed in the table are for two-bedroom apartments only

housing stock, another half a million vouchers have been issued to transfer former public housing tenants or tenants in other production programs to the voucher program (Schwartz 2010). Today a total of about 2.2 million households in the United States are using housing vouchers (HUD 2012c). The federal government spent about $19 billion on this program in 2010 (National Council of State Housing Agencies 2011).

One critical issue in administering the voucher program is how to determine the fair market rent since the government needs to subsidize the difference between the fair market rent and 30 % of the household income. Each year HUD determines the fair market rent for each metropolitan area based on the distribution of market rents in the area. In the United States a metropolitan area is drawn to reflect a single housing and labor market. Currently, HUD defines fair market rent as the 40th percentile rent in a given metropolitan area, which is the dollar amount below which 40 % of standard-quality rental housing units are rented on the market. HUD also allows the fair market rent to vary with the size of housing units. This calculation ensures that the fair market rent reflects local market conditions so that voucher households would have sufficient subsidy to rent decent housing units. Table 11.1 lists the fair market rent for a two-bedroom apartment for the ten largest metropolitan areas in 2010 and 2013. As Table 11.1 shows, the fair market rent varies widely from one housing market to another and also changes over time. Thus, the cost of the voucher subsidy also varies accordingly.

Despite the shift from production subsidies to demand subsidies in the 1980s, it would be a mistake to assume that the U.S. government has completely abandoned the production approach in its housing policy. In only 3 years after it discontinued the project-based Section 8 program and the public housing program, Congress would enact through its tax code a housing program that has produced more low-income housing units than either the public housing or the project-based Section 8 program ever did.

11.4 The Low-Income Housing Tax Credit Program: A Joint Venture Between the Public and Private Sectors

As part of the Reagan administration's efforts to cut government spending and streamline the tax code, the Tax Reform Act of 1986 aimed to wipe out all tax incentives for rental housing investment (Schwartz 2010). Panicked about how this might affect affordable housing production, a coalition of housing providers and advocacy groups pushed to include a hastily drawn up provision, Section 42, to provide tax benefits for the production of low-income rental housing (McClure 2000). The act was passed, thereby establishing the Low-income Housing Tax Credit (LIHTC) program. While intended as an emergency response, the program's resiliency has surprised those who crafted it. Since its inception, the LIHTC program has been popular among various interest groups and has sailed through several different administrations with steady growth. As a result, it has replaced the public housing program to become the nation's largest affordable housing production program. By 2009, almost 34,000 projects, about 2.1 million housing units, have been placed in service under this program (HUD 2011).

The LIHTC's popularity is largely due to its unique design. Unlike the public housing program that provides direct development subsidies, the LIHTC provides federal tax credits to owners and investors of low-income rental housing (Cummings and DiPasquale 1999). A project without federal tax-exempt bond financing can claim a tax credit of 70 % of construction cost or 30 % of acquisition cost if it rents at least 20 % of units to households with less than 50 % of the area median income (AMI) or at least 40 % of units to households with less than 60 % of the AMI. Developers who wish to build such housing have to apply for tax credit allocation from their state housing credit agencies, normally the state housing finance agencies. Once awarded, developers sell the tax credits to private investors who contribute equity to the development in exchange for an ownership position that allows them to use the tax credits and other possible tax benefits from the project. The equity contribution from investors is critical since the amount of debt that affordable housing projects can support is never adequate to cover their development costs (McClure 2000). By contributing equity into the project, investors become the legal owner of the affordable housing projects and can claim the tax credits in equal installments for the next 10 years.

With investors as limited partners, developers work as general partners to conduct the actual development and operation activities in return for development or management fees. Developers often do not work directly with investors. Instead, intermediate organizations, known as syndicators, have developed to facilitate the tax credit transactions. These syndicators not only help developers sell tax credits to investors but also help investors monitor the performance of the affordable housing projects to ensure that all program regulations are complied with so that investors can successfully claim tax benefits. Figure 11.2 describes the flow of investment in a typical LIHTC project.

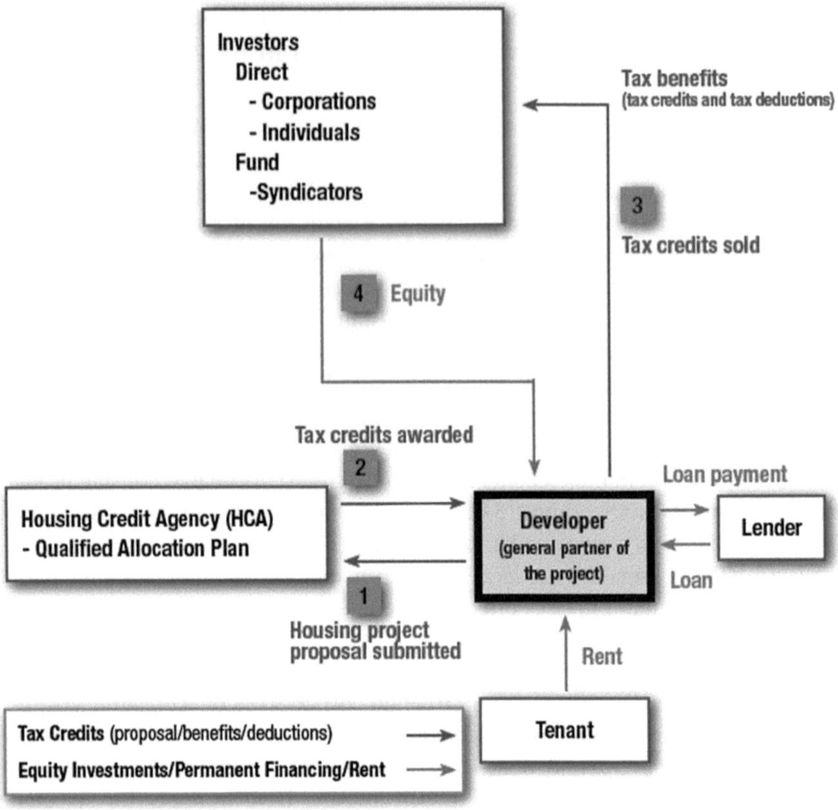

Fig. 11.2 Flow of tax credit and equity investment in a typical LIHTC project (Source: Adapted from Office of the Comptrollers of the Currency (2008))

When the LIHTC first took effect, investors were concerned about the risks associated with affordable housing development and were reluctant to buy those tax credits. The transaction cost for structuring the complicated tax credit deals, for example, the fees paid to syndicators, was also high. As a result, the price for tax credits was very low, with one dollar of tax credit traded for only about 30 or 40 cents. Because a large portion of the government funding was wasted in the transaction process, the program's efficiency was seriously questioned (Stegman 1991). However, over time the LIHTC has proved to be a sound investment for investors, especially for financial institutions that are looking for ways to meet their community reinvestment obligations as required by federal regulations. The price for tax credits steadily increased, reaching 80–90 cents per dollar in the last decade (Schwartz 2010). The LIHTC thus became an effective vehicle to raise development fund. The recent economic recession, however, has posed serious challenges on the program. Due to their income losses, many financial institutions that were formerly major buyers of tax credits withdrew from this market. With a significantly shrinking demand, developers could not find buyers for their tax credits. In response, the U.S. government had to provide temporary assistance by allowing developers to trade in unsold tax credits for direct development subsidies (Schwartz 2010). Since 2010 the LIHTC equity market has rebounded, but the degree of recovery varies across places.

While the LIHTC program subsidizes housing production, it differs from older production programs in several aspects. First, by awarding tax credits, the program spends future tax revenues and does not go through annual congressional budget authorizations. This reduces its visibility and makes it less vulnerable to budget cuts. Second, the program administration is decentralized. Unlike other major housing programs, the LIHTC is not run by HUD. Instead, the Internal Revenue Service (IRS) and state housing finance agencies jointly administer this program. Each year the program gives states the equivalent of nearly $8 billion in annual budget authority to issue tax credits. As long as the aggregate tax credits allocated do not exceed the cap amount, each state may set specific allocation criteria under very general guidelines issued by the IRS. This gives states the flexibility to address their own housing needs and priorities. In many states, the process of getting LIHTC funding has been very competitive. As a result, the state housing finance agencies have been able to select the projects that best match their policy goals, a critical reason for the program's success. Last but not the least, the program encourages the public and private sectors to work in partnership. The public sector, as represented by the state housing finance agencies, is in charge of allocating the LIHTC funding, while the private sector, including developers, syndicators, and investors, is responsible for developing and operating affordable housing projects. This brings efficiency and market discipline into the affordable housing production process (Deng 2005).

While encouraging public and private partnership, the LIHTC program has also played an important role in fostering the growth of the community development industry in the United States. In allocating the LIHTC funding, many state housing finance agencies have given preferences to nonprofit organizations. Nationwide, almost 30 % of the country's LIHTC projects were built by nonprofit housing developers, while the rest were produced by for-profit developers (Deng 2011). The funds and experience acquired from developing LIHTC projects have helped many community development organizations grow into a network of sophisticated developers and service providers (Freeman 2006).

Thus, the two most important housing programs in the United States today are the LIHTC, subsidizing housing production, and the Housing Choice Voucher program, subsidizing housing demand. Other major programs, including the public housing and the project-based Section 8 program, are no longer active, but the U.S. government still spends a significant amount of resources subsidizing the operation and maintenance of their existing stock. In particular, the HOPE VI program was created to redevelop the nation's most distressed public housing properties. Reflecting on the lessons from the public housing program, HOPE VI not only improves these properties physically but also promotes social and economic transformation in both the public housing complexes and the surrounding

Table 11.2 Summary of four major low-income housing programs in the United States

	Program	Total no. of units in the program	Federal expenditure in 2010	Income eligibility
Active housing programs	Housing choice voucher	2.2 million	$19 billion	Households with income equal or below 50 % of AMI are eligible, but at least 75 % of vouchers must be used by households with income equal or below 30 % of AMI
	LIHTC	2.1 million	$8 billion	Households with income equal or below 50 or 60 % of AMI are eligible
Inactive housing programs	Public housing	1.16 million	$7.2 billion	Households with income equal or below 80 % of AMI are eligible. But most public housing units serve households with much lower income, especially those living below the poverty line
	Project-based Section 8	1.11 million	$9 billion	Households with income equal or below 80 % of AMI are eligible. But at least 40 % of new admissions in those projects must be households with income equal or below 30 % of AMI

Source: Compiled by the authors with data from the U.S. Department of Housing and Urban Development (2011, 2012a, b, c) and National Council of State Housing Agencies (2011)
Note: *AMI* area median income, *AMI* is defined for a given metropolitan area by HUD

communities. From 1993 to 2007, HOPE VI demolished more than 150,000 units of distressed public housing and invested more than $6.1 billion in the redevelopment of 247 public housing projects (Schwartz 2010). Similar to both the LIHTC and the voucher program, HOPE VI also emphasizes the participation of the private sector in the redevelopment process. For example, while most public housing properties are managed by government entities, many HOPE VI projects have contracted private firms for property management. HOPE VI has dramatically improved the face of public housing (Schwartz 2010).

Table 11.2 summarizes the four major low-income housing programs in the United States. While it presents the amount of federal spending on each individual program in fiscal year 2010, it is important to note that this spending is not directly comparable across programs; that is, higher spending does not mean the program is more expensive. This is because the uses of funding are very different for different programs. For example, production subsidies and demand subsidies have different time paths of spending. The voucher program requires continuous funding to subsidize the ongoing housing consumption of low-income families, while a production program like the LIHTC provides up-front development subsidies. However, due to their high costs, affordable housing developments today are very likely to combine different types of development subsidies. Thus, while Table 11.2 shows that 2.1 million housing units have been placed in service through the LIHTC program, these units cannot be attributed to the LIHTC program alone. Other entities, such as state or local governments, have also provided important subsidies to those projects (Deng 2005). Moreover, as Table 11.2 shows for the public housing and the project-based Section 8 programs, production subsidies often do not end at the development stage. Major expenditures are needed to maintain and improve the aging assisted housing stock. This was less an issue for the LIHTC program in its early stage but has become increasingly important as the program matures.

Table 11.2 also identifies the maximum income eligibility for the four programs. However, the programs often choose to serve families with a lower income than what is required. For example, both the public housing program and the voucher program have been able to reach the poorest of the poor. In 2009 the average annual household income was about $13,234 among public housing residents and $12,591 among voucher holders, both well below the federal poverty line (Schwartz 2010). The LIHTC program serves households with much higher income. Studies of LIHTC developments show that without other rental assistance, such as vouchers, the average household income in those projects is about 40–50 % of the AMI, compared to 20–30 % of the AMI for most public housing or voucher tenants (McClure 2006; Schwartz 2010). However, some LIHTC units are occupied by voucher tenants. When combined with voucher subsidies, LIHTC projects can serve the very poor. The fact that the programs serve different income groups is another reason why the program expenditures, as reported in Table 11.2, are not directly comparable. Instead, studies have carefully compared program costs by controlling for family income and program benefits, as well as accounting for the different time paths of costs and benefits for different programs (Olsen 2000; U.S. General Accounting Office 2002; McClure 2000; Deng 2005).

11.5 Lessons from the U.S. Housing Policy Experience

Perhaps the most important lesson that can be learned from the history of U.S. housing policy development is on how to build support for housing programs that serve low-income households, given that this group is politically weak and cannot advocate for themselves. This has been a struggle for the public housing program in the United States, where ideological opposition and the political divide between the liberals and the conservatives constantly undermine program support (Freeman 2006). Recent housing programs have managed to expand the constituencies by including the private sector in the process. The LIHTC offers private investors the opportunity to invest in affordable housing production with a reasonable financial return – a way of doing good while doing well (Krumholz 2004).

The voucher program subsidizes the demand for privately owned rental properties, thus benefiting the developers and landlords of those properties. Both programs reward market winners while at the same time subsidizing the poor (Deng 2007). In doing so, they have built a broad-based coalition that includes not only affordable housing advocates but also the powerful private sector, which now has vested interest in seeing these programs continue (Freeman 2006). The programs' popularity shows that they are a good fit for the American political and economic environment. For emerging economies that seek to reformulate their housing policies, such as China, it is important that they find a way to build support for their affordable housing programs. They may or may not involve the private sector. However, without broad-based support, well-intended programs may fail.

Another lesson that other countries can learn from the U.S. housing policy experience is on what is the most effective approach to deliver housing subsidies, given that the United States has experimented with various housing programs. The debate on this issue has focused in particular on the comparison between production subsidies and demand subsidies. With a culture that emphasizes individualism, there is a strong belief in the American society that the market is the most efficient and least coercive allocator of goods and services and that government should play a secondary and supplementary role in regulating individual behaviors (Hayes 1995). Shaped by this belief, the basic tenet that has guided U.S. housing policy development in the last three decades is that demand subsidies are better than supply subsidies due to their lower cost, greater consumer freedom, and ability to leverage private production (Deng 2005). Empirical studies comparing program costs have often confirmed vouchers' cost advantages over production programs (Olsen 2000; U.S. General Accounting Office 2002). However, more recent studies have highlighted the powerful effects of local market conditions on program costs. These studies have found that vouchers are more cost-effective than production programs in soft housing markets, whereas in tight housing markets, vouchers may be as expensive as production programs since high rent inflation can significantly increase the cost of demand subsidies (Deng 2005; McClure 2000). This justifies the use of production programs in tight housing markets to relieve housing shortage and reduce rent inflation.

Besides cost efficiency, the other aspect of the debate between demand subsidies and production subsidies in the United States is the housing programs' spatial outcome, that is, how the spatial distribution of government-assisted housing units may help improve or hamper the socioeconomic opportunities available to low-income families. Housing is more than a roof over the head. Affordable housing is the foundation from which low-income households address the many other challenges they face. Where low-income families live affects not only their quality of life but also their access to socioeconomic opportunities, such as job availability or education quality. As our discussion shows, the public housing program in the United States has historically failed in this aspect. Concentration of poverty has plagued many public housing properties. Residents living in these properties have been physically and socially isolated from the mainstream society, which has had profound negative impacts on their education and employment outcome (Jargowsky 2002). Vouchers, by contrast, are favored for their ability to disperse poverty, offer recipients greater locational choices, and allow beneficiaries to take advantage of better education and employment opportunities (Deng 2007). As a result, the U.S. government has used vouchers as the main vehicle to distribute low-income housing assistance. Moreover, in redesigning its production programs, the U.S. government has also placed a greater emphasis on producing quality neighborhoods and promoting socioeconomic integration through affordable housing development. The HOPE VI program is a good example of such efforts. By providing both quality housing and comprehensive social services, HOPE VI transforms distressed public housing properties into mixed-income communities, with the goal of helping low-income families become self-sufficient. Research about the LIHTC program also shows that the program has performed much better than the public housing program in bringing affordable housing projects to low-poverty suburban neighborhoods, although some argue that it could have done more in dispersing poverty (McClure 2006; Katz 2004).

These changes in U.S. housing policy offer important lessons for emerging economies like China. As China plans to significantly expand affordable housing production for its population in need, it is important that it does not repeat the mistakes that the United States has made with its public housing program. China has a good opportunity to do it right. Because of its socialist heritage, public housing in China does not carry a stigma. Thus, the Chinese public does not (or not yet) have strong resistance against government-assisted housing developments. Still, China needs to be careful in its massive affordable housing development efforts, especially those targeting very low-income families. Without conscientious planning, concentration of poverty can easily take place. How can affordable housing projects provide opportunities for families to move up rather than trapping them in poverty? This is a question that emerging economies like China need to consider in designing their affordable housing policy.

While expanding affordable housing production may be necessary for many emerging economies, it is not the only solution to their housing problems. In China three decades of housing reform has resulted in significant improvement in urban households' living conditions. According to the Ministry of Housing and Urban-Rural Development of China, the average living space per capita among urban residents has risen from 6.7 square meters in 1978 to 28 square meters in 2008. At the same time, the ministry acknowledged that the main housing problem China faces today is no longer widespread overcrowding but urban poverty (Ministry of Housing and Urban-Rural Development of China 2009). The shifting nature of the current housing problem in China is somewhat similar to what the United States experienced in the 1970s. As previously discussed, the U.S. government responded by introducing demand subsidies into its housing policies. It may be the time for the Chinese government to examine the role of demand subsidies in its housing policy framework, given their cost advantages and ability to expand neighborhood choices for low-income families.

Whatever housing policies countries pursue, it is important to note that no single policy can fit all, especially in countries like China and the United States, which are large and diverse. Instead, local flexibility is important in achieving the desired policy outcome (Schill and Wachter 2001; Apgar 1990). Numerous studies in the United States have shown that local factors affect both program efficiency and effectiveness. For example, while vouchers offer low-income families greater choices of neighborhoods, their effectiveness can be limited by various local factors, such as housing market conditions, the spatial distribution of affordable housing units, and the existence of housing discrimination (Deng 2007; Pendall 2000). Thus, it is important that housing programs target local needs and are coordinated with local objectives. This local flexibility is a critical factor for the success of the LIHTC program in the United States. China has a long tradition to allow for local flexibility in the implementation of its economic reform. This tradition needs to be maintained in its housing policy development.

References

Apgar WC Jr (1990) Which housing policy is best? Housing Policy Debate 1(1):1–32
Cummings JL, DiPasquale D (1999) The low-income housing tax credit: an analysis of the first ten years. Housing Policy Debate 10(2):251–307
Deng L (2005) The cost-effectiveness of the low-income housing tax credit relative to vouchers: evidence from six metropolitan areas. Housing Policy Debate 16(3/4):469–511
Deng L (2007) Comparing the effects of housing vouchers and low-income housing tax credits on neighborhood integration and school quality. J Plan Educ Res 27:20–35
Deng L (2011) The external neighborhood effects of low-income housing tax credit projects built by three sectors. J Urban Aff 33(2):143–165
Freeman L (2006) Comment on Kirk McClure's "The low-income housing tax credit program goes mainstream and moves to the suburbs.". Housing Policy Debate 17(3):447–459
Hårsman B, Quigley JM (1991) Preface in housing markets and housing institutions: an international comparison. Kluwer Academic, Boston/Dordrecht/London
Hayes RA (1995) The federal government and urban housing, 2nd edn. State University of New York, Albany
Jackson KT (1985) Crabgrass frontier: the suburbanization of the United States. Oxford University Press, Oxford
Jargowsky P (2002) Sprawl, concentration of poverty, and urban inequality. In: Squires GD (ed) Urban sprawl, causes, consequences & policy responses. The Urban Institute Press, Washington, DC, pp 39–72
Katz B (2004) Neighborhoods of choice and connection: the evolution of American neighborhood policy and what it means for the United Kingdom. Brookings Institution, Washington, DC
Krumholz N (2004) The reluctant hand: privatization of public housing in the U.S. Paper presented to the CITY FUTURES conference, Chicago
Landis JD, McClure K (2010) Rethinking federal housing policy. J Am Plann Assoc 76(3):1–30
McClure K (2000) The low income housing tax credit as an aid to housing finance: how well has it worked. Housing Policy Debate 11(1):91–114
McClure K (2006) The low-income housing tax credit program goes mainstream and moves to the suburbs. Housing Policy Debate 17(3):419–446
Ministry of Housing and Urban-Rural Development of China (2009, 2009a) Press release for the conference on taking comprehensive measures to promote healthy development of the real estate market. http://www.mohurd.gov.cn/hybd/09hy/fdcscjk/fdcschjcl/200901/t20090106_184498.htm. Accessed 5 Feb 2010

National Council of State Housing Agencies (2011) Housing choice vouchers fact sheet. http://www.ncsha.org/resource/2011-housing-choice-vouchers-and-project-based-section-8-fact-sheet. Accessed July 2012

Office of the Comptrollers of the Currency (2008) Low-income housing tax credits: affordable housing investment opportunities for banks. Community development insights. http://www.occ.gov/topics/community-affairs/publications/insights/insights-low-income-housing-tax-credits.pdf. Accessed Dec 2012

Olsen EO (2000) The cost-effectiveness of alternative methods of delivering housing subsidies. Working paper 351. Thomas Jefferson Center for Political Economy. World Wide Web page: http://www.virginia.edu/economics/papers/olsen/costeffectiveness.survey.pdf. Accessed 13 March 2004

Olsen EO (2003) Housing programs for low-income households. In: Moffitt R (ed) Means-tested transfer programs in the U.S. University of Chicago Press, Chicago, pp 365–442

Pendall R (2000) Why vouchers and certificate users live in distressed neighborhoods. Housing Policy Debate 11(4):881–910

Rosen H (1985) Chapter 7: Housing subsidies effects on housing decisions, efficiency, and equity. In: Auerbach AJ, Feldstein M (eds) Handbook of public economics, vol 1. Elsevier, North-Holland, pp 375–472

Schill MH, Wachter SM (2001) Principles to guide housing policy at the beginning of the millennium. Cityscape 5(2):5–19

Schwartz A (2010) Housing policy in the United States, 2nd edn. Routledge, New York

Stegman MA (1991) The excessive costs of creative finance: growing inefficiencies in the production of low-income housing. Housing Policy Debate 2(2):357–373

Szylvian KM (1999) Industrial housing reform and the emergency fleet corporation. J Urban Hist 25(5):647–689

U.S. Department of Housing and Urban Development (2011) HUD National Low Income Housing Tax Credit (LIHTC) database: projects placed in service through 2009. http://www.huduser.org/portal/datasets/lihtc.html. Accessed July 2012

U.S. Department of Housing and Urban Development (2012a) Public and Indian housing: public housing capital fund. 2012 Summary Statement and Initiatives. http://portal.hud.gov/hudportal/documents/huddoc?id=PH_Capital_Fund_2012.pdf. Accessed July 2012

U.S. Department of Housing and Urban Development (2012b) Public and Indian housing: public housing operating fund. 2012 Summary statement and initiatives. http://portal.hud.gov/hudportal/documents/huddoc?id=PH_Opera_fund_2012.pdf. Accessed July 2012

U.S. Department of Housing and Urban Development (2012c) Picture of subsidized households 2009. http://www.huduser.org/portal/picture/picture2009.html. Accessed July 2012

U.S. Department of Housing and Urban Development (2012d) Fair market rents. http://www.huduser.org/portal/datasets/fmr.html. Accessed December 2012

U.S. General Accounting Office (2002) Comparing the characteristics and costs of housing programs. GAO–02–76. Washington, DC

Van Order R (2000) The U.S. Mortgage market: a model of dueling charters. J Housing Res 11 (2):233–255

Von Hoffman A (2000) A study in contradictions: the origins and legacy of the Housing Act of 1949. Housing Policy Debate 11(2):299–326

Zhu X, Deng L, Hu H (2009) Three models of public housing in the 20th century. First Chapter in: Housing: socioeconomic, availability, and development issues. Nova Science Publishers, New York, pp 1–44

Chapter 12
Social Housing in the United Kingdom

Mark Stephens

12.1 Introduction

Social rented housing[1] has played an important role in the United Kingdom for almost a century. From the introduction of central government subsidies in 1919 to the new Affordable Homes Programme, governments and landlords have faced trade-offs between the depth of subsidy and the scale of the new build programme; between rent levels and the quality and location of social housing; and between targeting housing on the poor and creating poverty neighbourhoods. These dilemmas are encountered in any country, but are played out through different institutional structures and within the wider context that includes demography, the labour market and wider economy, social security system and social attitudes.

The ability of governments to respond to changes is highly path dependent, and this chapter begins by providing an historical overview of the origins and development of social rented housing in the UK. It then examines the key changes since around 1980 that contributed to the changing nature of the sector: the Right to Buy, which was introduced in 1980 and led to many better off tenants becoming home-owners; and the changes in the way in which social rented housing is allocated, which led to a much greater emphasis on housing people in the greatest need. We then examine the factors that led to housing associations taking over from local authorities as the main providers of social rented housing: the transfer of local authority housing to the ownership of housing associations, and the promotion of housing associations as the main providers of new social rented housing from 1988.

[1] 'Social housing' is the term applied to housing that is let at below-market rents and allocated administratively according to need. It covers both public housing, which in the UK almost always takes the form of local authority housing, and housing provided by registered housing associations, which are private bodies, but operate on a not-for-profit basis.

M. Stephens (✉)
Professor, School of the Built Environment, Heriot-Watt University, Edinburgh, Scotland, UK
e-mail: M.Stephens@hw.ac.uk

J. Chen et al. (eds.), *The Future of Public Housing: Ongoing Trends in the East and the West*, DOI 10.1007/978-3-642-41622-4_12,

Finally, we examine the most recent challenges to the sector, which have arisen from the government's attempts to reduce the size of the budget deficit: the new model for financing "affordable" rental housing, and cuts to Housing Benefit (which is the UK's housing allowance).

12.2 Historical Overview

The United Kingdom was the first industrial nation (Mathias 1969). It was the first country where, as measured by the 1851 census, a majority of the population lived in urban areas. Urbanisation was associated with widespread overcrowding, poor sanitation and high levels of child mortality. The health problems arising from densely populated urban areas were compounded by the lack of understanding of the means by which diseases, notably cholera, were transmitted. Cholera was identified definitively as a water-borne disease only in 1854, by which time some 100,000 people had died of its consequences (Wootton 2006). Once the health effects of overcrowded and insanitary housing became clear, early state intervention treated housing as a health problem. Following a Royal Commission on Housing in 1885, legislation allowed local authorities to 'close' slum housing. Since clearance resulted in the problems of overcrowding tending to re-emerge in adjacent locations, local authorities were often reluctant to sanction clearance (Land Enquiry Committee 1913).

Before the First World War there was a marked reluctance to countenance public subsidy, particularly that provided by central government. Philanthropists made an appearance, providing sanitary housing for the 'respectable' poor, in part motivated by a belief that an improved physical environment would encourage higher standards of moral behaviour. There was also some housing provided by local authorities without central government subsidy. Although early social science had seemingly demonstrated that poverty was unavoidable for many households, no matter how prudently they budgeted (Rowntree 1901), there was nonetheless a tendency for progressive opinion stress the role of the land market in causing inadequate housing. By 1914 this view was changing although the enhancement of wages through a statutory minimum wage was seen as an alternative to subsidised housing (Land Enquiry Committee 1913).

Public rental housing subsidised by central government arrived in the aftermath of the First World War. The war-time Reconstruction Committee recognised the malfunctioning of the housing market, which was compounded by war-induced disruption to supply and the controls introduced on private rents in 1915 as a consequence of inflationary pressures. Moreover, the pre-1914 boom in infrastructure (schools, public transport and utilities) had created a (debt) crisis in local government finance (Offer 1981), such that central government equalisation grants became an inevitable and enduring feature of the system from 1929 (Lyons 2007).

Subsidised rental housing, introduced in 1919, was conceived as being a temporary measure, until market equilibrium was restored, and rent controls could be removed (Daunton 1984). Since shortages were not removed, rent control was retained until 1989, and by 1980 around one-third of the population lived in social rented housing, almost all of it supplied by local authorities.

Early 'council' housing was not intended for the poorest people. Rather, it was aimed at skilled working and administrative classes. Indeed, rents – although subsidised – were so high that it would have been impractical for the poorest people to afford them. A Medical Officer of Health found that the mortality rate among council tenants in one area was higher than among the slum-dwellers, and attributed this to the high rents (Daunton 1984).

This incident points to the enduring trade-offs in public housing: between size, quality and rent; between rent and quantity; and between location and density. These trade-offs became more acute, when, after 1930, the Government adopted council housing as the principal means of clearing slums. Relatively low-density suburban developments – chosen for the cheap land – moved households away from amenities and crucially their places of employment. The alternative was higher density housing in inner-urban areas, notably the Quarry Hill development of almost 1,000 apartments in the centre of Leeds (Ravetz 1974). A start to the remaining problems of affordability was made as legislation permitted local authorities to develop their own differential rent systems, i.e. varying the rent according to individual household's incomes. An advanced scheme (again in Leeds) caused much resentment among the tenants whose rents rose to pay for their poorer neighbours (Finnigan 1984).

Council housing resumed a leading role in social policy with the advent of the welfare state in the decades following the Second World War. Initially, the Government aspired to an ideal of high quality housing that could be occupied by a diverse range of classes. However, under the pressures of acute shortage and the persistence of slums, the Government reverted to essentially the position adopted in the 1930s. Building for 'general needs' gave way to prioritising slum clearance in the mid-1950s. With it, the size and quality of the housing declined, and its density increased. A clear signal was sent to the 'aspirational' working classes that their future lay in home-ownership, which became the majority tenure in 1970 as private renting continued to decline.

By the early 1970s the 'crude' housing shortages (measured by comparing the number of households with the numbers of houses) had been removed, and the Government moved to raise rents and to target subsidies on poorer tenants. This was to be achieved by the introduction of a national housing allowance system (called Housing Benefit), which replaced the schemes run by individual local authorities in 1972/73 and was extended to private tenants (Fig. 12.1).

The era of 'mass' public house building came to an end in the mid-1970s, when economic crisis led to assistance from the International Monetary Fund, and with it curbs on public spending. The ideological hostility of the Conservative Governments of the 1980s and 1990s towards local authority housing also contributed to a further decline in house building. Combined with the sale of properties at discounted prices under the Right to Buy from 1980, the sector shrank in absolute as well as relative size.

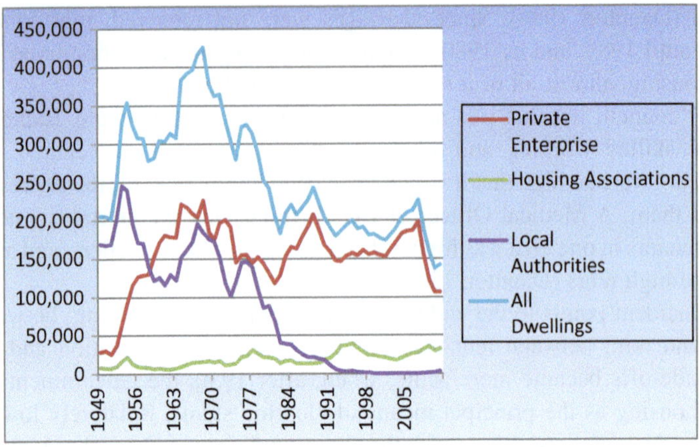

Fig. 12.1 Housebuilding in the UK 1949–2011 (Source: DCLG Live Table 241)

12.3 Right to Buy[2]

The Right to Buy was introduced by the first Thatcher government in 1980. The principal motivation was to promote owner-occupation, rather than to cut public spending. Governments since the 1950s had promoted home-ownership as the 'ideal' tenure for aspirational households, especially after the switch in the social housing programme away from 'general needs' housing and towards prioritising rehousing people from slum clearance programmes. Although the government made claims that it would save money, the policy remained uncosted until after 2000 (see Munro 2007).

Nearly all council tenants could exercise the Right to Buy provided that they had been tenants for 3 years. It was backed with strong financial incentives. Qualifying tenants could purchase a property with a minimum discount of 33 % from its open market value, and this rose by one percentage point for each year of tenancy up to a maximum of 50 %. Over time the terms became more generous: in 1984 the minimum residency requirement was dropped to 2 years and the maximum discount was raised to 60 %. More generous terms for tenants living in flats were introduced in 1986 with a minimum discount of 44 % rising by two percentage points for each year's residence to a maximum of 70 %.

Figure 12.2 shows how Right to Buy was an immediate success when it was introduced in 1980, but that sales fell dramatically after 2002/03.

An underlying reason for the affordability of the scheme for government the maturity of the local authority housing sector. Much social housing had been built in the 1930s and the high levels of inflation experienced in the 1970s helped to erode the real value of debts even on relatively recently built housing. The equity

[2] This section closely follows a section in Stephens et al. (2014) and is reproduced with permission.

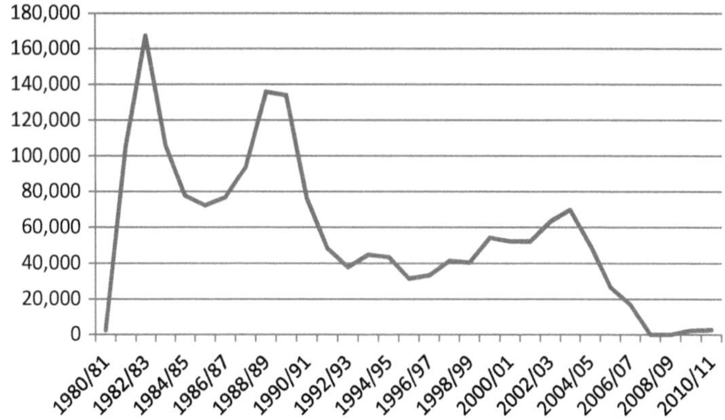

Fig. 12.2 Right to buy sales (England) 1980/81–2010/11 (Source: Department of Communities & Local Government: Live table 670)

that built up in the sector financed the discounts without any 'financial' subsidy needing to be inserted into the system. Indeed the capital receipts helped to reduce the level of government borrowing (Gibb and Whitehead 2007).

The transfer itself was probably on average 'progressive' in the sense that assets owned by the community as a whole were transferred to people who were mostly less well off than the average. But in the longer term, the limitation on using capital receipts for constructing new social housing eventually led to shrinkage in the availability of social housing.

Research suggests that the impacts of RTB have been quite complex. For example, the government has claimed that '... it has encouraged more affluent tenants to remain in the neighbourhood they have lived in for many years, helping to create stable mixed income communities' (DETR, quoted in Stephens (ed.) 2005). But the evidence is complex, and it is clear that RTB has probably impacted in different ways in different areas (see Munro 2007).

Until recently, it appeared that the policy – at least in its traditional form – had run its course, as sales have fallen throughout the UK. This was caused in part by restrictions, mostly in the form of maximum discounts that were introduced leading both to reductions in sales and the size of discounts. A maximum discount of £24,000 was introduced in Wales in 1999, then reduced to £16,000 in 2003. Regional maximum discounts ranging from £16,000 (in the high pressure south east) to £38,000 were also introduced in England (Wilcox et al. 2010). The 2004 Housing Act also lengthened from 2 to 5 years the period before a tenant becomes eligible to exercise RTB and extended the period during which the discount must be repaid from 2 to 5 years in the event of a re-sale. Moreover, the social landlord is given the right to repurchase the property if it is sold within 10 years of the RTB being exercised. Under the 'modernised' right to buy in Scotland, a reformed discount structure including a cash limit of £15,000 was introduced in 2002. However, sales declined less than elsewhere in the UK as the 'old' rights continued to be enjoyed by more established tenants (Wilcox et al. 2010). Under the 2010 Housing Act, the Scottish Nationalist government ended the Right to Buy for new tenants.

However, the UK's Conservative-led Coalition Government, formed in 2010, has sought to revive the right to buy in England, the one jurisdiction in which it controls housing policy. From April 2012, it raised the maximum discount to £75,000 (or 50 % of property value if it is a house; 70 % if it is a flat). Sensitive to criticisms that social housing stock will be lost, the Government has put in place incentives for local authorities to reinvest receipts in new housing. However, the new housing must conform to the new 'affordable' housing model under which rents are set at 80 % of market value. Local authorities not wishing to reinvest receipts will lose them to a national housing fund. Former local authority tenants, whose homes have been transferred to housing associations (see below), retain the right to buy and can participate in the new scheme. The new policy marks an important divergence from the rest of the UK.

12.4 Allocations and Role of the Sector

Local authorities have always enjoyed a good deal of autonomy in choosing tenants for social housing. As we have seen, early council housing was not affordable to the poorest and tended to house skilled working and clerical classes, but the emphasis on slum clearance in the 1930s and again from the mid-1950s changed that.

Particularly since the desirability of council housing varied according to its location, building type (house, walk-up, high rise, etc.), and quality the question of allocation was not just one of gaining access, but gaining access to what. The transition from private renting to council housing was bewildering for some households. Young and Wilmott's (1957) study of the East End of London records how mothers used to "speaking for" their daughters to persuade private landlords whom they knew to house them as they set up home with their husbands were bewildered when faced with the impersonal bureaucracy of the local authority housing department. Although the role of elected Councillors remained important until into the 1980s, and local authority housing could form part of a patronage system, it was primarily housing officers who operated allocation systems, and these were run to match households to "suitable" council housing, according to the family's status as well as their "objective" position. Thus housing officers would conduct household inspections to gauge the "respectability" of a household wanting to be re-housed. Until the "right to buy" removed much of the more attractive stock, there was a good deal of mobility within the system, so a household might enter the sector in an unpopular estate, but by good behaviour and regular payment of rent, make the case, perhaps with the help of a Councillor, into progressively more attractive accommodation. Filtering also occurred through the mechanism of thee "ability to wait" (Clapham and Kintrea 1984), whereby the less desperate households rejected offers of unpopular council housing until what they regarded as a suitable offer was made.

Discrimination became an issue with immigration from the British Commonwealth from the 1950s onwards, but was generally indirect: in other words allocation systems were constructed that had the effect of excluding or restricting access to certain groups. Thus the Greater London Council's "Sons and Daughters" scheme that favoured the sons and daughters of existing tenants clearly discriminated against newly arrived immigrants until it was abolished in the early 1980s (Glyn 2006). The system made a brief re-appearance in one London borough in the early 1990s (ibid.)

So council housing, whilst prioritising people needing to be rehoused as a result of slum clearance from the mid 1950s, housed a broad range of households, although there was differentiation within the sector. The change in the nature of the sector into one that was more "residual" began in earnest from the 1970s onwards.

In part this reflected changing attitudes towards allocations, with concerted efforts to become more "objective" and to base allocation more strictly on need. The landmark Homeless Persons Act of 1977 gave local authorities a statutory duty to house priority need non-intentionally homeless people in temporary accommodation until suitable settled accommodation becomes available (Fitzpatrick 2008). In practice settled accommodation nearly always took the form of a local authority tenancy (ibid.) creating an internationally unusual (and quite possibly unique) de facto right to housing. Whilst a recent change in England now means that local authorities can discharge their duty through private sector accommodation, the "priority need" limitation was abolished in Scotland in 2012 meaning that all non-intentionally homeless people have a right to settled accommodation. But here, the important consideration is that with rising homelessness in the 1980s, local authority housing, particularly in high demand areas, became increasingly focussed on the most vulnerable groups – leading to some resentment amongst others in great housing need. Needless to say, the situation was made considerably more acute by the relatively low level of new build in the social rented sector that has now pertained for four decades.

The right to buy not only removed much of the more attractive housing in the most desirable neighbourhoods from the sector, but took with it better off tenants, too. Meanwhile remaining tenants were also exposed to the economic restructuring that accelerated in the 1980s with widespread de-industrialisation that disproportionately affected the urban areas where council housing was concentrated. Unemployment and other forms of "worklessness" mean that the profile of tenants in the social rented sector as a whole is now decidedly disadvantaged. As Table 12.1 shows, incomes and levels of labour market participation are markedly lower than in the other tenures, with fewer than one-third of household reference persons in full or part-time employment, compared to more than 60 % of owner occupiers and nearly 70 % of private renters.

The pattern of "residualisation" in social housing is given a further twist by its concentration in so-called "poverty neighbourhoods." There is a live debate over

Table 12.1 Tenure profile (England, 2010–2011)

	Owner occupiers	Social renters	Private renters
Size of sector (number of households)	14.4 m	3.8 m	3.6 m
Proportion of household reference persons (HRPs) aged under 40	18.5 %	27.9 %	63.3 %
Mean weekly gross income[a] (HRP plus partner)	£786	£334	£558
Mean weekly gross income[a] (all members of household)	£836	£368	£627
Mean weekly mortgage payment/rent[b] (before Housing Benefit)	£143	£79	£160
Median length of time in current residence	12 years	7 years	1 year
Proportion of households receiving SMI[c]/Housing Benefit	0.3 %	62.6 %	24.6 %
Proportion of HRPs working full time	56.1 %	22.0 %	59.2 %
Proportion of HRPs working part time	7.4 %	10.4 %	10.1 %
Sample size	12,037	3,049	2,470

Source: DCLG (2012)
Notes
[a]Includes Housing Benefit
[b]Rent excluding services and rent-free cases
[c]Support for Mortgage Interest: a social assistance benefit to assist low income owner-occupiers with their mortgage interest costs

whether the concentrations of poor people in particular neighbourhoods exerts a further (independent) disadvantage on their residents. Possible causes might include the stigma associated with a particular estate, the development of cultures of worklessness as people have few role models who are in work, and the isolation of people from the social networks that would link them to labour markets. However, evidence of either neighbourhood effects or, if they exist, their causes remain inconclusive (Kintrea 2008). An associated thesis suggests that social housing itself might exert an independent effect on the outcomes of tenants. Although the socio-economic profile of social tenants is striking and there is evidence of diminishing life chances of people growing up in council housing (Lupton et al. 2009), that the tenure itself should be the cause lacks a convincing hypothesis. Another way to conceive of the sector, is that it provides a valuable "safety net" – secure and for the most part housing of a reasonable physical quality – for many low income households as their labour market position has worsened whilst both poverty and income inequality rose (Stephens et al. 2002).

12.5 Subsidies and Rents in Local Authority Housing

Since the 1930s local authorities have operated a system of rent pooling, under which the debts associated with building a particular estate are shared with others. This removes the anomalous position whereby newer estates with higher debts would have higher rents than older estates with lower debts. However, the system of local authority Housing Revenue Accounts (HRAs) does not tackle anomalies between local authorities, leading to inconsistencies in rents.

Central government has been able to exert influence over rent levels through subsidy. Local authority housebuilding has always been the subject of annual revenue subsidies, rather than up-front capital subsidies (in contrast to housing associations). In the 1980s, reductions in central government subsidies to local authority HRAs forced rents upwards until three-quarters of English local authorities received no subsidy at all (Wilson 2000). This process reflected the maturing of the sector, as very little new building was taking place and historic debts, already eroded by inflation, were repaid.

Until 1990, central government subsidy for Rent Rebates (the name for Housing Benefit for local authority tenants) was paid to local authorities separately from subsidies for the HRA. However, by merging the subsidy for the HRA with the subsidy for Rent Rebates, the Government once again gained control over rents. Thus local authorities with negative subsidy entitlement on the traditional HRA now lost subsidy associated with the payment of Rent Rebates. Any remaining surpluses were transferred to the local authority's General Fund. This system was unpopular with many tenants who objected that the poorest tenants' Rent Rebates were being paid for in part by other tenants, rather than by the community as a whole. Indeed, in 2000/01 the cost of Rent Rebates in England was £4.2 billion, of which more than one-third (£1.5 billion) was paid for by surpluses on HRAs (Wilson 2000). Revenue subsidies from central government to English local authorities declined from £4.3 billion in 1980/81 to£0.6 billion in 1992/93 (in 2003/04 prices), and then became negative, before small net subsidies re-emerged in the early 2000s (Hills 2007, Table 6.1).

The re-emergence of net subsidies reflected a reform to the system, which included an additional item of notional expenditure in HRAs – the Major Repairs Allowance, which was transferred by the local authority into a separate Major Repairs Reserve, where it could accumulate "to allow for more effective capital works expenditure planning" (Hills 2007, p. 61). Rent Rebates were taken out of the HRA, but in practice surpluses were redistributed between local authorities with the objective of removing anomalies in rent levels between local authorities – a national system of rent pooling. Rent restructuring also took place in the housing association sector with the grant distributing body (the Housing Corporation) assuming that applications from individual associations for capital subsidy would involve charging rents consistent with rent restructuring (Hills 2007). With various protections built into the system to prevent overly rapid rent rises, rent restructuring may be completed by around 2015.

Meanwhile the national HRA was tending towards surplus once again. In the mid-2000s, some 182 local authorities paid £615 million into the national HRA whilst just 52 received £694 million in subsidy (Wilson 2011). By 2009/10 a surplus was recorded (CLG Live table 651). Yet another reform then took place, which was intended to create a "final" settlement between local authorities and the central Government, and allow local authorities to become self-financing. This was achieved through a one-off redistribution of the outstanding housing debt between local authorities based on each authority's ability to service debt and maintain stock (Wilson 2011). This involved some very large redistributions with seven local authorities making payments in excess of £0.25 million and six receiving payments above this level (Pawson and Wilcox 2012). The Treasury also received a one-off payment of £8 billion (ibid.).

Many local authorities hoped that the settlement would allow them once again to build new social housing at a rate of perhaps 10,000 units a year. However, the Government's assumptions behind the introduction of "self-financing" in April 2012 reduced the scope of local authorities to build, and it seems that additional expenditure released through self-financing is more likely to be spent on repairs and stock improvement (Wilson 2011). Three-quarters of receipts from right to buy sales continue to be returned to central government. The government can also cap borrowing by local authorities, which (under UK accounting conventions) it does to control public spending. Moreover, the government has retained a provision that allows it redistribute debt again.

12.6 The Emergence of Housing Associations as the Main Providers of Social Rented Housing

Over the past quarter of a century the social housing sector has been transformed in another way. After central government subsidies for social housing was introduced in 1919, local authorities were chosen as the principal vehicle for the delivery of social housing. So, until the 1980s, almost all social housing was provided by local authorities. Housing associations, private non-profit (and usually charitable) organisations were often a legacy of nineteenth century philanthropy, and played only a niche role in the housing system, for example playing a leading role in neighbourhood renewal in the 1970s. In 1980, more than 90 % of social housing in the UK was provided by local authorities and just 7.5 % by housing associations (DCLG Live Table 101). In 2008, housing associations overtook local authorities as the main providers of social rented housing in the UK. In 2011, around 55 % of social housing in the UK was owned by housing associations and around 45 % by local authorities (DCLG Live Table 101).

Whilst local authorities have lost stock through the right to buy and demolitions, the shift in the balance between housing associations and local authorities was also attributable to new build by housing associations and transfers of local authority housing to housing associations (the later known as "stock transfers").

Stock transfers were prompted by the Government's changes to local authority Housing Revenue Accounts that came into operation in 1990 (see above). Some local authorities facing negative subsidy considered it to be beneficial to divest themselves of their hosing stock in order to avoid "negative subsidy" when Rent Rebate subsidy was taken into the Housing Revenue Account. These authorities made use of a provision that allowed them to transfer their entire stock to a housing association, which could be established for the purpose. These transfers are known as Large Scale Voluntary Transfers.

Fig. 12.3 Stock transfers (Source: Wilcox (2006), Tables 68a, 68d, 68e; Pawson and Wilcox (2010), Table 68)

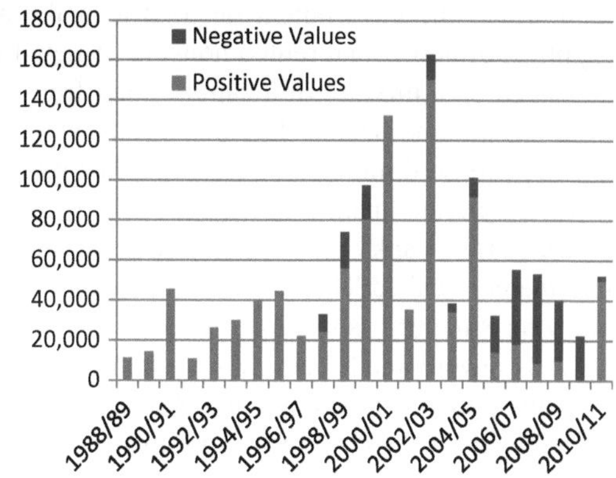

For a transfer to take place, tenants have to be balloted. The transfer value is based on the concept of tenanted market value, which is set at the net present value of net rental income over the next 30 years. Net rental income takes into account future repairs and maintenance obligations and the loss of rental income through right to buy. Since the local authorities with surpluses in the HRAs tended to be those with low levels of outstanding housing debt, their stock was also of positive value, i.e. its value was greater than the outstanding debt. These authorities were typically suburban or rural with stock of a generally high standard and with low housing debt. To reflect the loss of "negative" subsidy the Treasury introduced a "dowry" to be paid on transfer. Tenants retained their right to buy after transfer, and rents levels were usually guaranteed for a number of years. The upgrading of the stock was also a key attraction of transfer for tenants, and this was to become key to future transfer policy. Since housing associations are private organisations (albeit non-profit) they can borrow money without it scoring as public spending.

However, stock transfers were not viable in the areas where social housing was in the worst physical condition and in most need of renovation. In urban areas with problematic housing built in the 1960s and 1970s and high levels of outstanding debt, the transfer value of housing was too low to pay off outstanding debt. In the 1990s, the government introduced a subsidy programme called the Estate Renewal Challenge Fund which allowed local authorities to bid for subsidy to facilitate transfer and then upgrade the stock (Fig. 12.3).

These small-scale transfers gave way to some large-scale transfers of negative value stock. As part of its drive to improve the quality of social housing, the government was prepared to subsidise these transfers, the largest of which was the city of Glasgow with more than 80,000 properties. The Glasgow transfer involved the government writing off almost £1 billion of the city's housing debt, and heralded a large upgrading programme. However, whilst around 75 % of transfer ballots resulted in approval for transfer, this was not always the case. The Glasgow transfer was controversial and subsequent ballots in Edinburgh and Birmingham were rejected. After these, transfers of the entire stock of local authority housing in large cities ended. Transfers continue on a smaller scale, and the total transferred exceeds one million dwellings in England alone.

In 1988, the government decided to make housing associations the principal suppliers of new social rented housing. A new funding system was introduced that depended on a mixture of a capital grant from central government and borrowing from the private sector. Initially grants were very high (80 % or even more), although these diminished over time. For the first time housing associations had to access private finance on a large scale, which they did both in the form of loans secured from banks and bonds issued by individual associations or through an intermediary called The Housing Finance Corporation. This had the advantage of allowing smaller associations to access private finance, although the trend was towards development being concentrated among very large housing associations that emerged as regional associations merged with one another.

From 1990 onwards, use was made of planning obligations as a means of funding social and other forms of affordable housing. Development rights were nationalised in the UK in 1947, and when planning permission is granted for a developer to build on a particular site, the value of the site is enhanced. Since the 1970s, so-called "planning gain" was used to pass some of the costs of developing infrastructure on to the developers who benefited from them. From 1990, such obligations were also increasingly used to fund social and other forms of social housing. These "section 106 agreements" (named after the section in the Act that permitted their use) became an important source of subsidy for social housing (Crook and Monk 2011). The model worked well in the years of rising property values up until the credit crunch in 2007, but in the climate of a depressed property market, the government has suggested that developers' obligations to provide affordable housing might be reduced or even removed where they are an impediment to development.

12.7 New Supply in an Era of Austerity

The housing budget has been one of the principal casualties of the government's austerity programme. As a consequence of the 2010 Spending Review, the budget for housing development was cut by 60 % for the 4 years beginning in April 2011. Of the £4.5 billion that was allocated to housing, £2.7 billion had already been committed, leaving £1.8 billion to form the basis of a new funding model.

The new funding model is called the "Affordable Housing Programme" and is intended to make the limited public finds available to go further and to assist the construction of some 80,000 new dwellings. The grant per unit is being cut from an average of £60,000 per house to £20,000. (NAO 2012). "Social" rents are to be replaced with "affordable" rents that can be as high as 80 % of market rents. Housing associations themselves will become more dependent on raising private finance and cross-subsidising new developments.

The public funds for the programme were allocated by competitive bidding – and were oversubscribed – so there was no difficulty in persuading enough housing associations to participate. Rents so far have averaged 75 % of market levels, lower

(65 %) in London where market rents are much higher than the national average. Outputs are back-end loaded, so around 56 % of completions will occur in the final year of the programme. This has contributed to a collapse in social/affordable housing starts. These fell from 35,690 in 2010/11 to 12178 in 2011/12 (Housing and Communities Agency, Table 1a).

A key factor in the success of the programme is the ability of housing associations to raise sufficient private finance. It is expected that they will have to raise more finance in the 4 years of this programme than they have raised over the past two decades. They have achieved this so far, with an increasing use of bonds. However, there are doubts about the sustainability of the programme beyond the 4 year period. This is because some housing associations will reach the limits to their borrowing capacity, although others maintain that they could support another round (Stephens and Williams 2012). One consequence is that other ways of attracting finance into the sector are being explored.

12.8 Housing Benefit

A further controversy in the finance of social housing arises from changes to Housing Benefit (HB). More than 60 % of tenants in social rented housing receive HB to help them pay the rent. It is almost always paid directly to the landlord. It is widely believed that this arrangement helps to reduce rent arrears. However, the costs of HB have grown and the programme is being cut back.

In April 2013 a weekly overall benefit cap for working age people will be introduced of £350 for single people and £500 for couples and lone parents. The government's estimates suggest that half the 56,000 households likely to be affected live in London and almost half will live in social rented housing (DWP 2012a). Mean losses approach £100 per week (ibid.). Although not specifically a cut to Housing Benefit, the Government's estimates suggest that only tenants will be affected, so clearly HB entitlement plays a major role in lifting benefit "entitlement" over the cap. Moreover, the money will be recouped by cutting HB.

A "bedroom tax" will also be introduced in April 2013, with HB being cut for households judged to be under-occupying their social housing. If a household is under-occupying their house by one room, their HB will be cut by 14 %; if they are under-occupying it by two or more rooms, their HB is cut by 25 %. The measure applies only to working age households (i.e. pensioners are exempted). The measure is likely to affect 660,000 households (that is 30 % of working age social tenants on HB). They will lose on average £14 per week (DWP 2012b).

A third change involves the introduction of a new system of social security called Universal Credit. It will be phased in from October 2013, and will involve the incorporation of HB into a single welfare payment for working age households. One effect of this change will be the payment of all benefit income (including the housing cost element) to the claimant, rather than the landlord. Exemptions may apply for "vulnerable" households, but it is not yet clear how vulnerability will be defined. Of course, social landlords fear that the new arrangement will make it much more difficult to collect rents.

Overall, the changes to social security benefits threaten to undermine the security that HB has provided to the social rented sector in general, and to housing associations in particular. If housing associations begin to record higher levels of rent arrears, then it is possible that this affect the willingness of the markets to lend to housing associations and the terms of loans.

12.9 Conclusions

As the centenary of government subsidies for social rented housing approaches, it is possible to reflect on the changing role of the sector. Adopted as a temporary expedient, it became an enduring feature of the British housing system, being used as a tool to rid the country of slum housing and to provide decent housing for everyone. At its peak, it housed a third of households, but the removal of the overall shortages of housing in the 1970s and the growth of owner-occupation weakened the strong political support that the sector had once enjoyed. The economic crisis of the mid-1970s followed by the ideological hostility of the Thatcher governments ensured that the sector would decline. The success of Right to Buy was founded on the maturity of the sector and the fact that it had provided much high quality and popular housing. The shift towards a social rented sector provided by housing associations rather than local authorities, reflected both an ideological hostility to local authorities and the government's public spending conventions that count borrowing by local authorities as public spending, but exclude borrowing by housing associations. Although the sector has residualised and shrunk, much of it has also been refinanced in order to improve its quality. Within the context of growing poverty and income inequality since the 1970s, social housing has arguably provided a safety net for a substantial proportion of the population. This role may be threatened by the shift towards "affordable" rents and cuts in Housing Benefit, both of which may cause housing associations to focus on somewhat better off households.

References

Clapham D, Kintrea K (1984) Allocation systems and housing choice. Urban Stud 22(2):261–269

Crook ADH, Monk S (2011) Planning gains, providing homes. Hous Stud 26(7–8):997–1018

Daunton MJ (1984) Introduction. In: Daunton MJ (ed) Councillors and tenants: local authority housing in English cities, 1919–39. Leicester University Press, Leicester, pp 1–38

Department for Work and Pensions (2012a) Benefit cap (housing benefit) regulations 2012: impact assessment, 16 July. DWP, London

Department for Work and Pensions (2012b) Housing benefit: size criteria for people renting in the social rented sector. Equality Impact Assessment, updated, June. DWP, London

Department of Communities and Local Government (2012) English housing survey: households 2010–11. DCLG, London
Finnigan R (1984) Council housing in Leeds, 1919–39: social policy and urban change. In: Daunton MJ (ed) Councillors and tenants: local authority housing in English cities, 1919–39. Leicester University Press, Leicester, pp 101–153
Fitzpatrick S (2008) The contribution of the statutory homelessness system. In: Fitzpatrick S, Stephens M (eds) The future of social housing. Shelter, London, pp 39–52
Gibb K, Whitehead C (2007) Towards a more efficient use of housing finance and subsidy. Hous Stud 22(2):183–200
Glyn S (2006) Playing the ethnic card – politics and ghettoisation in London's east end. University of Edinburgh Institute of Geography Online Paper Series: GEO-018 http://www.era.lib.ed.ac.uk/bitstream/1842/1397/1/sglynn001.pdf
Hills J (2007) Ends and means: the future roles of social housing in England, CASE Report 34. London School of Economics, London
Kintrea K (2008) Social housing and spatial segregation. In: Fitzpatrick S, Stephens M (eds) The future of social housing. Shelter, London, pp 69–83
Land Enquiry Committee (1913) The land. Volume II: urban. Hodder & Stoughton, London
Lupton R, Tunstall R, Sigle-Rushton W, Obolenskaya P, Sabates R, Meschi E, Kneale D, Salter E (2009) Growing up in social housing in Britain. A profile of four generations, from 1946 to the present day. Tenant Services Authority, London
Lyons M (2007) Lyons inquiry into local government. TSO, London
Mathias P (1969) The first industrial nation: the economic history of Britain 1700–1914. Methuen, London
Munro M (2007) Evaluating policy towards increasing owner occupation. Hous Stud 22 (2):243–260
National Audit Office (2012) Financial viability of the social housing sector: introducing the affordable homes programme, HC 465. The Stationery Office, London
Offer A (1981) Property and politics 1870–1914. Landownership, law, ideology and urban development in England. Cambridge University Press, Cambridge
Pawson H, Wilcox S (2010) UK housing revue 2010/11. Chartered Institute of Housing, Coventry
Pawson H, Wilcox S (2012) UK housing review 2012 briefing paper. Chartered Institute of Housing, Coventry
Ravetz A (1974) Model estate: planned housing at Quarry Hill Leeds. Croom Helm, London
Rowntree BS (1901[2000]) Poverty: a study of town life. Macmillan, London [Policy Press, Bristol]
Stephens M (ed) (2005) Evaluation of individual policies and technical report: evaluation of English housing policy 1975–2000. Office of the Deputy Prime Minister, London
Stephens M, Williams P (2012) Tackling housing market volatility in the UK – a progress report. Joseph Rowntree Foundation, York
Stephens M, Burns N, McKay L (2002) Social market or safety net? British social rented housing in a European Context. Policy Press, Bristol
Stephens M, Elsinga M, Knorr-Siedow T (2014) The privatization of social housing: three different pathways. In: Scanlon K, Whitehead C, Fernández-Arrigoitia M (eds) Social housing in Europe. Wiley-Blackwell, Oxford (forthcoming)
Wilcox S (2006) UK housing revue 2006/07. Chartered Institute of Housing, Coventry
Wilcox S, Fitzpatrick S, Stephens M, Please N, Wallace A, Rhodes D (2010) The impact of devolution: housing and homelessness. Joseph Rowntree Foundation, York
Wilson W (2000) Rent rebates and local authority housing revenue accounts, House of Commons Library research paper 00/87. House of Commons Library, London
Wilson W (2011) The reform of housing revenue account subsidy, Standard Note: SN/SP/4341. House of Commons Library, London
Wootton D (2006) Bad medicine: doctors doing harm since Hippocrates. Oxford University Press, Oxford
Young M, Wilmott P (1957) Family and kinship in east London. Pelican, London

Chapter 13
"Everyone Should Be Housed": The French Generalist Model of Social Housing at Stake

Claire Lévy-Vroelant

13.1 Introduction

13.1.1 European Trends in Social Housing Systems

Today, in France as in most European nations (Houard 2011; Scanlon and Whitehead 2013), housing represents a highly strategic point where the ideas of justice, redistribution, and democracy are at stake. On the one hand, social housing systems are impacted by European regulations. Social housing is a SGEI in Community law, and the future of social housing may be shaped by the decisions of the European Court of Justice, as the recent Dutch case shows (Ghékière 2011). On the other hand, the debates are colored by national situations. In one way or another, housing has fully entered the national public arenas as a political object, with the socioeconomic transformations leading to the revision of the representations and shape of the whole social question. Currently, the French-subsidized rental housing system is clearly at the core of debates and decisions involving a large range of actors. Caught "between inertia and change" (Driant 2011), the whole sector is in a process of revision under a range of pressures (Levy-Vroelant and Tutin 2010b).

Given this situation, it is worth distinguishing the different issues that are currently a matter of debate. Most are not typically French; similar concerns are being discussed all over Europe. Beyond the heterogeneity of social housing systems (Ghékière 2011), major trends can be identified: the shift toward privatization and "residualisation," the redefinition of target groups, the reorientation of public funding from direct subsidies (the so-called brick and mortar) to personal allowances, the concentration and hybridization of social housing enterprises (Mullins et al. 2012), and the inflation of fiscal incentives (Pollard 2010). A parallel and paradoxical

C. Lévy-Vroelant (✉)
University of Paris, 8 Saint-Denis, Centre de recherche sur l'habitat,
UMR LAVUE 7281, CNRS, France
e-mail: clevyvroelant@gmail.com

J. Chen et al. (eds.), *The Future of Public Housing: Ongoing Trends in the East and the West*, DOI 10.1007/978-3-642-41622-4_13,

process takes place: the legal strengthening of housing rights *and* the weakening of collective protections in the context of the changing missions of the State (Lévy-Vroelant 2011), and the capacity to successfully deal with the homelessness under question (EOH report 2011). Last but not least, housing has become a tool for urban policies, through intensive fund raising at the local, national, and now European level. The urban renewal process, which operates almost everywhere in Europe, also uses social housing as a tool to reorganize urbanity and the spatial distribution households with various degrees of achievement. However, the people's effective power to choose their home and location remains uncertain.

13.1.2 The "French Model" at Stake

Such trends are also active in France where, as in other national contexts, path dependency determines specific configurations and answers (Lévy-Vroelant et al. 2013). The national distribution according to the tenure status is quite balanced: 56 % of households are homeowners (of which 80 % live in individual houses), 22.3 % are tenants in the private rental sector (70 % reside in apartments in collective buildings), and 17.3 % are social tenants (85 % live in apartments); 4.5 % have "other status" (such as furnished flats, free accommodations, etc.). Around ten million inhabitants live in a social housing unit.

The French social sector belongs to the "generalist" family (together with Austria, Germany, Belgium, Italy, Finland, Czech Republic, Poland, and Luxembourg) (Ghékière 2008). Such "model" is characterized by a large (but not universalist) targeting regarding the population to be housed, as well as the use of priority criterions. It also comprehends the domination of social landlords in the allocation process and the role of the State in providing funds and determining rent levels and income ceilings. However, such "model" is at stake. Contradictory pressures are operating in the social housing sector, which is required to be at the same time an instrument for implementing social cohesion, territorial equity, and the right to housing for all. Consequently, the population to be targeted, the level of prices, the relation between private and public supply, the implementation of the recently reinforced right to housing (Brouant 2011), the ongoing decentralization of financial and administrative powers, and the allocation process and its effects on both social and spatial equity[1] are crucial issues that, interestingly enough, are a matter of discussion in the academic milieu and among lobbying activists and have reached (again)[2] public opinion.

The French subsidized housing sector is a realm of various contradictions. In this chapter, we consider these contradictions as non-commonplace starting points. First

[1] In France, the "spatial equity" paradigm has been approved through the nomination of the ministry in charge of housing, called "*Ministère de l'Egalité des territoires et du logement*" (Ministry of Territories' Equality and housing).

[2] As in the postwar period (1950s and 1960s), during which housing was regarded as a national concern in opinion, if not in policy.

of all, far from being on the decrease, the social housing stock is quite large not only in number (between four and five million dwellings, according the perimeter considered; see Sect. 13.3) but also in proportion to the total stock (17–18 % of households) and to the rental stock (around 44 % of rental housing units belong to social landlords). Conversely to the trend generally observed in Europe, the social housing stock does not tend to decrease and seems rather to be experiencing a revival. At the same time, it suffers a bad reputation and is currently blamed for functioning as a filter and excluding (or even discriminating) on the basis of poverty, presumed insolvency, or "ethnic" background. These concerns are put in fast-forward on the national and European level by defenders of the right to housing for all (Feantsa reports 2008, 2011; Comité de suivi DALO report 2012; FAP report 2013). Scientific literature has also largely explored such hypotheses (Sala Pala 2005; Wacquant 2008; Pichon 2011). Those approaches seek to demonstrate that the French social housing system does not fulfill the expectations toward more territorial equity (Blanc 2010; Jaillet 2011) or even that it participates, with the excuse of getting rid of ghettos, in discriminative processes through "local methods for managing local diversity" (Kirszbaum 2011). The *de facto* concentration of households with migrant backgrounds in "sensitive" and mediocrely maintained social housing areas reveal a "hidden" filtering process (not solely income-based) that challenges not only the "generalist model" but also the "Republican model" (which supposes indifference to origins under any circumstances). Finally, the role of the subsidized sector in accommodating the poorest and those "most in need" is in line with its mission of general interest, but the State representatives (namely the prefects) are not always in a position to impose their views on the outcomes of the allocation procedure. *Are HLM to be burnt?*[3] Such a provocative and radical implicit assumption associates the 2005 riots to the housing question; in doing so, it embraces the large range of concerns (and hopes) of which housing, and more particularly social housing, has become a symbol.

13.1.3 Building Coalitions: Discourses and Practices

The HLM system has its critics, as well as some enemies,[4] but in most cases, these critics do not intend to deny its necessity. Some are clearly targeting a reform that should improve the sector, and, emblematically, the attribution process is pointed out for its lack of transparency and fairness (Bourgeois 2012; Houard and Lelévrier 2012); others are advocating for a general revision of housing policies. Considering the high level of housing rents (social and private) as the main factor favoring increasing inequalities, some propositions are converging toward a joint mobilization of both

[3] According to a recent book: Lefebvre J.-P., *Faut-il brûler les hlm? De l'urbanisation libérale à la ville solidaire*, Paris, l'Harmattan, 2008, 392 p.

[4] Mostly, the Private Real Estate Professionals' Union (UNPI) has been accusing social housing enterprises of distorting fair concurrence, and it has actually lodged a complaint against social housing with the European Commission.

public and private housing stocks to be opened to those most in need (Lévy and Fijalkow 2012). In this last case, it is no longer the housing unit that needs to be "social" (or better socialized) but the rent, with the duty of compensating for the shortage in rent falling to the State. However, beyond these critics, there is a remarkable consensus on the indisputable necessity of social housing that needs to be investigated in detail. Looking at the discursive practices of policy and decision makers is a rather promising way to make this understandable (Zittoun 2000, 2009). We consider that stakeholders' actions and discursive activities are coherent and that one may shed light on the other. Additionally, framing the public opinion serves as a tool in coalition building, where actors have to convince (and combat) each other to achieve a consensus. The interpretative pattern usually accepted in describing the evolution of policies from the period after the Second World War fits into the current opinion that the social housing sector has weakened as a consequence of the loss of public intervention and the vanishing welfare state. It is necessary to go beyond such pattern because it closes the possibility to understand how the sector is carrying out transformation and adaptation and does not provide an alternative for the future but only expects a continuation of the current trend. Perhaps it would be more pertinent to reintroduce the terms of the debate, as well as the alliances along which social housing is being reconfigured, either from a defensive position or a more proactive one.

We start with the statement that the social housing sector in France, unlike what is often said, is far from disappearing and is still very strong, and we look for the explanation for such a situation (1). We then analyze the interplay of actors (national politicians, local representatives, social landlords, the State). In doing so, we put the HLM at the center and envisage the tools (both discursive and concrete) that the social housing sector explores and implements to cope with the new context and react to the new challenges (second part). The social housing responses and resources in dealing with change are then developed (third part). In the conclusion, we try to reinstall the debate in the larger context to specify the more important issues being raised regarding social housing in the present times, the first of which is its (probably insufficient) role in ensuring that "everyone should be housed."

13.2 The Strength of the Social Sector in France

13.2.1 The French Social Housing Realm

According to the latest data from USH[5] (*Union sociale pour l'habitat*), out of the overall stock of 27.680.000 housing units (INSEE 2012), social housing, also known as HLM (*habitation à loyer modéré*), accounts for 4.5 million, and

[5] The USH is the umbrella federation of the 761 social housing bodies that make up the sector. See USH *Données statistiques* 2012, http://www.union-habitat.org/sites/default/files/Donn%C3%A9es%20statistiques%202011.pdf, consulted 4/01/2013.

accommodating 16 % of households. The rate is actually 17 % because there are in total 4.8 million housing units submitted to income considerations regarding their allocation (or with a "social" purpose), including 320,000 dwellings belonging to the private sector and 350,000 belonging to the non-profit sector (but not HLM) (see Sect. 13.4); charities belong to a third sector and receive public support. While the number of private rented dwellings has remained almost constant, and private renting has decreased in proportion to the stock, the numbers of owner-occupied *and* socially rented homes have both roughly tripled since the 1960s. The weight of social housing in the economic and financial landscape is far from negligible, with an investment capacity of 17 billion euros and 160.000 employments provided, according to USH.[6] Since the 1960s, three distinct types of social housing have been produced, targeted at households of different income levels. There have been various programmes, each with its own acronym; the current ones are standard social housing (PLUS),[7] "very social" housing for lower-income households (PLAI),[8] and upper-income social housing (PLS)[9] (Lévy-Vroelant et al. 2013). The proportion of upper-income social housing in the total construction of social housing has grown (from 25 % in 2003 to 32 % in 2010), confirming the general shift toward more expensive rents (see Sect. 13.3), while the "very social" sector has become increasingly specialized and cut off from common and regulated social housing (Lévy-Vroelant and Reinprecht 2013).

About 85 % of social housing units are flats, and due to the recent history, half of the stock was built before 1976 (and one fourth, 1.12 million units, between 1966 and 1975). This legacy of the industrial period, also called the "three glorious decades" because of the economic growth that favored the democratisation of the "consumption society", standardized domestic facilities and generated the "modern" way of living (and thinking) that now appears to be problematic. During the 1970s, more than 110,000 social housing units were completed yearly. Those estates are nowadays a matter of concern, not because they were intrinsically offering bad housing conditions but because the dynamic economic and social environment generating upgrades in social mobility had come to an end by the beginning of the 1980s. At the beginning of the twenty-first century, large estates of more than 500 dwellings represented less than 6 % of the stock nationally, and new construction was oriented toward small housing estates, except in the large cities, such as Paris, Lyon, and Marseille, where the densification of the urban fabric has become a new standard (and a discursive common place) in relation to the energy consumption concern. At the same time, the share of individual houses is

---

6 http://www.union-habitat.org/les-hlm-de-%C3%A0-z/pr%C3%A9sentation-du-secteur/l%E2%80%99habitat-social-une-mission-d%E2%80%99int%C3%A9r%C3%AAt-g%C3%A9n%C3%A9ral, consulted 5/2/2013.

7 PLUS for *Prêt locatif à usage social* (rental loan with social use); 68 % of households are eligible.

8 PLAI for *Prêt locatif aidé d'intégration* (rental loan for integration); 31 % of households are eligible.

9 PLS for *Prêt locatif social* (social rental loan); 82 % of households are eligible.

increasing, accounting for almost one fourth of new production. The average size of new social housing estates is around 23 dwellings per building.

After the 1970s, social housing construction went down (to less than 50,000 by the turn of the century). However, since then it has increased remarkably. "The net balance (construction minus demolition for urban renewal and 5,000 sales to tenants/year) was above 50,000 in 2011, which makes of France the only European country (with Denmark) where the social rental stock is increasing both in absolute and relative terms." At the same time, the funding of the current ambitious program (150 000 per year) appears to be quite uncertain.

13.2.2 Social Housing: A Historical Consensus

The social housing of today (and plausibly of tomorrow) remains framed within a specific historical pattern. French social housing has its heroes, emblematic places, and, under these idealized images, a project for solving the conflict between labor and capital. The French system has developed on the "traditional" ground of (1) centralized governance, (2) a strong individualistic ideology favoring individual property and responsibility (the famous slogan "*enrichissez-vous*" ("get richer") launched by Guizot, head of the King Louis Philippe's government in 1840), (3) division between assistance (charity and philanthropy) and insurance (gained through class struggle), and (4) dominance of entrepreneurs as crucial economic stakeholders. In short, between 1850 and 1912,[10] the French understanding of the relation between State, civil society, companies, and financial power led to a set of laws and dispositions that enabled public authority to intervene in the "private" domain of housing. Obviously, the legal system plays a role (and is reflected) in the definition of the mission of social housing. In the case of France, the Civil Code and the following legal dispositions clearly distinguish between private ownership and renting, with the first considered as superior and almost unlimited by law and as a social norm. All together, these items (superiority of home ownership, ancient centralized governance, powerful entrepreneurs, charity as ultimate safety net) are reflected in social housing outcomes and in one of their more emblematic features: "where allocation there [in France] is dominated by representatives of local interests empowered to refuse disadvantaged people" (Ball 2008).

After the devastation of the Second World War, housing became part of the welfare state duties. Supportive political and economic decisions have been undertaken in Europe rather simultaneously, including the use of housing for welfare purposes. The HLM Act (1949) was enacted to ensure decent housing conditions

[10] 1850: the first law in favor of public health allowed *ad hoc* commissions to enter the domestic realm to tackle unhealthy housing situations. The Expropriation Act in the name of general interest soon followed. Around 1900, laws enabling social housing were voted on; the Bonnevay Law in 1912 is considered one of the most important because it created the municipal social housing companies (HBM, the predecessors of the current HLM).

for "the wage-workers and their families." In France, perhaps more strongly than in other countries, the social housing history has been parallel to the country's industrial and economic development. As a consequence, the social stock is concentrated in large cities (Paris, Lyon, and Marseille) and former industrial areas, such as the coal and iron mines and textile industry centers of the first industrialisation period (northern and eastern parts of France), as well as in large cities' suburbs and in "new towns" developed according to a centralized master plan from 1965 in order to counterbalance the Paris region's dominance. In terms of urbanism and architecture, the ideas of the modern movement (Le Corbusier) are fully mainstream. Two thirds of the existing social stock is located in towns with more than 100,000 inhabitants. Most of these locations now suffer from the economic crisis and the general mutation of the production process. They then cumulate socioeconomic handicaps and experience geographic isolation, with dilapidated or badly maintained urban environment and housing conditions. This situation has led to an important shift toward the "*politique de la ville*" ("urban policy") decided, ruled, and monitored at the central level by agencies such as ANRU[11] and symbolized by the creation of the so-called "sensitive urban area,"[12] where 7 % of the French population (around 4.4 million) live and which is mainly characterized by the importance of the social housing stock, 60 % on average (Chevallier and Lebeaupin 2010).

French subsidized housing is also characterized by the importance of the supply provided through the intervention of enterprises. From the beginning, as previously noted, companies have been keen on providing social housing to their workers in order to control them and improve productivity by securing their living conditions, besides philanthropic reasons. In the reconstruction era (1953), a "1 % tax" on wages was introduced to provide ring-fenced funds for housing investment. In 2011, "*Action Logement*",[13] which owns 785.000 social and intermediary housing units (in ESH form, see below), counted up the total income from enterprises' participation as 3.5 billion euros. The major part of urban renewal actions has been supported through Action Logement funding (to ANRU and ANAH).[14]

---

[11] ANRU (*Agence nationale pour la renovation urbaine*) is a powerful agency that organizes, promotes, and funds urban redevelopment in delimited areas (ZUS, sensitive urban areas, and those decided at the government level according to the PNRU (*Plan national pour la renovation urbaine*); around 40 billion euros worth of investment in 2004–2013). France is now entering the Second PNRU, with uncertainties regarding funding.

ZUS, see Observatory of French Sensitive Urban Areas, 2011, http://www.ville.gouv.fr/IMG/pdf/rapport-onzus-2012.pdf, consulted 3/02/2013.

[12] ZUS, see Observatory of French Sensitive Urban Areas, 2011, http://www.ville.gouv.fr/IMG/pdf/rapport-onzus-2012.pdf, consulted 3/02/2013.

[13] "Action Logement" is the new name of the ensemble composed of 31 CIL (*Comité interprofessionnel du Logement*).

[14] ANAH stands for *Agence nationale d'amélioration de l'habitat*, which is in charge of improving the private stock. In 2012, 341 million euros worth of housing units improvement were distributed were distributed. http://www.anah.fr/

Table 13.1 Housing units provided under income ceiling conditions

HLM bodies	Public and semi-public landlords	Private landlords
OPHLM = 2.18 million	SEM = 0.25 million	"Private-social housing" provided through fiscal incentives = 0.07
ESH = 1.9 million	Charities, third sector = 0.10 million	Social housing provided through ANAH subvention = 0.25
Cooperatives = 0.02 million		
Total = 4.1 million	Total = 0.35 million	Total = 0.32
Total = 4.77 million units		

Source: USH, Données statistiques 2012

13.2.3 USH and Its Components: Social Housing Organization and Financing

Social rental housing programs are owned and managed by two main kinds of providers that fall under the remit of the umbrella organization *Union sociale pour l'habitat* (USH): OPHLM, public agencies (*offices publics pour l'habitat*) chaired by local authority representatives; and ESH (*entreprises sociales pour l'habitat*). Semi-public organisms (SEM) also intervene in the supply (SEM and charities accredited through "public service mission delegation"), as do individual private landlords who take part in the social provision because they have benefited from the large fiscal incentive for purchasing a dwelling, which they have then rented out under social conditions (lower rents). Of the total 4.77 million dwellings delivered under income conditions, as shown in Table 13.1, HLM bodies are dominant, representing 86 % of the supply.

The HLM bodies also manage foyer furnished rooms (around 300 000); these are very specific to the French system, which since 1954 has provided separate accommodations for immigrant workers (the so-called *Foyers de travailleurs immigrés*, FTM) and young workers (the so-called *Foyer de jeunes travailleurs*, FJT) to facilitate internal migration during the period of huge economic growth (Lovatt et al. 2006).

An additional portion (around 800 000 dwellings) is considered as social because it offers rents below the market rates. This supply has heterogeneous origins: one part is provided by municipalities and the State, and the other is composed of the stock covered by the so-called "1948 law," which was enacted in 1948 to block the inflation of rents for the existing stock while liberating newly built units and stimulating the market. As a result, part of the ancient stock retained low rents and remained accessible to anyone, whereas the new construction market was stimulated. Recently, this law has been suppressed (with tolerance for older occupants). Also called the "*de facto* social housing provision," this sector has played a very important role in the integration of the modest-income population, and its disappearance (also due to intensive real estate speculation: more than one million units covered between 1985 and 1995) must be mentioned as a factor that worsens the shortage of affordable housing. As a whole, subsidized housing amounts to around six million dwellings. From the structure of the whole sector, one can observe the importance of HLM bodies, the very minor role of cooperatives, the (growing) importance of the "very social" part, and the mixing of legal forms between public (OPHLM) and private (individual private landlords).

In brief, the strength of the HLM system lies in its long history, in the collaboration between a large range of stakeholders, including economical and financial ones, in the strong nationally driven regulation, in the durable consensus on the necessity to activate the construction sector, and in the large support from public opinion. Interestingly enough, social housing is considered as necessary and even *indispensable* in order to implement social justice and solidarity, but its reputation is not good enough to make it *desirable*: social housing is good, but for the others. This leads us to consider the challenges that the sector has to face.

13.3 Challenges

13.3.1 Social Housing Tenants: Still a Diverse but Impoverished Population

Having acknowledged the diversity of the social housing system, one would easily agree that the different social organisms will not encounter the same type of challenges and that the location will also matter a lot. It can even be an artifact to consider social housing as a whole. Still, we need to know to what extent the households living in social dwellings do belong to the most "in need" section of the population.

According to INSEE documentation, *"in 2002, households in the four highest standardized income deciles amounted to 20 % of social housing residents. This proportion, albeit not negligible, is lower than ever (30 % in 1984). High income social housing residents enjoy on average much better housing conditions than poor ones. Nor do the former live in the same districts as the latter"* (Jacquot 2007). This means not only that the social tenants have become poorer but also that the sector is fragmented between the provision of good quality and attractive location and that of dilapidated and stigmatized housing, with a large variation between these two extremes. This trend is not new, as Fig. 13.1 shows, but has been reinforced in the past years, with the new tenants (residents for less than 3 years)[15] having a lower level of income than those in place and with the territorial inequalities having increased.[16]

[15] Called *"aménagés récents"* (recently moved in), they refer to a category used to measure changes in the French National Housing Survey.

[16] The data used in this section are mainly from *Enquête Occupation Parc Social, DGALN, 2009, exploitation CRÉDOC, http://www.developpement-durable.gouv.fr/IMG/pdf/tome1c.pdf (consulted 5/02/2013), and the last ONZUS report (Observatoire national des Zones Urbaines Sensibles, 2012).*

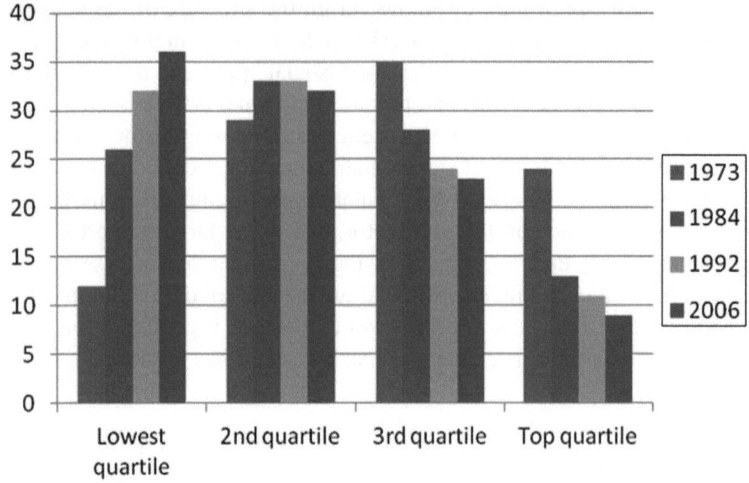

Fig. 13.1 Distribution of social housing tenants according to the income quartile, in 1973, 1984, 1992, and 2006 (Source: INSEE ENL (National Housing Survey), 1963–2006)

13.3.2 One or Several Social Housing Sectors?

The structure of the households also reveals the social housing sector's specificity: less couples, much more single-parent families, and also more dependent children; these trends have been accentuated in the last years. However, there are large differences according to the location, and the type of provider, as Table 13.2 shows. The non-HLM social housing sector (the park owned by semipublic and private social landlords) tends to be more similar to the national pattern, with couples with children being more numerous there than in the HLM sector (31.8 % versus 26.1 %); the same trends also hold for couples without children (13.4 % versus 15.3 %) and for single-parent families, which are expectably less numerous than in the HLM sector (17.7 % versus 19.2 %) despite being double the average in France (8.2 %).

Moreover, the social housing sector as a whole is not accommodating all households "in need": a large part of these households are housed in the private sector or own the flat where they live. Based on the distribution according to tenure status of the 6.9 million households considered as low-income,[17] 2.9 million own their flat (representing 20.4 % of owner-occupied housing), 1.9 million are accommodated in the private rental sector (36 % of the whole private rental market), and 2.1 million are present in the social sector (about half of social tenants). Even if the sector tends to accommodate more and more of the impoverished population, the lowest incomes are also distributed in other types of occupancy status.

[17] Low-income households: Those whose income is less than the half the median income; see Driant J.-C. and Rieg Ch., "Les ménages à bas revenus et le logement social," *INSEE première* n° 962, April 2004

Table 13.2 Structure of households in the social sector and in all sectors (France) and structure of social housing households in four regions (Ile de France, Alsace, Bretagne, and Languedoc Roussillon)

	France metropolitan		France metropolitan				
			All households	IDF	Alsace	Bretagne	Languedoc-Roussillon
	HLM Social housing tenants	*Other social landlords*	(2009, RGP)	HLM	HLM	HLM	HLM
Single	**36.4**	33	33.6	31.5	32.5	**46.5**	34
One parent families	**19.2**	17.7	8.2	19.4	16.5	20.7	**24.2**
Couple without children	**15**	15.8	25.9	14.4	16.9	12.1	13.1
Couples with children	**25.1**	30	27.1	28.3	29.8	18	25
Total couples	***40.1***	***45.7***	***53***	*42.7*	***46.7***	*32.2*	*38.1*
Other	**4.3**	3.8	5.2	**6.4**	4.3	2.7	3.7
Total	**100**				100	100	100

Source: Enquête Occupation Parc Social, DGALN, 2009, exploitation CRÉDOC and Insee, RP1990 sondage au 1/4 – RP1999 et RP2009 exploitations complémentaires

13.3.3 The Mismatch Between Demand and Supply

According to the recently published FAP annual report (FAP 2013), there are currently 1,179,857 social housing applicants (including the demand for internal mutation in the social sector), among which more than 400,000 are in the Paris region, where the tension is extremely high. In addition to the imbalance between demand and supply, the social housing allocation procedure is intrinsically opaque. Involving parties with reservation privileges, stakeholders of different kinds, and representatives of local authorities and (in theory) of the State, the Commission that rules on final attribution is often deemed discriminatory. Besides that, and in spite of the shortage, the application process sometimes results in refusals from the applicants when an offer comes. The USH has ordered a research to better understand the reasons for these refusals, which contribute to hampering the whole system.[18] The findings point to the existence of repellent dwellings that are difficult to rent out mostly because of their location. In addition, the refusals are also addressed to new and well-located housing, in which case the smaller spaces and higher rents discourage the applicant from accepting the offer. The new context of

[18] *Etude sur les refus d'attribution par les demandeurs de logement social.* Final Report FORS-Recherche sociale/CREDOC pour l'Union Sociale pour l'Habitat, November 2012, 76 p.

social housing production (increasingly through public-private partnership) negatively impacts "commercialization" because social landlords can lose control of the timing of the process. Finally, the applicants, who sometimes have to queue for years, could become aware of the market and develop different strategies; that is, refusals can happen simply because the applicant has changed his mind in the meantime.

The mismatch between offer and demand is also reflected in the difficulty of adapting the size of the household to the dwelling: there is a substantial fraction of social dwellings that are either under- or overcrowded. The numbers are difficult to estimate for several reasons, but generally, undercrowded units (650,000–800,000) are inhabited by elderly people do not vary according to the city size, whereas overcrowding (about the same number of dwellings but obviously concerning much more people), which touches mostly families with dependent children, displays a high prevalence in large cities and is associated with a low standardized income and unsatisfactory housing conditions (Jacquot 2007). Additionally, the proportion of inhabitants in place for less than 3 years in the total of social tenants is decreasing, down from 33 % in 2000 to only 27 % in 2009. The decreasing turnover, accentuated in the public sector (vis à vis the private one) and especially in large dwellings (three or more rooms), is both a result and a cause of the sclerosis of the housing provision dynamics. The rigidity of the allocation procedure can be considered to be aggravating the situation to a certain extent.

13.3.4 Less Public Direct Funding, More Fiscal Incentives

Preferential loans, granted by a specific bank (the *Caisse des Dépôts et consignations, CDC*)[19] are the main tools for producing social housing. The low interest rate is crucial, but even more important is the loan duration (usually 40 years). Besides the specific loans, social housing financing is a mix of subsidies, fiscal incentives, and consolidated equity capital. The nature of this mix has changed a lot over time. As a result of the move from brick-and-mortar subsidies to demand-side policies initiated in 1977, direct grants to social housing from the state budget are now limited. Consequently, additional funding is to be provided by municipalities (under direct subsidies or provision of cheap land), which makes it harder and uncertain for the social enterprises to achieve balanced budgets. However, at the same time, HLMs pay a reduced rate of VAT (7 % instead of 20 %) and benefit from a 25-year property tax exemption and from growing fiscal deductions so that one can consider that fiscal incentives have become the core of housing policies: between 1984 and 2006, direct subsidies to construction (brick-and-mortar

[19] The *Caisse des dépôts et consignations* is an old institution (founded in 1812) aimed at serving as a deposit bank for savings that are then oriented toward social housing construction (preferential loans).

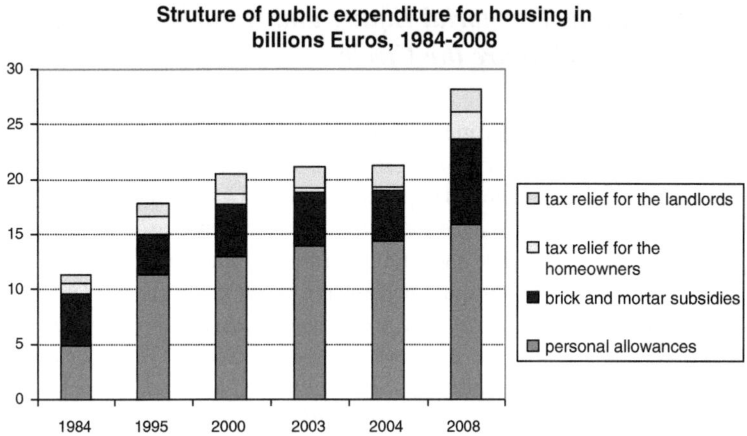

Fig. 13.2 Structure of public expenditure, 1984–2008, the four main social housing funding sources (Source: INSEE (2006) and comptes du Logement 2004 et 2008)

subsidies) have moved from 49 to 18 % (5.1 billion euros), whereas personal subsidies (to households) have moved from 34 to 51 % (14.7 billion euros), and fiscal deductions from 17 to 31 % (9 billion euros) (Pollard 2010) (Fig. 13.2).

To enlarge the supply and allow individuals to build up their assets, various fiscal incentives have been offered.[20] In exchange, investors had to agree to rent ceilings and minimum rental periods. These programmes have contributed to the provision of more affordable housing to quite a large extent (Pollard 2010), but this new provision's results are random, not sufficiently targeted both socially and geographically, and primarily benefit private investors. Besides the acknowledged trend consisting in the switch from brick and mortar to personal allowances (the latter still go to the social landlord as a complement to the rent), the other important shift is the generalized use of fiscal incentives, which appears to be less transparent, less controllable, and less socially fair. With market deregulation or reorganization (public-private partnerships, concurrence in the social sector itself, changes in the characteristics of the provision, etc.) and permanent intervention (social benefits, tax policies, real estate construction governance, etc.) being two faces of the same coin, the objective is then to analyse properly this apparent paradox by identifying the stakeholders' actions and discourses, as well as the alliances they establish among them.

[20] The different devices of tax exemption regarding housing received their name from their promoter, generally the Minister of Housing in place. These are more or less "social" according to the government's political orientations. There was the Périssol in 1996, the Besson in 1999, the de Robien in 2003, and Borloo in 2006. After Scellier in 2009, the current Minister, Cécile Duflot, also proposed a renewed device based on fiscal incentives.

13.3.5 *Providing Territorial Equity and Right to Housing: Trying to Square the Circle*

Social housing bodies are now in a delicate position because the change in funding sources forces them to liaise with financing consortia and negotiate for each project. They have to meet each financer's expectations (type of housing units, rents levels, environmental concerns). Because the central government has contractually delegated the distribution of brick and mortar to local authorities, the latter are in a position to rule on projects and again become prevalent in the game. "*This handover has partially altered the social housing production landscape by making more room for local and regional plans to increase available capacity. That was how in the name of 'social mix,' 'urban renewal', and 'controlled urban development', social housing production processes have been greatly diversified over the past decade, giving rise to new issues such as housing replacement, diversification and density management, in the agenda, alongside the original goal to merely increase capacity*" (Driant 2011, p.120). In other words, social housing enterprises have been "invited" to enter the urban renewal market, a highly competitive environment, and to act as a tool for the implementation of urban *and* social policies. They execute demolitions (18 000 in 2010), behave as developers, or even buy from developers: since 2000, social housing organisations have been authorised to buy housing units built by private developers and sold-off plans (*Vente en état futur d'achèvement*, VEFA), which has been the main sale option for French property developers since it was established in 1967 (Driant 2011).

Simultaneously, the main actors in housing policy (government, local authorities, national social housing federation, NGOs, experts, and media) have pushed for (or accepted) an enforceable right to housing. The so-called DALO Act[21] was debated on with passion (Was it a good means to improve the rights of those who could hardly access any right?) and voted on in 2007. When the time came to assess the situation, both hopes and frustrations were found to result from its difficult implementation. Emblematically, the 6th report of the monitoring committee published in November 2012 is entitled "*Rappel à la Loi*" ("Reminder of the Law") and showed unequal and dissatisfactory implementation (Houard and Lévy-Vroelant 2013). When the enforceable right to housing started to be considered by the government (2005), most local authority representatives were anxious that they could become individually accountable and that the State was taking an opportunity to shirk its responsibilities. The USH was internally divided. With the impoverishment of a portion of the social tenants, the "fight against the ghettos," and the call to provide poor people with housing solutions, the introduction of the enforceable right provided an opportunity to strengthen the image of HLMs as "providers of housing to the poor" (Houard 2011).

[21] See a recent law, the so-called DALO, on "opposable right to housing" (2007), which establishes the responsibility of the State to provide a home to everyone in need and the possibility for an individual to claim this right in court.

13.3.6 The Bad Reputation

In the context of post-welfare policies, social housing is then also concerned with urban policies. A large proportion of immigrants live in large social housing estates, which are precisely those targeted by urban renewal policies. Approximately more than one in five social housing units are located in ZUS. Social housing is thus *officially* connected with images of dilapidated urban landscapes and social exclusion and has become a top political priority. The rhetoric of the "ghetto" is used to support ideologically the vast (and sometimes contested) implementation of urban renewal policies, using and abusing the social mix rhetoric.

A victim and guilty at the same time, the USH pleads, with some reasons, for its social necessity. The representation of social housing in public opinion perfectly fits into this double-faced feature, as shown in a recent survey ordered by the USH,[22] in which 80 % of those interviewed regarded social housing as a necessity, and 74 % agreed that social housing has a bad image. On the one hand, social housing is popular because it is associated with security (of tenure) and the idea of the State as a provider of a certain level of protection and wealth. On the other hand, social housing is connected with negative representations. The impoverishment of the tenants and the spatial segregation associated with criminality nurture a bad image of the sector. The displacement of social policies (non-territorialized) into urban policies (territorialized) contributes to the negative reputation of social housing neighbourhoods. A boomerang effect is to be expected because urban renewal programs particularly target areas that include large-scale demolitions,[23] with the reduction of antisocial behaviours and criminality as official targets.[24] Additionally, the bad maintenance of most large estates built in the 1960s and 1970s (and sometimes even more recently) is a matter of deep frustration: successive national housing surveys show that social housing tenants have a higher degree of dissatisfaction. A last line of huge critics, with evident political background, targets the "privileged" part of the sector, which is well-located, well-designed, and still affordable, and points to it as a realm of uncontrolled clientelism and social injustice. Even so, social housing is considered as a common good that needs to be preserved.

---

[22] Baromètre d'image du logement social, TNS SOFRES 2011, http://www.tns-sofres.com/_assets/files/2011.06.08-logement.pdf, consulted 9/2/2013.

[23] The 2004–2013 plan envisages the demolition of 139,000 housing units. By the end of 2011, 73,000 housing units had been effectively demolished (93,700 planned) and only 39,7000 had been built (73,000 planned): http://www.ville.gouv.fr/IMG/pdf/rapport_onzus_2011.pdf, p. 264.

[24] See http://www.ville.gouv.fr/IMG/pdf/rapport_onzus_2011.pdf, pp. 141–165.

13.4 The Social Housing Sector's Retort

13.4.1 USH Gets a Handle on Its Destiny as a Mainstream "Social Housing Market"

The goal of accomplishing a "mission of general interest" is at the core of the USH communication strategy. The USH home page insists on the values, meaning, and coherence of such mission, especially in a context of increasing economic and social frailty combined with the inflation of real estate prices and rents on the private market.[25] A key sentence is: "Social housing's mission is essential to preserving social cohesion and for a better 'living together'".[26] The notions of solidarity, quality, and affordability, as well as of social mix, progress, and sustainable development contribute to the positioning of the USH as an alternative and indispensable "social housing market," "benefitting one French in six."

The rhetoric is quite habile in combining the contradictory challenges of serving social cohesion (being attractive and mainstream-oriented) and implementing the right to housing (showing solidarity and targeting those most in need); however, the emphasis is definitely on the first: *"social mix depends on the political will to promote, in a given geographical area, diversity in terms of socio professional categories, standard of living and/or lifestyle."* This topic is balanced by the emphasis on housing a large part of low-income households and, consequently, on promoting solidarity: *"one third of social tenants households earn less than 795 euros per month/person."*

The second argument goes back to the very origins and presents social housing as a pioneer in the field of architectural and technological innovation. Only the issue has changed; instead of promoting comfort and modern living standards (as was the case from the late nineteenth century to the 1920s and then again in the 1960s), energy saving has become a new paradigm: "*85 % of the new social housing units receive the label of energetic performance*."

The third argument refers to the general interest and is double-sided. On the one hand, social housing serves as a cost-of-living insurance that enables households to participate in the consumer society, *"enabling their goods and services consumption and their participation to local economy."* On the other hand, the emphasis is put on the economic importance of the sector as a provider of employment on the French labor market: *"the construction of one housing unit represents the creation of more than one non-relocatable employment on the national labor market."* This last argument is certainly very powerful in coalition building.

---

[25] http://www.union-habitat.org/les-hlm-de-%C3%A0-z/pr%C3%A9sentation-du-secteur/l%E2%80%99habitat-social-une-mission-d%E2%80%99int%C3%A9r%C3%AAt-g%C3%A9n%C3%A9ral, consulted 8/2/2013.

[26] Free author's translation from French for all USH website quotations.

13.4.2 The Agreement on Production and the Coalition Building

The objectives of the government (the call for more public money as direct investments and for recognition of the leading role of social housing in urban renewal) have received continuous support in the last decades, even though conflicts between the USH and the minister in charge of housing under the Sarkozy presidency have been highlighted by media. Today, nearly all the political parties in France consider it necessary to increase the production of new housing units. This option is clearly connected with the aim of reconfiguring neighbourhoods and achieving "social mix" and "social cohesion." Under these different aspects, as previously discussed, social housing is central. The choice of a member of the Green Party as minister in charge of housing (Cécile Duflot), may indicate the political will to combine environment concerns with the promotion of the construction. The current minister is in a position to push the sustainability issue as well, that is to say, to promote renovation instead of placing the whole bet on construction. However, the discourse remains very much production-oriented (with 500,000 new housing units/year as a repetitively announced objective), and the discussion now focuses on the share of social housing in the whole target (150,000 units) and, significantly, the proportion of "more social" housing (that is to say, those funded through PLAI and with lower rents) to the whole.

It is worth mentioning that the argument has been taken up at the European level. The promotion of social housing as "a lever for helping the European Union to end up with the economic, social, and environmental crisis" is making way.[27] The social housing federation's efforts to restore and improve its image can then be interpreted as a way to overcome the contradictions and challenges it has to face.

13.4.3 Changing Image and Reputation

As previously discussed, social housing as a whole has to tackle different negative representations. The first one is linked to images of dilapidated, insecure, and poor neighbourhoods. The challenge is to break down the stigma. In this regard, a large communication strategy is organized, sometimes with the commitment of the State or the local authority. Rich documentation is actively distributed during the urban renewal operations. At the national level, a document is proposed, with the idea of

[27] http://www.developpement-durable.gouv.fr/IMG/pdf/Dossier_de_presse_-_logement_socia2012-final.pdf

Consulted 10/2/2013. See also European Parliament, Karima Delli report for the Commission of Employment and Social Affairs (2012/2293(INI). http://www.europarl.europa.eu/sides/getDoc.do?pubRef=-//EP//NONSGML+COMPARL+PE-504.103+01+DOC+PDF+V0//FR&language=EN, consulted 1/2/2013.

"tackling 10 prejudices" about social housing. Interestingly enough, those prejudices all refer to the capacity of social housing to remain attractive or improve its attractiveness. In brief, the arguments are trying to cope with negative perceptions, which are those delivered by the "ZUS" label (noisy, crowded, located nowhere, ghettoized, anonymous, and banal), and to turn them upside down to promote the potentials of such supply in a disorganized market: greenness, conviviality, energy saving-orientation, and last but not least, professionalism, openness, and anticipation capacity. The *eco-quartiers*[28] are emblematic of such positioning. The USH quarterly journal *Habitat et Société* reveals the main knots and hopes of the social housing sector and shows how strongly the USH desires to deal with societal changes and be seen as a progress builder and lifestyle inventor in terms of young people's housing, mixing of communities, aging and housing, and gender and housing, among other issues. The USH is also very habile in converting its leading role during the past century's housing history into a symbolic capital. However, all these go together with the reconfiguring of the financial and managerial organisation of social housing organisms. This is definitely the strategic aspect of the on-going changes, considering that social enterprises, and primarily social landlords, have to successfully combine social *and* commercial goals.

13.4.4 Reconfiguring from Inside: Concentration, Hybridization, and Diversification

In 2007, a reform took place, and the historic OPHLM (municipal housing bodies) had to merge with the OPAC (public habitat bodies) and create a new structure, namely OPH (*Office public de l'habitat*). Beyond changing the labeling, the reform basically consisted in providing an optional choice for private accountancy in order to better fit the new obligations resulting from locally driven governance. In doing so, the Offices' management rules become more adapted to partnerships involving private companies.[29] Private operators can then enter the social housing market provision through public-private partnerships and acquisitions in VEFA. Middle-sized Offices are increasingly merging with each other or creating larger associations as a way to share technical departments and expertise in land, building, and commercial action (the newly composed "Paris Habitat," for instance, deals with 115,000 housing units).

To anticipate the diminution of direct funding, the 761 social housing organisations have also entered a process of mutualisation of their assets and equity funds. As stated by Marie-Noëlle Lienemann, the minister in charge of housing in the last

[28] Expected to be an exemplar of a sustainable city: http://www.developpement-durable.gouv.fr/Lancement-du-label-national,31489.html

[29] See GRIDAUH-USH report, "Le partenariat entre les organismes d'HLM et les opérateurs privés," September 2009

socialist government and currently the USH interim president, *"not a single euro must sleep in the cash of one single HLM body"* (73th USH Conference held in Rennes in September 2012). The consensus on the "optimal use" of capital equity is not so easy to realize due to competitiveness and diverging management options among the different organisms. Social housing bodies have therefore been reassessing their property portfolio management strategies and negotiating social benefit covenants with central and local governments. The employers' participation in social housing also shows the connections and collaborations between "social partners." The enterprise "*Foncière Logement*" is a result of public-private partnership. Funded mainly through Action Logement (fuelled by employers' contributions, formerly at "1 %"), it proposed "good standards housing" for wage workers whose enterprises participate in the employers' collection. The participation of Foncière Logement in the process of social housing production is emblematic of the recent orientations: in partnership with VINCI Construction, Foncière Logement buys the housing products in VEFA. In doing so, it opens preferential loans, such as PLS, with the private investor. Hybridization results in new competing organizational logics, trade-offs between social and commercial goals, and resource transfers (Czischke et al. 2012). It extends the boundaries of the playground to developers and investors.

In this context characterized by accentuated concurrence, and the "enabling state"-oriented governance, private developers (under SCI, SACI, and SCCV)[30] have become the more dynamic stakeholders in real estate construction. In 2005, they covered a third of the whole production. The share of public supply (social housing providers, local authorities, the State) in the housing production is now around 10 % of the total (compared to 25 % in the mid-1990s). Moreover, the usual credit tools dedicated to social enterprises are now open to private ones in the context of the urban renewal program. As well described in Vinci[31] documentation, the urban renewal program is an excellent playground for investors: *"Since 2005, the funds allocated by the State to the Urban renewal program have contributed to stimulate the real estate construction, where VINCI intends to strengthen its position."* In this context, social housing as a "product" serves, according to VINCI rhetoric, both private and general interests: it is a fructuous market allowing good profits and contributing, through social provision and more diversified "housing products," to the implementation of social cohesion. In this context, too, the conflict between stakeholders is related to the concurrence between developers who are pushed to seek out more convenient partnerships. On the side of social housing bodies, the recent transformation (2007) of their legal status, which enables them to adopt the rules of private accountancy and management, as mentioned above, goes together with the incentive to contract with the State and

[30] Different legal forms of private enterprises, called "civil societies," and composed of several individual or collective partners.

[31] VINCI is a well-known constructor that is active in different markets (mainly transport and construction), more recently in what we call the "social housing market." http://www.institut-entreprise.fr/fileadmin/Docs_PDF/travaux_reflexions/LLG07Financement/VINCI2presentation.pdf

territorial authorities and to adopt the regime of calls for bids and offers. European regulations, which encourage privatisation "under control" of social goods, play in the same direction (Ghékière 2011).

13.5 Conclusion

Since the last decade of the twentieth century, the French HLM system has been undergoing a metamorphosis. More recently, these transformations operate in a context where housing prices and rents have become increasingly unaffordable. French households are on average much better housed today than three decades ago, but the gap between those who can afford and those who cannot is increasing. In large cities, the concern is less about the housing shortage than on the uncontrolled level of real estate prices. The speculative bubble did not have the disastrous consequences verified in other countries. However, many issues, such as mobility and changing lifestyles, young people's needs, environmental stakes, and spatial inequity, combined with shrinking labour markets, have not found a satisfying resolution. The housing market is segmented and instable, especially in the Paris area and the largest cities. Households are rather expected to pay the full price and consent to personal sacrifices to secure themselves through homeownership. At the same time, the unequal participation of social groups in the distribution of goods is a matter of great concern that goes beyond the homelessness question. The achievement of "housing for all" does not seem to come any closer. Behind the housing question, the social question has reappeared.

At the same time, a "new deal" seems to be currently at work, displacing the mainstream historical relations between stakeholders and incorporating a new *modus operandi*. In this configuration, the State is no longer fully the leader or provider. It has become a *facilitator* that enables private actors to participate on the floor, while "social partners" alternate between protest and cooperation. In such context, the role of the social housing sector is crucial and, more than ever, symbolizes public concerns and hopes. While concentrating on and strengthening its assets, the sector is also currently reconfiguring its identity. Under the cover of mutation of financial devices, the reforms have reshaped the sector and reconfigured alliances; they have blurred the borders between the traditional subsidized sector and the private one, as well as fragmented the social housing provision. On the one hand, this has contributed to moving the two sectors closer to each other; however, it has also rigidified the housing provision into separate *and* competing markets. Actually, the main point is probably the continuity of a secular trend. In contrast with the idea of a "neoliberal" turn, it seems that ancient alliances between building companies, the social housing sector, and the government are gaining strength again. At the moment, the government is studying a way to increase and generalize fiscal facilities and to reduce the VAT from 5.5 to 5 % in social construction (and the renovation of dilapidated buildings), with a possibility to renounce the VAT increase for the whole building sector (from 7 to 10 % in

2014). Different contexts, different tools, same objectives: similarly to the decades following the Second World War, housing is a leading element of the whole economy and urban (re)development. Building has become a goal in itself as an instrument to tackle unemployment and boost economic growth. In this respect, social housing is in a good position.

The debate about how public money and common goods should be collected, allocated, and redistributed has nevertheless gained renewed importance. In spite of its efforts and strength, the social housing sector alone does not seem to have the capacity to meet housing needs or to insure the right to housing. In the near future, the more important task could be to re-embed the housing question into the achievement of the general interest. The social housing sector, with its legacy and legitimacy, could then play a leading role again, on condition that it operates under enlightened democratic control. After all, European social housing of the origins has been a leader not only in terms of security of tenure but also in architectural innovation and social integration. The question is certainly not whether to throw the baby out with the bathwater but rather how to re-enchant it. Recasting the social realm will entail discovering *new forms of social property* that are likely to guarantee that housing is something that everyone, in both the present and future generations, can enjoy. Precisely because the economic, biological, and natural environments are instable, and the resources of energy and space are limited, individualistic approaches to property, protection, and sociability need to be challenged by alternative ones. A much greater range of *habitat* possibilities regarding conception, construction, tenure, financing, lifestyle, and social relations must be explored. From this renewed knowledge and collective imagination, solutions may appear.

References

Ball J (2008) Housing disadvantaged people? Insiders and outsiders in French social housing. Routledge, Abingdon

Blanc M (2010) The impact of social mix policies in France. Hous Stud 25(2):257–272

Bourgeois C (2012) Quand expertise, normes et délibérations conditionnent l'accès aux droits sociaux : le cas des commissions Droit au logement. In: Bureau M-C, Sainsaulieu I (eds) Les configurations pratiques de l'Etat social. Septentrion, Paris, pp 133–151

Brouant J (2011) Implementation of the enforceable right to housing (DALO) confronted to local practices and powers. In: Houard (ed) Social housing across Europe. La Documentation Francaise, Paris, pp 278–291

Chevalier C, Lebeaupin F (2010) La population des zones urbaines sensibles. INSEE première n°1328

Czischke D, Gruis V, Mullins D (2012) Conceptualising social enterprise in housing organisation. Hous Stud 27(4):418–437

Données statistiques (2012) http://www.union-habitat.org/sites/default/files/Donn%C3%A9es%20statistiques%202011.pdf. Consulted 4 Jan 2013

Driant J-C (2011) The inertia and metamorphosis at work in France's social housing sector. the HLM system at the turn of the decade. In: Houard (ed) Social housing across Europe. La Documentation Francaise, Paris, pp 116–131

Ghekiere L (2008) Le développement du logement social dans l'Union Européenne. *Recherches et Prévisions* n° 94

Ghékière L (2011) How social housing has shifted its purpose, weathered the crisis and accommodated European Community competition law. In: Houard (ed) Social housing across Europe. La Documentation Francaise, Paris, pp 135–151

Houard N (2011) A change of direction towards the residualisation of social housing? In: Houard (ed) Social housing across Europe. La documentation française, Paris, pp 334–356

Houard N, Lelévrier Ch (2012) Mobilité et choix résidentiels : quels enjeux pour les politiques publiques ?. In: Politique de la ville. Perspectives françaises et ouvertures internationales, Centre d'analyse stratégique, Rapports et document n°52, La documentation française, Paris, pp 99–110

Houard N, Lévy-Vroelant C (2013) The (enforceable) right to housing: a paradoxical French passion (1990–2012). Int J Hous Policy, London, Routledge 13(2):202–214

Jacquot A (2007) L'occupation du parc HLM. Eclairage à partir des enquêtes logement de l'INSEE. Direction des Statistiques Démographiques et Sociales, document de travail n° F0708

Jaillet M (2011) Mix in French housing policies: a "sensitive" issue". In: Houard (ed) Social housing across Europe. La Documentation Francaise, Paris, pp 318–333

Kirszbaum (2011) Social housing in the unthought of the multi-ethnic town. In: Houard (ed) Social housing across Europe. La Documentation Francaise, Paris, pp 292–217

Lévy J-P, Fijalkow Y (2012) Une autre politique du logement est-elle possible ? Le monde, Tribune, 1.03.2012. http://www.lemonde.fr/idees/article/2012/03/01/une-autre-politique-du-logement-est-elle-possible_1649893_3232.html

Levy-Vroelant C (2010) Housing vulnerable groups: the development of a new public action sector. Eur J Hous Policy 10(4) pp 443–456(14), Routledge

Lévy-Vroelant C (2011) Housing as welfare? Social housing and the welfare state in question. In: Houard (ed) Social housing across Europe. La documentation française, Paris, pp 191–214

Lévy-Vroelant C, Reinprecht C (2013) Housing the poor in Paris and Vienna, the changing understanding of 'social'. In: Scanlon K, Whitehead C (eds) Social housing in Europe. LSE/Wiley, London (forthcoming)

Levy-Vroelant C, Tutin C (2010a) Le logement social en Europe au début du 21ème siècle : la révision générale. Presses Universitaires de Rennes, France, 247 p

Lévy-Vroelant C, Tutin Ch (2010b) France: un modèle généraliste en question In : Lévy-Vroelant C, Tutin Ch (eds) Le logement social en Europe au début du XXIe siècle, La révision générale. Presses Universitaires de Rennes, Rennes, 247 p

Lévy-Vroelant C, Reinprecht C, Robertson D, Wassenberg F (2013a) Learning from history: 'Path dependency' and change in the social housing sectors of Austria, France, the Netherlands and Scotland, 1889-2012. In: Scanlon K, Whitehead C (eds) Social housing in Europe. LSE/Wiley, London (forthcoming)

Lévy-Vroelant C, Schaefer J-P, Tutin C (2013b) Social housing in France. In: Scanlon K, Whitehead C (eds) Social housing in Europe. LSE/Wiley, London (forthcoming)

Lovatt R, Lévy-Vroelant C, Whitehead C (2006) Foyers in the UK and France – comparisons and contrasts. Eur J Hous Policy 6(2):151–166

Mullins D, Czischke D, van Borter G (2012) Exploring the meaning of hybridity and social enterprise in housing organisations. Housing Stud 27(4):405–417, 2012 Special Issue: Social Enterprise, Hybridity and Housing Organisations

Pichon P (2011) Housing policies for the homeless. Or what a closer look at moving off the streets and into a real home shows. In: Houard (ed) La documentation française, Paris, pp 263–277

Pollard J (2010) Soutenir le marché : les nouveaux instruments de la politique du logement. Sociologie du travail, n°52

Sala Pala V (2005) Social housing policy and the construction of ethnic borders. A comparison of France and Great Britain. Political science doctoral thesis, Rennes, Rennes 1 University

Scanlon K, Whitehead C (2013) Social housing in Europe. LSE/Wiley, London (forthcoming)

Wacquant L (2008) Urban outcasts: a comparative sociology of advanced marginality. Polity Press, Cambridge
Zittoun P (2000) Quand la permanence fait le changement. Coalitions et transformations de la politique du logement. Politiques et management public 18(2):123–147
Zittoun P (2009) Understanding policy change as a discursive problem. J Comp Policy Anal Res Pract 11(1):65–82

Reports

Droit au logement, rappel à la Loi (2012, November) Comité de suivi du droit au logement opposable, 142 p. http://www.cnle.gouv.fr/IMG/pdf/6e_rapport_Dalo_def-1.pdf
Housing policy and vulnerable social groups (2008) Report and guidelines prepared by the Group of Specialists on Housing Policies for Social Cohesion (CS-HO). Council of Europe Publishing, Strasbourg
Le rôle du logement dans les parcours d'exclusion liée au logement. Logement et exclusion liée au logement, Thème annuel 2008 (2010) Rapport Européen, Feantsa, Thorne European service, 29 p
L'état du mal-logement en France en 2012, 18ème rapport (2013, February) Fondation Abbé Pierre pour le logement des personnes défavorisées (FAP), 242 p. http://www.ladocumentationfrancaise.fr/var/storage/rapports-publics/124000639/0000.pdf
Overview of Housing policies. Housing in the EU member states (2006) Directorate General for Research, Working document, Social affairs, series W 14. European Parliament, Brussels
Social Housing Allocation and Homelessness (2011) European observatory of homelessness, EOH comparative studies on homelessness, Feantsa. Pleace N, Teller N, Quilgars D (eds) Brussels, 80 p. http://eohw.horus.be/files/freshstart/Comparative_Studies/2011/Feantsa_Comp_Studies_01_2011_WEB.pdf

Chapter 14
Maturation of the Dutch Social Housing Model and Perspectives for the Future

Peter Boelhouwer

The Dutch social rented sector has acquired an international reputation because of its social nature and the way it has evolved. With around 32 % of the total stock, the size of the sector is much bigger than in other western European countries. Also, the development of the sector after the Second World War is unique. The current position is determined by the specific structure of the Dutch welfare state and the country's distinct housing policy. It is also the result of the shifting balance of supply and demand in the national housing policy. In this chapter, we explain the development of the Dutch social rented sector on the basis of the above-mentioned characteristics. We start with an international comparison regarding the position of the Dutch social rented sector. We will also pay attention to the background of the successful development of this sector: the financing system, the unique guarantee system, and the interplay between the central government and local housing associations. The chapter concludes with an exploration of the future of the social rented sector in the Netherlands. Due to all kinds of processes and developments, the social rented sector in the Netherlands is now at a crossroad, and important policy decisions have to be made.

14.1 Introduction

The housing system of the Netherlands has acquired an international reputation because of its unique nature and the way it has evolved. Over the past years, the Dutch housing system has been a source of inspiration for policymakers far and wide, including scholars and officials from some of the former socialist states in Eastern Europe and several Asian nations. Researchers and policymakers in those

---

P. Boelhouwer (✉)
OTB Research for the Built Environment, Faculty of Architecture and the Built Environment, Delft University of Technology, P.O. Box 5030, 2600 GA, Delft, The Netherlands
e-mail: p.j.boelhouwer@tudelft.nl

J. Chen et al. (eds.), *The Future of Public Housing: Ongoing Trends in the East and the West*, DOI 10.1007/978-3-642-41622-4_14,

countries have shown a keen interest in the way social rented housing is operated in the Netherlands. In particular, they are intrigued by the strong position of social housing in the country. This sector accounted for 41 % of the total housing stock of the Netherlands at the beginning of the 1990s; in contrast, the share of this sector in most other West European countries rarely reaches 20 %. Thus, the Netherlands clearly stands out in this sense. The strong position of Dutch social housing has its roots in the long period when housing was influenced by the national government. Of course, public intervention had been common practice throughout Western Europe for decades. However, the Netherlands eventually came to steer its own course. Whereas most other West European countries veered toward privatisation in the early 1970s, the Netherlands did not start to move in that direction until the 1990s.

The objective of this contribution is to explain how the Dutch social rented sector came to have the specific character for which it is renowned. To place this social institution within its societal context, a theoretical perspective is provided in Sect. 14.2. More specifically, the characteristics of the different welfare states in Western Europe are presented. The presented welfare state typology makes it possible to structure the position of the social rented sector in Europe and the Netherlands from a theoretical perspective. Section 14.3 elaborates on the direction in which Dutch housing policy developed and the role that the social rented sector played in that overall policy. The existence of clear links with the transformation of the welfare state will be shown, as described in the preceding section. This also clarifies the special position of housing as a policy field between the state and the market or, as Harloe (1995) and Torgersen (1987) had previously characterised, of "housing as the wobbly pillar under the welfare state." One of the success factors of the social rented sector in the Netherlands is the institutional structure and, more specifically, the way the financing of the sector is organised. The inventive interplay between state guarantees and the revolving fund principle created a unique situation that allowed housing associations to flourish and initiate more than half of the building production in the Netherlands in 2012, without any direct financial state aid. Section 14.4 explains this unique collaboration between housing associations and the state. As in many other West European countries, the welfare state, as well as the position of the intermediate sector in the Netherlands, is under pressure. The different policy options are discussed in Sect. 14.5. This sketch is specifically concerned with the development options for the social rented sector in the next few years. In that light, it emphasises the strategic decisions that will have to be made soon. Finally, this chapter ends with some concluding remarks.

14.2 Theoretical Perspective

The development of the social rented sector in Europe has been described by several authors in the past (Boelhouwer and van der Heijden 1992; Danermark and Elander 1994; Harloe 1995; Murie 1992). As many of these authors have noted (see, for an overview, Danermark and Elander 1994, p. 2), the concept of social housing, although used as if its meaning was self-evidently clear, takes on different meanings in various national contexts. It is sometimes connected to council housing (such as in the UK), sometimes regarded as publicly subsidized housing irrespective of ownership (such as in Germany), sometimes considered as intermediate housing (such as in the Netherlands), or sometimes viewed as an umbrella concept covering various types of housing in terms of ownership and tenure. Nevertheless, despite these and other differences, the term social housing has historically been ascribed some dimensions that are quite similar from country to country, thus making comparative discussion meaningful (Danermark and Elander 1994, p. 2). As summarized by Harloe (1995), social rented housing can be very broadly characterized as having three major characteristics: First, it is provided by landlords at a price that is not primarily determined by considerations of profit. Second, it is administratively allocated according to some conception of "need." Third, government control over social rented housing is extensive and has become more so over time. With regard to this last characteristic, things have changed in the last decade. Social landlords in the Netherlands, for instance, are much more independent from the government than they were before.

In Boelhouwer and Hoekstra (2012, pp. 369–370), we constructed an adjusted welfare state typology to explain this new position of the social rented sector. This typology is based on that of Esping-Andersen (1990) and Kemeny (1995). On the basis of the changing role of the central government in many Western European countries in the 1990s, we subdivided Kemeny's capital-led corporatism into two types: conservative and modern. Conservative corporatism corresponds with corporatism as defined by Esping-Andersen. In this definition, the state is fairly active in the provision of welfare services. However, this does not lead to income redistribution because the preservation of the existing hierarchy in society is the starting point for welfare policies at the state level. Consequently, the welfare provision is segmented; different groups are entitled to different welfare services, and the traditional family is often explicitly favoured. Furthermore, the state is definitely not the only provider of welfare services. In this respect, the family and private nonprofit organisations also play an important role. Modern corporatism refers to a more indirect style of governance in which the central government defines the policy frameworks within which the local authorities and the private actors operate. Thus, next to liberalism, we distinguish three different kinds of corporatism: labour-led, conservative, and modern.

Table 14.1 shows how the various welfare state regimes in the modified theoretical framework differ with respect to these characteristics.

With the above-explained adjusted welfare state typology, it is also possible to structure the position of the social rented sector more precisely. Kemeny's distinction between home-owning and cost rental societies could be the starting point. In his article "Corporatism and Housing Regimes" (Kemeny 2006), he argued on the basis of a division between capital-led and labour-led corporatism that there is a connection between the specific corporatist welfare state and the existence of an integrated rental market with a strong social rented sector. Kemeny contended that

Table 14.1 Main characteristics of the four welfare state regimes according to the modified theoretical framework

	Labour-led corporatist	Conservative-corporatist	Modern corporatist	Liberal
De-commodification	High	Relatively high	Relatively high	Low
Influence of central government	High and direct	Quite high and often indirect	Quite high and often indirect	Low
Degree of political corporatism	Many corporatist structures and processes	Many corporatist structures and processes	Many corporatist structures and processes	Few corporatist structures and processes
Fragmentation in the provision of welfare services	Fragmentation on the basis of measurable criteria	Fragmentation on the basis of occupation and/or social status	Fragmentation on the basis of measurable criteria	Fragmentation on the basis of measurable criteria.
Treatment of the traditional family in welfare policies	No preferential treatment for the traditional family	Preferential treatment for the traditional family	No preferential treatment for the traditional family	No preferential treatment for the traditional family
Role of State, market, and family in the provision of welfare services	Dominant position of the State	Important (if not dominant) position of the family	Welfare services are provided by both market and State	Dominant position of the market

the corporatist power system induces the need to achieve compromises. Corporatist compromise solutions entail a political solution that takes into consideration several different interests. The fragmentation of political parties, resulting in coalitions and minority governments being the norm, may be part of the explanation for the rise of an integrated market and a strong social rented sector. The latter can take many shapes and forms, such as municipality-owned companies, voluntary or charitable societies, trusts, rental cooperatives, and even privately owned nonprofit enterprises (Kemeny 2006, p. 12). For right-wing hegemonic coalitions that could be classified as liberal welfare states, it is quite clear that there will be a choice for a dualist rental system, in which nonprofit activities are restricted and nationalised. Social rented housing is incorporated into a publicly controlled planned economy and shaped into a low-income housing sector (command economy means-tested public renting). Examples of such states are the USA, Canada, Australia, New Zealand, and, to a lesser degree, the UK. Corporatist welfare states are more related to an integrated rental market with a specific leading role for the social rented sector (Kemeny 2006, p. 13). In conservative corporatist countries, we could expect right-wing parties with a still-strong influence and a social rented sector that is limited and has limited impact on the rental market. We could also expect a variety of ownership forms of social rental housing. Examples of these countries include Germany and Switzerland. In labour-led corporatist countries, we would expect a bigger and more uniform social rented sector and a very small profit rented sector. The social rented sector would be more than big enough to have a leading position in the rental market. Also, the influence of the tenant and/or the state could be more explicit. Clear examples of this type of corporatist states are Sweden and Denmark. In modern corporatist welfare states, the role of the state is smaller, and the role of the market, as well as the social rented sector, is bigger than in labour-led corporatist states. A clear example of this is the social rented sector in the Netherlands, which, with 32 % of the housing stock, still has a dominant position not only in the Dutch rental market but also in the overall housing market. The state largely confines itself to creating the conditions and formulating the policy frameworks within which local government authorities and private actors operate. This new policy framework brought the housing associations in the Netherlands into a very powerful position. They are financially very strong and are positioned in the bigger cities, where they dominate the local rental market in terms of their housing stock and play a crucial role in urban renewal developments. A relevant question for the future is whether more corporatist welfare states will develop in the direction of modern corporatist welfare states and whether right-wing parties and liberal-oriented neoclassical economies will approve such development. More specifically, the role of the European Commission and the way the policy of free competition is implemented in the near future by specific laws from Brussels will probably answer the question of whether corporatist welfare states in general will have a bright future.

14.3 Developments in Dutch Housing Policy and the Role of the Social Rented Sector in the Context of the Welfare State

The constant tension between government intervention and market influences becomes apparent when we study the development of the social rented sector in the Netherlands. Immediately after World War II, the Netherlands had to deal with serious housing shortages, in common with most Western European countries. The situation soon deteriorated because of the rapid growth in the number of households and low production levels in residential construction in the early postwar period. The shortages that became apparent soon after 1945 made an exceptionally high level of government intervention in homebuilding programs broadly acceptable. Policymakers were faced with escalating costs, ranging from the cost of living to construction costs and interest rates. Thus, substantial object subsidies were needed to contend with the massive housing shortage. A high level of government intervention was called for; this was entirely fitting in a period when the welfare state was gaining ground. In comparison with the rest of Europe, housing production in the Netherlands rose to an unprecedented level after the 1960s. This rapid rate of construction was necessary; during this period, the number of households in the Netherlands increased much more rapidly than in the rest of Europe. The decline in the birth rate came to the Netherlands very late; there was also a postponed, but nevertheless intense, decline in average household size. In contrast with the period before 1940, the need to build cheaply and quickly led to an emphasis on the social rented sector. These driving forces helped the sector to expand. The sector's share grew from 12 % in 1945 to 41 % in 1975 and to no less than 44 % of the total stock by the early 1990s. No other Western European country attained such a high share. The eventual turning point in Dutch housing policy was reached in 1989. The remainder of the new policy is strongly geared to the promotion of the market (Heerma 1989). The Memorandum on Housing for the 1990s *[Nota Volkshuisvesting in de jaren negentig]* puts particular emphasis on deregulation, decentralization, and self-sufficiency. This new policy line includes the decentralization of authority. The transfer of responsibilities and risks from the State to the local authorities and provinces and the independence of housing associations and (organizations of) housing consumers are featured. For the housing associations, this shift meant that the existing regulations operating in advance were replaced by retrospective accountability (Heerma 1989). Financial freedom was also markedly increased, in addition to freedom in terms of policy. The government decided to phase out the object subsidies for new construction as rapidly as possible. Rents in the period 1990–1994 were raised annually by 5.5 %, a far greater margin than the general level of inflation, and this increase in revenue strengthened the financial position of the associations. The Grossing and Balancing Operation constituted a second important episode marking the move towards financial independence. The State wanted at one and the same time to redeem the long-standing subsidy commitments (15.9 billion euros) and simultaneously call in early the loans that the associations still had outstanding (18.6 billion euros). In this way, the continuous pumping of money around the social housing circuit could be brought to an end. After intensive consultations with the sector, an agreement was reached that the Grossing and Balancing Act would take effect in 1995. The advantages for the State were evident: savings were made on the object subsidies, the administrative bureaucracy could be substantially reduced, and the housing budget could be subjected to a stringent cleanout operation. Moreover, the State could take an independent position with respect to the housing association sector in the discussions concerning the annual rent increase. The Act also brought certain advantages for the associations. They traded in supposed savings at one and the same time, became capable through their greater independence in carrying out a more flexible and thus market-oriented rental policy, and assumed new responsibilities in the management of their property. The increased rents and the Grossing and Balancing Operation have ensured that the associations have sufficient financial resources at their disposal to be able to carry out the housing task quite independently. In the Netherlands, this is referred to by the term *revolving fund.*

The government considers the social rented sector in its entirety as a revolving fund that should be capable of functioning without government subsidies. The idea of a revolving fund implies that current and future reserves generated in the social rented sector are put to use within that sector; in this manner, the housing associations subsidize themselves. The revolving fund applies both to the sector as a whole and to the individual associations. Each of these associations has to use the yields of its operations in the current stock to pay for (non-cost-effective) new instruments in the quality of the stock, new construction, and improvements in liveability. For the sector as a whole, the yields of the prosperous and the poor associations can be balanced. Prosperous associations could, for instance, support their poor counterparts by lending them funds at below-market interest rates.

When we look at the situation of the social rented sector in the Netherlands around the second half of the last decennium, the following observations could be made (Boelhouwer and Hoekstra 2009).

- The pressure on the housing market puts associations in a strong position. The rentability of their housing is excellent. A few years ago, housing associations worried about empty accommodation, whereas now supply exceeds demand right across the board.
- Towards the end of the 1990s, the national government stated that new housing production should concentrate on the market sector. As a result, the associations built very little social rented housing during the period 2002–2007.
- The financial position is robust. More capital than the minimum amount needed has been accrued, creating room for investment. The composition of the housing supply (age, quality), the development of demand on the housing market, and the shift in the attitude of the national government all lead towards a substantial investment programme (2007–2011). There are huge differences in the financial positions of the various associations.
- The image of the sector is decidedly poor. Much of the publicity is negative in tone (high salaries, arrogance, fraud, low housing production in the past).
- The European Union has asked that attention be paid to a fair competitive position in relation to commercial landlords and project developers, as well as to the size of the target group of the social rented sector.

On the basis of these characteristics, one can conclude that the housing associations had become used to not being held accountable for their actions. The organisations had become distanced from their "natural owners," the tenants and the government, and they are neither "disciplined by the market" nor "disciplined by the Government." There was no structural incentive for the associations to make socially acceptable investments. It is important to realise that in practice, housing associations were making a lot of socially acceptable investments. The amount and direction of the investments, however, were not controlled or steered by government bodies. On the other hand, most associations felt stifled by the State-dictated policy framework and the legislation and regulations. They found themselves trapped in a bureaucratic web and wanted more room for enterprise. To face up to the problems described above, a deluge of reports and recommendations appeared in the Netherlands in the period 2004–2006. Alongside all these reports and recommendations, the stance adopted by the European Commission was just as significant in terms of the future positioning of the housing associations. Within the context of the European regulations on market efficiency and competition, all forms of State assistance that cannot be termed as a service of general interest must in principle be reported to the European Commission. In this respect, the European Commission's decision on 13 July 2005 to grant the housing sector a general exemption from the obligation to report State assistance is important. This "exemption from notification" can be given because, according to the European Commission, there is only a very limited risk of causing disruption on the internal European market. This means that associations do not have to report to the European Commission every project they undertake involving State assistance. Another condition specified in the decision is that associations must make an administrative distinction for any activities undertaken that do not benefit the public interest. The decision applies to all Member States. One day later, on 14 July 2005, Minister Dekker received a supplementary letter from the European Commission. The Commission was of the opinion that the Dutch Government should introduce the following three measures:

- housing associations activities with State assistance should be directly linked not only to the maximum value of houses but also to socially deprived households;
- any commercial operations undertaken by the housing associations should be subject to market conditions, and profits made from commercial activities must be reinvested in the social house building sector; and
- excessive and structural overcapacity of social housing should be prevented by selling these houses, and the overcapacity should be restricted to a small percentage of the total housing supply.

The Brussels rules were formally introduced in the Netherlands on 1 January 2011. In June 2011, Minister Donner also sent a first draft of a new Housing Act to the parliament. This document was based on 6 years of discussion and several letters and policy documents of three former ministers. The housing associations were given two concrete tasks: the primary allocation of regulated rented housing to targeted income groups and investment in house building and restructuring. The primary allocation to targeted income groups is based on an income of 33,614 euros per year (1 January 2011 and indexed every year); approximately 39 % of all Dutch households have an income below this threshold and approximately 76 % of the current allocations is beneath this ceiling. Ten percent of the yearly allocations of the housing associations may be directed to households with a higher income (especially meant for households with an urgent request, with specific needs, and from restructuring areas). Households in social rented accommodation that receive an increase in their income are not directly obliged to move. New housing should provide a sufficiently attractive alternative for these people, according to the Minister.

Another important proposal is to change the role of the Central Fund into a Housing Authority (for an elaboration of the Central Fund, see Sect. 14.4). In the case of a bad functioning housing association, the Authority will have the possibility to give instructions to the management board of the housing association. The financial monitoring and control role of the current Central Fund will not be changed. A new task for the Authority is to control the regulations on state support (the Brussels rules). On the basis of this last aspect, housing associations have to make a division in their bookkeeping between commercial activities and activities under state control (organising housing for the target group and real estate for the use of societal organisations, such as schools and community centres). Also important is that housing associations still have the opportunity to be active in commercial activities, such as building housing for middle-income groups and developing more expensive rented and owner-occupied houses. The only conditions are that there will be no state support involved and that these activities are organised under the same conditions as those conducted by commercial firms. The Minister of Housing will maintain supervision on the integrity, governance, and performance of the housing associations. Also, the position of the internal supervisory board is strengthened. The board's approval is required for important decisions, such as the selling of houses and the acceptance of big investment proposals. The board is also responsible for the functioning of the management board of the housing association. When the internal supervisory board is not functioning well, the minister has the authority to fire the board.

The draft of the new Housing Act is more or less in line with the government maxim "Freedom and responsibility," as published by the centrum right-wing government in October 2010. It is remarkable that the reforms and proposed budget cuts are mostly focussed on the (social) rented sector. The home-ownership sector is almost not mentioned in the agreement, and the huge fiscal subsidies to homeowners (deduction of mortgage interest) are not discussed at all. In the rented sector, the policy of yearly rent adjustment by inflation is continued. The most important reason for the government to not introduce a more market-oriented rent adjustment system is that such a policy would lead to negative effects on the purchasing power of tenants. Only renters with an income above 43,000 euros per year will be confronted with a rent increase of 5 % plus inflation (at present, 2 % in the Netherlands). This strong rent increase will, however, only affect about 15 % of the total households in the rented sector. A practical problem is how to check the income level. Tax authorities are the only institutions that can check income data, and they are already complaining about an overload of commitments. Checking the incomes of 2.4 households in social housing is costly, time-consuming, and sensitive to fraud. The plan is to implement this rent increase in July 2013.

The coalition agreement has the most far-reaching consequences for the social rented sector in the Netherlands. First of all, tenants in the social rented sector receive a right to buy, after a similar policy that has been in effect in Great Britain since 1980. This proposal is introduced to further stimulate home ownership and to compensate the landlords for a large property tax that will be introduced in 2014, which is intended to raise 760 million euros every year (620 million euros for housing associations, 140 million euros for commercial real estate investors). The government wants landlords to pay part of the costs of housing allowances. The suggestion to introduce a right to buy is quite new and was not discussed before the election. At present, the government is quite hesitant about making a firm statement in this regard. It is obvious that the housing associations in the Netherlands are private organisations that cannot be expropriated without compensation (Boelhouwer 2007). The coalition government had to resign in April 2012 and announced that new elections would be

Table 14.2 Key Statistics Dutch Housing Associations (2011)

Housing stock (in housing units, end of 2011)	2,414,300
New dwellings for rent	28,600
New dwellings for sale	6,700
% New dwellings, sold at a discount	34.4
Dwellings demolished	11,900
Sale units in housing stock to households	14,300
% Dwellings in housing stock, sold at a discount	43.0
Housing units renovated (more than €20,000 per unit)	18,800
Expenses to quality of environment, per housing units (x €1)	115

Source: Centraal Fonds Volkshuisvesting (2012: 14)

Table 14.3 Rents, quality, turnover, Dutch Housing Associations (2011)

Number of quality points (*wws-punten*) per housing unit	136.8
Monthly rent per housing unit (x €1)	440
Rent in % of maximum allowed rent (in %)	70.2
Real Estate Value per housing unit (x €1000), as of January, 1	154
Turnover rate housing units (in %)	7.7
% Allocations to target group (EU-standard): housing units with monthly rent until €652.52, allocated to households with taxable income of €33,614 per year	93.5

Source: Centraal Fonds Volkshuisvesting (2012: 14)

held in September 2012. To reduce the government deficit to below 3 %, after the fall of the government, a coalition of government and opposition parties agreed to cut another 12.4 billion euros from the government budget for the year 2013. There were also some remarkable housing market reforms introduced. The most noteworthy is to mitigate the mortgage tax relief for first-time buyers. For the rented sector, not many new proposals were presented. The most important change is that renters with a yearly income between 33,000 and 43,000 euros will be confronted with a rent increase of 1 % plus inflation. For the housing associations, this means that that there will be three different rent increases, depending on the income of the household.

To complete this overview of the development of the Dutch social rented sector, Tables 14.2 and 14.3 and Fig. 14.1 provide some key statistics. In 2011, 389 housing associations were active in the Netherlands, owning a total of 2,414,300 housing units. In 2011, these housing associations received rents in the total amount of €12.8 billion (€5.164 on average per housing unit). The financial result was +€1.9 billion (+€779 on average per housing unit). Figure 14.1 shows that the housing associations in the Netherlands since WW II have accounted for a substantial part of the Dutch housing production, with fluctuations depending on the economic development. The production of these housing associations has been anti-cyclical to the general economic circumstances.

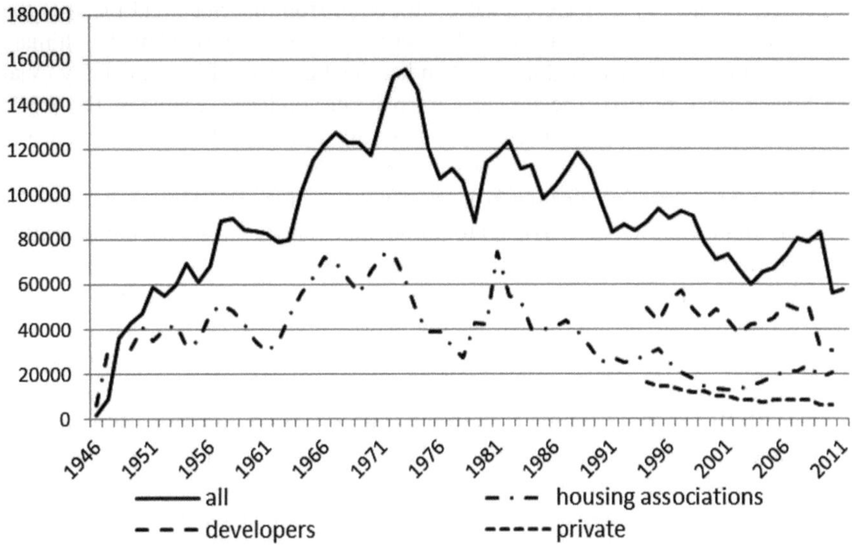

Fig. 14.1 Housing production in the Netherlands by owner (1946–2011) (Source: Central Bureau of Statistics (CBS))

14.4 Financing in the Social Rented Sector

Until the beginning of the 1980s, the financing needs of the Dutch housing associations were covered by loans granted by the State. These loans exerted a direct pressure on the national budget. In the 1980s, the government came into serious financial problems, saw the national debt rising rapidly, and thus decided in 1984 to abolish the provision of loans to associations and the counter-guarantees provided by the State for loans borrowed from the capital market. In 1983, the Social House-Building Guarantee Fund (WSW) *[Waarborgfonds Sociale Woningbouw]* (WSW) was set up as a private law institute to enable the coverage of the financing needs of associations. At first, only guarantees for housing improvement were provided. Five years later, however, it became possible to obtain guarantees for the financing of the construction of new dwellings. The WSW endeavours to provide the participating associations with access to the capital market at the lowest costs. Since then, the WSW has granted guarantees to moneylenders for loans for new construction, housing improvement, acquisition of dwellings, and nursing and retirement homes. The WSW is not, however, the only institute that makes guarantees available. Local authorities also grant guarantees for housing associations' loans, albeit on a limited scale.

When housing associations borrow with loan guarantees provided by the WSW, there is a triple guarantee. The primary security is formed by the financial resilience of the association itself and of the entire sector through the participation of the Central Fund (see below). The secondary security consists of the capital assets of the WSW, which are created by a single capital contribution from the State and the fees the associations pay to obtain guarantees. The tertiary security is formed by the ultimate responsibility of the State and the local authorities that share this task equally (Van der Schaar 1991, p. 404). The attractive interest rates on loans secured by the WSW demonstrate the great confidence that lenders have in the fund. Their confidence is largely due to the ultimate security provided by the State (Priemus 1995).

A housing association wishing to use the facilities of the WSW must first register with the fund. Before the WSW approves an application, it tests the creditworthiness of the applicant. Before 2007, the evaluation of the financial position of an association was based on its assets. Since 2007, however, the basis has been that the yearly cash flow of the housing association must be positive. This means that even associations with a high solvency (but in which the money is mainly bounded in stone) could have problems in attracting loans.

The WSW has received the highest possible ratings from the world's leading rating agencies: AAA from Standard & Poor's and Aaa from Moody's Investors Service (WSW 2011). By the end of 2010, most of the social landlords in the Netherlands were registered with the WSW, and the total secured capital of the institute had risen to around 85.1 billion euros. Between 2011 and 2016, the Dutch housing associations expect to invest a total of around 40.4 billion euros, most of which will be funded externally (WSW 2011).

The WSW also has an important monitoring function and is keeping watch of all developments that affect social housing. Therefore, the WSW:

- assesses its participants' financial positions and overall quality,
- devotes attention to its participants' cash flows,
- analyses the market on an ongoing basis,
- requires participating housing associations to provide information twice a year and asks for both actual and forecast figures,
- advises participants on the range of products available in the market, and
- is actively involved in developing new financial products for the sector (WSW 2011).

In addition to the WSW, the Netherlands has a second important institute: the Central Housing Fund *[Centraal Fonds voor de Volkshuisvesting]* (CFV). This fund is responsible for two important tasks: financial supervision (since 1998) and financial reconstruction (since 1988). Associations in poor financial position can appeal to the CFV for assistance. According to the draft Housing Act, the Central Fund will be transformed into a new housing authority.

The CFV is a mutual fund established by and for the associations. Its purpose is to support financially weak associations and, when necessary, help them restructure their operations. To this end, each association contributes annually to the fund. The size of the contribution required from an association is calculated on the basis of its financial situation and, since 2001, on whether it has given financial assistance to another association that does not have enough capital to finance some specific projects. An association that fails to qualify for (further) participation or guarantees from the WSW can appeal to the CFV for help. The CFV will provide an interest-free loan to an impoverished association on the condition that it becomes self-supporting within 3 years. Sometimes, this condition requires the restructuring of an association. In many cases, a member of the CFV takes over the management of the association. In principle, the CFV contributes half the cost of such an operation. The other half is usually borne by the local authority that is also ultimately responsible for housing. The conditions for support imposed by the CFV closely reflect those applied by the WSW in assessing an association's creditworthiness (Gruis 1997, p. 18). Since the establishment of the CFV, financial support amounting to over 500 million euros has been granted to 18 housing associations.

In addition to its financial reconstruction task, since 1998 the CFV has also undertaken a supervisory task that includes early-warning monitoring. By providing a timely signal of an association's financial weakness to the national government, the institute can intervene as a formal supervisor. As a result, any financial problem affecting an association can be avoided as far as possible. In this context, the CFV has been given a number of specific new tasks. One is the signalling task related to the assessment of the likelihood of future cases needing financial reconstruction. For this purpose, the CFV compiles reports on the financial position of individual associations. These reports are based on the associations' annual reports and any supplementary information they may provide. Furthermore, the CFV advises the State on the financial aspects of new admissions, mergers, and any changes in the statutes. The CFV also gives annual reports on the financial situation of the housing associations as a whole. It was announced that the financial position of the sector in 2010 could be considered healthy. Only four housing associations had a solvency position that was regarded to be in jeopardy; the value of their assets was too low for their investment plans.

The operation costs are another point of attention for the CFV. These have been far above inflation in the last few years and differ between 5 and 10 %. On the basis of these figures, one could wonder if the housing associations do operate efficiently. After a lot of criticism from the CFV and the central government, the operation costs finally went down to "only" 3 % in 2009 (much less than in the years before but still higher than the inflation rate of 1,2 %). The umbrella organisation AEDES is also aware of this problem. In fact, it ordered that the operation costs of the housing associations be brought down by 20 % in the years to come. The yearly report from the CFV also stated that the housing associations were quite successful in combating the economic crisis and were able to invest on an anti-cyclical basis. The years 2008 and 2009 were in many ways excellent years, during which the production of owner-occupied and rented accommodation, renewal activities, and the spending on liveability all boomed. The year 2010 can be seen as turning point. After 2010, mainly because of less income and taxing by the government, the activities of the housing associations were expected to go down substantially (Central Fund 2011, p. 7).

As a summary, Table 14.4 presents an overview of the most important characteristics of the operation of the social rented sector in the Netherlands.

Table 14.4 Key points of the operation of the social rented sector in the Netherlands

Guarantee of construction and improvement activities by Social House-building Guarantee Fund (WSW)
Financial supervision and financial reconstruction by the Central Housing Fund (CFV)
No direct bricks and mortar subsidies by the central government; revolving fund principle
58 % of total housing production in 2010 and 2011
Housing associations are private organisations who fulfil a public task and are controlled by the central Government
EU rule that housing associations activities with State assistance should not only be directly linked to the maximum value of houses, but also to socially deprived households
Any commercial operations undertaken by the housing associations should be subject to market conditions, and profits made from commercial activities must be reinvested in the social house building sector
Huge property tax for social rented housing starting in 2013

14.5 The Future of the Social Rented Sector

Encapsulated in the above description is a warning that, over the next few years, the Dutch social rented sector must reconsider its position. This follows from the changes in the arrangements of the Dutch welfare state and the subsequent shifts in the redistribution of income because of the new Brussels rules on competition, as well as from the autonomous developments in the housing market. Another important reason is the financial mismanagement of some housing associations in recent years. Several housing associations have gotten themselves into huge problems by speculation with financial derivatives (interest swaps). For instance, the biggest housing association in the Netherlands (Vestia) lost around 2 billion euros in 2012.

There are several possible scenarios for the future of the Dutch housing associations, which are connected to the future development of the welfare state.

14.5.1 Continuation of the Current System

Perhaps the most likely outcome of the debate about the future of the Dutch housing associations is the adjustment of the current system to the new Brussels rules to avoid any further disasters. This direction fits perfectly well with the consolidation of the modern corporatist welfare state and is also in line with the recent proposals to modify the Housing Act that were introduced by the Minister of Housing and approved by the Dutch parliament in July 2012. To solve the current governance problems and avoid future financial disasters, the governance by the central government will be tightened a little bit, and treasury rules will be more restrictive in general and more specific for the use of financial derivates (more or less in the same way that municipalities are treated). In addition, the tasks of the housing associations will be divided in into a for-profit and a not-for-profit part. There could be an administrative distinction in the housing association between activities for the target group (with a household income below 33,600 euros) and those for the non-target group. For the latter group, there will be no state assistance, such as WSW support or cheap land provided by municipalities. This separation of activities will create a level playing field with the commercial sector. Also, the internal governance of the housing associations could be further improved and professionalized.

14.5.2 Opting Out

An opposite policy direction is that the government will retreat completely and the housing associations will become nonprofit organisations without any government support. This is an extension of the Grossing and Balancing Operation from the 1990s. It also means that the government support for the WSW will be ended and that housing associations, like those in Germany, will be treated like commercial landlords. The revolving fund will ensure that housing associations will still be able to house low-income and other deprived groups. For many housing associations, this will mean a bright future: they will no longer be squeezed by government regulations and instead have freedom to act. Also, the recently introduced taxes for housing associations could be ended. Two years ago, a housing association tried to leave the nonprofit system. This move, however, was opposed in court. Against this background, it is highly doubtful if the central government will support such move to opt out. This will only be negotiable if housing associations will hand in a huge part of their financial reserves to the central government. Furthermore, the government is by constitution still responsible for also housing vulnerable groups in society. It will be very difficult for the government to fulfil this task if there are no possibilities left in terms of its steering the housing associations.

14.5.3 Functional Organisational Split

In the *split-function variant*, a division is created between the actual activities of the housing association and its capital (see also Boelhouwer and Priemus 2012). Some scholars (Conijn 2011) have argued that social landlords are far from efficient, should work in a more cost-effective manner, and should be more influenced by market forces. Most of the housing associations in the Netherlands currently have the legal form of a foundation. To create a legally valid division between capital and management activities, the foundation will have to set up a new company to which all real activities of the housing association (ownership of property, management, and development) can be transferred. The foundation will then only hold shares in this company. The new company will act as a regular commercial asset management company and strive to achieve good profits on the exploitation and development of the rental property. The profits will be either distributed as dividend to the shareholder (the foundation) or invested with the aim of increasing profits in the future, which will also go to the shareholder. The original housing association (the foundation) will thus be converted into an investment fund and asset management firm; the only link between the foundation and the company will be that the former holds the shares in the latter. One possibility is that the fund will still be governed by the provisions of the Social Rental Sector Management Order *[Besluit beheer sociale huursector]* (BBSH). In accordance with the terms of this Order, surpluses are to be used in the interest of social housing in conformity with guidelines drawn up by parliament. The obligation to use the housing association's capital in the interest of social housing is thus also preserved in this variant.

14.5.4 From Real Estate Manager to Capital Manager: The Opting in of Private Capital

An extension of the organisational split is to fully integrate private investment capital in the housing associations sector. This variant is in line with the development from a modern corporatist welfare state to a more liberal-orientated welfare state and will result in a firm paradigm shift. Such a shift does not seem very likely against the history of the Dutch welfare state. In this variant, there will be a new business firm that owns more than half of the shares in the company. These shares will be sold to private investors, such as pension funds and insurance companies, which will receive their share of the company's dividends. Of course, the housing associations will be compensated for the transfer of shares and will be transformed into a trust that can invest in all kinds of societal demands not served by the market (for instance, lower rents for low-income groups or investment in liveability measures). The shares of the new business firm are in principle freely tradable, and more private capital is welcome to invest in the firm. The funds (foundations) will sell part (preferably the greater part) of their shares to the new firm and invest the yield in other equities, thus creating an economic as well as a legal separation between activities and capital. As in the functional organisational split, the economic separation has an advantage in that an external shareholder can exert more effective pressure on the management to operate efficiently. Pension funds are typically likely to be interested in acquiring such shares as long as the relationship between yield and risk is favourable. Because there are benefits of scale in asset management, it is conceivable that the funds (foundations) might be interested in making use of one or more common asset management companies. In 2012, such a proposal was launched by a group of housing experts, former politicians, and investors (Forum for Housing and Living 2012). However, Boelhouwer and Priemus (2012) pointed out some negative consequences of this choice. One is that the more liquid nature of the capital will increase the temptation to squander the assets. Another potential problem is that the politicians will have to relinquish their discretionary control of rental policy to attract new potential shareholders.

As previously mentioned, the continuation of the current situation with a stronger role of the government as external supervisor best fits the current modern corporatist welfare state in the Netherlands. We can only interpret the functional organisational split function and the opting-in and -out variants as a prelude to the complete transformation of the housing association from a nonprofit organisation with a hybrid character, where the orientation towards a target group and the obligation to devote its capital to a specific (social) purpose in conformity with the Housing Act remain essential components, into a fully fledged commercial market player, where the interests of the shareholders will in the long run prevail over the dedication to a particular target group and the obligation to use the funds for a particular purpose. In my opinion, this comes down to throwing out the baby with the bathwater. In the past, housing associations have made an essential contribution to maintaining social housing in the Netherlands at a proper level. They can continue to do so if certain conditions are met. I am therefore convinced that the adapted current system is preferable over the split-function and opting-in variants.

14.6 Conclusions

The central question posed at the outset of this chapter is how to explain the position of the Dutch social rented sector in the country's housing system. It has been established that the position of the social rented sector is strongly influenced by developments in the society at large. In particular, its specific position may be explained with reference to the emergence and transformation of the Dutch welfare state. For example, until the 1950s, the social rented sector in the Netherlands was quite modest (12 % of the dwelling stock), even compared to other European countries. After the Second World War, the welfare state, a phenomenon that at first was only weakly developed in the Netherlands, grew to maturity at an extremely rapid pace. In fact, the Dutch "lag" behind other countries in Western Europe turned into a comfortable "lead" within a few decades. Moreover, the welfare state remained in full glory much longer in the Netherlands. The turning point did not come until the mid-1990s. In most other West European countries, government influence on processes in civil society had already been radically reduced in favour of market forces during the 1970s. In the Netherlands, the development of the social rented sector coincided with the vigorous build-up of the welfare state. The sector continued to grow in the Netherlands for a longer period than in most other West European countries. Ultimately, the share of the Dutch social rented sector reached its highest point, 41 % of the stock, at the beginning of the 1990s.

Against this development perspective, this chapter has shown the uniqueness of the maturation of the Dutch social rented sector from an international perspective. The Netherlands has, with 32 % of the total housing stock, not only far and away the largest social rented sector in Europe but also independence and substantial accumulated capital in the existing stock. Thanks to the opportunities of rent pooling, the input of the accumulated capital, and the freedom to dispose of real estate so that capital invested in bricks and mortar can be put towards other objectives, the housing associations are able to rent out newly constructed social rented dwellings at well below the cost price. The usual unprofitable top of 70,000 euros for the construction of a social rented dwelling is currently substantially higher than the object subsidies that the State government had granted at the beginning of the 1990s. Financing needs can also be met entirely by the WSW so that, in addition to being able to obtain sufficient capital, borrowing on the international capital market is against keen tariffs. This unique situation has been brought about through mutual cooperation and solidarity, and not least through the safety net function of the State. Impoverished associations are also restructured by the CVF through the sector itself. In the future, however, the strong financial position of the associations may also constitute a danger. Now that the national government is being threatened by financial difficulties because of the economic crisis, politicians in particular are looking covetously at the associations' accumulated capital. A first attack on their financial position is the 620 million euros the housing associations have to pay from 2014 onwards on the basis of a new property tax for landlords. Also, municipalities are in financial bad weather and increasingly trying to transfer costly activities to the housing associations.

References

Boelhouwer PJ (2007) The future of Dutch housing associations. J Housing Built Environ 22 (4):383–391

Boelhouwer PJ, Hoekstra J (2009) Towards a better balance on the Dutch housing market? Analysis and policy proposition. Eur J Housing Policy 9(4):457–475

Boelhouwer P, Hoekstra J (2012) Housing and the state in Western Europe. In: Smith SJ, Elsinga M, Fox O'Mahony L, Seow Eng O, Watcher S, Hamnett C (eds) International encyclopedia of housing and home, vol 3. Elsevier, Oxford, pp 363–373

Boelhouwer P, Priemus H (2012) Housing system reform: the opinion of advisory board versus political reality in the Netherlands. J Housing Built Environ 27(4):527–542

Boelhouwer PJ, van der Heijden HMH (1992) Housing systems in Europe: Part I, A comparative study of housing policy, Housing and urban policy studies 1. Delft University Press, Delft

Centraal Fonds Volkshuisvesting (Central Housing Fund) (2011) Jaarverslag 2010 (Annual Report 2010). CFV, Huizen

Centraal Fonds Volkshuisvesting (2012) Sectorbeeld realisaties woningcorporaties. Verslagjaar 2011 (Picture of sector realisations housing associations. Year 2011). CFV, Baarn

Conijn J (2011) Woningcorporaties op een kruispunt. Amsterdam School of Real Estate, Amsterdam

Danermark B, Elander I (1994) Social rented housing in Europe: policy, tenure and design, Housing and urban policy studies 9. Delft University Press, Delft

Esping-Andersen G (1990) The three worlds of welfare capitalism. Polity Press, Cambridge

Forum for Housing and Living (2012) Woningcorporaties op eigen benen: verdienen om te kunnen dienen. Forum for Housing and Living, Naarden

Gruis V (1997) The Netherlands. In: Boelhouwer PJ (ed) Financing the social rented sector in Western Europe. Delft University Press, Delft, pp 7–20

Harloe M (1995) The people's home? Social rented housing in Europe and America. Blackwell, Oxford/Cambridge

Heerma E (1989) Nota volkshuisvesting in de jaren negentig (Memorandum on Housing in the 1990s). The Hague (ministerie VROM)

Kemeny J (1995) From public housing to the social market: rental policy strategies in comparative perspective. Routledge, London

Kemeny J (2006) Corporatism and housing regimes. Housing Theory Soc 23(1):1–18

Murie A (1992) Public rented housing in Britain. In: Danermark B, Elander I (eds) Social rented housing in Europe: policy, tenure and design, Housing and urban policy studies 9. Delft University Press, Delft, pp 77–94

Priemus H (1995) How to abolish social housing? The Dutch case. Int J Urban Reg Res 19(1)

Torgersen U (1987) Housing: the wobbly pillar under the welfare state. In: Turner B, Kemeny J, Ludqvist L (eds) Between state and market: housing in the post-industrial era. Almqvist & Wiksell International, Stockholm, pp 116–127

van der Schaar J (1991) Volkshuisvesting een zaak van beleid (Social housing: a matter of policy). The Spectrum, Utrecht

Waarborgfonds Sociale Woningbouw (Social House-building Guarantee Fund) (WSW) (2011) Jaarverslag 2010. WSW, Huizen

Chapter 15
Understanding Variation in the Size of the Public Housing Sector Across Swedish Municipalities: The Role of Politics

Roger Andersson

15.1 Introduction

From the 1940s and into the 1990s, public housing in Sweden was a key element in the Social Democrats' ambition to construct a housing system that would secure high quality, affordable housing for all. Municipally owned housing companies still control 17.5 % of the Swedish housing stock and provide housing for about 14 % of the population but their key role has been contested and their privileged position has eroded in the wake of a stepwise change in the regulatory system over the past 20 years.

It is often said that the best way of trying to understand what future might bring about is to study history (Malpass 2005). Although historical lessons are often helpful, dramatic changes are not easy to anticipate. Few Swedes living in the 1930s could probably foresee the dramatic expansion of hitherto almost unknown public housing that eventually followed as part of the modernisation project gaining momentum after WWII. Modernisation went hand in hand with fast urbanisation, rapid economic growth, and social reforms. That municipally owned housing would become an important part of this development was not easy to foresee even for the political left which dreamt of a stronger State and strived for better housing and more redistribution of wealth and welfare (Elander 1991). And it had probably not been possible without the administrative reforms that enabled cities to grow bigger as they incorporated land from adjacent municipalities and formed larger and more resourceful local governments.

In only 23 years – from 1951 to 1974 – the number of municipalities in Sweden was reduced in two steps, from 2,281 to 1,037 to around 280, and while they grew bigger they were given a pivotal role in reconstructing and expanding the production of social services, infrastructure and housing (Nielsen 2003, p. 23). However,

R. Andersson (✉)
Professor, Institute for Housing and Urban Research, Uppsala University, Uppsala, Sweden
e-mail: Roger.Andersson@ibf.uu.se

J. Chen et al. (eds.), *The Future of Public Housing: Ongoing Trends in the East and the West*, DOI 10.1007/978-3-642-41622-4_15,

as the role of the central State was to establish different kinds of legal and financial frameworks for this development, much power has been and still is in the hands of local politicians. This tends to produce local variations which are partly the result of structural demographic and socioeconomic differences but partly also of a more ideological character.

Not all political parties have supported the expansion of public housing and it can be hypothesized that municipalities controlled by the political left have been more pro-public housing. The Swedish economist Pettersson-Lidbom (2008) has found that left-wing local governments spend and tax 2–3 % more money than right-wing governments. They also employ more workers and therefore also have lower unemployment rates. It is very likely that such politically produced variations in spending and employment occur also with respect to public housing, historically as well as today.

Lee et al. (2004, p. 807) state that there "are two fundamentally different views of the role of elections in policy formation. In one view, voters can affect candidates' policy choices: competition for votes induces politicians to move toward the center. In this view, elections have the effect of bringing about some degree of policy compromise. In the alternative view, voters merely elect policies: politicians cannot make credible promises to moderate their policies, and elections are merely a means to decide which one of two opposing policy views will be implemented". In their analysis, using voting record data from the U. S. House (1946–1995), they find support for the latter hypothesis, i.e. that voters elect policies. If this holds in the Swedish context, we can expect a positive correlation between local support for the left and the volume of public housing.

This chapter will contribute to the discussion of the future of public housing by focusing on the Swedish case and in particular developments over the past two decades. Two empirical questions are asked: (1) which local political, demographic and socioeconomic conditions can explain the size of the public housing sector across Swedish municipalities, and (2) can such conditions and changes of such conditions also explain changes over time in the relative size of the public housing sector? However, before engaging with these empirical questions the chapter briefly outlines the historical background and recent trends in Swedish public housing.

15.2 Historical Background

According to the political scientist Bo Bengtsson (2012), a combination of four elements have characterized the Swedish housing regime for almost half a century (1960s to 2010): (1) a universally oriented housing policy without individual needs or means testing; (2) a public rental sector with housing companies owned by the municipalities and professionally managed at arm's length distance from political influence; (3) an integrated rental market with formal links between rent-setting in the public and the private rental sector; (4) a 'corporatist' system of centralized rental negotiations between (public and private) landlords and representatives of a

Table 15.1 Tenure composition of the Swedish housing stock 1945–2006, percent of all dwellings

Year	Owner occupied	Cooperative	Public rented	Private rented	Total
1945	38	4	6	52	100
1960	34	9	14	43	100
1970	34	13	23	30	100
1975[a]	40	14	24	22	100
1980[a]	42	16	23	19	100
1985[a]	43	16	24	17	100
1990[a]	43	17	23	16	100
2002[b]	42	19	22	17	100
2011[b]	41	23	18	18	100

[a]Source: Statistics Sweden Census 1975, 1980, 1985 and 1990
[b]Source: Statistics Sweden, Estimated housing stock December 31, 2002 and 2011

strong and well organized national tenant movement. In the same paper, Bengtsson argues that these characteristics "are strongly interrelated, almost in terms of necessary and sufficient conditions" (p. 1).

In other work Bengtsson (2006) has employed a path dependency perspective on Swedish housing, analysing developments from an early "establishment phase" (limited housing reforms in response to early urbanization; from the early 1900s to the 1940s), a "construction phase" (comprehensive and institutionalized housing policies aimed at reducing housing shortage; 1950s to the mid 1970s), a "management phase" (housing needs had been saturated; mid 1970s to the early 1990s), and finally thereafter a "retrenchment phase" with diminishing state engagement in housing provision. Table 15.1 shows that although some public (municipal) housing emerged during the establishment phase, most municipal rental housing companies were set up after World War II and the bulk of public housing was built during the 1950s and 1960s, i.e. during the heydays of the Social Democratic hegemony over Swedish politics.

Although other actors than the municipalities up to 1974 could be declared to be what in Swedish is called "*allmännyttig*" (*gemeinnützig* in German, and "for the benefit of everyone" in English) – and thereby in different ways privileged by the State – this particular form of public rental housing had until recently four characteristics (Hedman 2008, p. 7): it was operated without profit motifs, it was owned by municipalities, it was accessible for all households irrespective of income, and it was rent leading for all rental housing in each local housing market.

The political ambition behind the socially oriented housing policy in Sweden was to provide good housing for all regardless of income, and to break the link between income and housing outcomes. From the 1940s and into the 1990s, public housing in Sweden was a key element in the Social Democrats' ambition to construct a housing system that would secure high quality, affordable housing for all (Elander 1991). It was not the only instrument – substantial municipal land ownership, interest rent subsidies, rent regulation and housing allowances also played important roles – but it provided local governments with a great deal of influence over housing construction and housing allocation.

15.3 Recent Developments

Municipally owned housing companies still own about 20 % of the Swedish housing stock and provide housing for about 14 % of the population but their key role has been contested and their privileged position has eroded in the wake of a stepwise change in the regulatory system over the past twenty years. As stated by Turner and Whitehead (2002, p. 201): "Housing policy has been undergoing rapid change across Europe and the industrialized world. This change has been particularly dramatic in Sweden where housing has traditionally been a core element of the welfare state." As pointed out by van Gent in a study on Spain and the Netherlands, "The politics of welfare reform are related to the discourses of homeownership ideology. The ownership of (housing) assets agenda serves as a means to change the relationship between state, market and individual households" (van Gent 2010, p. 735). Table 15.2 shows that home ownership per se has not increased in Sweden (slight increase if cooperative housing is grouped together with home ownership) but it is without doubt so that the political right in Sweden has its voting base among home owners and among those preferring less State involvement and more market solutions in both the welfare and housing sectors.

The Conservative-Liberal national government of the early 1990s initiated important changes of housing policy in Sweden (see Lindbom 2001) and opened up for local decisions concerning tenure conversion, i.e. the conversion of public rental housing into market forms (cooperative housing). The formal decision was taken in 1992 but it was at least partially based on ideas proposed by the UK Conservative government more than ten years earlier (Forrest and Murie 1988). In some Swedish municipalities, predominantly those having a Social Democratic majority, this decision had no or small effects in the housing market. In other it had a very profound effect as conservative political majorities decided to completely sell off substantial parts and in some cases all municipal housing either to private rental companies or to cooperative associations (tenure conversion). The Social Democratic governments ruling between 1994 and 2006 introduced measures intended to make it more difficult to sell out public housing (the requirement of having a 75 % majority instead of a simple majority of residents in favour of buying and a law stopping municipalities from selling the municipal housing company to private interests) and these measures

Table 15.2 Overview of the tenure composition in Sweden 1990 and 2008. Percent of all residents

Tenure	1990	2008
Per cent residing in public housing	16.3	14.1
Per cent residing in cooperative housing	12.4	15.7
Per cent residing in home ownership	54.8	54.9
Private rental or unknown tenure	16.5	15.3
Total	100.0	100.0
Total pop.	*8,591,000*	*9,237,000*

Source: Geosweden database, Institute for Housing and Urban Research, Uppsala University

clearly had effects and conversions were radically reduced (Swedish Board of Housing, Building and Planning, 2011)

With the return of a Liberal-Conservative government in 2006, these counter measures were abolished and sell-outs and conversions have regained momentum. In 2010 alone, 15,000 dwellings were sold out in Sweden, equal to the number the year before and to volumes in the early years of the decade. According to the Swedish Board of Housing, Building and Planning, the Stockholm region continues to lead this development and in contrast to municipalities elsewhere most of the dwellings in the capital region are sold to cooperative associations. Elsewhere in the country, buyers are predominantly private rental companies. Over the period 2000–2011, 155,000 public and private rental units in Sweden have been converted into cooperative tenure. Of these, 112,000 were in Stockholm County and approximately 40 % of these were public rented dwellings (Statistics Sweden 2012).

Public housing continues to be a politically contested tenure form and most Social Democratic municipalities – like Gothenburg and Malmö – continue to maintain and develop public rental housing. In Stockholm however, the political majority has shifted in almost every election, causing radical shifts in housing policy (and, one might add, an ever increasing shortage of housing).

Conversions from public rental housing to other tenure forms are but one example of a reduced role of public housing in Sweden. As described above, the public housing sector used to play an important role in the soft rent regulation system, i.e. in negotiating rents based on a dwelling's utility value. Rents for the rental sector were negotiated between public housing companies and the local tenant's association. This rent was based on costs, with less emphasis on location and more on standard (see, however, Lind 2007 and Wilhelmson et al. 2011). Equally and in some cities even more important, the rents set after negotiation was the baseline also for private property owners, who could not establish market-based rents for different neighbourhoods and locations within a city. In June 2010 the sitting government managed to pass a bill through parliament whereby the municipality owned public housing companies no longer are rent leading. It is also so that their function of being *allmännyttig* has been undermined also by the fact that they now have to run their operation on businesslike principles, which in fact "represents a deviation from the principles embodied in the Local Government Act requiring operations to be run on a cost price basis and prohibiting undertakings being run for profit" (SABO 2010). At the same time, the new Act clarifies that "a businesslike perspective is compatible with active social responsibility". (Government Proposition 2009/10, p. 185) However, little is known regarding how this will work out in reality. Christophers (2013) argues that Sweden now represents "a monstrous hybrid" with clear signs of neo-liberalization but with considerable regulatory framing still in place. He identifies the increasing housing shortage, due to undersupply of rental units, along with increasingly-unaffordable prices for housing for purchase, as the two biggest challenges and problems of contemporary Swedish housing.

What will happen from now on is difficult to know but it will certainly be equally important in the future to study not only the overall national effects of the new regulatory framework for public housing but also to focus closely on local variations in outcome (see also Musterd, 2014, who stresses the same point for the Netherlands). As I stated in the introduction, it is likely that local politics continues to influence both the size and function of the public housing sector in Sweden. In what way politics has affected developments during the State housing policy retrenchment phase starting in the early 1990s will be illuminated in the next sections.

15.4 Local Politics and Public Housing: Selection and Description of Variables for the Empirical Study

Two research questions are focused in this chapter: (1) which local political, demographic and socioeconomic conditions can explain the size of the public housing sector across Swedish municipalities, and (2) can such conditions and changes of such conditions also explain changes over time in the relative size of the public housing sector?

Addressing the first of the two research questions I will use cross-sectional data on all Swedish municipalities, measured at two points in time, 1990 and 2008. The same set of variables will be used for estimating the impact of a range of local characteristics at both points in time. It is of course fully possible that we have to do with what many researchers would call path dependencies so that contemporary conditions have only marginal explanatory value (Bengtsson and Rounavaara 2010). By applying the same set of independent variables for 1990 and 2008 respectively, we can hopefully test whether their explanatory power changes over time. In analysing the second research question I will use a difference approach, measuring changes over time in variables that have explanatory value for estimating the relative size of the public housing sector.

Ideally, one would prefer long data series. This is however difficult to establish in this particular case and the primary reason is the administrative reforms mentioned in the introduction to this chapter. Public housing expanded rapidly during the 1950s and 1960s. Sweden at that time had more than 1,200 municipalities. An administrative reform in the early 1970s meant amalgamations and a substantial reduction of the number of municipalities. There were 277 municipalities shortly after this reform. Since then some of them have split up so that the country now has 290 primary municipal units. Some of the variables used in the forthcoming analysis cannot be measured back in time without considerable work and some are probably impossible to find data for. This and the fact that major reforms affecting the sector have taken place after 1990, are the two most important reasons for narrowing the study to the 1990–2008 period.

One should of course be aware of the fact that if the present day size of public housing is a result of the political majority situation in the 1950s and 1960s (when new housing construction peaked), attempts to explain the sector's importance using contemporary data might fail. However, two circumstances speak against being so pessimistic. Firstly, despite the fact that the political landscape changes over time, most localities see relative stable political tendencies decade by decade. With some exceptions, regions that were predominantly voting left in the 1950s and 1960s continue to do so but sometimes at a lower level of support. In cases where majority conditions have changed, the growth of the middle class – typically following de-industrialisation and sub-urbanisation – is probably the most important explanation. Such changes have typically been concentrated to the bigger cities, leaving much of the traditional class structure intact in less urbanized parts of the country. Secondly, construction of new public housing continues and the selling out and conversions taking place during the past two decades also lead to an uneven development of the public housing sector. If the size of the public sector in 1990 was due to a historical political legacy, nothing speaks against presuming that later developments are the result of more current politics and of contemporary structural conditions. Berg and Berger (2006) find support for a structural break on the Swedish housing market due to policy shifts around 1990. These shifts "have resulted in a more market driven demand for housing investment in Sweden". This might speak against the idea that local politicians can affect housing investments, including deciding on the volume of public housing.

As will be shown below, there has been a political swing from left to right during the period covered here. Among many political changes, the reduction of central state housing subsidies from 1992 onwards has substantially affected the level of new housing construction and few – if any – OECD countries have seen so little new housing emerge since 1990 (see for example OECD 2012, providing per capita data on housing investments in 20 countries 1980–2008; Sweden is at the bottom). This is the primary reason for the fact that tenure composition – despite conversions from private and public rental to cooperative housing – by and large is rather similar 1990 and 2008 (see Table 15.2).

As can be expected, tenure composition including the role of public housing varies across municipalities of different size (see Table 15.3). Some of these variations have to do with the degree of urbanisation and the general population development. Municipalities having experienced population decline since the 1960s are often rural, deviate demographically from the rest of the country, and seldom have much multifamily housing. And public housing has always been almost exclusively constructed in the form of multifamily housing. As was discussed above, an important period for housing construction in Sweden was the 1950s, 1960s and 1970s. Public housing companies took an active part in the so called Million Homes Programme (1965–1974). It was a period of extensive housing construction but of course more so in the big cities and in rapidly expanding middle-sized cities.

The relative size of public housing decreases 1990–2008 in most municipalities but the most radical development takes place in Stockholm (Andersson and Magnusson 2014), which saw a decrease from 32 to 21 %. The reduction is seldom due to demolition although this can and has affected some of the smaller and more rural municipalities (facing housing surplus in the wake of negative population

Table 15.3 The relative proportion (per cent) of the population in municipalities (ranked according to population size) residing in public housing, 1990 and 2008

Municipality size	1990	2008
Stockholm	32.2	21.4
Gothenburgh	29.5	26.0
Malmo	15.8	15.5
100,000–200,000 in.	20.3	15.6
50,000–100,000 in.	18.7	14.3
20,000–50,000 in.	14.6	11.5
Less than 20,000 in.	10.1	8.4
Total (Mean)	12.7	10.2
Weighted mean	16.3	14.1

Source: Geosweden database, Institute for Housing and Urban Research, Uppsala University

change). In some municipalities experiencing population growth the reduction is due to lack of new public housing construction so that the sector's relative size undergoes change when other tenure forms expand. In yet other, like in Stockholm, the decrease is primarily caused by the selling out of public housing to sitting tenants, who form cooperatives that formally take over ownership.

The subsequent multivariate statistical analyses of the relation between local politics and public housing will make use of two sources of data; (1) election data and (2) population register data. The two sources are briefly described below.

15.4.1 Election Data

I have downloaded from Statistics Sweden's public website election statistics by municipality (i.e. number of seats per political party in local parliaments) for two separate elections, 1988 and 2006. These data have been used for calculating the proportion of seats for the political left (the Social Democratic party and the Left Party). This can be argued to provide relevant information about the influence of the political left but it is by no means perfect.

Sometimes, local governments are based on broad coalitions (for an overview of coalition theory and Swedish practice, see Bäck 2003) and sometimes the left-right divide is crossed by the forming of coalitions between for instance the Center Party (liberal), or the Liberal Party, and Social Democrats. Furthermore, it is not unusual that local politics see a small oppositional party emerge as the result of a particular issue (such as the closure of a school or a hospital, construction of a highway, etc.). In some cases such a local party can be based on former Social Democratic voters so that the left can be politically stronger on for instance housing issues than is indicated by the two traditional leftist parties' proportion of the seats. It should also be pointed out that the Social Democrats – with or without support from the Left Party – often form the majority with support from the Green Party. This has become more common during the period studied here.

Without very time consuming data collection for keeping track of all these locality-specific political conditions, the simple calculation of the relative strength of the political left is both a straightforward and relevant option. It should be added that in municipalities having a bourgeois majority (often comprising four political parties) (the conservative/liberal Moderate Party, The Liberal Party, The Center Party, and the Christian Democrats) the non-left will typically control the local agenda and decision-making. Both nation-wide and in most cases locally, the Moderate Party is dominant in this group of political parties. Until quite recently, the Moderate party has persistently been arguing for neo-liberal values: lower taxes, deregulation, privatization of publicly owned property, delivery of welfare services, etc. In municipalities where this party dominates local politics, public housing typically has a marginal position and home ownership is the dominant tenure form.

Six municipalities have been added since the 1988 election so the empirical analyses carried out for 1990, and for changes 1990–2008, make use of 284 units. The 2008 analysis is based on all 290 municipalities (see Table 15.4). As transpires from Table 15.4, the left had a much stronger position in 1990 (election in 1988) than in 2008 (election 2006). More than 120 municipalities had a Left majority in 1990 but it should be noted that only three out of 13 of the most populous municipalities were controlled by the political left. In 2008, only 68 municipalities had a Left majority and none of the 13 largest. Meanwhile, the number of municipalities voting overwhelmingly non-Left increased substantially.

15.4.2 *Population Register Data*

The analyses will also make extensive use of the Geosweden database, which comprises a wide range of annual individual, longitudinal, geo-coded register data for the entire time period 1990–2008. The database is used for calculating all

Table 15.4 Election results 1988 and 2006 by type of municipality (population size). Proportion of seats for the left (Social Democratic Party and the Left Party)

City/population size	Minority position						Majority position					
	Under 30 %		30–40 %		40–50 %		50–60 %		60 % or more		Total N	
	1988	2006	1988	2006	1988	2006	1988	2006	1988	2006	1988	2006
Stockholm	0	0	0	1	1	0	0	0	0	0	1	1
Gothenburgh	0	0	0	0	1	1	0	0	0	0	1	1
Malmö	0	0	0	0	0	1	1	0	0	0	1	1
100,000–200,000 in.	0	0	0	3	5	7	2	0	0	0	7	10
50,000–100,000 in.	2	4	3	8	12	15	12	3	1	2	30	32
20,000–50,000 in.	4	10	11	22	26	29	29	12	10	2	80	75
Less than 20,000 in.	15	20	38	51	42	48	37	31	32	20	164	170
Total	21	34	52	85	87	101	81	46	43	24	284	290

Table 15.5 Descriptive statistics for variables used in the multivariate analyses

		1990					2008			
Variable type	Variable	N*	Min.	Max.	Mean	Std. Dev.	Min.	Max.	Mean	Std. Dev.
Dependant variable	% in public housing	290	0.00	63.33	12.68	8.04	0.00	49.04	10.24	6.18
Political balance	% left seats	290	17.78	74.36	47.81	11.41	8.89	82.86	43.29	11.86
Demography	% immigrant background	290	2.48	45.88	9.41	5.81	4.27	52.10	13.38	7.27
	% age 80+	290	1.04	7.04	4.50	1.23	2.05	10.31	5.99	1.44
	% age 20–34	290	13.82	28.36	19.01	2.16	10.02	29.21	15.13	2.98
(Size of) Municipality	Stockholm	290	.00	1.00			.00	1.00		
	Gothenburg	290	.00	1.00			.00	1.00		
	Malmö	290	.00	1.00			.00	1.00		
	100,000–200,000 in.	290	.00	1.00	.02	.15	.00	1.00	.03	.18
	50,000–100,000 in.	290	.00	1.00	.10	.30	.00	1.00	.11	.31
	20,000–50,000 in.	290	.00	1.00	.27	.45	.00	1.00	.26	.44
	Lowest to 20,000 in.	290	.00	1.00	.58	.50	.00	1.00	.58	.49
Housing market condition	Tobin's Q	290	.37	2.44	.84	.34	.18	3.37	.89	.53
Socio-economic structure	% employed	290	68.17	90.63	84.36	2.94	63.06	86.63	79.15	3.71
	% low household disposable inc.	290	18.35	41.95	27.49	4.26	19.17	36.41	25.69	3.11
	% high household disposable inc.	290	13.20	45.40	22.95	6.00	11.74	49.37	21.88	6.66
	% received housing allowance	290	4.41	19.92	13.58	2.52	2.83	14.23	8.23	1.73
	% low work income	290	19.21	40.54	25.61	2.91	15.66	38.83	23.78	3.72
	% high work income	290	12.41	40.60	22.08	5.66	12.23	47.61	22.19	6.17

*The N is 284 for 1990

variables listed in Table 15.5 except for the election data just discussed. Individual data records showing housing, demographic and socioeconomic positions have been aggregated to the municipal level.

Table 15.5 displays descriptive data for all variables used in the subsequent multivariate analysis. They show for 1990 and 2008 the minimum, maximum and mean values (and standard deviation) for both the dependant and all independent variables. It can be noted that the dependant variable – percentage of the population in municipalities residing in municipal public housing – gets lower maximum and mean values in 2008 compared to 1990. This indicates a relative overall reduction of the public housing stock (see also Tables 15.2 and 15.3). In terms of the independent variables, some deserve a more elaborated comment.

First of all, Sweden had a Social Democratic government in 1990, supported by the Left Party. They lost this majority in the early 1990s, but regained power in 1994, maintained it in 1998 and in 2002 but lost again in the 2006 election. These country-wide majority swings are visible also at the local level (see also Table 15.4). The average support for the left in the municipalities was higher in 1990 than in 2008 but we can also notice a tendency towards polarization so that the minimum and maximum values for the left are both higher in 2008.

Secondly, the proportion of residents having foreign background (born outside of Sweden or having two foreign-born parents) increases substantially from 1990 to 2008. The municipal mean grows from 9.4 to 13.4 %. These values are far below the national means for respective year which indicates that it is the larger municipalities that tend to have high proportion of immigrants (Andersson 2012). This indicator is included here because of the substantial over-representation of immigrants in the public housing sector.

Thirdly, like elsewhere in countries having completed the demographic transition the proportion of elderly people grows in the population. This however occurs geographically very uneven so that some municipalities have five times as many aged 80 or above as have some other municipalities. Historically, rental housing is more common among the elderly but also among young adults. The latter category is taken into consideration here by including a dummy for the 20–34 year old. Their proportion decreases during the period but the variance increases.

Fourthly, the number of inhabitants changes over time but the overall structure remains stable. Stockholm, Gothenburg and Malmö are the three largest municipalities and they are analysed separately (dummies). Municipalities in the population range 100,000–200,000 inhabitants constitute only a couple of percentage points of all 290 municipalities while the smallest (under 20,000) form the biggest group. Many but not all of these are rural and have normally low population density.

Fifthly, Tobin's Q is included in order to take the general strength of the housing market into account (see for example Berg and Berger 2006). Tobin's Q contrasts the costs of producing new housing with the local price level for existing housing (ibid). Values under 1 indicate that construction activity is low because costs of producing new housing exceed the market value of already existing housing. Values over 1 are normally found in the larger cities and in hot spots that experience economic and population growth. This indicator thus measures not only the housing supply and demand balance but indirectly also local and regional long-term labour market conditions. The mean value is below 1 in both years which indicates that more than half of all municipalities have a weak housing market with tendencies towards increasing housing vacancy rates or simply reduction of housing units.

Finally the table reports on a series of socioeconomic indicators such as the percentage employed and work income (both measured for those aged 20–64), disposable household income (measured for age 15 and above), and the percentage of all having received some kind of housing allowance during the year. Both disposable household income and work income are defined as the relative share of people in the lowest quartile while high income correspondingly refers to the upper quartile. It is hypothesized that the proportion residents with low disposable income would on average demand more public rental housing. The proportion of residents receiving housing allowances decreases substantially over the period. This has primarily to do with politically decided changes in the regulation system; fewer nowadays qualify for such allowances (Enström-Östh 2010). The indicator is included in order to identify local concentration of the most needed households, who could also be hypothesized to be over-represented among public housing tenants.

15.5 Results

The analyses are carried out in three steps, using three models for each step (running the SPSS Linear Regression option). The first model includes only one control variable, the percentage Left seats in local parliaments. In the second model, I add the percentage having immigrant background, the percentage of each of two age groups (80 plus and 20–34) and the population size of municipalities (seven groups with Stockholm, Gothenburg and Malmö treated separately). The final model in each step contains information also on housing market conditions (Tobin's Q) and socioeconomic control variables (employment, income and housing allowances).

Step 1 is to run the analyses for 1990, step 2 for 2006, and step 3 is the difference models aiming at explaining change in all variables 1990–2006. The presentation of results follows this sequence.

15.5.1 The 1990 Model

Model 1 in Table 15.6 shows that the political balance contributes to explaining the variation in the dependent variable (percent public housing). The estimate is highly statistically significant but only 10 % of the variation is explained (R2 adjusted, see bottom line). The political balance variable remains statistically significant also after adding controls for demographic characteristics and for population size. Most of these new control variables are also statistically significant and contribute to increase the explanatory value; now 38 % of the variation is explained. Adding the final set of control variables (model 3) substantially increases the power of the model (R2Adj. = .56) but neither the political control variable nor municipal size are now statistically significant. The local support for the Left is however close to being significant and one particular city, Malmö, has much less public housing than could be expected given the political, demographic and socioeconomic attributes of the city. Tobin's Q is positively related to the share of public housing which means that this sector was bigger in strong housing markets than in weaker.

Table 15.6 Parameter estimates for explaining variation across Swedish municipalities in the percentage living in public housing, 1990

		Model 1			Model 2			Model 3		
Variable type	Variable (1990)	B	Std. error	Beta	B	Std. error	Beta	B	Std. error	Beta
	(Constant)	1.842	1.964		−24.780	12.661		34.466	49.117	
Political balance	% left 1988	.227	.040	.321***	.221	.035	.311***	.080	.052	.113
Demography	% immigrant background				.401	.080	.289***	.241	.083	.174***
	% age 80+				.605	.621	.091	−.891	.719	−.134
	% age 20–34				.580	.312	.187*	.576	.317	.186*
(Size of) Municipality	Stockholm				16.286	6.500	.120**	4.710	5.864	.035
	Gothenburg				13.486	6.488	.099**	−.604	5.811	−.004
	Malmö				−1.389	6.478	−.010	−14.601	5.765	−.107**
	100,000–200,000 in.				7.160	2.529	.138***	−.152	2.334	−.003
	50,000–100,000 in.				5.496	1.384	.209***	.376	1.325	−.014
	20,000–50,000 in.				3.489	.906	.195***	.3881	.861	.022
Housing market condition	Tobin's Q							12.485	1.846	.517***
Socio-economic structure	% employed							−.281	.475	−.102
	% low household disposable inc.							−.446	.273	−.235
	% high household disposable inc.							−1.477	.255	−1.084***
	% received housing Allowance							.900	.310	.278***
	% low work income							−.564	.524	−.203
	% high work income							.865	.255	.604***
R square adj.				0.10			.38			.56

P > | z |: * = p < 0.05, ** = p < 0.01, *** = p < 0.001

What is worth noticing is that a bigger share of high income households correlates negatively with the dependent variable but also, and surprisingly, that the share of people having a high work income increases the probability of finding more public housing. One should also notice that the proportion of people with foreign background is related in a statistically significant way to the relative size of the public housing sector; i.e. the presence of immigrants means that it is more likely to find public housing. It is very likely that causality also works the other way around so that only municipalities having a reasonable big public housing sector have attracted immigrants. The same reasoning probably applies for the category young adults. Municipalities that in 1990 had a big proportion of the 20–34 years old tend to have more public housing.

15.5.2 The 2008 Model

The final 1990 model explains more than half of the variation in the dependent variable. When the same set of independent variables is employed for the 2008 data, the explanatory value drops to 40 % (see model 3 in Table 15.7). Interestingly, it is not the political or demographic variables that produce less effective estimates but rather the decreasing effect of adding socioeconomic control variables. Model 2 for 1990 and 2008 gives about the same R2 values, while model 3 obviously does not.

For 2008, the relative strength of the Left turns out to be statistically significant for the level of public housing: support for the Left has decreased compared to 1990 but municipalities having a higher proportion of leftist voters are definitely more likely to have a bigger share of public housing.

Estimates for the other control variables comes out very much similar to the 1990 models, meaning that the percentage young adults, immigrants and housing allowances recipients, are positively correlated with public housing. The same applies for Tobin's Q. Malmö still has a negative sign and so has the influence of having a big proportion of households with high disposable incomes.

15.5.3 The 1990–2008 Difference Model

The idea with a difference model is to focus on statistical relationships between variables that change over time. In this case, the only time invariant input variable in the models is the stratification of municipalities according to population size; not much happens here. The difference model therefore excludes this information but population change is instead introduced. The models thus measure change in all dimensions, including the dependent variable. It is thus relative change 1990–2008 in the local proportion of public housing that now constitutes the dependent variable.

Table 15.7 Parameter estimates for explaining variation across Swedish municipalities in the percentage living in public housing, 2008

		Model 1			Model 2			Model 3		
Variable type	Variable (2008)	B	Std. error	Beta	B	Std. error	Beta	B	Std. error	Beta
	(Constant)	5.607	1.350	***	−12.668	3.096	***	−3.463	51.298	
Political balance	% left 2006	.107	.030	.205***	.125	.0254	.239***	.086	.039	.164**
Demography	% immigrant background				.238	.0489	.279***	.248	.0587	.291***
	% age 80+				.199	.247	.0463	−.496	.363	−.116
	% age 20–34				.834	.166	.401***	.529	.178	.254***
(Size of) Municipality	Stockholm				1.009	5.234	.010	1.612	5.258	.015
	Gothenburg				2.884	5.300	.027	3.515	5.256	.033
	Malmö				−9.800	5.345	−.0930*	−9.527	5.352	−.090*
	100,000–200,000 in.				−1.318	2.083	−.039	−1.459	2.146	−.043
	50,000–100,000 in.				1.067	1.186	.054	.496	1.237	.025
	20,000–50,000 in.				1.828	.737	.130**	1.382	.797	.098*
Housing market condition	Tobin's Q							3.124	1.117	.266***
Socio-economic structure	% employed							.376	.504	.226
	% low household disposable inc.							−.402	.281	−.202
	% high household disposable inc.							−.632	.300	−.680**
	% received housing Allowance							.759	.317	.213**
	% low work income							.282	.551	.169
	% high work income							.315	.248	.313
R square adj.				0.04			.37			.40

P > | z |: * = p < 0.05, ** = p < 0.01, *** = p < 0.001

It is clear from both the 1990 and 2008 analyses that the selection of explanatory variables makes sense. Many but not all give a statistically significant contribution to explaining why the relative importance of public housing varies over Swedish municipalities. The question now is whether they have capacity to explain not only relationships for particular years but also dynamic developments. Table 15.8 displays the results.

All three difference models produce statistically significant positive estimates for the political balance measure. This means that where the left has been relatively stronger the change in public housing has been less negative or more positive than elsewhere. Part of the explanation of the local importance of public housing is therefore politics, and the main hypothesis is therefore supported.

The relative presence of immigrants explained part of the variation in public housing in the cross-sectional analyses and this variable remains statistically significant (albeit at a lower level of confidence) also when changes in the relative share of immigrants are applied for explaining variations over time of the public housing sector. The same applies for the young adults: increasing proportion of the 20–34 years old predicts increasing shares for public housing.

Interestingly, the former strong statistical relationship between Tobin's Q and public housing now disappears. Whether a local housing market gets stronger or weaker over time seems to lack importance for predicting changes in the role of public housing.

Finally, two socioeconomic variables produce statistically significant relations with the dependent variable. And both behave as could be expected: it is detrimental for public housing if a municipality experience a relative growth of households having high disposable income while public housing fare better if the relative share of low work income people increases. This means that public housing remains a social class issue: the sector is stronger where the left has more influence and even with this taken into account, the sector is an important housing option for low income people and for ethnic minorities.

15.6 Conclusions

Bengtsson et al. (2006) identify four historical phases of housing provision in the five Nordic countries: an establishment phase with limited housing reforms in response to the early urbanization; a construction phase with comprehensive and institutionalized housing policies aimed at getting rid of housing shortage; a management phase where the more urgent housing needs had been saturated; and a retrenchment phase with diminishing state engagement in housing provision (ibid., pp. 21–24). This study focuses attention to Sweden and to the last of these phases. Whether diminishing state engagement should be seen from the perspective of shifting political power balance or to other factors deserves further research attention. It could very well be that Malpass (2008) statement that housing is a 'tool or lever of change rather than a driver of it' may turn out to be true also for Sweden.

Table 15.8 Parameter estimates for explaining variation across Swedish municipalities in the change of percentage living in public housing, 1990–2008

		Model 1			Model 2			Model 3		
Variable type	Variable (change 1990–2008)	B	Std. error	Beta	B	Std. error	Beta	B	Std. error	Beta
	(Constant)	−1.616	.341	***	2.010	1.200	*	−5.467	2.797	**
Political balance	Change % left 1988–2006	.192	.045	.245***	.177	.045	.226***	.122	.043	.156***
Demography	Pop. change 1990–2008				−.000	.000	−0.216*	.000	.000	−.065
	% immigrant background				−0.128	.115	−.075***	.212	.119	.124*
	% age 80+				−0.452	.427	−.065***	−.311	.441	−.045
	% age 20–34				.584	.180	.218	.555	.175	.207***
Housing market condition	Tobin's Q							.483	1.131	.027
Socio-economic structure	% employed							−.378	.274	−.225
	% low household disposable inc.							−.393	.161	−.233**
	% high household disposable inc.							−1.056	.214	−.476***
	% received housing allowance							−.402	.286	−.254
	% low work income							.916	.216	0.419***
	% high work income							−.136	.173	−.056
R square adj.				0.06			0.12			0.28

P > | z |: * = p < 0.05, ** = p < 0.01, *** = p < 0.001

One consequence of the retrenchment of national housing provision policy is however obvious: it will most certainly open up for more local variation and this is even more likely in a country such as Sweden, where municipalities are institutionally strong, resourceful and exercise influence on a range of issues.

The presumed variation is the background for this chapter, and two empirical questions were asked in the introduction: (1) which local political, demographic and socioeconomic conditions can explain the size of the public housing sector across Swedish municipalities, and (2) can such conditions and changes of such conditions also explain changes over time in the relative size of the public housing sector?

Sweden has experienced political changes since the early 1990s. Some of these are without doubt of an ideological nature which can be but not need to be caused by alterations in the class structure and subsequently in voting behaviour. Others have taken place very much in agreement over the left-right divide, including many important changes of housing policy that was triggered by the Swedish State budget crisis in the early 1990s. However, the policy to gradually diminish the role of public housing has clearly been driven both nationally and locally by the political right (Turner 2007). The key question is whether politics matters for explaining variations in the size of public housing across Sweden's 290 municipalities.

Three empirical analyses have been carried out using election data and population register data for 1990 and 2008. While local politics seemed not to explain much of the overall variation in 1990 – especially not after controlling for a range of other factors – it is clear that politics matters for explaining the occurrence of public housing in 2008 and also changes in the role of public housing 1990–2008. This result confirms what seems logical: when national regulations are relaxed, internal geographical variation gets bigger; local politics becomes even more decisive for future developments.

Public housing has been and remains a social class issue in Sweden: the sector is stronger where the left has more influence and the sector is an important housing option for low income people and for ethnic minorities. Whether the sector will survive in its present form, where municipalities own and control their housing company is therefore also a political issue but it is also an issue that partly will depend on decisions at the European Union level (and Swedish adjustments to such decisions). Housing as such is not included among the European Union's competence areas (i.e. it rests with the member states) but it is indirectly affected by many EU regulated policies and most importantly rules concerning the free market and fair competition. Social housing is excluded from such regulation because it aims at servicing particular categories of weak consumers (Boverket 2012). Swedish public housing is however open for anybody and public housing companies therefore compete with private actors. The decision taken by the Swedish parliament in 2010, to require that public housing companies operate according to business-like principles, was a means to mitigate EU criticism concerning the Swedish public housing system violating the principles laid down in the EU act on fair competition. It is also so that the historically privileged influence concerning rent setting that the public housing companies were exercising until 2010 was doubtful from an EU perspective (Boverket 2012). It is without doubt so that many reforms that lately have weakened the role of public housing in Sweden have been initiated by the political right but – conveniently – often with reference to what is demanded from membership in the EES/EU.

As shown by Magnusson and Turner (2008) and Andersson and Magnusson-Turner (2011) for Sweden, and recently by Musterd (2014) for the Netherlands, the gradual down-sizing of public housing risks leading to residualisation, i.e. a situation where the relative proportion of weaker housing consumers increases in the sector. This may in turn lead to more stigmatisation and to making the sector less attractive for middle income households. The result of this may very well be that Swedish public housing gradually takes on a role more similar to countries having social housing.

References

Andersson R, Magnusson Turner L (2011) Segregation, gentrification, and residualisation: from public housing to market driven housing allocation in inner city Stockholm. Paper presented at the Symposium on Public Housing Futures, City University of Hong Kong and Fudan Centre for Housing Studies, Fudan University, 22nd – 23rd Aug 2011

Andersson R (2012) Understanding ethnic minorities' settlement and geographical mobility patterns in Sweden using longitudinal data. In: Finney N, Catney G (eds) Minority internal migration in Europe. Ashgate, Aldershot, pp 263–291

Andersson R, Magnusson Turner L (2014) Segregation, gentrification, and residualisation: from public housing to market driven housing allocation in inner city Stockholm. Forthcoming in Int J Hous Policy

Bäck H (2003) Explaining and predicting coalition outcomes: conclusions from studying data on local coalitions. Eur J Polit Res 42:441–472

Bengtsson B (2006) Sverige — kommunal allmännytta och korporativa särintressen (Sweden — municipal non-profit housing and corporative interests). In: Bengtsson et al (eds) Varför så olika? Nordisk bostadspolitik i jämförande historiskt ljus [Why so different? Nordic housing policy in comparative historical light]. Égalité, Malmö, pp 101–157

Bengtsson B (2012) Path dependence or historical juncture? The Swedish housing regime before and after adjustment to the European competition policy. Paper presented at the ENHR 2012 conference 'Housing: Local Welfare and Local Markets in a Globalised World', Lillehammer, Norway, 24–27 June 2012

Bengtsson B (ed), Annaniassen E, Jensen L, Ruonavaara H, Sveinsson JR (2006) Varför så olika? Nordisk bostadspolitik i jämförande historiskt ljus [Why so different? Nordic housing policy in comparative historical light]. Égalité, Malmö

Bengtsson B, Rounavaara H (2010) Introduction to the special issue: path dependence in housing. Hous Theory Soc 27(3):193–203

Berg L, Berger T (2006) The Q theory and the Swedish housing market – an empirical test. J Real Estate Financ Econ 33(4):329–344

Boverket [Swedish Board of Housing, Building and Planning] (2011) Bostadsmarknaden 2011–2012, Karlskrona. http://www.boverket.se/Global/Webbokhandel/Dokument/2011/BME-2011-2012.pdf. Retrieved Dec 2012

Boverket [Swedish Board of Housing, Building and Planning] (2012) EU och bostadspolitiken 2011 – Rättsutveckling och samarbete inom EU av betydelse för svensk bostadspolitik Rapport 2012:4. Karlskrona. http://www.boverket.se/Global/Webbokhandel/Dokument/2012/EU-och-Bostadspolitiken-2011.pdf Retrieved Dec 2012

Christophers B (2013) A monstrous hybrid: the political economy of housing in early-twenty-first-century Sweden. New Polit Econ. doi:10.1080/13563467.2012.753521
Elander I (1991) Good dwellings for all: the case of social rented housing in Sweden. Hous Stud 6 (1):29–43
Enström Öst C (2010) Housing policy and family formation, Economic studies 123, Uppsala University
Forrest R, Murie A (1988) Selling the welfare state: the privatisation of public housing. Routledge, London
Government Proposition 2009/10:185) Allmännyttiga kommunala bostadsaktiebolag och reformerade hyressättningsregler [New Public Municipal Housing Companies Act], Stockholm
Lee DS, Moretti E, Butler MJ (2004) Do voters affect or elect policies? Evidence from the U. S. House. Q J Econ 119(3):807–859
Lindbom A (2001) Dismantling Swedish housing policy. Gov Int J Policy Admin 14(4):503–526
Lind H (2007) The municipal housing companies in Sweden: current situation and future prospects. Paper presented to the 2007 ENHR International Conference, http://www.enhr2007rotterdam.nl/documents/W16_paper_Lind.pdf Retrieved Dec 2012
Malpass P (2005) Housing and the welfare state. The development of housing policy in Britain. Palgrave MacMillan, Basingstoke
Malpass P (2008) Housing and the new welfare state: wobbly pillar or cornerstone. Hous Stud 23 (1):1–19
Magnusson L, Turner B (2008) Municipal housing companies in Sweden – social by default. Hous Theory Soc 25(4):275–296
Musterd S (2014) Public housing for whom? Experiences in an era of mature Neo-Liberalism: The Netherlands and Amsterdam (Forthcoming in *Housing Studies*)
Nielsen P (2003) Kommunindelning och demokrati: Om sammanläggning och delning av kommuner i Sverige [Municipality division and democracy: amalgamation and secession of municipalities in Sweden]. Statsvetenskapliga föreningens skrifter 157, Uppsala
OECD (2012) Economic outlook analysis and forecasts. http://www.oecd.org/eco/economicoutlookanalysisandforecasts/42150567.pdf. Retrieved Dec 2012
Pettersson-Lidbom P (2008) Do parties matter for economic outcomes ? A regression-discontinuity approach. J Eur Econ Assoc 6(5):1037–1056
SABO (Swedish Association of Public Housing Companies) (2010) The Riksdag has passed the new Public Municipal Housing Companies Act. http://www.sabo.se/aktuellt/nyheter_s/2010/juni/Sidor/Riksdagen_nyalagen.aspx Retrieved Dec 2012
Statistics Sweden (2012) Press release from Statistics Sweden, No 2012:760. Kalkylerat bostadsbestånd 2011. http://www.scb.se/Pages/PressRelease____335520.aspx. Retrieved Dec 2012
Turner B, Whitehead CME (2002) Reducing housing subsidy: Swedish housing policy in an international context. Urban Stud 39(2):201–217
Turner B (2007) Social housing in Sweden. In: Whitehead C, Scanlon K (eds) Social housing in Europe. London School of Economics and Political Science, London, pp 148–164
Van Gent WPC (2010) Housing policy as a lever for change? The politics of welfare, assets and tenure. Hous Stud 25(5):735–753
Wilhelmson M, Andersson R, Klingborg K (2011) Rent control and vacancies in Sweden. Int J Hous Mark Anal 4:105–129

Chapter 16
"Unorthodox" Housing Policy in Hungary: Is There a Way Back to Public Housing?

József Hegedüs

16.1 Introduction – The Emergence of the Unorthodox Economic Policy

The global economic crisis had a severe impact on the Hungarian economy at the end of 2008 due to the high public deficit and large FX debt/GDP ratio. Hungary had to take out emergency loans from the IMF and introduced measures such as cutting government expenditures (housing subsidies, pensions, etc.) and levying special taxes. The interim Hungarian government launched an austerity program that consolidated the budget and brought down the deficit to 3.8 % of GDP by 2009. After the election in 2010, the new government, which received 53 % of the votes and has two-thirds majority in Parliament, introduced "unorthodox" economic measures, provoking widespread discussion and criticism both in Hungary and abroad. The economic basis of this policy is a modified neo-Keynesian economic policy that tries to boost economic growth through state expenditures or tax cuts. The "unorthodox" economic policy aims to restore economic growth and fiscal balance without austerity measures.

Unorthodox economic policy must be clearly distinguished from unorthodox monetary policy, which has been an integral part of the financial governance of numerous countries in the aftermath of the Great Financial Crisis of 2008. Unorthodox monetary policy applies tools that aim at maintaining the financial system and credit supply to avoid a depression. ***Unorthodox economic policy***, however, does not have systematically organized elements, although the Argentinian and Venezuelan models, among others, which seem to provide examples for Hungarian policy makers, might help us to identify a master plan behind the seemingly chaotic measures. There are two approaches to the current "unorthodox" economic policy in Hungary. The majority of economists argue that this policy is a set of unrelated

J. Hegedüs, Ph.D. (✉)
Managing Director, Metropolitan Research Institute, 1093 Lónyay 34, Budapest, Hungary
e-mail: hegedus@mri.hu

J. Chen et al. (eds.), *The Future of Public Housing: Ongoing Trends in the East and the West*, DOI 10.1007/978-3-642-41622-4_16,

economic decisions motivated by shortsighted political gain, rooted in a misunderstanding of the main principles of economics. Others believe that the government is following some type of "master plan" (Szelényi 2012; Valentinyi 2012).

I argue in this chapter that a consistent economic policy framework is conceivable, which is intrinsically associated with a quite autocratic political framework. There is no theory of "unorthodox" economic policy, and what we have is closer to "propaganda" texts. These are based on general guidelines and governing principles rather than a detailed program, and in practice they will contain a set of ad hoc, spontaneously created ideas that will roughly match the master plan framework.

From a sociological point of view, the key question is how the new policy will change the political and economic setup of the institutional structure and how it may contribute to solving social tensions arising from the economic crisis. While we cannot ignore that the measures have the motivation of maximizing voter support (which is the most important aim of politics), our main focus is on their wider structural impact.

The aim of economic policy (be it orthodox or unorthodox) is to reinforce economic growth and ensure a sustainable economic balance. In the post-recession period, its aim is to provide the sources to kick-start growth, for which a budgetary deficit may be an effective tool. The ambition of the newly elected government after 2010 to increase the public deficit in order to boost economic growth was thwarted by strict EU regulations, which meant that the government had to find an alternative solution. The problem in 2010 was that the international market did not tolerate the increase of the deficit as a consequence of an unpredictable economic policy. The government (and Fidesz, the ruling party) did not give up on economic policy based on demand-side interventions, but to achieve this, they had to use "unorthodox" policy measures. This was when the unorthodox methods were introduced, which had four pillars.

Firstly, private resources were confiscated to decrease the deficit and the state debt. Private pension funds were nationalized, and new taxes were levied on banks (targeting, first of all, foreign-owned banks), as well as on monopolistic energy providers and large retailers. The politicians of the ruling party thought that the international market would appreciate the strong government and the "unorthodox" measures and that they could finance the deficit without IMF support. The government refused to cooperate with the IMF in 2010, but the expected economic growth did not materialize, and, according to the financial market evaluation, Hungarian borrowing presented a high risk. At the end of 2011, the government asked the IMF to negotiate a loan, but at the end of 2012, the negotiations stopped again.

Secondly, the central government initiated massive centralization, practically renationalizing the local municipality system, which had been decentralized in the past 25 years: hospitals and schools, which used to take up 60 % of the local authorities' budgets, are now nationalized; and public policy functions formerly fulfilled by local governments are to be delegated to the newly created districts, administrative divisions under direct central government control. The water sector is undergoing a similar reform, with the providers pressed to adopt an easily controllable centralized system, while formerly locally controlled functions are relocated to the Hungarian Energy Agency.

Thirdly, the engines of economic growth are the remaining multinational companies (automotive industry) and EU structural funds, which are monopolized by a particular economic interest group with close ties to the current government (KÖZGÉP – Construction and Metal Structure Manufacturing Company). The central government buys up strategic companies and buys a share in energy providers to reinforce its direct influence on the economy. The government also took steps to gain control over the Hungarian National Bank, but the planned measures were withdrawn after the EU Commission and the Central European Bank expressed their concern about the central bank's independence. From the middle of 2013, however, the government will have control over the HNB anyway through the appointment of Mr. Matolcsy, the "father" of unorthodox economic policy, as head of the HNB. Furthermore, the Prime Minister announced (in July 2012) the aim to achieve 50 % Hungarian ownership of the banking sector; as a first step, the Hungarian Development Bank bought shares in savings banks. Moreover, the government aims to replace the profit-making companies in the public service sector with nonprofit companies.

Fourthly, the transformation of the society was just as radical. A flat rate income tax was introduced to favor higher income groups (thus risking the budget balance), large-scale public work programs were launched for the vulnerable groups that had lost their livelihoods as a result of the GFC, and social transfers and privileges were revised. The goal of the central government is to cut transfers to those living in deep poverty, with the hope that the resulting new resources will be absorbed by the middle class, and strengthen its solvency. The most recent measure of decreasing utility costs by 10 % across the board was conceived along the same lines, its motive being to reinforce higher income groups' financial means. At the same time, this logic requires the limitation of central financing in health care and education because the economic contraction makes a balanced budget unsustainable. To maintain the political support of the middle class, the government did not use measures that directly increased the burdens of this group. This poses a challenge for the public relations department of the government, which has to hide the consequences of the economic measures, which, in the end, will result in higher prices and lower welfare for the middle class as well.

The success of the unorthodox economic policy, which implements a radical redistribution of the economic burden brought about by the crisis among different stakeholders, hinges on whether it succeeds in triggering economic growth or leaves the economy in its current stagnation, as well as on the economic actors' reaction to the unusual austerity measures.

The central questions addressed in this chapter are: What constitutes the housing policy of the new government? What are the chances of a new approach in social housing as a consequence of the financial crisis and "unorthodox" economic policy? In the first part of the chapter, we will give an overview of developments in the social housing sector in Hungary; in the second part, we will analyze mortgage market developments in the last 12 years, focusing on the factors that led to the accumulation of the risky FX loan portfolio. Next, we will provide an overview of the housing market after 2009 and summarize housing policy concepts and the institutional dynamics behind them. In the fourth part, we will analyze the mortgage rescue programs and their results (until the end of 2012). Finally, we will evaluate the developments from the point of view of the future of social housing in Hungary.

16.2 Social Housing in the New Post-socialist Systems – The Case of Hungary

The transition from the East European Housing Model[1] (Hegedüs and Tosics 1996) towards a market-based housing system took place in the last two-and-a-half decades. However, these processes were more complicated than the mainstream approach in the 1990s presumed (World Bank 1993; Hegedüs et al. 1996; Buckley and Tsenkova 2001; Tsenkova 2009; Hegedüs 2013b, c) because the market creation policy measures were corrected both by market correction strategies (different safety net approaches to lessen the difficulty of the transition) and by social forces that were supported by the socialist welfare tradition. The adaptation of the different actors (public institutions, private organizations, and households) took place in a conflicting environment, where the coping strategies involved elements of informal economies, extended families, social and political networks, etc.

Attempts to generalize on the main trends of the welfare regime development proved to be non-conclusive and resulted in categories of mixed regimes that combined elements of liberal, social democrat, and family-based South European regimes (Tomka 2005; Ferge 2002; Cerami 2005; Tausz 2009). The reasons for the uncertainty in the evaluation of the new regimes are that public sector reforms (education, health care system, etc.) are incomplete, policy and institutions in different welfare sectors follow different principles even within a single country, and there is a big gap between the rhetoric of the programs and their actual implementation. The fact is that welfare policies in different sectors tend to change incrementally; they follow different tracks and dynamics (Kasza 2002, p. 282).

Consequently, the development of a welfare policy in the region did not originate from a consistent ideological model; policy makers did not follow a "master plan." Instead, welfare policies evolved in direct reaction to specific societal problems. The various areas of welfare policy (income benefit programs, education, pension system, etc.) were generally modified with loosely coordinated measures (Hegedüs and Szemző 2010). This type of "trial and error" or

[1] The main characteristics of the East European Housing Model were: one-party political control over the housing sector, the subordinate role of market mechanisms; the absence of market competition among housing agencies (bureaucratic coordination), and a broad control of the allocation of housing services (huge, nontransparent subsidies). However, under this model, several "sub-models" (versions) emerged; these were the responses of individual countries to particular challenges in the development process of the socialist economy (Hegedüs 2013c).

"scrambling through" approach was more or less a general phenomenon in the region (Tsenkova 2009).

Social housing policies in the region are still undergoing a process of transition. However, they have three important elements in common: the limited role of social landlords due to privatization, an affordability problem due to the divergence in incomes and housing costs in both the public rental and the homeownership sector, and an accessibility problem in both rental and owner-occupied housing for low-income groups. The institutional answers to these structural problems have differed from country to country, but they nevertheless form subspecies of the same model rooted in the EEHM (Hegedüs 2013a).

The development of social housing policy in Hungary brought changes in the following three areas of the housing and welfare sector: (a) the social rental sector, (b) housing allowances and income benefit programs, and (c) low-cost housing opportunities (both rehabilitation and access to new/existing units). These are discussed in turn in the succeeding sections.

16.2.1 The Social Rental Sector

As a consequence of the privatization by 2007, only 140,000 housing units (3 % of the total stock) have remained in the public rental sector (from 721,000 23 %, in 1990); moreover, the housing privatization has not stopped because social landlords (municipalities) still have incentives to get rid of the stock. Public rental housing is concentrated in the cities: 69 % of the stock is found in Budapest and in larger cities.

As a consequence of the privatization, municipalities were left with low-quality housing stock, which stood in need of major rehabilitation, and tenant households generally had multiple social problems. The remaining social rentals were often concentrated in the worst parts of the cities, and the allocation system also contributed to the residential segregation of disadvantaged households. The cost of maintaining the municipal rental stock is not supported by the central budget. The maintenance of social housing is thus costly for the municipalities because the rents do not cover their expenses. Consequently, many municipalities would like to get rid of their social rental housing and the social problems frequently posed by housing concentrations of poor tenants.

In 2000, the government launched a grant program for local authorities, which made the latter eligible for a grant of up to 75 % of the cost of investments; as a result, 12,800 units were built. However, the program had several weaknesses. The average costs were considered to be very high, the allocation criteria for new tenancies were not regulated, and consequently, the allocation was dependent on the municipal governments, which typically preferred the low-to-middle class households. Moreover, during the period of operation of the scheme, the privatization process continued; thus, local authorities privatized 25,000 units but built, bought, or renewed only 8,900 rental units.

In 2004, the government stopped the social rental program due to fiscal pressures, citing the high cost per unit as the reason. The government proposed a rent allowance program as a substitute for the budget-financed rental program. The proposal failed (was not introduced) because the guaranteed rent level required by investors was unacceptably high, twice the actual market rent, because of the high construction cost. However, the importance of the social rental sector was never questioned in government documents. In 2005, a new rent allowance program was finally introduced, which aimed to use the private rental sector for social purposes. Local governments could apply for rent allowance for low-income families with children that had private rental contracts. The program was a failure: very few local authorities put forward a proposal because they did not want to take on the responsibility and risks for the management of the private rental units.

16.2.2 Housing Affordability and Housing Allowances

Housing affordability has become the main housing problem. From the social housing policy point of view, the basic questions are how the poor are housed and what kind of public programs help them to afford housing consumption at a socially accepted level. The majority of the poor live in the private sector as low-income homeowners or low-income private renters. Of total household expenditures, housing-related spending increased from 9 to 20 % in the first 10 years of the transition, while the income disparity (the ratio of the average income of the lowest income decile to that of the highest income decile) increased from 4.7 to 7.3 (CSO 2007). Energy-related expenditures represent the biggest segment of housing costs: in 2007, they constituted almost 70 % of housing-related expenditures.

The Social Law (1993) introduced a housing allowance scheme financed through the local governments' discretionary budget. Local governments used this program only on a limited scale because it was financed exclusively out of their own budgets, unlike other income benefit programs. In 2004, the government introduced a new housing allowance program, which received 90 % of its financing from the central budget. Beyond the housing allowance system, households' affordability was supported by indirect (across the board) subsidies, of which the energy consumption subsidy was the most important. In 2006, the total indirect energy price subsidy was HUF 208 billion, 12 times more than the total cost of the housing allowance. On January 1, 2007, the government introduced a new energy allowance subsidy, which followed the logic of a means-tested consumption subsidy as households in the higher income band were given less subsidy. Its cost was HUF 110 billion in 2007, but the targeting was very poor. The energy allowance subsidy was decreased from HUF 109 billion to 63 billion between 2007 and 2010 and was integrated into the housing allowance scheme in 2012.

The design of the subsidy system cannot guarantee that low-income households can pay their housing costs after providing for their basic needs. Subsidies only cover a small proportion of the housing cost, which poses a further problem.

16.2.3 Construction Subsidies

From 1990 to 1998, housing construction dropped to 20,000 units/year (25 % of the 1980s construction rate). Because most state subsidies were cut, access to housing became less affordable. The only exception was the housing construction allowance, a cash grant for new construction.

The housing construction allowance was first introduced in 1971, and its function has changed several times. It is a cash grant that helps with the down payment of home buyers. The size of the subsidy depends on the number of children in the household; it is not a means-tested grant, and only buyers of newly built homes or “self-builders” – households that build or organize the building themselves – are eligible. Among the further criteria are that applicants do not own a dwelling of their own at the time of their application and that the standard of the new home is below the centrally decided standard size and cost limit. In 1995, the amount of the grant was increased for families with two or three children, which made it possible for low-income households to build new “low-cost” housing without substantial savings or loans. Interestingly enough, although it was not the intention of the policy makers, this subsidy scheme was used by large, poor families (for example, Roma families) with the help of intermediaries (builders, lawyers, contractors, and Roma NGOs). It was particularly significant in less developed regions, where the grant covered almost the total cost of the construction. Private developers emerged, who specialized in using the advantages of this scheme (Zolnay 2002). The program had several negative effects. Many of the homes built in this manner were of poor quality. Furthermore, much of the construction took place in less developed regions with higher unemployment. According to some estimates, 10,000 homes were built using the allowance between 1995 and 1997, which was the largest, albeit unintentional, Roma housing program after 1990 (Hegedüs 2013a). However, the social effect of the program was much less than it could be. For example, the fact that the size of the construction subsidy depended on the number of children explicitly contributed to the segregation of the poor Roma families, which, through the mediation of private developers, used this opportunity to move to areas with lower land prices. The housing construction allowance served fewer and fewer poor households because its value was inflated after 2000.

16.2.4 Rehabilitation Program

The rehabilitation program (under the housing policy objective to improve the quality of housing) became important after 2004, especially the “panel program” to rehabilitate buildings constructed with prefabricated technology. This was a politically popular program because it reached wide strata of the society and was relatively cheap from a fiscal point of view. Constant expansion of the “panel program" has taken place since 2004, as a result of which 25 % of this stock (190,000 housing units) was renovated to some degree by 2009. There are more serious social problem areas in segregated housing estates and run-down urban areas with a high share of Roma population, which require more social attention and fiscal resources. Some programs were started in 2006 but mostly on a pilot scale. Urban rehabilitation programs were launched slowly after 1990 under the control and support of the local governments, but in most cases, the urban poor were forced to move out of the renewed neighborhoods. The first urban rehabilitation program aimed at improving the living conditions of the "sitting poor" was started in 2006.

16.2.5 Conclusion

We can conclude that the most important housing policy measures after the transition favored the higher income group the most: these include housing privatization, mortgage subsidy programs (including the contract savings schemes), and partly, the implicit energy price subsidy (which in the years 2002–2007 supported the higher income groups much more than the poor). However, there were important programs that aimed at smoothing the consequences of income inequalities, such as housing allowance programs (especially after 2006), programs for social rental housing (although they failed after 4 years), and panel refurbishment programs (helping mainly the lower-to-middle income groups living in housing estates).

The housing policy, however, could not halt the exclusion process caused by the interplay of the labor and the housing market; thus, the social segregation of the poor has increased in the last two decades. Moreover, certain programs reinforced trends towards segregation. Housing policy (the actual implemented measures and programs, not the rhetoric in white papers) has been the result of different social forces: there was no master planning behind them (Hegedüs-Somogyi 2005) The analyses showed that, step-by-step, income benefit programs and social services are responding to a wide spectrum of social problems.

16.3 Hungarian Mortgage Market Development Between 2000–2009

In Hungary, economic performance improved after the transition recession, as a result of the austerity program of 1995–1996. The real GDP grew at an average rate of 4.4 % over the period 1997–2002, and the GDP reached the level of the pre-transition period by 2001. Unemployment had been on the decrease from the middle of the 1990s and stabilized at 5–7 % at the turn of the century although the employment rate remained low. Inflation stabilized and the interest rate decreased at the end of the 1990s as a clear sign of the macroeconomic stabilization.

The right-wing government (1998–2002) introduced major changes in housing policy in 2000. The most significant element of the program was the support for housing mortgages. Two interest rate subsidies were introduced beyond the already existing demand-side construction grant for families with children: (a) an interest rate subsidy for mortgage bonds (supported by the "bank lobby") and (b) an interest rate subsidy for loans connected to new construction (supported by the "construction lobby").[2] The third element of the subsidy program was the personal income tax (PIT) mortgage payment allowance.

In the original proposal (in 2000), the size of the mortgage subsidies and PIT allowance were at a low level, which gave a fiscally manageable impetus to the development of mortgage finance. However, the government was under constant pressure by lobbying groups; thus, the conditions and eligibility criteria for the two interest rate subsidy schemes were relaxed between 2000 and 2002. Additionally, in the spring of 2002 (before the election), the personal income tax deduction was expanded to loans for buying existing housing units, opening up a huge market for mortgage banks. By the end of 2002, it became clear that the volume of housing loans had increased very quickly as a consequence of the subsidies. In 2002, the outstanding loans more than doubled and reached 4.5 % of GDP.

There were two important drawbacks of the program: fiscal consequences and the equity effect. Firstly, the fiscal effects of the mortgage programs had been substantially underestimated, the actual cost being three times higher than projected (Hegedüs 2011, p. 119). Moreover, the socialist government (2002–2006), for political reasons, kept postponing decisions to cut the subsidies. The leading political parties got into a "game" of promising more and more support to the housing sector without understanding the fiscal and social consequences of the proposed programs. Secondly, the social consequence of the housing subsidy program was regressive income redistribution. The net value of the mortgage subsidy in 2002–2004 was 50–70 % of the loan (taking into calculation the two interest rate subsidies and the PIT allowance), which could be accessed without means testing. The regressive equity effect of the mortgage program is shown clearly by the allocation of the PIT allowance in 2004, where the upper 20 % of households in the income distribution received 60 % of the total subsidy, and the upper 40 % received 80 % (Hegedüs and Somogyi 2005, pp. 199–202).

After a long political debate, the government changed the conditions of the mortgage program in 2004. The interest rate subsidies were decreased, and tax exemptions in PIT for mortgage repayment were first cut severely and then

[2] See the social aspects of the programs in Hegedüs and Somogyi (2005) and the technical description in Szalay and Tóth (2003).

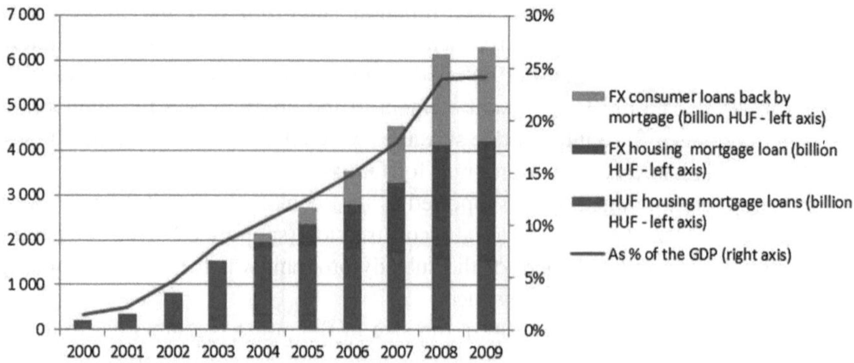

Fig. 16.1 Mortgage development in Hungary, 2000–2009

abolished in 2007. Housing credit grew very quickly in Hungary between 2000 and 2004, and the cut in subsidies did not halt the expansion of the market because foreign exchange (FX)-dominated loans successfully replaced the subsidized HUF loans. The share of FX loans went from close to zero in 2004 to 90 % of new lending in 2008. There were no direct fiscal burdens in relation to the loans issued in FX. The availability of cheap funds and the exceptionally high spread gave a high motivation for the banks and mortgage brokers to expand the market to consumer loans (Fig. 16.1).

The politicians ignored the risk that FX meant for the economy. There were no regulations on FX loans because of the strong connections between the government and the bank lobby. Regulatory agencies – the HNB, the Bank Supervisory Agency, and the Consumer Protection Agency – did not have the political support to intervene, but from time to time, they indicated the possible risk of FX loans. Even the opposition party did not support restrictions on economic growth.

The most important driving force of the over indebtedness in FX loans was the loose fiscal policy, which resulted in a huge difference between the interest rates on FX loans and those on HUF loans. Because of the high deficit, the HNB had to keep the interest rate high to give incentives to finance government debt.

The competition was high among banks, but instead of price competition, risk-based competition dominated the market and led to a worsening credit portfolio. "Strong loan expansion made the banking systems vulnerable: the ratio of FX denominated loans, the banks' loans/deposit ratio and their dependence on foreign funding all increased significantly. These accumulated imbalances increased the vulnerability of these countries to the coming crisis" (Banai et al. 2009, p. 12) The "creative" role of the banks (without real control by the HNB and the Bank Supervisory Agency) was an important factor in explaining the expansion of lending (new products, aggressive advertising, and the important role of individual mortgage brokers (Csányi 2007)). However, no house price bubble developed in Hungary; although house prices had increased in the last 10 years, they were far from those in countries with similar mortgage expansion.

16.4 Housing Market and Housing Policy After the Great Financial Crisis

16.4.1 Housing Market Decline – The Crisis

The consequences of the financial crisis on the housing sector in Hungary were very much like those experienced elsewhere (Scanlon et al. 2012; Deloitte 2012). However, the decline in the Hungarian housing market seems to have been among the most pronounced:

- Housing construction: New housing construction decreased from 36,200 to 10,600 thousand between 2007 and 2012; the decline was more severe when measured in terms of building permits (from 44,300 to 10,600).
- House prices: The year-by-year decrease in house prices between 2008 and 2009 was 8 % in nominal values and 12 % in real values. The decline continued such that, at the end of 2012, the real house price was more than 25 % lower than in 2008 (FHB price index).
- Housing market transactions: Housing transactions decreased by 40 % during 2008 and 2012 and is expected to reach 94,000 or 2.3 % of the housing stock, in 2012.
- Nonperforming loans: The stock of nonperforming mortgage loans (i.e., loan payments overdue by more than 90 days) increased from 2.6 to 6.3 % of the total outstanding balance between 2008 and 2009; the downward trend continued, with the figure reaching 12.3 % by 2011 (Q1).

The Hungarian government's initial response to the crisis focused on managing the fiscal deficit, which was one of the conditions of the IMF loan. The government cut housing subsidies drastically as part of the fiscal adjustment program. Both the interest subsidy and the homeownership down payment grants were abolished.

Both governments in Hungary after the crisis (a coalition of socialists and free democrats in 2008–2010 and the right-wing Fidesz party from 2010) tried several programs, but the approach of these two governments were very different. The first government, in keeping with the conditions of the IMF loans of 2008, introduced an "orthodox" policy: it cut housing subsidies and, step-by-step, launched rescue programs targeted at the vulnerable groups, negotiating with banks and construction companies. The programs were very cautious for fear of their possible uncontrolled fiscal effects; consequently, their results were modest as well.

The Fidesz government's approach was very different. With strong political support, their room to maneuver was much wider, and when the government's fiscal plan to increase the deficit was rejected by the EU, the leading political party (the Prime Minister) started a "freedom fight" against foreign-owned banks and international companies. The approach became "unorthodox" in the sense that the government preferred programs helping the wealthier and exploited the public's hostility towards the banks, which helped the government to transfer the cost of the program to the banking sector without considering the possible macroeconomic effects.

16.4.2 Politics of the Mortgage Rescue Program – Between Orthodoxy and Unorthodoxy

The mortgage rescue programs aim to slow down the negative effects of macroeconomic changes. The international experience shows that very different solutions have been implemented depending on the causes and extent of the default, such as legal changes (foreclosure procedure to promote out-of-court restructuring), tax and loan forbearance, temporary ban on evictions, rent-to-own schemes, etc. (Wilcoxs et al. 2010; Long and Wilson 2011; Howard 2011; UC 2011). The "orthodox" approach of the mortgage rescue programs specifies that the government or any large-scale public institution should intervene only if there is enough evidence that market-driven solutions did not work; this is because the cost of the interventions could easily exceed the benefits as there is always a danger to "create opportunities for politicization and capture by special interests" (Erbenova et al. 2011). This orthodox approach targets the subsidies for social groups in difficulty, but with a prospect to overcome the difficulties, pushing back the risk of moral hazard behavior, etc.

The "unorthodox" solution is not easy to define, but it seems to be open towards "blanket debt forgiveness schemes," which puts an unexpectedly high burden on the economy (depending on who picks up the costs) or distorts the behavior of the players. In our (Hungarian) case, the unorthodox approach means that the burden of the crisis should be put on the banking sector (as much as possible on foreign-owned banks) and support the middle class to generate purchasing power (decreasing their budget pressure) in order to boost the economy. This policy is based on the expectation that the cost of the rescue program can be absorbed by the banking sector without risking the economic recovery.

The key questions in the "solution" to the housing credit crisis are: Who is going to pay for the rescue program, and how will the burden be allocated between the government (taxpayers), banks (both foreign-owned and Hungarian), and the different groups of the borrowers? One of the most important elements of the problem is that defaulted borrowers have very few options to escape because there is no substantial social housing stock, and the private rental sector is very unpredictable. Thus, if the value of the loan is higher than the value of the home, the borrower, who cannot pay the mortgage, is in a critical situation. This is why mass eviction causes a huge political problem.

The mortgage rescue program is very important for the Fidesz government (supposing the government follows the master plan) because it necessarily risks the devaluation of the HUF and a further increase of the burden of FX borrowers. Politically, it would be very difficult to manage the protest against an economic policy that increases the burden of 20–25 % of households that typically belong to the middle class. Until the problem of FX loans is resolved, no recovery in the housing market can begin.

The previous Hungarian government initially followed the mainstream approach. It put a moratorium on foreclosures up to September 1, 2009, which was extended first until the end of June 2010 and later, by the new government, until

July 1, 2012. The 2-year moratorium posed a risk to the stability of the financial system because it gave the borrowers in financial stress less incentive to meet their loans given that nonpayment did not have consequences. The moratorium in itself and the parallel expectation that the government would help the defaulted households increased the share of nonperforming loans (HNB 2010).

The moratorium had an effect on arrears in utility payments as well. Between 2009 and 2012, the number of households having arrears of more than 12 months increased from 231,000 to 292,000 (25 %) (Herpai 2010; NFM 2012).

The foreclosure moratorium, which was phased out gradually, was applied through a quota: banks were allowed to sell foreclosed properties worth over 30 million forint and to carry a mortgage of 20 million forint; the quota was 3 % of all foreclosed homes in the fourth quarter of 2012 and is expected to reach 4 % in 2013 and 5 % in 2014. The actual foreclosures reached 80–85 % of the quota in the first two quarters of 2012 (PSZAF 2012b). However, the moratorium has remained at the center of discussion because the new ombudsman (appointed by the minister of National Economic Development in 2012) has again raised the possibility to re-introduce a moratorium until his new plan is accepted.

The policy of the previous government was to give incentives to banks and borrowers in order to solve the problem without too harsh an intervention from the government and to help only those households in the most critical situation to keep the cost as minimum as possible.

The interest of banks was to restructure the loans to keep up the performance of their portfolio. After the GFC, the banks improved their loan management departments and offered different forbearance options for borrowers in financial difficulty, such as increasing the modification of loan terms, reducing payments, capitalizing arrears, etc. The government between 2008 and 2010 put forward different suggestions and even subsidies (although very cautiously) to give incentives for borrowers and banks to reach a restructuring agreement. For example, in early 2009, the Hungarian government gave households experiencing loan repayment difficulties due to unemployment the option of paying reduced installments on their mortgage loans for a maximum of 2 years. Thereafter, borrowers would have to cover the cost of their increased debt. The repayment of deferred installments to lenders is guaranteed by the government. However, the qualification criteria for this program are so strict that very few borrowers are deemed eligible. The government was very cautious in determining the eligibility criteria in order to avoid being left responsible for much of the "bad loans" issued by Hungarian banks in the past. In 2010, only 3,000 out of 24,000 restructured loans qualified for this government program.

The banks reacted to the government model by developing their own solutions, which were administratively simpler and financially more advantageous for them. Consequently, the banks persuaded their clients to choose their (rather than the government's) restructuring products.

The volume of the FX loan stock presented a high risk for the economy; thus, from the beginning, one of the aims of the mortgage rescue programs was to convert FX loans into HUF loans but without a huge fiscal cost. The law forced the banks to convert FX loans into HUF loans at the market price of the foreign currency, but very few households used this option because they hoped that the HUF would recover its value.

The previous government established a crisis fund, to which well-off individuals and companies were expected to contribute on a voluntary basis. The crisis management fund would provide one-off assistance to some 30,000 of Hungary's most disadvantaged families whose members had lost their jobs after October 1, 2008 or for whom loan repayment installments had increased by more than 20 %. The program was stopped in 2010 because it proved to be ineffective and costly.

The Fidesz government's policy concerning the mortgage crisis was very different from that of the previous government, which was irreconcilable with the new "unorthodoxy." First of all, they blamed the crisis on previous governments and the banks, and they communicated a readiness to rescue borrowers from the outset. However, faced with the cost of such a program, the government realized that this would be impossible to achieve without risking the monetary stability of the economy. Consequently, their strategy was to put as much of the burden as possible on the banks. However, this conflict would involve a macroeconomic risk if the banking sector were to stop making loans. Secondly, the new government did not want to limit the program to the needy population because its political supporters come from the middle class. Thus, the programs offered possibilities to well-off groups, households facing economic hardship, and households that were unable to repay their loans. An important element of the history of the mortgage rescue programs is that there was no detailed master plan; different programs were negotiated with the banking sector, and even nongovernmental, civil organizations had some role in the negotiations. The program details changed frequently according to the experiences. Thirdly, it is worth mentioning that, similarly with other unorthodox programs, the government used war rhetoric to describe the program, for instance, "fight against the banks." The common element in the communication strategies was that they always contained "half-truths," which served as a supporting element.

16.4.3 The Fidesz Government's Mortgage Rescue Program

16.4.3.1 Early FX Loan Repayment Scheme

The program, which ran from September 2011 until the end of February 2012, made it possible for borrowers to repay their FX mortgages in full at only HUF 180 to the franc when the franc was trading at HUF 235–250.

As a result, almost one quarter (23.3 %) of mortgage loans were repaid, 984 billion HUF at the discounted exchange rate and HUF 1.355 billion at the current exchange rate (PSZAF 2012a, b). The new loan was on 30 % of the source of the early repayment, with the remaining 70 % representing the households' savings

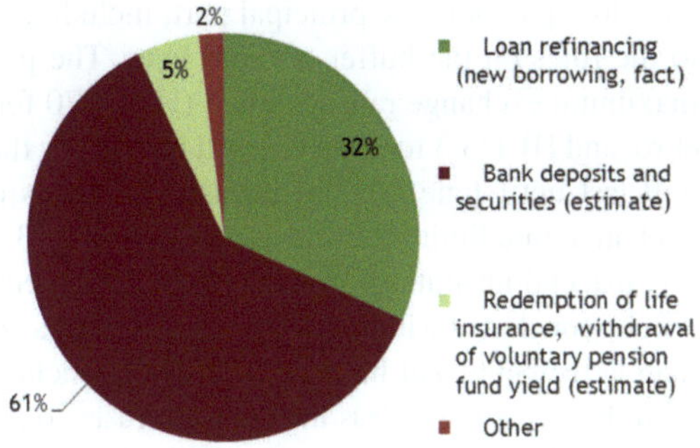

Fig. 16.2 The source of the "early repayment programs" (total amount: 980 billion HUF) (Source: HNB 2011)

(life insurance, securities, etc.). This indicates that it was the better-off families that were able to take advantage of this opportunity. Of course, the interest rate increased as the early repayment scheme started, but it was justified by the increased risk of the loan portfolio of the bank (Fig. 16.2).

According to the analyses, 15 % of the repaid sum was connected to the informal economy. Actually, the law stipulated that the Tax Office cannot check the source of the early repayment in connection with the untracked wealth increase (Law CXXX, 2011).

The banks were forced to carry the cost of the discount, writing off a gross loss close to HUF 400 billion (0.5 % of GDP). Later, an agreement between the banks and the government allowed 30 % of the loss to be rewritten from the special tax on banks; consequently, the cost of the program was shared 70/30 % between the banks and the government. This implicit subsidy was "given" to those households that could finance the repayment (either from savings or loans), which had a regressive effect on the income distribution.

As a consequence of the ERS, the quality of the remaining stock is expected to worsen, as shown in a recent report on K&H Bank: the share of NPL (loans with more than 90 days of payment arrears) in the stock of mortgage loans increased from 10.7 to 13.4 % in the last 3 months (see HNB 2011, for a detailed analysis).

16.4.3.2 FX Loan Rate Cap Scheme

In 2012, the government introduced a program that put an exchange rate cap on repayments and opened a special account for the exchange rate differential. Clients could apply to participate in the exchange rate limit scheme by the end of 2012 at the credit institutions disbursing their loans. The program is available to clients who have taken out FX loans worth a maximum of HUF 20 million, are behind with their payments by no more than 90 days, and are not part of a repayment assistance program. Banks will temporarily apply an exchange rate of HUF 180 to the Swiss franc, HUF 250 to the euro, and HUF 2.5 to the yen during the scheme. The balance compared to market rates will be recorded in a special buffer account. The interest component from the part of the monthly repayment above the exchange rate limit will be paid by the bank and the government (at a ratio of 1/3–2/3); borrowers will have to repay only the principal part, including the interest on the latter, according to the rules on the buffer account loan. The part of the repayment exceeding the maximum exchange rate specified (HUF 270 for the Swiss franc, HUF 340 for the euro, and HUF 3.3 for the yen) will be paid by the state. The preferential rate period will last until June 2017 at the latest. Clients can initiate the termination of the exchange rate limit after the expiry period of 3 years.

Financial institutions must do their best to ensure that the credit limit agreement will be concluded within 60 days of receipt of a complete application. Buffer account loan agreements that have already been concluded will be amended in accordance with the new rules unless the debtor refuses to give his/her written consent.

According to estimates, 75–90 % of eligible borrowers will join the program. However, the program has had a slow start: only 11,000 out of 610,000 possible contracts have been transferred into the special scheme (Palkó 2012). The expected cost of the program is HUF 25 billion per year (HNB 2012) or HUF 65–107 billion over 5 years (Palkó 2012).

16.4.3.3 Rent-to-Own Schemes – The National Asset Management Company

The previous government also launched a mortgage-to-rent scheme that offers preferential loans to local authorities so that they can buy repossessed homes and let the original owner remain as a tenant in the property. However, many local authorities have refused to participate in this scheme because there is no long-term guarantee that the central government will continue to support this newly created rental stock.

The Fidesz government announced the introduction of the National Asset Management Company (NAMC) in 2010, which, according to the original plan, will buy the homes of borrowers who are in default and then rent these back to them.[3] However, soon after the announcement, the government realized that it did not have the resources to buy the debts on a mass scale. Nevertheless, the law was not enforced until the end of 2011, and the NAMC started to operate in the middle of 2012.

In 2011, after a long period of political discussion and preparation with banks, the government set up the National Asset Management Company, which can buy a limited number of delinquent loans and offer a renting option to the debtor. In the beginning, the plan was to purchase up to 5,000 units; the maximum number was later increased to 8,000 in 2012 and to 25,000 by 2014. The NAMC will pay 55 % of the value given in the original mortgage contract in Budapest, 50 % in cities of county seats and 35 % in other settlements. Both the banks and the debtors have to

[3] There is another program for households who have taken out FX loans of less than HUF 20 million and have arrears of more than 90 days. Such borrowers have the possibility to convert their loans into HUF loans with a 25 % deduction. They were allowed to apply until August 31, 2012. However, it seems that only a limited number of borrowers would have chosen this option because the payment after conversion would remain higher than what most of them could afford to pay.

initiate the transaction; however, there are strict eligibility criteria, which have been changed several times.

In summer of 2011, the government introduced another program: to build a greenfield housing estate 60 km from Budapest (Ócsa Social House-Building Project) for those who are at risk of eviction due to nonpayment. After a wide debate, construction started in 2012, and 80 units had been built by the end of 2012; these are intended as social rental units under the management of the NAMC.

16.5 Conclusion: Could the Unorthodox Mortgage Rescue Program End with a New Social Rental Sector?

16.5.1 Mortgage Rescue Programs and the Support of the (Upper) Middle Class

By 2012, the mortgage rescue programs covered all borrower subgroups; however, these subgroups enjoyed different priorities in terms of "time and money." The wealthiest families have enjoyed the highest subsidies, having were forgiven 25 % of their debt, at a cost of around HUF 450–500 billion paid at a 1/3–2/3 ratio by the government and the banking sector. The banks initially protested against the plan, but they eventually accepted it with the concession that 1/3 of the cost could be written off from the extra bank tax introduced as part of the unorthodox policy. This placed a major administrative burden on the banks because they had to deal with several thousand clients in a short period. The cost of the program was open-ended so the banks tried to slow down the process and limit the size of the loan that could be used for early repayment. It was a question of solidarity among the banks in that they were expected to limit the loans issued for other banks' clients to pay back their loans. The government accused the banks of "price rigging," and the Bank Supervisory Board initiated proceedings to check the possibility that the banks had formed an "interest rate cartel."

As part of the war on banks, the government used several measures to encourage early repayment, such as tax advantages for companies that transferred resources to their employees in order to repay loans (up to HUF 7.5 million). One of the most dubious measures was to guarantee that the Tax Office would not check the origin of the money spent on repayment. Decreasing the outstanding FX loans was more important for the government than keeping the rule of law. Observers highlighted the fact that a significant part of the resources was untraceable and definitely came from the informal economy.

One of the consequences of the early repayment scheme was that the best-paying 15 % of loans disappeared from the portfolio of the banks, and the share of nonperforming mortgage loans increased from 4.1 % in the first quarter of 2009 to 16.2 % in the second quarter of 2012 (HNB 2012).

16.5.2 Is the National Asset Management Company Prepared for Its Task?

A politically critical element of the mortgage rescue program concerns the policy towards the most vulnerable debtors, those with arrears of more than 90 days. Banks can terminate the contracts of such debtors and start foreclosure procedures following a court decision. The households are defenseless because they typically have arrears on utility costs as well as loans (sometimes more than one loan). The government promised to help starting in 2010, but nothing actually happened until the middle of 2012. First of all, there was no systematic research that identified the causes of the arrears. The financial statistics clearly show that the number of households with arrears has increased significantly in the last 2–3 years, partly because of the increased payment burden but also because of the political message that guaranteed that the government would rescue borrowers with arrears (According to experts, the 3-year moratorium on foreclosure ensured that this would be the case.). The idea of the National Asset Management Company was raised immediately after the Fidesz government was formed, but government experts soon realized that the bad loans were too expensive for the government to buy. The basic idea of helping the most vulnerable group was formed and accepted at the end of 2011. Initially, this policy aimed at buying 8,000 bad loans (from a total of 140,000) under the special rental scheme, but even the experts did not have a clear idea of who would be eligible for the program and how it would be administered.

The selection was based on entitlement, meaning that the NAMC has to buy (up to the limits set by the law, that is, 8,000 in November 2011 and 25,000 set in May 2012) every bad loan that is eligible according to the selection procedure. Thus, the NAMC did not have discretion over the selection. Consequently, in the first half of 2012, the government gradually changed the eligibility criteria, being careful not to open it too wide so as to avoid taking on an overly great burden.

A strong element of the political message was that the program would enable debtors to buy back their homes, which seemed very unrealistic. If the debtors are unable to buy back their homes, the program will have the effect of expanding the social housing stock more than any other program since 1989.

The other issue is how the new rental stock would be managed. By 2014, 25,000 units will represent 10 % of the public housing presently owned by the municipalities. In the beginning, there was a clear vision that the housing units in the property of the NAMC should be transferred to the municipalities, which would manage them according to the rules and procedures developed in the last two decades, placing housing under the control of the management companies. However, the government did not want the municipalities be involved in managing the stock, although this possibility has not been excluded entirely.

The law set the yearly rent at 1.5 % of the value of the home as established in the original loan contract, which is a lower level than the existing social rents. There is no central regulation with regard to the municipal rental stock. During the discussion of the law in Parliament, MPs from cities responsible for social housing criticized the program because the rents were too low to cover maintenance costs, which would also make it difficult to integrate the stock into the existing municipal rental sector.

An important new element in the program (in contrast to the regulation of existing municipal social housing) is that the law defined the household eligibility criteria: (a) a minimum of one child in the household (thus excluding single and pensioner households) and (b) participation in the housing allowance program or in job-seeking income benefit programs (in other words, the household has to be preselected by the municipality for a welfare program). This is necessary because the NAMC does not have the capacity to control the eligibility, thus the existing local government programs will have to provide the necessary information.

The real problem is that the NAMC does not have any idea what will happen if the new tenants are unable to pay the rent and utility costs. The legal rule is clear: after 3 months, the contract is broken, and an eviction procedure will begin. However, it is unclear whether the government is willing to pay the political price for evicting people who cannot pay before the next election (spring of 2014).

16.5.3 The Pressure on Social Housing in the Absence of Economic Recovery

The unorthodox economic policy (if we suppose the existence of a "master plan" for an unconventional economic policy) has not achieved the results that the government expected. There has been no economic growth, increasing poverty, youth out-migration, a low employment level, relatively high inflation, and low investments despite the government's stable financial situation (low deficit, no increase in the loan/GDP ratio).

The slow economic recovery has an important effect on housing policy and the housing market. First, there are limited budgetary resources for housing subsidies, which means that the housing program will not be enforced. Secondly, without economic growth, the share of NPL loans will rise, which means that the pressure on the NAMC will also increase.

However, both households that have FX mortgage arrears and households that do not have loans but have difficulties in meeting their housing costs will put pressure on social housing. During the 20 years of the post-transition period, housing poverty has become one of the most important social issues. The mortgage rescue program has been very important, but we should not forget that its benefits accrue mainly for better-off households: "Since 50 per cent of the bank loan portfolio is concentrated in wealthy households, the amendments to the taxation system will have a positive effect on portfolio quality of the banks on the whole" (HNB 2010, p. 17).

Housing affordability is a very serious social problem. Today, 14–18 % of households have serious difficulties in paying their housing-related expenditures, which leads to a growing number of arrears and to insecurity of tenure in both the public and the private sector. "Only" 3 % of households account for the mortgage arrears.

In 2010, the government froze the cost of district heating and water supplies to prevent the expansion of housing cost arrears and even planned to decrease households' utility costs. It was a typical "unorthodox" solution: putting the burden of the price increase on the service providers, which cannot be maintained for long, and a regressive allocation of the implicit subsidy. The real social problem is the low level of employment, in which the lack of social housing policy plays an important role. Unemployed people cannot move to growth regions, partly because of high housing costs, and there is a severe lack of social rental housing.

16.5.4 The Need for New Models

The policy responses to housing poverty issues have been very weak (Hegedüs 2013c). There is a proposal for new social housing construction (supported by the construction industry lobby), which is not realistic due to government expenditure constraints. Moreover, the expansion of the local government stock is constrained not only by the scarce financial resources of the municipalities but also by the lack of interest in extending the social housing stock in municipalities. Social housing is on the defensive in Hungary, and political support for it is very weak. The lack of demographic pressure on the housing market allows municipalities to draw on the private rental market and the empty housing stock for the expansion of social housing. The private rental sector is mostly part of the informal economy. Its size is estimated to be 12 % of the housing stock, according to the census of 2011. One possible solution is for local authorities or registered NGOs to develop social rental agencies, which would rent housing units to socially needy people, financed by a rent allowance scheme that would be much more cost-effective than new building programs. The chances of success for the new system is uncertain because government policy is unpredictable, and it is not yet clear how the pressure from the lowest 20–30 % of the society (which has struggled to pay the cost of housing) will force the government to use budget resources for the program and take a step towards building up institutions. However, there is no alternative model open for any government in the near future because of the budgetary pressure, the lack of demographic pressure, and the present state of the housing stock. Consequently, doing nothing will push the housing system into a situation in which housing will become one of the most important sources of social conflicts.

Biography: József Hegedüs, Ph.D., is a founding member of the Metropolitan Research Institute, a think-tank in urban and housing policy, established in 1989 in Budapest, Hungary. He has been a co-organizer of the East European Working Group of the European Network for Housing Research since 1989 and a member of the Housing Policy Council, a high-level advisory group in housing policy matters since 1996 in Hungary. Since 1994 he has been a part-time Associate Professor at Corvinus University Budapest. His research focused on urban and housing issues after the transition in Eastern-Europe with a special attention to the social issues. He has published extensively on housing policies in transitional countries and new member states.

References

Banai Á, Király J, Várhegyi E (2009) A special aspect of the past 20 years: dominance of foreign banks in emerging Europe with special regard to Hungary. Presentation at the CICM conference of 16–18 September 2009, London. http://services.bepress.com/cgi/viewcontent.cgi?article=2052&context=eot&z=1260557057

Buckley R, Tsenkova S (2001) Housing market systems in reforming socialist economies: comparative indicators of performance and policy. Eur J Hous Policy 1(2):1–34

Cerami A (2005) Social policy in central and Eastern Europe. The emergence of a New European model of solidarity. Dissertation zur Erlangung des Grades eines Doktors der Sozialwissenschaft der Universität Erfurt. Manuscript

Csányi S (2007) A verseny és transzparencia kérdései a bankszektorban. Presentation Verseny és transzparencia, II. Bankkonferencia, Visegrád, 6–7 Nov

CSO (2007) Household Budget Survey. Central Statistical Office, Budapest

Deloitte (2012) Property index (Overview of European residential market). http://www.deloitte.com/assets/Dcom-Belgium/Local%20Assets/Documents/EN/be_deloitte-property-index-2012.pdf

Erbenova M, Liu Y, Saxegaard M (2011) Corporate and household debt distress in Latvia: strengthening the incentives for market-based approach to debt resolution. IMF working paper WP/11/85 http://www.imf.org/external/pubs/ft/wp/2011/wp1185.pdf

Ferge Z (2002) Social structure and inequalities in old socialism and new capitalism in Hungary. Rev Sociol, The Hungarian Sociological Association 8(2): 9–34

Hegedüs J (2011) Housing policy and the economic crisis – the case of Hungary. In: Forrest R, Yip N-M (eds) Housing markets and the global financial crisis: the uneven impact on households. Edward Elgar Publishing Limited, Cheltenham, pp 113–130

Hegedüs J (2013a) Hungary – ideas and plans without political will. In: Hegedüs J, Lux M, Teller N (eds) Social housing in transition countries. New York, London, pp 180–194

Hegedüs J (2013b) Housing privatization and restitution. In: Hegedüs J, Lux M, Teller N (eds) Social housing in transition countries. New York, London, pp 33–49

Hegedüs J (2013c) The transformation of the social housing sector in eastern Europe: a conceptual framework. In: Hegedüs J, Lux M, Teller N (eds) Social housing in transition countries. New York, London, pp 3–32

Hegedüs J, Somogyi E (2005): Evaluation of the Hungarian mortgage program 2000–2004. In: J Hegedüs, Struyk RJ (eds) Housing finance: new and old models in Central Europe, Russia and Kazakhstan. OSI/LGI, Budapest, pp 177–208

Hegedüs J, Szemző H (2010) Shaping the new welfare regime in transition countries: the interplay of public policies and households' strategies (Case of Hungary). Comparative housing research: approaches and policy challenges in a new international era, 24/25 March 2010, OTB Research Institute and the Faculty of Architecture, Delft University of Technology, The Netherlands

Hegedüs J, Tosics I (1996) Disintegration of East-European housing model. In: Clapham D, Hegedüs K, Kintrea K, Tosics I (eds) Housing privatization in Eastern Europe. Greenwood, Westport

Hegedüs J, Mayo ES, Tosics I (1996) Transition of the housing sector in the east central European countries. Rev Urban Reg Dev Stud 8:101–136

Herpai BA (2010) lakossági díjhátralékok alakulása egy felmérés tükrében (Households' utility cost arrears) Esély, 2010/6, pp 22–40
HNB (2010) Report on financial stability. November 2010. Hungarian National Bank, Budapest
HNB (2011) Report on financial stability. November 2011. Hungarian National Bank, Budapest
HNB (2012) Report on financial stability. November 2012. Hungarian National Bank, Budapest
Howard J (2011) Long term safety nets to protect mortgage borrowers. Building Societies Association, London
Kasza G (2002) The illusion of the welfare "regime". J Soc Policy 31(2):271–287
Law CXXX (2011) Law on extensions of protection measures in connection with the amendment of Law CXII 1996 on Credit Institution and Financial Enterprises
Long R, Wilson W (2011) Mortgage arrears and repossessions. Library House of Commons, London, June 9
NFM (2012) Utility cost arrears – report to Parliament downloaded from http://www.parlament.hu/irom39/09104/09104-0001.pdf
Palkó I (2012) Nem tudják a devizahitelesek, miről maradnak le? (The FX borrowers do not know what they loose?) Portfolio http://www.portfolio.hu/vallalatok/penzugy/nem_tudjak_a_devizahitelesek_mirol_maradnak_le.170699.html
PSZAF (2012a) Gyorselemzés a végtörlesztésről. 2012 március 12. http://www.pszaf.hu/data/cms2334451/gyorselemzes_vegtorlesztes_120312j.pdf
PSZAF (2012b) Kényszerértékesítésre kijelölt ingatlanok adatai. 2012. Május 16. http://www.pszaf.hu/bal_menu/jelentesek_statisztikak/statisztikak/kenyszerertekesites
Scanlon K, Lunde J, Whitehead C (2012) Post-crisis mortgage and housing markets in Europe: a comparative review. Copenhagen, London
Szalai G, Tóth G (2003) A lakásfinanszírozás gyakorlata, kapcsolodó kockázatok és azok kezelése a Magyar bankrendszerben (The finance of home purchase and construction, the risks involved and their management in the Hungarian banking system) Hungarian National Bank, Report on Financial Stability 2003 December, Budapest, pp 100–115
Szelényi I (2012) Az argentin model (The Argentine model). HVG, 15. January 2012. http://m.hvg.hu/hvgfriss/2012.02/201202_szelenyi_ivan_az_argentin_modell
Tausz K (2009) From state socialism to a hybrid welfare state: Hungary. In: Schubert K, Simon Hegelich S, Bazant U (eds) The handbook of European welfare systems. Routledge, London
Tomka B (2005) Determinants of East Central European welfare systems a comparative perspective, 1945–2000. Paper presented at the 20th ICHS conference, Sydney, 3–9 July 2005
Tsenkova S (2009) Housing reforms in post-socialist Europe. Lost in transition. Springer, Heidelberg
UC (2011) National measures and practices to avoid foreclosure procedures for residential mortgage loans. Commission Staff Working Paper. Brussels. http://ec.europa.eu/internal_market/finservices-retail/docs/credit/mortgage/sec_2011_357_en.pdf
Valentinyi Á (2012) Ortodox kalauz IMF nélküli kormányoknak (Orthodox guide for government without IM?F): downloaded from http://index.hu/gazdasag/penzbeszel/2012/01/02/ortodox_kalauz_imf_nelkuli_kormanyoknak/?cp=1
Wilcox SA, Wallace G, Bramley J, Morgan F Sosenko, Ford J (2010) Evaluation of the Mortgage rescue scheme and homeowners mortgage support. The Centre for Housing Policy, University of York School of the Built Environment, Heriot Watt University, New York
World Bank (1993) Housing: enabling markets to work/with technical supplements. World Bank, Washington, DC
Zolnay J (2002) A Housing Program of the social housing PBC set up by the Nation-Wide Roma Self Government. http://www.romaweb.hu/romaweb/cikk.jsp?p=7

Part III
Concluding Part

Chapter 17
Reflections

Ray Forrest

17.1 Introduction

This book has explored the state of public housing at the beginning of the twenty-first century across a wide range of societies. In doing so, two key messages emerge. First, public housing systems are embedded in, and are shaped by, distinct social pressures, economic circumstances, political institutions and cultural norms. Temporally and spatially public housing is highly differentiated. This may seem an obvious point but in general discussion of housing systems there is a tendency to assume that markets produce diversity and government and quasi-governmental interventions are intrinsically bound to produce uniformity. In housing debate there is regular reference to the differentiated nature of home ownership but references to public housing still generate a strong monotone image-to extend the metaphor, we tend to think of home ownership in colour but public housing in black and white. National public housing systems have, however, emerged along particular paths, under different circumstances and this means that they will have different trajectories in changing times. A second message relates to uniformity of purpose as opposed to diversity of approach or outcome-namely, public housing as the vehicle to provide accommodation to people who cannot afford to buy in private housing markets or pay market rents. Over time and over space the precise nature of the housing question will vary but public housing always has a social purpose in the broadest sense of addressing a societal need (e.g. better housed workers as part of economic strategy; better housing conditions as better public health; better housing as visible price to pay for political support). The societal need will be multilayered with different interconnected motivations and purposes. Thus, there is unlikely to be a mono-causal explanation for the emergence of public housing. But however

R. Forrest (✉)
Department of Public Policy, City University
of Hong Kong, Hong Kong, China
e-mail: safray@cityu.edu.hk

J. Chen et al. (eds.), *The Future of Public Housing: Ongoing Trends in the East and the West*, DOI 10.1007/978-3-642-41622-4_17,

nuanced, the role of public housing is to provide housing which would be absent or of unacceptably low quality if left solely to market processes.

We are inevitably and immediately into terminological difficulties here. Private, market, social, state, public are terms which are used in different combinations with regard to housing. ‘Social’ and ‘public’ are often used interchangeably in western contexts although public housing is typically taken to mean direct provision and management by a government provider, central or local. ‘Social’ often denotes some other kind of provider such as a housing association or charity. In both cases, it usually refers to rental housing. The terminological difficulties are compounded by problems of translation as well as variations in form and function. Other analysts have spent considerable time and effort in distinguishing the different forms and hybrids of this type of housing provision (see, for example, Harloe 1995). For the purposes of this concluding reflection, however, the intention is to keep things relatively uncomplicated. Public housing here generally refers to direct provision of housing by central or local governments for low or lower income households. This could include rental for sale schemes, public home ownership schemes as well as long term renting. It originates as housing funded, owned and managed by governments although the dwellings may end up in some other tenure. The assumption is that public housing is for collective use and is allocated on some bureaucratic calculus of need. Access to market based provision is primarily dependent on ability to pay-albeit sometimes, indeed often, aided by direct or indirect subsidies.

Against that background this brief concluding chapter is organized in three sections. First, it reflects on the past of public housing. Second, it examines the key dimensions of the present, as a period which has seen the scale and scope of public housing systems in general decline. Third, it reflects on future trajectories. In a post-crash world, where do we go from here given the uneven impact of recent economic crises and the varied institutional forms and policy histories of existing public housing systems? Economic crisis has generated a more general social crisis of trust and legitimacy in many core institutions. Debates around public housing are caught up in these contemporary narratives, positively and negatively. It is also indicative of a changing world, and consistent with a core message of this text, that Asia figures more strongly in the discussion as we move from the past to the future.

17.2 Public Housing Pasts

In thinking about public housing eras in terms of past, presents and futures the period between the end of WW2 and the mid 1970s is typically seen as capturing its golden age. And the three subsequent decades encompasse much of what has shaped the present. We are currently in a transition to a different era occasioned by the aftermath of the global financial crisis in the west and the increasing social and economic pressures of accelerated urbanization in the east. The emerging era for public housing provision will be shaped by the political and social fallout of a global financial crisis. The early period for public housing was embedded in *Les Trentes Glorieuses* of relatively stable postFordist capitalism and was shaped by the aftermath of global conflict. There was a strong, unionized working class and devastated cities. In the same period, European planning and particularly the British council housing model was influential in the postcolonial/colonial enclaves of Singapore and Hong Kong. And surprisingly perhaps, it is in these two cities that the public housing model seems to have survived in different but equally robust forms.

In a post war Europe, as after the First World War, there was a powerful 'homes for heroes' political rhetoric and pressing strategic and economic needs to provide better living conditions for the general population. There are numerous fading photographs of Ministers and local dignitaries proudly visiting these new public housing estates. There was much to be proud about as the new houses represented a significant transformation of living conditions for substantial sections of the working class. Here we had apparently benevolent states rewarding the sacrifices of their working classes with better housing and better health. There were also, of course, strong grassroots pressures for better housing, a wave of post war squatting and endemic homelessness (and see Malpass 2003 for a nuanced account of this period).

These housing interventions, as has been emphasized, inevitably took different forms in different European countries. But the common and undeniable impact was to achieve a major improvement in living conditions and housing opportunities. In the UK, for example, the vast majority of new public tenants were moving from private landlordism where in the late 1940s relatively few were living in accommodation with running hot water or bathrooms. They moved to public housing where almost all dwellings had such facilities (Lupton et al. 2009). But part of the critique of the public housing of this era is that this housing was most typically for the privileged labour aristocracy-the skilled working class rather than the poor. The poor remained generally elsewhere and typically in the low quality, low amenity private rented sector. The skilled working class had political muscle and were strategically important in the industrial resurgence after the war. At that time access to home ownership was only achievable for a slowly expanding professional and middle class.

Even in the USA, where public housing has played a very limited role in providing working class housing, there was considerable political agitation in the post war period. The 1930s depression had devastated many careers and household incomes and new construction had fallen dramatically. By the mid 1940s the housing situation was even worse and there were calls for a major public housing programme as part of a new deal. Indeed, the 1949 Housing Act, passed despite considerable resistance from the real estate lobby and political conservatives, promised a public housing programme of over 800,000 dwellings (see interesting discussion in Hackworth 2003).

The USA never developed an extensive public rental sector but the general point is that physical, social and economic conditions combined in the late 1940s to generate wide support for subsidized state rental housing. As the decades passed, these conditions changed markedly. In particular, absolute housing shortages eased, housing conditions and amenities improved, home ownership became more accessible and political support for mass public rental housing waned. Public rental housing was a victim of both success and failure. Across a number of societies, it made an enormous contribution to upgrading lives and opportunities. In particular, it severed or considerably eroded the link between income and housing condition and it had a major impact on illnesses associated with damp and decay. It became possible to enjoy decent housing without a relatively high household income. Public tenants escaped private landlordism with its insecurities, uncertainties and often unacceptable conditions. Moreover, public housing proved popular-unsurprisingly. In a later era, it was often argued by 'modernisers' that public tenants wanted to be home owners-that they were trapped in an unpopular tenure. However, the expressed desire for home ownership was not to be interpreted as a reflection of the unpopularity of public rental housing (Forrest and Murie 1990). Quite the contrary, the wave of new building for public rental in the post war period often provided a popular route into home ownership in a later era.

There were also mistakes associated with excessive social control and excessive spatial concentration. These were often a product of the constraints, exigencies and attitudes of the times-easily condemned in retrospect. The excessive scrutiny of prospective tenants, the often evident paternalism and superciliousness of officials, the lack of freedom and choice seemed to be intrinsically flawed elements of early public housing systems found in many countries. But rules, procedures and behaviours which seem unacceptable today need to be set in their contemporary social and cultural contexts. Moreover, they typically received little comment from those entering the public housing sector. You can put this down to blind gratitude, incorporation or whatever but it was the new housing opportunities, and often the quality of these opportunities which were to the forefront of concerns for many new tenants in the post war Europe. Concerns with tenant choice and freedom emerged much later and were not disconnected with the decline in the quality and quantity of public sector tenancies- the freedom to make more choices in conditions of greater scarcity.

The management and maintenance of public housing stocks were also often woefully inadequate. Low rent regimes were often low maintenance regimes. This was particularly true in the mass housing estates of communist Eastern Europe and in China. Tenant purchase and related tenure transfer policies in some countries included the addition of good quality dwellings to the owner occupied stock. But the 'shock doctrine' (Klein 2007) privatizations in parts of Eastern Europe, and particularly in Russia, were more typically of a very different nature involving dwellings which were as likely to be liabilities as assets. The highest levels of home ownership are now to be found in Europe's post socialist states rather than in the longer established and more affluent market economies. States may have managed to unburden themselves of these responsibilities in the short term but the longer term consequences for individual owners and governments are still to impact and could prove expensive, fiscally and socially. As became very evident in the late 2000s, low quality, low value home ownership is not necessarily a step up from public or private tenancy.

17.3 Public Housing Presents

As this book has underlined, we are now entering a new phase for public housing. Privatization, in the form of tenant purchase or open market sales of state housing, has generally run its course. In most cases, there is little left to transfer or sell and fewer takers for what remains. By and large, the tenure transfer moment has passed and is irreversible and probably unrepeatable. There has also been an ideological shift or, at least a more cautious approach towards public sector restructuring and so-called modernization. The post-privatisation era for public rental housing will be one with new housing forms and different geographies. In western welfare states there is little evident support for substantial new investment in public rental housing. Political preferences remains market oriented but with a distinct inclination towards private renting given the difficulties of providing sustainable home ownership for lower income households. The UK provides a striking example of this retreat from home ownership for the current generation of younger households. In 1991, 60 % of 16–34 year olds were in owner occupation. In 2011, the comparable percentage was 36 % (Survey of English Housing 2010/2011/2012). Moreover, the UK is not exceptional. Across a wide range of societies there has been a marked increase in the proportion of younger households entering private renting or remaining in the parental home well into adulthood (Forrest and Yip 2013).

Younger and lower income households have found themselves squeezed between a shrinking public sector and an unaffordable home ownership market. In much of Asia including China, Korea and India concerns about rising housing problems and associated social tensions have generated support for substantial new policy interventions in the housing system. In Hong Kong, for example, where house price rises continue to be fuelled by rising affluence and speculative inward investment, and where squalid cubicle private renting remains a reality, the housing problem is the top government priority. Here there remains a strong commitment to a sustained public rental programme as well as new assisted home ownership schemes. In general, the pressures of rapid and polarizing urbanization in Asia combined with a more pragmatic and less ideological approach to housing provision means there is less political queasiness about investment in public housing and a recognition that the expanding middle classes will need to be helped into home ownership. One interpretation of these developments, and of the contrasts which are emerging between East and West in terms of housing responses, is that the rapidly expanding cities of Asia or Latin America are facing the same kinds of pressures of rural–urban migration and rising affluence faced by European cities a century earlier. Investment in public rental housing was an eventual response then as it is now. Public housing provision emerges in particular historical conjunctures associated with proletarianisation, quantitative rather than qualitative housing problems, rural–urban migration and strategic concerns about economic competitiveness. The history of housing provision in Europe shows that outcomes are specific and path dependent and that appalling housing conditions for urban populations do not necessarily generate ameliorative government responses.

In passing, and with reference to the supposedly distinctive developmentalism of East Asian societies, it is also of some interest to quote from Wheatley, British Minister for Health in 1924. In a debate in Parliament he referred to the increasing competitive pressure on the British economy and urged his political opponents to "recognize that it is impossible to produce in the housing conditions of today workers who can successfully compete in the world's markets of tomorrow."(p. 6) Of course, the world is a very different place today. One difference is that we have a legacy of public housing intervention which provides the context in which any new interventions are judged. But perhaps equally significantly, after the crash, home ownership policies and aspirations are also being reevaluated. In this reevaluation, the symbiotic and supportive role of public rental housing in the history of the development of home ownership becomes more evident. Home ownership became the dominant tenure across a number of countries because of, not despite, the existence of vibrant public rental sectors. Sometimes this support was in the form of discounted purchase and small incremental transfers over a long period. In other cases, as referred to above, it involved large scale transfers of properties and people from the state rental to home ownership sectors over a very short period. Sometimes it offered desirable and sustainable home ownership, sometimes not. Patterns and policies of housing provision in one era set the conditions and possibilities for the next. Periods in which there is a strong commitment to market processes in housing provision can lead to more interventionist policies in a subsequent period if social tensions become more acute and social and economic priorities change. Equally, extensive direct provision or extensive subsidy offer the possibilities of tenure conversion and/or reduced support in a new round of policy initiatives. There is, as would be expected, an element of Polanyian double movement in the shaping of housing policies.

17.4 Public Housing Futures

We often speculate about the future role of public housing, and in particular, public rental or welfare housing, as if it is a residual concern once majority needs are taken care of. There is also a tendency to view the future in terms of past experiences-of social demands, of urbanization, of migration, of demography, of employment and so on. But, of course, the conditions which prevailed in post war Europe bear little relation to the urbanization pressures and migration flows evident in China or Latin America at present. And within Europe there are now very different circumstances in relation to social mobility, labour markets and population structures. In all societies, aspirations and expectations change with regard to housing opportunities and standards.

Social surveys in most countries would still indicate a general aspiration for home ownership but the forms of home ownership envisaged and the routes necessary to achieve it will vary within and between societies. And, as has been suggested, the future of home ownership is closely tied to the future of public housing. It is not only a matter of welfare provision for a minority but the way in which collective resources are to be mobilized to address the housing needs of majorities and future generations. We are currently emerging from a period in which housing opportunities have become more restrictive for new and younger households. Neoliberal experiments in providing affordable housing have stalled, perhaps terminally. Public housing is generally scarcer and home ownership less affordable. What is to be done? If home ownership is not affordable for large sections of populations what is to be on offer? Or to put it another way, how is the promise of a middle class future to be sustained with home ownership as a central ingredient? Both public rental housing and publicly assisted home ownership will have to play a role. The nature of those interventions will be shaped by policy and economic histories as well as by current events and conditions. As is already evident from new policy developments in China and South Korea, unrestrained housing commodification has social costs which have to be ameliorated. New and younger households need assistance. Good housing is also one of the most effective ways to temper general inequality. Societal fractures have widened in recent years-whether north or south, post socialist or postindustrial, developed or developing. Therborn (2012) has observed that a twentieth century of inequality between nations has given way to a twenty-first century of inequality within nations… "nations are converging whilst classes are diverging" (p. 12). Most measures of income inequality would certainly point in that direction. In that context, the housing sphere can play a critical ameliorative role.

There are two other broader issues which deserve mention. First, there is demographic aging. The housing interventions of the past were typically focused on low income families. Elderly households were a marginal concern with small numbers of specially designed dwellings available for the aging poor. Many existing public tenant populations are aging fast and the differential resources among other tenure groups means that there will be greater demands for collectively provided and funded forms of provision. The market can take care of the better resourced aging home owners but poorer, older households in private renting and home owners with low equity and low marketability will represent a source of growing housing demands on public resources. The nature of these housing needs will change and become more complex as the elderly age. Moreover, whatever the cultural context the gender balance will shift progressively towards higher proportions of elderly women. These developments are likely to be a key driver of public housing initiatives in the future.

Secondly, there is the issue of who is providing the housing and for what purpose. We have already referred to the overweening paternalism and unnecessary rules and controls of some public housing sectors of the past. However, there is another side to this, typically captured in references to a 'public sector' or 'public market' ethos. To put it another way, does it matter if employees are use value or exchange value oriented in their work? Are employees in public sector institutions more likely to regard their work as a 'cause' rather than a business, or merely their source of income? Is societal accountability a more important value in a public rather than a private organization? (see Jorgensen 2007 for a useful discussion).

Institutional values are also embedded in wider sets of social values and this will vary over time and space. It would be wrong to assume a set of public sector values and operating norms which are constant across cultural and national borders. Nevertheless, future debates about the way housing is to be provided and for whose benefit are bound up with questions of housing rights, housing justice and the overriding priorities of the providers themselves. In a post privatization world, there is a closer examination of the social benefits and social costs of marketization, corporatization and load shedding and of how these calculations are made. With regard to housing, there are social, economic and political risks involved if there is overreliance on organisations dominated by cost recovery and ability to pay imperatives. Housing remains near the top of many political agendas-in both rich and poor countries in terms of affordability and welfare issues. On a global scale, in simple quantitative terms, the housing problem is arguably greater now than it was half a century ago. Engaging with this challenge cannot be reduced to an economic discussion concerning the efficiency of different sectors. In whatever national or cultural context, the nature of housing provision will continue to be a highly politically charged debate. It is a 'special' commodity with a pivotal position in our everyday lives and in relation to national economies. The need for public housing interventions in some form is unlikely to diminish in the future although labels and structures will undoubtedly change subject to political fashion and policy imaginations. And, as this book has suggested, the scale and global geography of these interventions is likely to be very different over the next few decades.

References

Department of Communities and Local Government (2010, 2011, 2012) English housing survey. Office for National Statistics, London

Forrest R, Murie A (1990) A dissatisfied state-consumer preferences and council housing in Britain. Urban Stud 27(5):617–635

Forrest R, Yip N-m (2013) Young people and housing-transitions, trajectories and generational fractures. Routledge, London

Hackworth J (2003) Public housing and the rescaling of regulation in the USA. Environ Plan A 35:531–549

Harloe M (1995) The people's home: social rented housing in Europe and America. Basil Blackwell, Oxford

Jorgensen TB (2007) Public values, their nature, stability and change. Case of Denmark. Pub Adm Q 13:365–398

Klein N (2007) The shock doctrine. Metropolitan Books, New York

Lupton R et al (2009) Growing up in social housing in Britain. Tenant Services Authority, London

Malpass P (2003) The wobbly pillar? Housing and the British postwar welfare state. J Soc Policy 32:589–606

Therborn G (2012) Class in the 21st century. New Left Review 78:5–29

Wheatley J (1924) Houses to let. Trades Union Congress and the Labour Party, London

MIX
Papier aus verantwortungsvollen Quellen
Paper from responsible sources
FSC® C105338

FSC
www.fsc.org

If you have any concerns about our products,
you can contact us on
ProductSafety@springernature.com

In case Publisher is established outside the EU,
the EU authorized representative is:
Springer Nature Customer Service Center GmbH
Europaplatz 3, 69115 Heidelberg, Germany

Printed by Libri Plureos GmbH
in Hamburg, Germany